T0251130

Building a
Global Information
Assurance Program

Building a Global Information Assurance Program

Raymond J. Curts, Ph.D.
Douglas E. Campbell, Ph.D.

CRC Press
Taylor & Francis Group
Boca Raton London New York

CRC Press is an imprint of the
Taylor & Francis Group, an **informa** business

AN AUERBACH BOOK

CRC Press Taylor & Francis Group
6000 Broken Sound Parkway NW, Suite 300
Boca Raton, FL 33487-2742

First issued in hardback 2017

Library of Congress Card Number 20020278

ISBN-13: 978-0-8493-1368-4 (pbk)
ISBN-13: 978-1-138-43700-5 (hbk)

Library of Congress Cataloging-in-Publication Data

Curts, Raymond J.
    Building a global information assurance program / Raymond J.
Curts, Douglas E. Campbell.
        p. cm.
    Includes bibliographical references and index.
    ISBN 0-8493-1368-6 (alk. paper)
    1. Computer security. 2. Data protection. I. Campbell, Douglas E., 1954–
II. Title

QA76.9 .A25 C874 2002
005.8—dc21   20020278
                                                                                    CIP

Visit the Taylor & Francis Web site at
http://www.taylorandfrancis.com

and the CRC Press Web site at
http://www.crcpress.com

Contents

Acknowledgments

The authors would like to thank Mr. Rich O'Hanley, who convinced us that we could actually produce this tome, and who facilitated by gently nudging us along the way. We are also indebted to and very appreciative of our families, who were supportive and understanding throughout the long hours of research, writing, and editing.

Introduction

There are no rules here. We're just trying to accomplish something.

Thomas Edison

This book is the result of a collaboration between the authors on a large number and variety of information technology (IT), information assurance (IA), systems engineering (SE), information system interoperability, and related issues. Because of their long and diverse backgrounds, the authors bring a unique perspective to current IT issues. Both authors started out, directly after graduating from under-graduate programs, in the U.S. Navy. Dr. Campbell went into Intelligence, while Dr. Curts became an aviator and eventually migrated to airborne Signals Intelligence (SIGINT) platforms and, hence, the Intelligence field as well. After the Navy, both authors entered the government contracting arena. Dr. Campbell eventually started his own small company, while Dr. Curts went to work for larger, established, defense contractors in the Washington, D.C. metropolitan area. Their paths first crossed while supporting the Information Warfare (IW) Directorate (PD-16) of the Space and Naval Warfare Systems Command (SPAWAR) in Crystal City, VA, where they worked on the Navy's IW Master Plan and IW Strategy. Later, Dr. Curts chaired a subcommittee, in which Dr. Campbell participated, on the Contingency Theatre Air Planning Systems (CTAPS) during a National Defense Industrial Association (NDIA) study on interoperability for Mr. Emmett Paige, then-Assistant Secretary of Defense for Command, Control, Communications, and Intelligence (ASD(C3I)). Next, they collaborated on another NDIA study commissioned by Mr. Paige's successor, Mr. Arthur Money; that research looked into the potential for industry involvement in vulnerability assessments and so-called "red teams." Again, Dr. Campbell participated in a subcommittee chaired by Dr. Curts; this time, on the operational aspects of such efforts. Both of these reports resulted in presentations to a variety of government officials within the Department of Defense (DoD) and other agencies. At about the same time, Dr. Campbell and associates were completing a study of the Naval Safety Center (NSC) as a model for much-needed processes in the world of Information Security (InfoSec).

It was during these initiatives that the authors began to formulate the concepts presented herein. It started with presentations to the Command and Control Research and Technology Symposia (CCRTS) in 1999, 2000, 2001, and 2002. Meanwhile, the authors were completing work on similar topics for several of their customers, including the U.S. Navy, the Federal Aviation Administration (FAA), and the National Aeronautics and Space Administration (NASA). The ideas formulated here began to gel into a complete, comprehensive, "womb-to-tomb" systems engineering approach to information assurance. Bits and pieces have been published over the years in technical forums of one sort or another. The pieces have only recently been grouped together and melded into a comprehensive whole.

This book is intended for anyone interested in the construction and operation of an Information Assurance (IA) or Information Security (InfoSec) program. Specific concepts, processes, and procedures will be presented within these pages. But, while our approach is compete and comprehensive, it is not, nor could it be, all inclusive. The overall, high-level concepts presented here should remain relatively constant and will provide a solid foundation for any IA program for many years to come. Individual technical and system solutions, however, come and go. We will touch on all aspects of a good IA program. However, the specific, technical aspects of individual technology solutions shall be reserved for other publications. The reader will walk away with a step-by-step process for building IA policies, processes, procedures, and organizations and the data to support them (Exhibit 1). An in-depth program will, no doubt, take years to build and perfect. However, by following the steps presented here, a broad spectrum of IA issues can be addressed quickly. Depth can be added to any or all of the individual areas as the program matures.

This book is organized into 12 chapters with several appendices (Exhibit 2). The first chapter, Introduction to Information Assurance, provides the underlying motivation for this volume. Here we discuss the ultimate goals and basics of IA

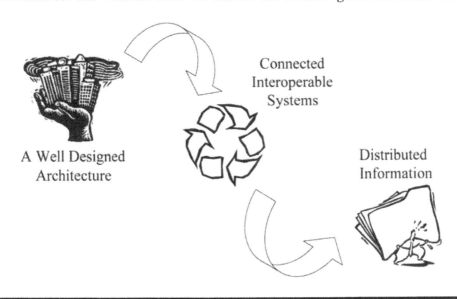

A Well Designed Architecture

Connected Interoperable Systems

Distributed Information

Exhibit 1   Information assurance, interoperability, and architecture

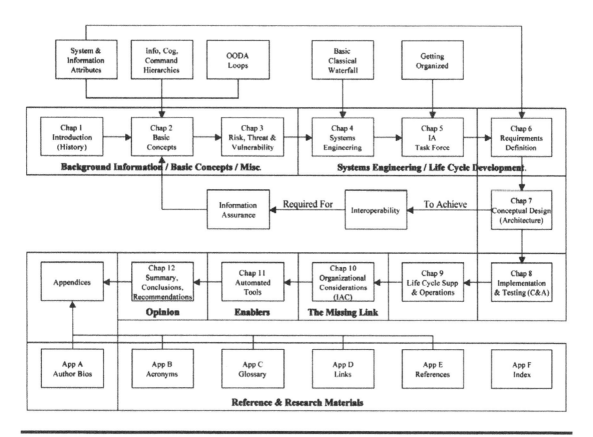

Exhibit 2 Volume organization

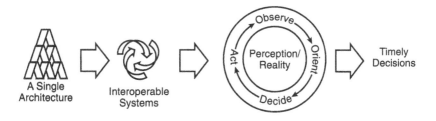

Exhibit 3 Information assurance process

(Exhibit 3). This chapter is, in essence, the blueprint for building the rest of the book. In Chapter 2, Basic Concepts, we provide a solid foundation for what follows. Here we set the framework with a brief discussion of the attributes of information and information systems: information, cognitive, and decision hierarchies; interoperability; architecture; the observe, orient, decide, and act cycle or "OODA" loop; and other important decision-making issues. Next we address risk, threat, and vulnerability (Chapter 3) and their applicability to information systems. Because we propose a structured systems approach in this volume, Chapter 4 contains a brief introduction to proven systems engineering concepts to prepare the reader for the discussion to follow. In Chapter 5, we present a systems engineering methodology beginning with getting organized, selecting a team, and mapping out the game plan. Chapters 6 through 9 progress through the development of an information infrastructure using standard systems engineering methods with direct application to information and information systems. Here we begin, after pulling together a small implementation group, to determine the requirements for our particular scenario and produce our plan. IT architectures and other conceptual design considerations are discussed in Chapter 7. In Chapter 8, we address implementation and testing, followed by life-cycle operations and maintenance in Chapter 9, and some specific implementation ideas in Chapter 10. Automated tools are an important aspect of any task if it is to be completed within a reasonable length of time using manpower and other resources efficiently. Tools to aid in various aspects of the previous sections are discussed in Chapter 11. Finally, our conclusions and recommendations finalize the discussion in Chapter 12.

Whether we are constructing a building, an aircraft, or an information system, any good acquisition and development process starts with the foundation (requirements) and builds upward and outward. We have taken that exact approach here. Though much more complex, global information systems can be likened to the worldwide electrical grid or the international telephone system. The infrastructure is an exceedingly important and expensive piece of the transport mechanism. Consequently, it is likely to be around for a very long time and must be robust, reliable, interoperable, and adaptable to new requirements, standards, and processes. As shown in Exhibit 4, without good systems engineering, something rather more mystical is often necessary (AMHH: a miracle happens here). But, the ultimate goal is not the building of an intricate, complex, interconnecting

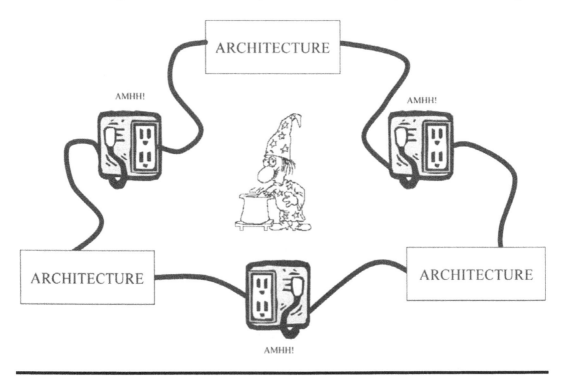

Exhibit 4   Global harmony

network of wires, computers, relays, and the like; rather it is the reliable, accurate, timely delivery of good, clean, quality electricity, voice, or (in the case of our discussion here) data.

Several appendices are included listing acronyms, definitions, references, internet links, and a short biographical sketch of the authors. These appendices are a valuable reference in and of themselves. The introductory section (Chapters 1–4), with its background information, is useful also as a stand-alone piece. The remainder will likely make more sense if read in the order it is presented.

Chapter 1

Introduction to Information Assurance

> The superior man, when resting in safety, does not forget that danger may come. When in a state of security he does not forget the possibility of ruin. When all is orderly, he does not forget that disorder may come. Thus his person is not endangered, and his States and all their clans are preserved.
>
> **Confucius**

There is very little information that exists today that will not at one time or another be stored or transmitted electronically. Even information that already exists in hard copy, such as paper, will eventually be faxed or scanned into a computer; thus, it enters the electronic realm. From here the information can be changed, deleted, or broadcast to the world. Information in electronic format must be readily available when needed and must be trusted. Sometimes there are confidentiality concerns. Ensuring the confidentiality, availability, and integrity of all electronically held information is the goal. *Information assurance* is the term used to describe this goal [CESG, 2002].

Through the use of appropriate security products and procedures, every person in the information assurance (IA) field hopes to achieve reasonable confidence that the electronic information he is responsible for is always available to those who need it and is adequately protected from unauthorized change or dissemination. Helping the owners of electronic information to determine the procedures and to some extent the products to achieve information assurance is the purpose of this book.

The U.S. Air Force defines IA slightly differently. "Information assurance represents measures to protect friendly information systems by preserving the availability, integrity, and confidentiality of the systems and the information contained within the systems" [ADW, 2002].

The National Defense University (NDU), located in Washington, D.C., prefers the following: "Information assurance is defined as information operations (IO) that protect and defend information systems by ensuring their integrity, authentication, confidentiality, and nonrepudiation. This includes providing for restoration of information systems by incorporating protection, detection, and reaction capabilities" [NDU, 2002].

A similar definition comes from the Pentagon's Office of the Secretary of Defense: "Information assurance is the component of information operations that assures the Department of Defense's operational readiness by providing for the continuous availability and reliability of information systems and networks. IA protects the Defense Information Infrastructure against exploitation, degradation, and denial of service, while providing the means to efficiently reconstitute and reestablish vital capabilities following an attack" [C3I, 2002].

Larry Loeb, author of *Secure Electronic Transactions,* states, "Information assurance is a technique used by large organizations, such as the military, to deal with the large volumes of information. Its goal is to make sure the information used is transmitted and computed in a noncorrupted state" [Loeb, 1999].

The U.S. Navy, in its Secretary of the Navy Instruction (SECNAVINST) 5239.3 [SECNAV, 1995], states that a fundamental information security policy is that data processed, stored, and transmitted by information systems shall be adequately protected with respect to requirements for confidentiality, integrity, availability, and privacy.

In these definitions, we can derive the aspects of information assurance services as being based on availability, integrity, authentication, confidentiality, and nonrepudiation. These basic building blocks of information assurance can be defined and described as follows (Exhibit 1) [Loeb, 2002]:

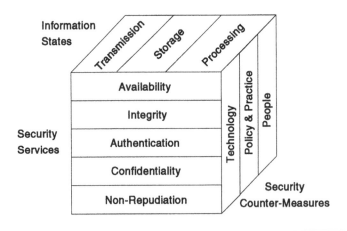

Exhibit 1   Information Assurance Model [Loeb, 2002]

Availability

Availability is the state when data or a system is in the place needed by the user, at the time the user needs it, and in the form needed by the user [PL 100–235]. Fundamentally, availability is simply the prevention of the unauthorized withholding of information or resources.

Integrity

Integrity is the assurance that the information that arrives at a destination is the same as the information that was sent, and that if any changes occurred, they are detected and reported. This is typically accomplished by running a hash function over the data to create a message digest that is then encrypted using a one-way encryption algorithm. The encrypted message digest is sent along with the original data, and the receiver can execute the same hash and encryption functions on the data received and verify that it matches the encrypted message digest received. Digital certificates, for example, make use of public key cryptography and message digest techniques to ensure the integrity of the certificate contents. In public key cryptography, a pair of asymmetric keys is used. The first key is the private key that is kept secret by the owner. The second key is the public key. The owner publishes this public key to everyone with whom he wishes to communicate. Data encrypted with the private key can be unencrypted with the public key, and vice versa.

Another important aspect of integrity is content control: examining the content of a data stream to ensure it is free of viruses, junk mail, and confidentiality breaches. This is especially important when dealing with e-mail but can also be applied to other data types. Because of the need to encrypt data that flows over the Internet, it becomes necessary to do the content scanning at the end nodes, as opposed to the gateways (like firewalls) where it may be done more efficiently. There are several commercially available software products for content scanning, e.g., IBM's Antivirus and MIMEsweeper from Content Technologies.

Exhibit 1 delineates three of the four dimensions of information assurance (the fourth being time). Over time (and change), there can be several of these discrete "McCumber-like" models (so named from John McCumber's paper on InfoSec [McCumber, 1991]) along the timeline of an organization. Each of the models might not link to others, but they still reflect the concerns associated with information assurance.

Authentication

Authentication is the assurance that the people (or systems) at each end of the connection are really who they claim to be. Two primary mechanisms are typically used to provide authentication on the Web: (1) user ID and password authentication and (2) digital certificate authentication. An often-used example of user ID and password authentication is the HTTP (Hypertext Transfer Protocol) basic authentication used by many Web servers today. HTTP basic authentication requires clients (usually a browser user) to pass user IDs and passwords to identify themselves to a protected server. There are normally two types of users that can be validated in this way. The first is a standard system user with valid user profiles. This user is allowed to use granted authorities to access objects within the system. The second is a user who is a member of a validation list. This user is able to obtain access only to resources that are authorized to the Web server or applications running on behalf of the Web server. This allows one to control access by the type of Web site user without concern for a Web user getting access to objects outside the scope of the Web server.

Another authentication method that is emerging is called digital ID or digital certificate. Digital ID support relies on a third-party certification authority to vouch for the identity of the client by providing him with a signed certificate. When users connect, they pass their certificate to the server, which then checks the certificates and verifies that each certificate was issued by a trusted authority. A digital certificate can be used to establish identities online and define relationships or privileges within a certain business, group, or community, much like a driver's license or passport can be used for identification in face-to-face transactions.

Digital certificates also allow users to encrypt and send information over open or private networks with the confidence that unauthorized persons cannot open the data, and that any compromise to the data en route can and will be detected. These concerns become magnified when transacting business electronically over unsecured public networks, such as the Internet, because it is more difficult to detect or prevent fraudulent transactions. Public key infrastructure (PKI) technology is fast emerging as the preferred trust mechanism for addressing these concerns. PKI consists of a certificate authority that provides digital credentials to participants, and a public key cryptographic system that uses these digital credentials to ensure overall message integrity, data privacy, signature verification, and user authentication. Together these technologies provide the trusted infrastructure required for secure electronic transactions.

User ID and password authentication is considered weak authentication because passwords typically flow in the clear and can be easily compromised. Digital IDs are considered strong authentication because the certificates are digitally signed by the authority and are protected with digital signatures.

Confidentiality

Confidentiality means that anyone who might be able to intercept the data is unable to interpret its meaning. Encryption techniques are used to scramble the data that is transferred between two machines so that eavesdroppers will not be able to understand the information. Only the intended receiver has an appropriate key that can be used to decrypt the data that was sent. A variety of encryption algorithms can be employed by different techniques to ensure confidentiality.

Encrypting of the data to be transported can be done at several levels: at the application itself, at the application programming interface (API), or in the network layer.

- *Application encryption:* Certain encryption services are available to various applications. One example is the common cryptographic services (CCS). These services are used by an application to perform application-controlled encryption. Most financial and banking applications have a need to control the encryption, and therefore use these interfaces. Another example of application-based cryptography is e-mail. Encrypted mail support can be provided, for example, via Domino's support of S/MIME (secure multipurpose internet mail extensions). S/MIME uses RSA public key encryption techniques to ensure secure transmission of e-mail.
- *Application programming interface encryption:* Some applications do not want to control the encryption, but do want to ensure that data sent and received is always encrypted. Key servers such as HTTP, Telnet, Management Central, LDAP, Java servers, Client Access, DDM, and DRDA support Secure Sockets Layer (SSL). The application interface uses SSL to take over the responsibility of providing encryption for the application's data.
- *Network-based encryption:* The use and growth of the Internet appears to be limitless. Beyond customer access, many companies are also using the global reach of the Internet for easy access to key business applications and data that reside in traditional information technology systems. Companies can now securely and cost effectively extend the reach of their applications and data across the world through the implementation of secure virtual private network (VPN) solutions.

Nonrepudiation

Nonrepudiation means that senders cannot deny at a later date that they actually sent a particular set of data. Requiring the use of a cryptographic technique called a digital signature accomplishes this. The digital signature is part of the digital certificate described earlier in the authentication section. A digital signature is created using a secret key only known by the signer. However, anyone can verify that the digital signature is valid by using a well-known public key associated with the signer. Digital signatures also provide users with a reliable method to decide what Web content (e.g., e-mail) they can trust. Nonrepudiation typically requires other information in addition to the digital signature, such as a digital time stamp.

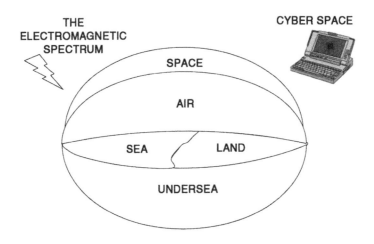

Exhibit 2   The Functional Environment

Summary

So, what really is this thing we call information assurance? By itself, information security is usually implemented in large organizations as a threat-reactive process. Information security (InfoSec) deals with the abnormal, which is measured relative to what is agreed to be the normal configuration of something, e.g., someone hacks into your network and you respond to the hack. Information assurance is more than this. It includes information security, of course, but as a metric, and it functions in a very large environment (Exhibit 2). In information assurance situations, the outcome of security processes must be measured, and the results of those outcomes reported so that they can be effectively acted upon. This closes the loop on an organization's information flow. Any organizational researcher will testify to the importance of providing feedback to a group effort, and that is what information assurance should be doing on a global scale.

The large organizations that are trying the IA approach hope to automate the underpinnings of information collection, while at the same time implementing any of the security services that might be needed. As with many such initiatives, government agencies lead the way. Exhibit 3 shows several significant events over the past ten-plus years that have influenced this process. Some are as simple as the release of instructions, directives, manuals, and handbooks on how to perform in the IA arena. Others are direct, and sometimes rather uncomplimentary, criticisms of departments, agencies, or processes. Over the years, several military and political events had significant impact on IA matters. And finally, in recognition of these new concerns, massive reorganizations or realignments of resources were undertaken. These historical events (and many more too numerous to mention) will not be discussed in detail within these pages but they are a valuable resource for those who are seeking to understand the evolution of IA. The interested reader

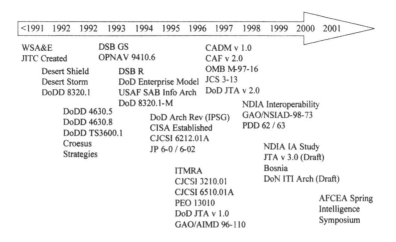

<1991	1992	1992	1993	1994	1995	1996	1997	1998	1999	2000	2001

WSA&E   DSB GS   CADM v 1.0
JITC Created   OPNAV 9410.6   CAF v 2.0
   Desert Shield   DSB R   OMB M-97-16
   Desert Storm   DoD Enterprise Model JCS 3-13
   DoDD 8320.1   USAF SAB Info Arch   DoD JTA v 2.0
                DoD 8320.1-M
     DoDD 4630.5   NDIA Interoperability
     DoDD 4630.8   DoD Arch Rev (IPSG) GAO/NSIAD-98-73
     DoDD TS3600.1   CISA Established   PDD 62 / 63
     Croesus   CJCSI 6212.01A
     Strategies   JP 6-0 / 6-02   NDIA IA Study
                              JTA v 3.0 (Draft)
               ITMRA   Bosnia
               CJCSI 3210.01   DoN ITI Arch (Draft)
               CJCSI 6510.01A
               PEO 13010   AFCEA Spring
               DoD JTA v 1.0   Intelligence
               GAO/AIMD 96-110   Symposium

Exhibit 3 Recent Events

can find references and links to these documents and organizations in Appendix C (Links) and Appendix D (References).

At this high level of data flow, automation of some processes is both desirable and necessary. Otherwise, decision makers become drowned in data, as the reader will see in the cognitive hierarchy model later in the book. What decision makers need is available, authenticated information that may have been encrypted and decrypted correctly at the highest levels of integrity with assurances that the decision maker can reach back to the originator who sent it. As an example:

- Security is having an intrusion detection system (IDS) ringing the system administrator's pager.
- Information assurance is, in addition, having the IDS post the event to a feedback file (not just a temporary console log) for later review. Whatever the system administrator does in response should also be picked up and put into the same feedback file [Loeb, 2002].

Ideally, all the security efforts in a system are integrated into the IA review. One can easily see how building a global information assurance program is possible, given that the highest orders of the building blocks are essentially the same.

Chapter 2

Basic Concepts

Everything that can be invented, has been invented.

Charles H. Duell, 1899

This book is a culmination of research in the areas of systems engineering, cognitive science, information assurance, information architectures, and interoperability. It is the first attempt, we believe, to show a step-by-step systems engineering approach to information assurance (IA). An IA overview was presented in Chapter 1. After a discussion of other basic concepts here and in the next chapter, we start, in Chapters 4 and 5 to lay out a plan of action and milestones (POA&M) to build an IA program from the ground up following accepted systems engineering "best practices."

The current wealth of globally distributed information is both a blessing and a curse. Today we have better, faster access to vast quantities of information. It is as if nearly every library in the world were physically located in our offices or homes — huge quantities of data at our fingertips. The good news is that we have easy access to just about any information that is available in the public domain and this ubiquitous information store is even more readily searchable, retrievable, and instantly available than it would be in a traditional, physical library. Unfortunately, this rapid access, the proverbial "drinking from a fire hose," may, in fact, be worse than no information at all. Without an effective way to organize and parse all of that data, we rapidly find ourselves in a state of data or information overload. When too much data comes in, especially when some of it is contradictory or less reliable, the human mind simply cannot make sense of it all. Thus we need a way to get organized — some method of filtering out unwanted or unnecessary data, and organizing the rest into meaningful information that can then lead to knowledge, understanding, decision making, and, as we will see, wisdom.

But the difficulty continues. Once we have arrived at the relevant data set and organized it into something meaningful, we still must ensure that the information is available to the people who need it, in a timely fashion, with some reasonable expectation of security (integrity, confidentiality, authenticity, etc.). As we saw in the previous chapter, IA is more than just information security (InfoSec), and it cannot be accomplished without interoperability of information and information systems. Interoperability, in turn, relies heavily on information, and information system architectures and standards. To better understand the environment in which we operate, let us first take a closer look at the information itself. Thus we arrive at a basic discussion of information, information attributes, and the attributes of the information systems on which they reside.

Attributes

The term *attributes* refers to the qualities, characteristics, and distinctive features of information and information systems. These attributes are derived from analyses of the roles that systems play in successful execution of missions across the organization. At the highest level, these attributes serve to guide technical requirements development, and help identify organizational interactions that will be key to fielding and supporting equipment. To be complete, attributes must address both the ephemeral qualities of the information being handled, as well as the enduring qualities of the hardware, software, processes, and procedures associated with the information support system itself. A number of authors have listed and categorized numerous attributes associated with systems and information. Each of these attributes can be related to specific systems or information types, and other related system-specific attributes can be created to describe any environment. Here we will briefly discuss the more commonly identified, generic attributes and their relationships. We affectionately call these the "ilities" of information and information systems. Both system and information attributes are concerned with ensuring that communication of information occurs in a manner that ensures that the "correct" information is communicated to authorized recipients only, and in time for the recipient to use it effectively. Summary-level attributes defined later form the basis for further decomposition and allocation of program-specific attributes. Rather than make up our own definitions and further the state of confusion, we have chosen, wherever possible, to simply adopt attribute descriptions offered by others. It should be noted that the literature abounds with seemingly different and distinct attributes. However, if we pull them all together, as we have tried to do here, we note a significant amount of overlap. Many different words have been used to convey the same or very similar meanings and describe the same functional capability. The reader is left to choose those found most appealing or appropriate to the individual and the situation. Sources have been referenced for those who are interested in a particular venue. First, we will address information attributes, followed by system attributes.

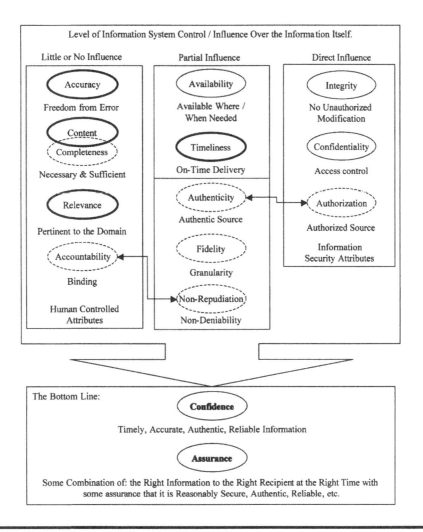

Exhibit 1   Information Attributes

Information Attributes

Information attributes are primarily concerned with the qualities of the information itself, as opposed to the system in which the information resides. Thus, information attributes contribute to one or more of the critical aspects of information "goodness" and the confidence we place in it. Exhibit 1 represents a summary of information attributes and groupings most often cited in the literature. Arguably, some categories are arbitrary and, in addition, some named attributes seem to overlap. Many authors consider some subset of the following information attributes as key. We have divided information attributes into three basic categories:

- Pure information attributes
- Attributes partially influenced by the system
- Attributes directly influenced by the system

Pure Information Attributes

Pure information attributes refers to those attributes on which the system or implementation has little or no influence. They include qualities of information that are not impacted by the storage or transportation mechanisms. These attributes are controlled by the individuals who create or compile the information, and they apply whether the information is transmitted verbally, electronically, in written hard copy, or by any other means. The relative importance of these attributes is debatable and dependent on the situation, so we will synopsize each in alphabetical order. These so-called pure information attributes are shown in the left-hand column in Exhibit 1.

Accountability

Accountability is a security goal generating the requirement that actions of an entity (individual or system) may be traced uniquely to that entity. This supports nonrepudiation, deterrence, fault isolation, intrusion detection and prevention, and after-action recovery and legal action [Stoneburner, 2001].

On an individual level, signed documents, approved actions, and business agreements should be binding. Parties should be able to receive receipts and notarize documents, and should not be able to deny the existence of an agreement or approval of an action nor repudiate that the exchange took place [Entrust, 2000].

Accuracy

Accuracy, of course, is the ability to ensure freedom from error, and to convey, in a usable format, the true situation at the required level of detail or granularity as related to programs, operations, and machine capabilities. This attribute is critical to validating the calculation of results from information assets. Accuracy is not "ground truth," rather it is a measure of precision. Concepts for ensuring accuracy are not mature. The levels of confidence in accurate results are generally obtained from experience and testing [FM 100–6].

Completeness/Content

Completeness of information (sometimes referred to as content) can be defined as the ability to assemble necessary and sufficient information on which to base a rapid, active information presentation and operational decision. Information encompasses all that is necessary and sufficient about the operation, task, or situation at hand to form a rapid, active presentation and decision. This attribute is important to the decision maker at the time of the decision. It is an attribute that has temporal connotations which later events could deny [FM 100–6].

Relevance

Information that is not related to the matter at hand is of little or no use. All too often our information systems provide large quantities of useless facts. Some facts are inherently more germane to the situation than others. Given the overabundance of data and the speed and bandwidth with which we are capable of transmitting it, confining the scope to only that information which directly bears on the matter at hand can significantly reduce our information handling problems and clarify what could be an overly detailed and ambiguous picture.

Attributes Partially Influenced by the System

Other attributes, though peculiar to the information itself, can be and are influenced by the system in which the information resides: electrical, mechanical, biological, or otherwise. Some are directly or heavily affected, while others are only partially influenced. The following (shown in the middle column in Exhibit 1) are partially or indirectly influenced by the underlying transport mechanism.

Authenticity

Authenticity has been defined as the ability to ensure that the information originates from or is endorsed by the source to which it is attributed. This attribute is critical to ensuring that unauthorized agents (individuals, other systems, or system segments) are precluded from inserting false information into the information stream. Concepts for ensuring authenticity have classically included challenge/response using known information which is not likely to be held by an unauthorized individual. Within the area of information technology, this same feature can be provided by encryption wherein the keys are used for digital signatures, signed messages where the signature will only decrypt with a unique public key, and layered encryption (wrappers) where each authenticator applies his encryption to the information [FM 100–6].

In short, the identities of the parties involved in electronic communications and transactions should be verified to ensure the privacy of interactions and to provide only authorized access to high-value or sensitive applications and transactions [Entrust, 1999, 2000].

Availability

As one might suspect, availability is the capability to ensure that the information is on hand and accessible when needed by decision makers during the decision process; or, from a systems engineering perspective:

> The probability that a system is available to operate when called on to do so for a particular mission or application [Eisner, 1997].

The likelihood that a system will operate successfully at the beginning of a mission [Eisner, 1987].

This attribute is critical in the context of having information where it is needed, when it is needed. Concepts for ensuring availability are not mature beyond the concept of building redundancy into the information system.

Alternatively, availability can be defined as the ability to support user needs any place, any time, in any operational environment. Availability (for the intended use and not for any other) is the security goal that generates the requirement for protection against intentional or accidental attempts to perform unauthorized insertions, deletions, or modifications of data, or to otherwise cause denial of service or data [Stoneburner, 2001].

Fidelity

The dictionary defines fidelity as accuracy, exact correspondence to truth or fact, the degree to which a system or information is distortion-free. Given that our information is accurate, as defined previously, we can accept the dictionary definition of fidelity as the quality, clarity, or precision of that information.

Nonrepudiation

As mentioned previously, nonrepudiation is an attribute that is closely associated with accountability. It refers to the inability of the source to disown, deny, disavow, disclaim, fail to recognize, or to reject information as invalid or untrue.

Timeliness

As we have already mentioned, timeliness, the ability to ensure the delivery of required information within a defined timeframe, is important in any information system and critical to some. In a military context, timeliness has been defined as the availability of required information in time to make decisions and permit execution within an adversary's decision and execution cycle or Observe, Orient, Decide, Act (OODA) Loop. Though conceived in a military context and used most often to describe military engagements, the OODA concept applies equally to all interactions. The OODA Loop is the way a business can achieve organizational intelligence with agility, where agility is defined as the ability to thrive in an environment of continuous change [Farrell, 2002]. We will discuss the OODA Loop in more detail later.

Timeliness is important in supporting the availability attribute. It is also important in maintaining the information flow for noncritical processing. Timeliness attributes are measurable and therefore quantifiable. The distinguishing difference between timeliness and availability is that availability is dependent on achieving a goal, while timeliness is concerned with duration or "time late." Concepts for ensuring timeliness are relatively mature with respect to processing speeds and communication rates.

Attributes Directly Influenced by the System

The remainder of the information attributes are those that are directly or substantially influenced by the transport mechanism. In Exhibit 1, they are shown in the right-hand column.

Authorization

Authorization applies to the legitimacy of the user or viewer of the information, "...the granting or denying of access rights to a user, program, or process" [Stoneburner, 2001]. The concern here is that information should be available only to those who possess the proper permissions to access it. This attribute is related to authenticity discussed earlier. Whereas authenticity applies to the sender, authorization applies to the receiver.

Confidentiality

Confidentiality is the ability to ensure that only authorized individuals are able to read specific information. This attribute is critical to preventing disclosure of information to outsiders who may choose to attack or exploit information assets. Confidentiality is primarily concerned with the ability to read or view information. Concepts for ensuring confidentiality through encryption are mature; concepts for ensuring confidentiality through trusted computing technology are available and mature at lower levels of assurance. The concept of confidentiality is akin to authorization.

Confidentiality (of data and key system information) is the security goal generating the requirement for protection from intentional or accidental attempts to perform unauthorized reads, and applies to data in storage, during processing, and while in transit [Stoneburner, 2001]. Data in transit over the network or in storage (such as files on a personal computer or credit card numbers on a Web server or back-end database) should not be disclosed to unauthorized persons [Entrust, 2000].

Integrity

The ability to ensure that the information is protected from unauthorized modification is generally considered to be the integrity of the information. This attribute is important to supporting evidence of correctness and authenticity, and is primarily concerned with the ability to write information. Concepts for ensuring information integrity are mature in the area of trusted technology.

Integrity (of the system and the data residing on that system) is the security goal that generates the requirement for protection against either intentional or accidental attempts to violate either [Stoneburner, 2001]:

- *Data integrity:* The property that data has not been altered in an unauthorized manner while in storage, during processing, or while in transit.
- *System integrity:* The quality that a system has when it performs its intended function in an unimpaired manner, free from unauthorized manipulation.

Data (such as e-mail messages and signed forms) should not be changed, altered, tampered with, or compromised by unauthorized manipulation [Entrust, 2000].

All of these information attributes culminate in a certain level of confidence that we can place in the information; an assurance that our information is timely, accurate, authentic, and thus reliable.

Confidence

Confidence, then, is based on some measure of the "goodness" of the other information attributes. It is a level of trust that all of the other attributes have been satisfied to a level that is appropriate under the circumstances. Confidence is more emotion than fact; thus, given the same information with the same attributes, no two individuals are likely to react in exactly the same way. Confidence in electronic interactions can be significantly increased by solutions that address the basic requirements of integrity, confidentiality, authentication, authorization, and access management or access control [Entrust, 2000].

Assurance

Information assurance is the term applied to the entire collection of attributes that we have been discussing and the measure of effectiveness of each. Assurance is grounds for confidence that the other security goals (integrity, availability, confidentiality, accountability, etc.) have been "adequately met" by a specific implementation [Stoneburner, 2001]:

- Functionality performs correctly
- Sufficient protection against unintentional errors (by users or software)
- Sufficient resistance to malicious penetration or bypass

Reach and Richness

The concept of information reach and richness originated with Philip B. Evans and Thomas S. Wurster in 1997 [Evans, 1997]. They described *reach* as "...the number of people, at home or at work, exchanging information." Reach is a measure of distribution (how far and how many) or the degree to which information is shared.

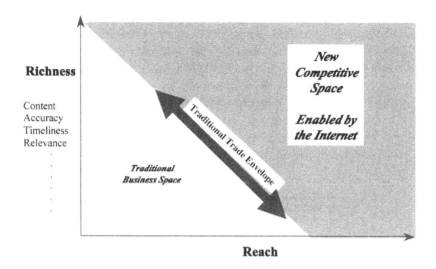

Exhibit 2   Reach and Richness [Alberts, 2000]

Richness, on the other hand, was defined by three aspects of the information itself: (1) bandwidth (the amount of information), (2) the degree to which the information is customized, and (3) interactivity (the extent of two-way communication).

In June, 2000, at the Command and Control Research and Technology Symposium (CCRTS), Dr. David Alberts presented a modified version of reach and richness as they might apply to today's information environment. While the concept of reach was unchanged, Dr. Alberts modified the definition of richness as follows:

> Information richness is an aggregate measure of the quality of battlespace information, and the quality of the interactions among entities [Alberts, 2000].

As shown in Exhibit 2, he specifically enumerates four of the "ilities" that we discussed previously, namely, content, accuracy, timeliness, and relevance, but it seems clear that all information attributes contribute to richness.

While Evans and Wurster did discuss the impact of networks on reach and richness, they did not include them in the original version of Exhibit 2. As we can see, however, Dr. Alberts has enhanced the original, summarizing the contribution of networks. According to Dr. Alberts [2000], networks create value by:

■ Bringing together information from multiple sources to be fused and thus enhance richness
■ Providing access to and facilitating the sharing of information which enhances reach and creates shared awareness
■ Enabling collaboration which transforms shared awareness into actions that can achieve a competitive advantage

In summary, Exhibit 1 lists the information attributes and groupings we have been discussing: so-called pure information attributes are shown on the left, attributes that can be influenced by the system are shown in the middle (partial or indirect influence) and on the right (direct or substantial influence). These are the attributes most often identified in the literature. We also note that the attributes specifically mentioned as components of richness are also included. These attributes pop up in various combinations from author to author. All of the attributes support one another and many are interdependent. Exhibit 3 shows some of these interdependencies as described by the National

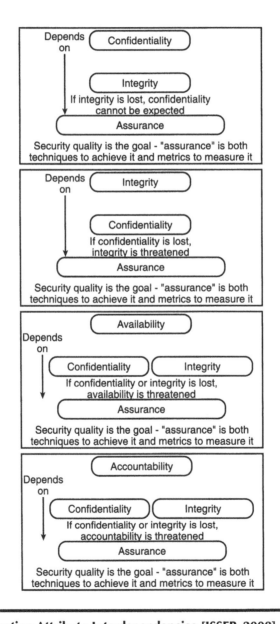

Exhibit 3   Information Attribute Interdependencies [ISSEP, 2000]

Institute of Standards and Technology (NIST) in its Information System Security Engineering Principles [ISSEP, 2000].

However, the bottom line is the confidence that we can place in the information that we have; that "warm fuzzy" feeling that we can use the information with some level of assurance that all, or at least most, of the attributes discussed here have been adequately satisfied. i.e., the information is timely, accurate, relevant, authentic, etc.

System Attributes

System attributes are concerned with specific hardware and software systems themselves as opposed to the information residing in the system. As with information attributes, the number, grouping, and relative importance of system attributes varies by author. We will discuss five major categories as shown in Exhibit 4: security, versatility, continuity, simplicity, and planning principles.

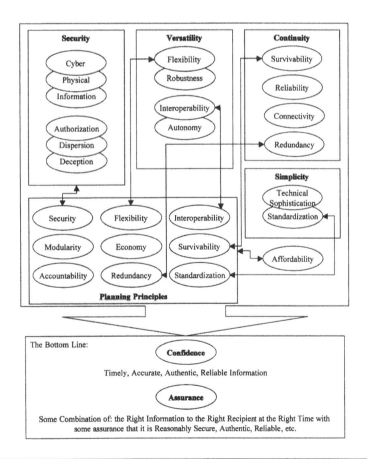

Exhibit 4   System Attributes

Security

The security attributes include cyber security, physical security, information security (InfoSec), authorization, dispersion, deception, and others. Security can be defined as [FM 100–6]:

- Protection from information compromise, including unauthorized access to information or services
- Prevention of denial of service, including loss or disruption of information exchanges or services

The level of security required depends on the nature of the information to be protected and the threat (or perceived threat) of interception or exploitation. Security of information systems is generally achieved by a combination of physical access control, user authentication, and protection of electronic, online communication. Security maintains the integrity of the organization and the information system, but must be balanced by the need to disseminate critical information quickly. If absolute security is our primary concern, we can simply sever all connections to anything outside the system itself, isolate it in a safe or secure room, lock the door, and post a guard. A system thus protected is not likely to be compromised. However, it is also very nearly useless. A delicate balance exists between the level of security that is necessary or desired and the need for usability. There is no such thing as a totally (100 percent) secure system; vulnerabilities always exist. The questions then are:

- What level of risk is acceptable?
- What level of security is achievable?
- What is the value of the information or the cost of compromise?
- What is the cost of the required protection measures?

Cyber Security

The term *cyber security* has been used to include both the physical security of the system and the electronic security of the information residing in the system. Traditionally, security best practice has advocated a layered security approach, and the layers almost always start with limiting physical access [TCSEC, 1985].

Physical Security

The best way to protect an information system and the information on that system is to prevent unauthorized access to that system. The physical security of the system typically includes a number of layers of access control from perimeter security (fences, guards, surveillance), facility security (building access control, monitoring), and hardware security (physical access to workstations themselves) to user authentication and authorization.

Information Security

Distributed information security rests on the following foundations [ISSEP, 2000]:

- *System assurance:* Assurance is the system characteristic enabling confidence that the system fulfills its intended purpose. It is fundamental to security that the system implementation is of sufficient quality to provide confidence in the correct operation of security mechanisms and in the system's resistance to deliberate or unintentional penetration. Technology has been developed to produce and measure the assurance of information systems. System assurance can be increased by using simple solutions, using higher assurance components, architecting to limit the impact of penetrations, and including trustworthy detection and recovery capabilities. System assurance both supports the architecture and spans it.
- *Operating system (OS) security services:* System security ultimately depends on the underlying operating system mechanisms. If these underlying supports are weak, then security can be bypassed or subverted. System security can be no stronger than the underlying operating system.
- *Distributed system security services:* While some services reside in a particular logical level of the system hierarchy, many are implemented via mechanisms that span the system both physically and logically.

Security Domains

A foundation for information systems security (ISS) is the concept of security domains and enforcement of data and process flow restrictions within and between these domains [ISSEP, 2000].

- A domain is a set of active entities (person, process, or device), their data objects, and a common security policy.
- Domains can be logical as well as physical; dividing an organization's computing enterprise into domains is analogous to building fences (various types of security barriers), placing gates within the fences (e.g., firewalls, gateways, and internal process separation), and assigning guards to control traffic through the gates (technical and procedural security services).
- Domains are defined using factors that include one or more of the following:
    - Physical (e.g., building, campus, region, etc.)
    - Business process (e.g., personnel, finance, etc.)
    - Security mechanisms (e.g., NT domain, network information system (NIS), UNIX groups, etc.).

The key elements to be addressed in defining domains are flexibility, tailored protection, domain interrelationships, and the consideration of multiple perspectives of what is important in information system security.

Authorization

Authorization is a system attribute, as defined here, and an information attribute, as defined earlier. Individuals should only be able to execute transactions or perform operations for which they have been granted permission (such as approving a purchase or withdrawing cash at an ATM); in other words, only if they have the appropriate signing authority [Entrust, 2000]. The intent here is to prevent deception, the intention or tendency to mislead or deceive.

Versatility

Versatility is the ability to adapt readily to unforeseen requirements. It is some combination of system autonomy, flexibility, interoperability, and robustness. Often, these are contentious.

- *Autonomy* represents the ability of systems to function independently. Most information systems, especially large-scale systems, require some interconnectivity to perform the operations for which they were intended. However, when planned or unplanned service interruptions occur, systems should be able to carry on, at least in some limited capacity.
- *Flexibility* is responsiveness to change, specifically as it relates to user information needs and the operational environment. Planners must be flexible in supporting information systems requirements in changing situations. They should anticipate the possibility of changes in the organizational mission or situation and build a plan to accommodate these changes.
- *Interoperability* can be defined as the ability of systems, units, or organizations to provide services to and accept services from other systems, units, or organizations, and to use the exchanged services to operate effectively together. Interoperability is the capability of information systems to work together as a system of systems. Interoperability implies compatibility of combined and organizationally common information or data elements and procedures, and is the foundation on which information systems capabilities depend. An interoperable information system is visible at all functional levels; a secure, seamless, cohesive infrastructure that satisfies system and information connectivity requirements from the highest levels of management to the lowest information request. Information systems should comply with the organization's formal information system technical architecture. Adherence to the standards and protocols defined therein helps ensure interoperability and seamless exchange of information between organizational components. Older, legacy information systems that do not comply with the system architecture and accepted standards will require special planning and may not be interoperable [FM 100–6].

■ *Robustness* refers to the system's ability to operate despite service interruptions, system errors, and other anomalous events. It requires the graceful handling of such errors and should be resilient in the face of unexpected disturbances.

Continuity

Continuity is the uninterrupted availability of information paths for the effective performance of organizational functions. Applying the subordinate elements of survivability, reliability, redundancy, and connectivity results in continuity. Global reach is achieved electronically, quickly, and often with a seamless architecture to support the requirements of the managers and their staffs. Connectivity is absolutely essential to the deployment and agility required of real-time systems [FM 100–6]. Continuity is a measure of the systems availability or readiness.

Connectivity

Connectivity is very similar to interoperability. In order to function in a widespread, diverse computing environment, the system must be connected to and communicate with that environment in some fashion, and remain so for the required duration of the operations requiring interaction with other systems.

Redundancy

Duplication of functional capability is generally built into information systems. The amount and complexity of that redundancy is usually dependent on the criticality of the system and the information resident in the system, or both. Redundancy can be complex and expensive, but is essential, at some level, for critical systems.

From an information systems network perspective, planners provide diverse paths over multiple means to ensure timely, reliable information flow. From an equipment perspective, planners ensure that sufficient backup systems and repair parts are available to maintain system or network capabilities [JP 6–0, 6–02; FM 100–6].

Reliability

Reliability is a measure of system dependability. From a systems engineering perspective, it can be defined as:

■ The probability that a system successfully operates to time t [Eisner, 1997].
■ The likelihood of mission success, given that a system was available to operate at the beginning of the mission [Eisner, 1987].

Some systems operate continuously, others remain idle for long periods of time until they are needed. In either case, it is important that a system is up and operating when called on. Reliability is closely related to availability.

Survivability

Survivability is a measure of the system's ability to function under less-than-optimal, degrading circumstances. Information systems must be reliable, robust, resilient, and at least as survivable as the supported organization. Distributed systems and alternate means of communication provide a measure of resilience. Systems must be organized and positioned to ensure that performance under adverse conditions degrades gradually and not catastrophically [FM 100–6].

Simplicity

Simplicity is a measure of the complexity of the environment. It includes standardization and technical sophistication.

Standardization

Standardization can be both a blessing and a curse. Systems, in general, are not built as a single, unified whole, nor are they constructed, integrated, and operated by any one entity; the very few, large, complex, global systems that are, must still interface with other systems or components. In order to facilitate this interaction and interconnectivity, some minimal set of hardware and software interface standards must be adopted. As we shall see later, one of the biggest issues with interoperability of systems today is the lack standards or lack of adherence to existing standards.

On the other hand, standards can stifle creativity and technological advancement. If we are bound to an existing and (by definition) aging standard, we are often precluded from inventing and adopting a better mouse trap. There must be an informed, technically sound trade-off between these two extremes.

Examples of successful application of standards to large-scale, diverse, ubiquitous systems abound. Electrical power distribution grids, and telephone systems come to mind. In addition, the computing world has successively adopted standards for computer boards, serial and parallel interfaces, modems, local networks, and the World Wide Web. Unfortunately, not all global information systems have been similarly successful.

Technical Sophistication

Like standards, technology can be both a help and a hindrance. Not enough technology can keep systems from performing at desired or required levels. Too much technology can overly complicate the system, requiring an inordinate

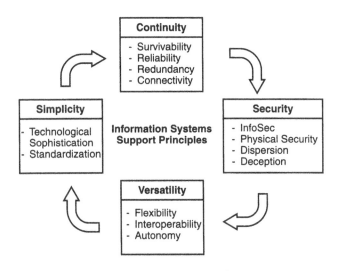

Exhibit 5   Information System Attributes

amount of time, money, manpower, and other valuable resources to keep it running smoothly. In addition, advanced technology is not always a good thing. Examples abound of technologically advanced or superior products that failed to attain widespread acceptance. Sony's Beta video technology and IBM's PC Micro-Channel Architecture (MCA) are good examples. While both were generally recognized as technically superior standards, they failed to proliferate and gain market share, and consequently fell into virtual disuse (as with MCA) or niche use (Beta). The result is difficulty supporting, expanding, and implementing such systems.

An alternative view of how these attributes might interrelate is shown in Exhibit 5.

Information System Support Planning Principles

When planning or designing any system, the first and probably the most critical step in the entire process is the collection, definition, and analysis of requirements. Each of the attributes described within these pages embodies one or more requirements that must be taken into account. Thus, system planning principles include most of the system and information attributes described previously in addition to many others too numerous to mention here. Despite a certain level of redundancy with the foregoing discussion, we have chosen to present nine principles that seem to be central to a solid foundation. The information systems planning principles discussed here are derived from Department of Defense Joint Publications [JP 6–0, 6–02], but represent a solid foundation for all information system planning and design. These principles focus the planner's attention on what is important to the user. Accountability, flexibility, interoperability, redundancy, security, standardization, and survivability have been addressed already and will not be repeated here. However, in addition to these we have the following:

Economy (of Scale)

Scalable system packages ease the application of economy. Space, weight, or time constraints limit the quantity or capability of systems that can be deployed. Information requirements must be satisfied by consolidating similar functional facilities, integrating commercial systems into organizational information networks, or resorting to a different information system.

Modularity

Modularity is distinguished by small packages consisting of sets of equipment, people, and software adaptable for a wide range of missions. Planners must understand the mission, the leader's intent and operational plan, the availability of assets, and the information structure required to meet the needs of each operation. These packages must satisfy the organization's informational requirements during the execution phases of the mission. Modular information systems packages must be flexible, easily scaled, and tailored with respect to capability.

Affordability

Affordability is the extent to which information system features are cost effective on both a recurring and nonrecurring basis. It is perhaps the major factor in system procurements. From the federal government to industry, cost has always been a driving concern. The important point here is to match the cost with the benefits of the system. Cost benefit analyses are routinely conducted for all manner of purchases, acquisitions, and updates. The one area where this trade-off is lacking, however, is in the area of systems and information security features. This will be discussed in greater detail when we talk about risk, threat, and vulnerability in Chapter 3.

All of the attributes discussed thus far have appeared in a variety of other IA-related works. However, there is one system attribute that the authors have not seen discussed elsewhere.

Maintainability

All systems require maintenance of one sort or another ,and the concept of maintainability may be implied in some of the other "ilities" we have presented here. However, for clarity, let us break this attribute out so that it can be addressed specifically. Maintainability, in systems engineering parlance, is defined as "the general ease of a system to be maintained, at all levels of maintenance" [Eisner, 1987].

Most new, major hardware system acquisitions today (such as aircraft, ships, automobiles, etc.) are specifically designed with maintainability in mind. Information systems are no different. There are a number of steps that can be taken, from both the hardware and software perspectives, that will decrease the maintenance costs, while increasing reliability and availability. Though a detailed discussion of these issues is beyond our scope here, maintainability issues should receive the same consideration as other requirements from the very beginning of system development.

The Bottom Line, Revisited

Assurance (that the other goals are sufficiently met) is grounds for confidence in our system implementation and its resident information.

We refer to IA repeatedly because it is the goal for all information systems. At this point, the interested reader may wish to review Chapter 1, where we discuss IA in more detail. Let us now take a closer look at how these attributes relate to IA.

Information Assurance

The term *assurance* can be defined in many ways, depending on the specific aspect being examined or the viewpoint adopted. However, in the majority of cases it can be said that IA includes the notions of trust and confidence. Information technology security refers to assurance in many contexts. At the very highest level, it can be characterized as the confidence or trust that a customer can have that an organization, system, product, or service will perform as expected.

A more refined version of this notion, and one that is more specific to security, is the confidence that an organization's product or system will fulfill its security objectives. From the customer's point of view, this may be expressed as "the organization, product, system, or service will comply with my security needs."

As seen in Exhibit 6, assurance needs can be generated in several different ways. Ten different types of assurance are shown [Menk, 1999].

- *Guarantee assurance* can be gained as a result of the guarantee offered by the vendor.
- *Evaluation assurance* can be gained as a result of a third-party evaluation.
- *Certification and accreditation assurance* can be gained by performing a system certification and accreditation.
- *Capability maturity assurance* can be gained from the capability maturity of the organization.
- *Recommendation assurance* can be gained from a recommendation.
- *Warranty assurance* can be gained from a warranty associated with a product or service.
- *Quality assurance* can be gained from a quality assurance program.
- *Track record assurance* can be gained based on the past history of performance.
- *Process assurance* can be gained from the process used to perform the tasks.
- *Reputation assurance* can be gained from the willingness of the organization to preserve its reputation.

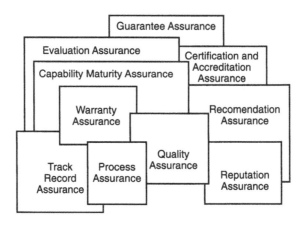

Exhibit 6   Assurance Source Framework [Menk, 1999]

In the security domain, assurance currently is most commonly generated by an evaluation, or by a system certification and accreditation (C&A). Evaluation of a product or component, and certification of a system provides the technical analysis that permits accreditation and visibility into known threats, vulnerabilities, impacts, risks, and safeguards. The risk taker would ideally like to have assurance that the risks have been minimized or mitigated to the best extent possible. Some of this assurance can also be generated by the policies, processes, and procedures used to develop, integrate, and manage the product or system. Further, activities performed by an organization implementing a standard, rigorous methodology, such as the Software Systems Engineering Capability Maturity Model (SSE-CMM), the Systems Engineering Capability Maturity Model (SE-CMM), or the new Capability Maturity Model Integrated (CMMI), and conducting appropriate assessments can form the basis of a process assurance metric. Assurance in an organizational process translates into assurance in the product, system, or service that will result from the process, and that will satisfy the security needs established. This therefore represents a further method by which assurance can be generated and another form of assurance, that of process assurance, seen in Exhibit 6.

Much work is being performed to establish metrics for different types of assurance and the interrelationships between different types of assurance. Some of the origins of current theories related to assurance are shown in Exhibit 7. However, it is also important to understand who is the user of assurance, how assurance might be used and why.

From the risk taker's perspective, it is possible to make a judgment of whether a security-related event, i.e., the threat or the vulnerability, should be protected against and safeguards implemented, based on the likelihood of the event and the impact of an occurrence. If, however, a large measure of uncertainty is associated with the likelihood, as is often the case, this determination becomes much more difficult. Increased assurance directly reduces the uncertainty associated with vulnerability. It thus has a significant effect on reducing the uncertainty associated with the risk of an event.

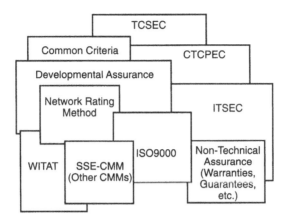

Exhibit 7 Assurance Overview Model

Assurance can make a significant contribution to the decision of the risk taker, and the security of the organization, and assist in focusing resources on those places that will have the greatest benefit to the organization. Similarly, when consumer organizations select a safeguard to mitigate risks, a certain amount of assurance can be attributed to the processes a supplier organization has in place to provide those safeguards. Process assurance, the degree of confidence gained through analysis of process evidence that security needs are satisfied, is a powerful mechanism for contributing to the total assurance in a manner different from evaluation assurance and certification and accreditation assurance.

Commercial Capabilities

The availability of commercial information systems often offers a guide as well as an alternative means to satisfy informational needs. Further, it may reduce the number and size of deployed modular packages; however, security must be considered. Operational use of a commercial system allows planners to compensate for system shortages and to meet the surge of information requirements in the early stages of deployment. However, planners have to ensure that deployed modular information systems packages implement open, nonproprietary, commonly accepted standards and protocols to interface with commercial systems [JP 6–0, 6–02; FM 100–6].

Security

The level of security required will depend on the nature of the information to be protected and the threat of interception or exploitation. Communications security (ComSec) is usually provided by electronic, online encryption devices. Security of information systems is achieved by a combination of control of physical access to terminals, by software, and by control of disks. Security

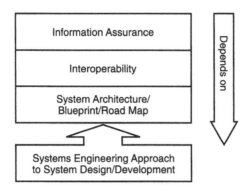

Exhibit 8   Security Goal Interdependencies [ISSEP, 2000]

must be balanced by the need to disseminate critical information quickly [ISSEP, 2000]. Security goal interdependencies are presented in Exhibit 8 from both a "top-down" and a "bottom-up" perspective.

In the past, many large organizations, most notably military organizations, gave great emphasis to security. In many instances, they expected complete and totally secure environments. We will show how total security is probably not attainable. Security is a relative term. The bottom line usually boils down to how much the information is worth, hence, how much we are willing to commit to its protection. To reiterate, with respect to computer-based information systems, the security of information residing on the computer can probably best be achieved by unplugging the unit, locking it in a strong safe, and posting a guard behind several layers of high-tech surveillance and intrusion-detection equipment. The information thus protected is very safe, but utterly useless; therefore the issue becomes one of information assurance and not, strictly speaking, security.

Network Views

An organization's intranet is typically dispersed physically and interconnected by circuits that are frequently not controlled by the organization [ISSEP, 2000].

Internally, an organization should consider compartmenting its intranet in a manner analogous to the watertight doors on a ship (hatches that are closed and sealed in an emergency against the intrusion of water). This supports the enforcement of organizational policies and the limitation of damage in the event of a breach of security.

"External" is no longer easy to determine. It is important to distinguish between transactions that are truly from "outside" and those that are the equivalent of being internal. The use of end-to-end encrypted paths is advisable for the latter.

The ability to detect and respond to insecurity is an essential part of an effective information system security capability. This is best achieved via incorporating detection, analysis, and response components into the organization's intranet.

Risk Management

Chapter 3 will discuss risks, threats, and vulnerabilities in detail. At this juncture, suffice it to say that risk management has become a major issue with respect to information systems, and the more connected and interoperable that they become, i.e., the farther the reach, the greater the risks. Few if any systems are free of vulnerabilities, thus they all have some degree of risk. Risk cannot be eliminated. However, if we are careful to identify, define, and measure the vulnerabilities of our systems, we can usually manage the risk to some acceptable degree.

Information Concepts

Next we look at data, information, and knowledge, and how they are used to arrive at conclusions and make decisions. There have been a number of versions of this discussion used by the authors and others for a variety of purposes. We will confine ourselves here to four distinct issues, consisting of

1. The cognitive or information hierarchy
   - The information domain and the cognitive domain
2. The decision or, as used by the military, the command hierarchy
3. The Observe, Orient, Decide, Act (OODA) Loop
4. The decision timeline (or battle timeline for military applications)

Cognitive Hierarchy

The cognitive hierarchy deals with the steps that humans take, i.e., the processes that we go through to collect, refine, categorize, and understand facts about our environment. It is an attempt to explain how we go from a collection of small, seemingly insignificant facts to some form of understanding, awareness, decisiveness, and wisdom. Typically, there are three distinct sections to the cognitive hierarchy: the information domain, the cognitive domain, and reality.

Information Domain

The beginnings of the cognitive hierarchy are based in the information domain which usually starts with a large variety of data points or facts that we have managed to accumulate via whatever means are at our disposal. However, data by itself is unintelligible until it is joined to a person's image of reality or frame of the decision situation (frame of discernment). It is at this point that data becomes information and knowledge [Sage, 1990]. What, then, is knowledge?

Unfortunately, these terms as used here, especially "data" and "information," are applied differently than one might expect from common, everyday conversation. Webster defines data as "information, esp. information organized

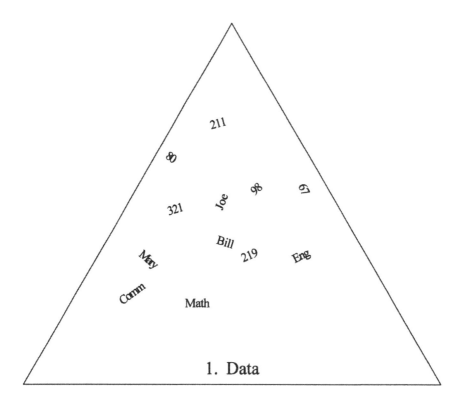

Exhibit 9   Data

for analysis," and information as "facts learned." With respect to the information domain, these definitions are essentially reversed. For purposes of this discussion, the terms data, information, and knowledge hold specific meaning and shall be defined as follows:

- *Data:* An unordered, unorganized collection of facts (Exhibit 9)
- *Information:* Data arranged in some logical, orderly, organized fashion
- *Knowledge:* Insights created by the application of the rules of logic and "real-world" facts to the available information.

In its raw form, data is simply a random collection of facts (Exhibit 9). In this natural, essentially chaotic state, it is of marginal, if any, use. In order to be meaningful, we must somehow arrange the data in a fashion that provides practical information.

As we can see, data means very little without some method of organizing, viewing, and interpreting it. However, it is not always obvious whether these facts are in any way related and, if so, how. The first task is to establish some logical connection between and among the data that we have collected, and then organize that data into a meaningful format. The result is meaningful, useful, coherent information (Exhibit 10).

Comparing Exhibits 9 and 10, we can see that somehow we have come to the conclusion that the data we have collected pertains to students, courses that

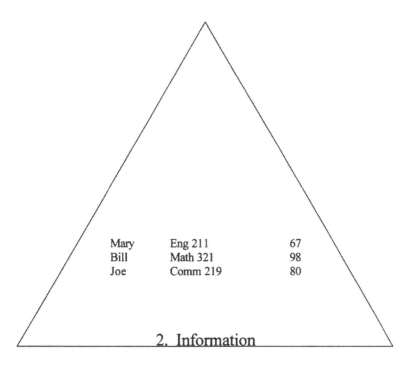

Exhibit 10   Information

they have taken or are taking, and their grades in those courses. But the big question is, how did we get here? What did we have to do or assume in order to make this connection? How do we know that it is correct? We obtained information from the collected data by organizing it into some recognizable form. How we came to this recognition, however, is debatable. Most likely, our real-world experience and environment lead us in a particular direction. Perhaps the person responsible for organizing this particular data set inhabits a university or some other educational environment; that being the case, it takes little effort to realize that the data of Exhibit 9 fits the information mold of Exhibit 10. Unfortunately, the connection is not always as easy to make. Nonetheless, more often than not the collector of the data is working within a specific domain, knows what he is collecting, and therefore knows how to fit the pieces together.

So we now have useful information, but not much. Knowledge must then be extracted from the available information. We know that Mary, for example, has a 67 in Eng 211, but what does that mean? What is Eng 211, and is a 67 good or bad? Without more information to put this into perspective, we really do not have any knowledge of what that means from any particular point of view such as Mary or the school. But when we combine the information that we have collected, with additional information from our environment, we can come to the conclusion that Mary is not doing well in this class (Exhibit 11). Combined with other information concerning the school's grading policies, her own study habits, and a host of other variables, one might also conclude that Mary is not working hard enough and is in danger of failing. However, in order to come to these conclusions, we had to apply logic and additional

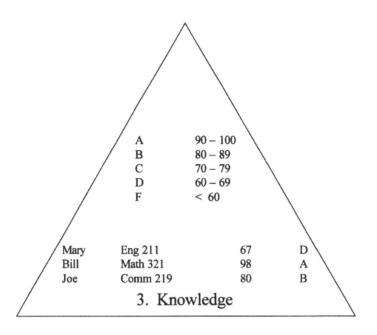

A	90 – 100		
B	80 – 89		
C	70 – 79		
D	60 – 69		
F	< 60		

Mary	Eng 211	67	D
Bill	Math 321	98	A
Joe	Comm 219	80	B

3. Knowledge

Exhibit 11   Knowledge

information about how the real world operates, and assume information not currently available from the facts given. How, then, do we know when the combined information from several sources is sufficient?

Consider the following example. A number of years ago, a freshman at the University of Illinois brought his grades home during the winter break. His parents were ecstatic; their son had achieved a grade point average of 3.85 during his first semester in a very demanding engineering curriculum. Because he had always been an honor roll student with a solid A/B average in high school, averaging between 3.75–3.9, it was obvious that he was doing equally well in his new educational environment. Unfortunately, the parents were missing a vital piece of additional information. The University of Illinois was using a five-point grading scale rather than the typical 4-point scale used by most other colleges, universities, and high schools. The student had a solid C average, but not the high B average that his parents assumed. Although we usually can and often do make these assumptions, things are not always what they seem. Consider another example: today, in the Fairfax County, Virginia, public school system, students must rank in the 94th percentile or above to achieve a grade of A, as opposed to the typical grading scale where anything greater than or equal to 90 is an A. In Fairfax County, 93 is a B.

So, we have navigated the first part of the cognitive hierarchy, namely, the information domain (Exhibit 12), and have managed to collect, analyze, categorize, organize, and interpret raw facts to arrive at some level of knowledge with respect to the domain of discourse. Note that most of what we have accomplished so far has been rather mechanical. We have collected facts from one or more sources (Exhibit 9); we have organized the facts into something recognizable (Exhibit 10); and, we have combined the resulting

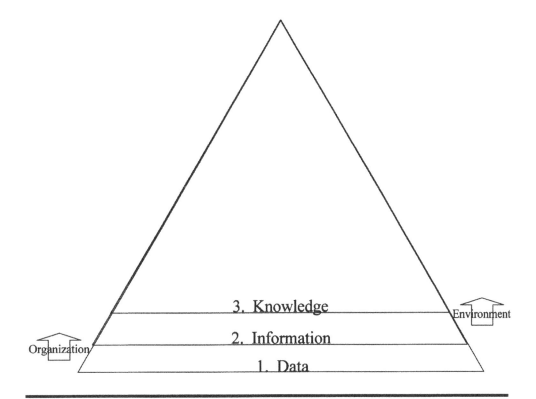

Exhibit 12 The Information Domain

information from multiple sources to arrive at some level of knowledge (Exhibit 11). Webster defines the term *knowledge* as "understanding acquired through experience." Here again, our usage diverges; we use the term to indicate a realization of the information.

At this point, we have exhausted all of the "mechanical" steps that we can take to refine the facts that we have available. Through the cognitive hierarchy, we use experience to build understanding from knowledge. Now we arrive at the daunting realization that we must take the next step. Now we must actually start to become "SMART": more *s*pecific, *m*easurable, *a*ccurate, *r*eliable, and *t*imely.

Cognitive Domain

The cognitive domain builds on the data, information, and knowledge we have previously gathered. If we think about the knowledge we have acquired, we can begin to interpret what we see and achieve some level of understanding. The depth, breadth, and quality of our understanding generally depends on the quantity and quality of the underlying knowledge on which it is based, and our cognitive abilities with respect to that knowledge. In Exhibit 13, we have begun to interpret what we know or think we know using deductive, inductive, and abductive reasoning techniques, which we touch on briefly at the end of this discussion.

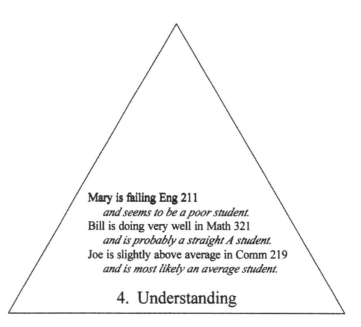

Mary is failing Eng 211
and seems to be a poor student.
Bill is doing very well in Math 321
and is probably a straight A student.
Joe is slightly above average in Comm 219
and is most likely an average student.

4. Understanding

Exhibit 13   Understanding

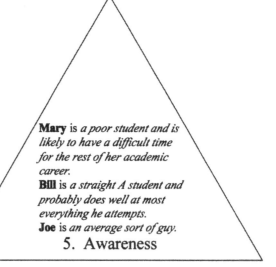

Mary is *a poor student and is
likely to have a difficult time
for the rest of her academic
career.*
Bill is *a straight A student and
probably does well at most
everything he attempts.*
Joe is *an average sort of guy.*
5. Awareness

Exhibit 14   Awareness

This is where we begin to make assumptions, draw conclusions and generally try to extend our understanding of the situation or environment based purely on thought processes applied to the underlying knowledge. By working through these thought processes and analyzing what we find, we can build a better awareness of our surroundings (Exhibit 14).

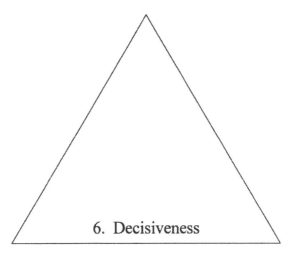

Exhibit 15   Decisiveness

Exhibit 16   Wisdom

Being aware of the situation, however, does not necessarily mean that we are willing or able to act on our beliefs; that decisiveness comes from a level of confidence in all that has gone before. How good is our data, information, knowledge as measured by some set of attributes as discussed earlier? How confident are we in our assessment of that knowledge, and the understanding and awareness that results? Decisiveness (Exhibit 15) is also heavily dependent on the individual characteristics of the decision maker, but although it may be vastly different from individual to individual, some comfort level must be achieved before we can claim a decisiveness to our state of mind and a willingness to take action.

From here, the next step is far from clear. Indeed, many authors would debate some aspects of our discussion thus far. However, at some point we reach a lofty, somewhat magical state of wisdom (Exhibit 16). What that is and how we get there has been a mystery since the beginning of mankind. Here, the common dictionary definition of wisdom is as accurate as any:

Exhibit 17   The Cognitive Domain

insightful understanding of what is true, right, or enduring; native good judgment.

We should also mention that within the cognitive domain, our usage of terms follows common definitions much more closely than in the information domain discussion. For clarity and completeness, we present those dictionary definitions here:

> *Understanding:* The ability to comprehend, perception; the capability to think, learn, judge; individual judgment or interpretation; accord of thought or feeling
> *Awareness:* Being mindful or conscious of
> *Decisiveness:* Marked by firm determination; resolute; unquestionable

But despite reaching this illusional state and rounding out the cognitive hierarchy (Exhibit 17), we are not done yet. So far, our discussion has been confined to the facts that we can discern about our domain or environment, our interpretation of those facts, and the conclusion we can draw from them. But there is still at least one piece missing. Why have we gone to all of this trouble collecting and mechanically orchestrating facts, then exercising our brains trying to decide what it all means? The simple answer is that we do all of this in an effort to better understand reality. Out there somewhere is the real world. Clearly, what we are trying to do is to build an understandable, unambiguous picture that accurately represents that reality (Exhibit 18).

Where reality fits with the rest of the hierarchy is debatable. The authors prefer to show reality somewhere between awareness and wisdom, as in Exhibit 19.

The question still remains, How do we use what we have learned? To answer this question, the U.S. military has adopted what it refers to as the command hierarchy or, more generically, the decision hierarchy.

Exhibit 18   Reality

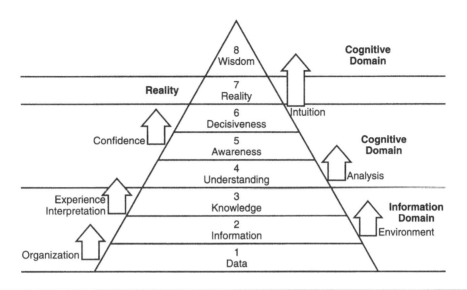

Exhibit 19   The Cognitive/Information Hierarchy

The Command/Decision Hierarchy

The decision hierarchy is an attempt to map human decision processes to the information and cognition processes just described, and fits closely with the OODA Loop battlefield concept developed by Colonel John Boyd, USAF, in the mid-1980s. Referring to Exhibit 20, in any situation, military or civilian, we generally start by trying to collect as much information about our situation

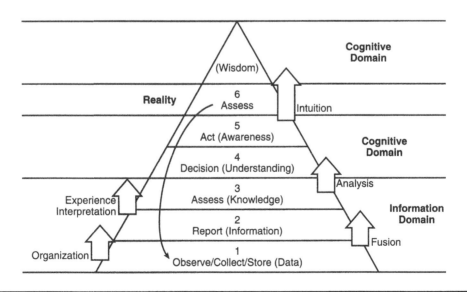

Exhibit 20   The Command/Decision Hierarchy

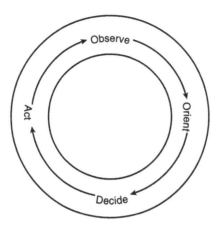

Exhibit 21   The OODA Loop

as possible. We observe our environment and collect facts. We then collate the resultant information into some form of report. This may be an entirely internal, informal, and perhaps even subconscious process or, in any large organization, it is more likely to be formalized and written. Reports thus generated are generally read and assessed to formulate a decision on which some action is then taken. Typically, the results of this action are then monitored to determine impact or change in the facts of the environment or situation and the process starts all over again. This is the process that Boyd dubbed the OODA Loop (Exhibit 21).

> Machines don't fight wars. Terrain doesn't fight wars. Humans fight wars. You must get into the mind of humans. That's where the battles are won.

> **Colonel John Boyd**

Boyd's theory was that a fighter aircraft with better maneuverability and superior speed characteristics should generally win the majority of "dog fight" engagements. However, this was not happening in actual air-to-air engagements during the Korean War. U.S. fighter pilots, despite flying aircraft with wider turn radii, were consistently beating adversary pilots and their aircraft. Based on an in-depth study, Boyd came to the conclusion that it was not necessarily the characteristics of the aircraft that was the deciding factor in winning a "dog fight," at least not the only factor. It was the ability of the pilot to acquire the adversary first, and the speed with which the pilot's decision-making inputs reached the aircraft's control surfaces. Boyd's hypothesis was that a U.S. fighter pilot would win the "dog fight" because he could complete "loops" of decision-making quicker than his adversary. Boyd surmised that quicker was better than faster. Boyd's loop occurred in four distinct steps [Boyd, 1986]:

- *Observe:* U.S. pilots could see their adversaries better and more completely because the cockpit design of their aircraft ensured better visibility.
- *Orient:* Because U.S. pilots acquired the adversary first, they could then react by orienting themselves toward the adversary faster.
- *Decide:* After reacting with their initial orientation, the U.S. pilot's level of training then allowed him as a decision maker to act quicker, proceeding to the next combat maneuver.
- *Act:* With the next combat maneuver decided on, U.S. pilots could then rapidly "input" aircraft control instructions, with the resultant quicker initiation of a desired maneuver.

A more in-depth look at the OODA Loop concept can be found in Chapter 9.

Reasoning

We have discussed the decision maker forming a mental picture. It is much easier for humans to do that than to manipulate and interpret text in one's mind. Simply, a picture is worth a thousand words, and a decision maker understands the significance of an icon much faster than having to read a couple of pages of text. Over the years, most of our early, text-based automated systems (e.g., CPM, DOS, Unix) have been converted to or augmented by a graphical user interface (GUI) (e.g., Windows, X-Windows, Apple OS) for just that reason. The authors believe that this and the emergence of the object-oriented paradigm (Chapter 6) are empirical indicators that humans find it easier to describe "views of the world" through the notion of objects rather than text.

The graphic shown in Exhibit 22 was originally developed for a Navy case study in which the authors participated. Consequently, it depicts Navy Command and Control systems, but the concepts are sufficiently generic to apply to any organization, and it makes the connection between individual systems, information systems, cognitive hierarchy, OODA Loop, and timeline concepts.

Virtually every operation, platform, system, and individual is heavily dependent on timely, accurate, reliable data and the infrastructure through which it moves. Consequently, that data and the infrastructure must be connected and interoperable so that the information can be shared, protected, trusted, secure, and assured. Data is at the center of everything. It is shared among those who need it via the communications and computers infrastructure. Whether we talk about the OODA Loop or the battle timeline, there are a number of functions that are routinely performed. We sense the environment and store the data that we collect. We use the data to construct models and simulations of the known environment and plan our actions. Decision makers use this wealth of information, and the infrastructure on which it flows, to command and control their organizations, deploying and directing them as necessary. Finally, we conduct assessments (or in military terms, BDA, battle damage

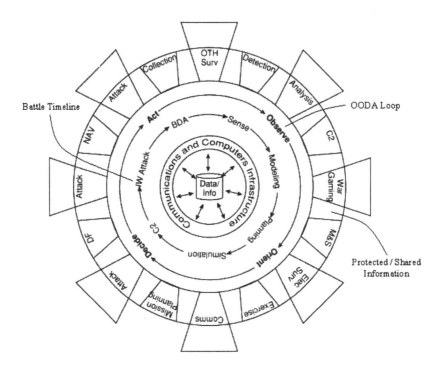

Exhibit 22   The Information Pinwheel

assessment) to determine what affect we have had and how the environment has changed; which brings us back to sensing the environment. This cycle, of course, is recursive, and in any actual engagement there are a number of people performing these functions simultaneously. The trick is to do it better, faster, and more reliably than the adversary, or get "inside his OODA Loop," as the saying goes.

Inferential Reasoning

Inferential reasoning is a broad and complex topic, well beyond the scope of this book. However, because we briefly mentioned reasoning concepts with respect to the cognitive hierarchy, we include very short and cursory descriptions of three basic reasoning concepts here: deduction, induction, and abduction. The interested reader can find significantly more detail in the references. In particular, Professor David A. Schum at George Mason University (GMU) in Fairfax, Virginia, is probably one of the leading experts in the world and has produced several seminal works in this area [Schum, 1986]. A short summary follows.

Exhibit 23   Inference Examples

Deduction:

>*Rule:* All the beans from this bag are white.
>*Case:* These beans are from this bag.
>*Result:* These beans are white.

Induction:

>*Case:* These beans are from this bag.
>*Result:* These beans are white.
>*Rule:* All the beans from this bag are white.

Abduction:

>*Rule:* All the beans from this bag are white.
>*Result:* These beans are white.
>*Case:* These beans are from this bag.

Types of Logic

Logic can be divided into three basic types (Exhibit 23) [Curts, 1990b]:

1. *Deductive:* The process of reasoning in which a conclusion follows necessarily from the stated premise. Inference by reasoning from the general to the specific [Morris, 1976].
2. *Inductive:* A principle of reasoning to a conclusion about all the members of a class from examination of only a few members of the class. Inference by reasoning from the particular to the general [Morris, 1976].
3. *Abductive:* A form of deductive logic that provides only a "plausible inference" [Firebaugh, 1988]. The conclusion is *possibly,* but not necessarily, *true.*

Notice that these three types of logic are ordered by the confidence one can place in the new knowledge inferred from the given data. The assessment of the validity of a hypothesis is inductive in nature. However, the generation of new hypotheses and the determination of evidence relevant to these hypotheses involves deductive and abductive reasoning [Sage, 1990]. It is much easier to implement a decision support system on the rules of deduction than to use induction to derive general truths from a database full of particular facts. Abduction appears to be more difficult by yet another order-of-magnitude.

Deduction

New knowledge based on deductive reasoning is *always true* if the assumptions on which it is based are true. One basic rule of deductive inference is *modus ponens,* if X is true and if X being true implies Y is true, then Y is true:

All women are female.
Sally is a woman.
Therefore, by deduction, Sally is female.

Induction

New knowledge based on the observation of many specific cases (induction) is *generally* true as long as the systems studied are well-behaved. More formally, for a set of objects, $X = \{a, b, c, d,...\}$ if property P is true for object a, and if P is true for object b, and if P is true for c, then P is true for all X:

IF $1 = 1^2$
AND IF $1 + 3 = 2^2$
AND IF $1 + 3 + 5 = 3^2$
AND IF $1 + 3 + 5 + 7 = 4^2$
THEN, by induction, $\Sigma(n$ successive odd integers$) = n^2$

Abduction

The term *abduction* was first introduced into philosophy and science by the renowned American philosopher Charles Sanders Peirce (1839–1914) to designate a special kind of logical reasoning. In his view, abduction, deduction, and induction are the three fundamental logics of scientific inquiry [Peirce, 1934, 1955]. The *Encyclopedia Britannica* describes abduction as "reasoning that derives an explanatory hypothesis from a given set of facts." Though loose and informal, this definition captures the basic meaning of the term.

> Abduction makes its start from the facts. Induction makes its start from a hypothesis. Abduction seeks a theory. Induction seeks for facts. Abduction is, after all, nothing more than guessing. Abductive inference shades into perceptual judgment without any sharp line of demarcation between them.
>
> **Charles Sanders Peirce**

The first starting of a hypothesis and the entertaining of it, whether as a sample interrogation or with any degree of confidence, is an inferential step called abduction (sometimes called retroduction). Abductive inference shades into perceptual judgment without any sharp line of demarcation between them. Abduction is a heuristic for making plausible inferences. It is heuristic in the sense that it provides a plausible conclusion consistent with available information, but one which may, in fact, be wrong. Formally, if Y is true and X implies Y, then X is true [Peirce 1934, 1955]:

All successful entrepreneurs are rich.
Sally is rich.
Therefore, by abduction, Sally is a successful entrepreneur.

It is intuitively obvious that the conclusions thus reached, while certainly possible, are by no means unquestionable. Abduction, though much less commonly found in automated systems, is the primary reasoning method attributed to Sherlock Holmes by Sir Arthur Conan Doyle:

You know my method. It is founded on the observation of trifles.

Deduction versus Abduction

Human diagnostic reasoning differs from the deductive inference methods used in most existing decision support systems in that it is an abductive logic, which is considered to be a nonmonotonic logic. There are at least three differences that distinguish deduction and abduction [Peng, 1986]:

1. The relationships among entities are categorical implications in deduction. They may be nondefinitive or probabilistic in abduction.
2. In deduction, the hypothetical statement to be proven is given. In abduction, hypotheses first have to be constructed during the inference process before they are "proven" or accepted.
3. In deduction, any inference chain leading to the proof of the theorem is acceptable. In abduction, however, a disambiguation process chooses from among all hypotheses those which are most plausible according to some criteria. Disambiguation is a complex process involving not only the use of associative knowledge, but also some meta-level criteria which are often global and context-sensitive. Empirical studies of human cognitive psychology have shown, and most researchers agree, that disambiguation in abductive inference is based on a repetitive hypothesize-and-test process [Peng, 1986].

Summary

In this chapter, we have covered a number of topics associated with information and information processing as a foundation on which to build. The rest of this book will consider methods to design and build information systems and to protect those systems and the information residing therein.

Chapter 3

Risk, Threat, and Vulnerability Assessments

Take calculated risks. That is quite different from being rash.

General George S. Patton, Jr.

In this chapter, readers will learn that the post implementation/program support phase occurs after the program has been implemented, and continues for the life of the program until phase-out. Management, users, and program developers need to continuously monitor the implementation phase to ensure that it measures up to the expectations and requirements developed in previous phases, and to enhance the program as needed to increase its useful life. This phase includes continuously monitoring, maintaining, and modifying the program to ensure that it performs as expected, and continues to meet the user's dynamic needs. Continuous risk, threat, and vulnerability assessments help identify and prevent potential problems, pinpoint where maintenance costs can be minimized, and determine when modifications or replacement activities should begin. This chapter begins with an in-depth look at a history of terrorist activities against information assets and concludes with a quick look at managing (planning, implementing, and maintaining) the risk.

One reason that risk, threat, and vulnerability assessments need to be so dynamic is that terrorists and terrorist organizations are becoming more intelligent. Their use of technology is growing and their sophistication in terrorist actions has increased, as this chapter will show. In the future, terrorist organizations may expand even further away from assassination, bombing, hijacking, and hostage taking, and toward high-technology terrorism [Icove, 1991]. The Coordinator for Counterterrorism for the Department of State said,

"We anticipate that terrorists will make greater use of high technology in their attacks" [Busby, 1990].

The problem for the information assurance staff is that terrorists already realize that a small bomb or fire at a computer center can do more damage in a short amount of time than any other single event.

Terrorists have historically established a need to continue their destruction of computer resources. To date, "terrorists and activists have bombed more than 600 computer facilities. Terrorism is a pervasive threat against computer facilities worldwide" [Cooper, 1989]. Computers are rapidly becoming a favorite target for terrorists. "Already, terrorists have bombed hundreds of computer sites around the world" [TF, 1988]. Thus, most of this chapter is concerned with establishing and validating the historical precedence.

Terrorism has been on the increase over recent years because of the availability of new targets. The term *new targets* means that the vulnerabilities in advanced, open, industrial societies make suitable targets for terrorist attacks. These include large aircraft, supertankers, international power grids and pipelines, transportation hubs, commercial and communications centers, motorcades, offshore oil rigs, liquefied natural gas facilities, nuclear power facilities, and computerized information and management systems [Laquer, 1987]. Computer centers are likely to be targets for future terrorists in the United States.

Computer attacks already account for some 60 percent of all terrorist attacks in the world. It would be expensive and inconvenient to guard every office and factory, but some changes will have to be made to reduce their vulnerability to crippling terrorist attacks [Cetron, 1989].

Federal Bureau of Investigation (FBI) agent Neil Gallagher, who led an antiterrorism unit in Boston, said more than 15 years ago:

> Bombings against computer centers reached a peak last year, with 24 centers bombed in West Germany alone. What is frightening is that the more our society depends on computers, the greater the risk. The increasing reliance on computers for the normal operation of society has resulted in the creation of critical nodes whose destruction would be comparable to brain death. Thus we have greatly increased the potential for major disruption and economic loss stemming from sabotage of computer facilities or interference with computer operations [Kupperman, 1979].

Also, "a well-directed terrorist attack on 100 key computers could bring the American economy to a standstill" [Sitomer, 1986]. Winn Schwartau, Executive Director of International Partnership Against Computer Terrorism (Interpact), has written a novel, *Terminal Compromise,* fictionalizing a series of devastating computer terrorist attacks against the United States [Schwartau, 1991a]. He writes:

> Computer terrorism provides the ideal mechanism for waging invisible remote control warfare, inflicting massive damage, and leaving

no tracks. Government policies and actions have created this country's most profound weakness: 70,000,000 computers, the mainstay of America's information society, are virtually defenseless against invasion.

Fiction has already become fact.

Nearly a quarter of a century ago, the Foreign Affairs Research Institute of London published a ten-page report on the problem of "intelligent terrorists" by Dominic Baron. It described how to cripple a modern industrialized state through a terrorist attack on its computer systems. Clearly, Baron said:

> ...access to major computing facilities will be open as much to the malefactor as to the good citizen, so it will not be difficult for the "electronic terrorist" to use these facilities to plan optimal strategies for his attacks on the weakest points of some security system [Clark, 1980].

The means of breaking into a computer are the same, whether for personal profit or destructive purposes. For example, a step-by-step description of a method used to divert goods is explained in one book [Hsaio, 1979]. The same method could be used by a terrorist group to steal weapons from an armory.

The need for continual risk, threat, and vulnerability assessments is also shown by the fact that many self-proclaimed computer hackers are very intelligent and some of their actions should be considered terrorism. Terrorism through computers can be done in two ways: when the computer is the target and when it is the instrument of the operation. The first method would involve its destruction or temporary denial of use through, for example, sabotage. The second would involve altering or copying the data. It is the hacker who gets involved with the second scenario. Some hackers attack computer systems by planting computer viruses or breaking in and stealing information — rather than bombing the centers as traditional terrorists have done in the past. The number of computer viruses is increasing by 47 percent per year [NCSA, 1991]. "At the rate things are going today, the "Carlos" of the future more likely will be armed with an IBM PC than a Czech-made VZ61 machine pistol" [Livingstone, 1990].*

U.S. military systems continue to need vulnerability assessments as well. One example is illustrated when a group of West German hackers infiltrated a wide assortment of computers at U.S. military installations and corporations using telephone lines. Three men were convicted in February 1990 of selling some of that information — reportedly none of it classified — to the Soviet Union [Suplee, 1990]. Perhaps the most blood-curdling threat to computer

---

* The "Carlos" referred to is Ilich Ramirez Savchez, better known as "Carlos the Jackal." He is one of the most infamous of all terrorists. The Czech-made Skorpion VZ61 submachine pistol is perhaps the most popular terrorist weapon in the world. Carlos carries a VZ61. Mr. Livingstone is president of the Institute on Terrorism and Subnational Conflict.

security is the vulnerability to terrorism found in most commercial information systems. Arguments by authorities (in the field of computer terrorism) have generally failed to draw much attention to the problem. As a form of intentional destruction, terrorism would seem the most pervasive and unpredictable. Terrorism can seem pervasive by applying levels of force beyond normal vandalism, industrial sabotage, or burglary [Baskerville, 1988].

The most recent problem is that terrorists themselves are using computers. Police raids on terrorist hideouts in South America, Europe, and the Philippines have revealed that terrorists are also using computers, modems, and communications and database software. In a report released in December 1990, the National Academy of Sciences warned: "Tomorrow's terrorist may be able to do more damage with a keyboard than with a bomb" [Ognibene, 1991].

Winn Schwartau states: "We don't normally think of the computer as a weapon. But in the wrong hands, our information processing systems can be turned against us" [Schwartau, 1991b].

The overall problem is that terrorists are becoming more intelligent — where they once were smart enough to understand the damage that could be done through the destruction of computer resources belonging to others, they are now using computer technology to further their causes. Modern electronics technology is providing terrorists with the means to create new variations on some of their oldest techniques: intimidation, kidnapping, murder, and bombing. For example, modern digital electronics provides the ability to construct bombs with digital timers that can be set for a delay of weeks, months, or years [Rawles, 1990a]. A computer chip found in the bomb wreckage of Pan Am Flight 103 at Lockerbie, Scotland, matched the configuration of electronic components of explosives seized in February 1988 from Libyan agents traveling in Senegal [Rowley, 1991]. It is alleged that terrorists used a microprocessor to detonate the powerful bomb in Brighton, England, that almost killed Prime Minister Margaret Thatcher. Four others lost their lives and more than thirty people were wounded. Technological terrorism is a growing problem [Bequai, 1987].

This is a problem that will continue to escalate, and a very real problem if the IA staff does not take action to remain at least as computer-literate as the terrorists. The Information Assurance staff needs to remember:

> In the tradition of spectacular heists, there's an element of art to the more clever computer-assisted thefts, with none of the heavy-handedness involved in marching into a bank toting a gun [Dotto, 1979].

An entire terrorist movement could be financed from the receipts of computer theft. Vital data could be stolen from computer information banks and ransomed back to the rightful owner [Livingstone, 1982]. Terrorism by itself should be ample enough reason to keep your risk, threat, and vulnerability assessments up-to-date.

Lawrence J. Fennelly, chief consultant to Assets Protection Training Institute, a security company, states it even better: "Part of the problem is that more than 60 percent of all corporations have no computer security programs whatsoever, and over half of these (corporations) have been ripped off" [Sitomer, 1986].

When it comes to writing your assessments, you may find it somewhat difficult to rely on historical precedence. For the most part, companies do not wish to "air their dirty laundry." "Companies hit by computer crime believe that the less the public knows about their misfortunes, the better it is for business" [CW, 1982]. In a mass mailing of 418 letters requesting information from companies on terrorist attacks against their overseas branches, nearly every company declined to acknowledge that anything had ever happened to them. However, through third-party sources (books, newspapers, Internet, etc.), the authors found material to show that the damage and destruction of computer resources had historical precedence. The need for assessments is quite real. Clearly, many companies underestimate the media in a free society:

> **IBM**'s offices in Dusseldorf were attacked in 1982. In June of that year, **Control Data Corporation**'s complex in Dusseldorf was blown up. That same month, one of **McDonnell-Douglas**' West German facilities was also hit. Two months later, in September 1982, **Sperry**'s offices in West Berlin were the target of a terrorist raid. In December 1983, **NCR**'s building in Vitoria and San Sebastian, Spain, were hit by terrorists. And **Honeywell**, whose offices in Athens were rocked by an explosion in 1981, came under another attack in July 1982, this time in Venice. In January of 1985, **IBM**'s offices in West Berlin were bombed [Lamb, 1986]*

Why Perform an Assessment?

Simply, enough incidents have occurred to warrant concern on the part of the IA staff responsible for their data and information anywhere in the world.

> One of the aims of terrorists is to intimidate people by making them aware of their personal vulnerability. To a degree, they have been successful [Long, 1990].

> Attacks on computers must escalate as society becomes more computer literate. Once terrorists wise up to the fact that a computer center is a sensitive part of a company, we can expect to see more of this kind of thing [Lamb, 1986]**

Since the early 1970s, numerous cases of physical attacks against government, commercial, and educational computer centers have been documented

---

* Boldface by authors for emphasis only.
** Article quotes Ken Wong, a security specialist with the British consulting firm BIS Applied Systems.

[DRC, 1986]. In the last decade, at least 57 computer centers in Europe, including six bank computer centers, have been attacked by terrorists [Rozen, 1988]. In certain countries, there is strong evidence that local terrorist groups are systematically trying to attack computers in industry and government. Our social fabric has become more critically dependent on the thread of technology as its binder. If this technology is fragile, it is an obvious terrorist target. As computer applications in many countries have become increasingly sophisticated, the operators of these systems have become increasingly concerned about the unforeseen consequences of total reliance on them [Hoffman, 1982]. There is no guarantee that computer facilities will continue to escape the notice of terrorists groups as an ideal target for the disruption of the basic structural elements of a society [Menkus, 1983]. Indeed, one person has stated:

> Based on material gathered and analyzed, the author estimates that by the end of 1982, over 100 terrorist attacks against computer targets of data processing personnel were committed. This estimate contradicts the general belief of those engaged with information systems' security, that the danger of terrorist attacks against those targets is low [Pollak, 1983].

Since 1982, the attacks have continued. For example, at about 3 a.m. on Monday, September 2, 1985, two German software houses (Scientific Control Systems and *Mathematischer Beratungs und Programmierungsdienst*) had major computer center bombings within minutes of each other. The credited terrorist group considered the development of data processing systems as oppressive to workers [Lamb, 1986].

During a computer conference in Rome in 1986, it was claimed that more than 60 cases of serious acts of terrorism had been committed against computers or computer centers [Arkin, 1992].* Exhibit 1 provides a historical look at one such incident.

Around the world, other computer centers have also suffered terrorist attacks. In a 30-month period between May 1976 and December 1978, the Red Brigade carried out bombing attacks against at least ten computer centers located in Italy. The losses averaged about $1 million per attack. According to the statements made by the Red Brigade, the computer centers were singled out because they were "instruments of the capitalist system" and must be destroyed. The Red Brigade manifesto specifically includes destruction of computer systems as an objective [Brushweiler, 1985]. The attacks, which were conducted by the Red Brigade, are as follows [Norman, 1985]:

- *May 1976:* Five terrorists held employees at a Milan warehouse at gunpoint, set fire to the warehouse, and destroyed the Honeywell

---

* Section 11.02[3][c]. The reference quotes its source as coming from page 94 of the International Computer Crime Proceedings (ICCP) Report entitled Computer-Related Crime: Analysis of Legal Policy, published by the Organization for Economic Cooperation and Development (OECD), Paris, 1986.

Exhibit 1 Computer Incident in Northern Ireland

The Belfast Cooperative Society, Ltd., located in Ireland, had been using computers since 1948, starting with a Powers-Samas punch card and advancing to a Honeywell 200 system installed in 1967. Its data disks were stored in a Chubb fire protection safe.

The Society began backing up its data once a week when civil disturbances in Northern Ireland began escalating in 1971. The Society had a standing arrangement with Irish Hospitals Trust in Dublin for backup because its computer configurations were similar.

The computer room was located on the fourth floor of the building and was protected by a water sprinkler system, fire detection equipment, and a carbon dioxide fire suppression system. While members of the Society were prepared for a fire in the computer room, they failed to envision total destruction of the building by terrorist bombs.

The first attack came in March 1972 when three armed men gained access to the building after overpowering the security guard. They placed one bomb on the first floor and one on the second. Only one exploded; the other was defused by demolition experts. A hole was blown in the second floor, but the company was able to place a barricade around it and proceed with business as usual.

However, on Wednesday, May 10, 1972, at 3:45 p.m., the company received a telephone call from a local newspaper. The newspaper reported that it had received a call from a person who claimed a bomb had been planted in the Society's building. Because the building was closed to the public on Wednesdays, the guard assumed that the only way the bomb could have gotten in was through the loading docks. Company personnel and police checked the receiving department and then searched the building.

With a limited number of people searching through a 300,000-square-foot area, members of the group limited their search to looking for anything out of the ordinary. They found nothing. Because the company had been receiving an average of three telephone bomb threats per week, this threat was chalked up as just another hoax.

The bomb exploded at 4:40 p.m. on the second floor. The chief accountant, along with some of his people, rushed back to the office and went up though the building to the fourth floor where computer personnel were working. On the way up, they noticed a small fire on the second floor. However, the fire department was already on its way, so they passed the fire without fighting it.

Company personnel, and in particular computer center personnel, had practiced for such an event. When the chief accountant and his staff arrived, they found that the computer center personnel had remained calm, even though one of the punch card machines had been overturned by the force of the explosion. The staff had powered down the computer, put the tapes away, and locked the safe. The staff then walked across the flat roof and went down the fire escape stairway.

When the chief accountant went back into the building, he discovered that police were evacuating the building because they had received a call that a second bomb was about to go off. The building was sealed off at 4:50 p.m. At 5:15 p.m., heat from the enlarging fire began breaking the windows on the second floor. At 6:15 p.m., the building was an inferno.

The fire department fought the fire for two days before it was brought under control, and by that time there was nothing left but a shell and some twisted metal. Ten days later, the demolition crew found the company safe, which had fallen two floors down into the heart of the fire.

Forty tapes locked in the safe were recovered with minimal damage to only three tapes due to a blow torch which was used to burn off the hinges. However, the company had lost all its program listings and documentation, a number of transaction files had to be rerun, systems under development were a total loss, and manual operations were required for five weeks [Norman, 1985].

Exhibit 2   Anti-Imperialistic Military Movement Leaflet

Today we have hit and destroyed another counterrevolutionary and anti-proletarian center of the government which stored information and names.

We have shown the true face and the imperialistic design of the multinational Honeywell, engaged in the process of infiltration and leading to the center of data information of the bourgeois state.

The power of the repressive and counterrevolutionary system is today based upon friendship and technical collaboration between the bourgeois apparatus and U.S. imperialism.

Gendarmes, police, and other uniformed slaves use the electronic information systems, in particular the Honeywell system.

The methods have changed, the goals remain the same: yesterday, the CIA system, today, the multinationals.

The target remains: exploitation and oppression.

The chase after the imperialistic structure, until their successful destruction, is being continued by the militant forces.

Smash and destroy the product of contra revolution of the U.S. multinationals.

We are building the movement of anti-imperialistic resistance! [Pollak, 1983][a]

---

[a] Mr. Pollak is quoting his source as an internal report from the International Operations of Data Security Holdings, Inc.

---

computer center. At this time, they called themselves *Movimento Armato Anti-Imperialista* (Anti-Imperialistic Military Movement). They left behind the leaflet excerpted in Exhibit 2.

- *May 1976:* 15 men, armed with handguns and submachine guns, invaded a local government office in Rome and threw ten Molotov cocktails among computer equipment installed there, destroying eight IBM 2740 terminals [Whiteside, 1978].
- *October 13, 1976:* Plastic explosives destroyed the computer center at the De Angeli pharmaceutical firm in Milan.
- *December 19, 1976:* A security guard at Data-Montedison were tricked into opening a gate only to be overpowered by three men and a woman. These members of the Red Brigade explained that they were carrying birthday presents for an employee and that they wanted to come in and give him a surprise party. A communications controller was set on fire after being doused with gasoline. This one incident was given a closer look by another researcher, who depicts much larger destruction at the hands of the terrorists (see Exhibit 3).
- *January 17, 1977:* At the Sias steel manufacturing plant, a bomb placed above a computer center damaged the IBM 370/135 on the floor below.
- *April 15, 1977:* Four armed terrorists forced their way into the Liquechimica petrochemical company in Calabria, doused a production control center with gasoline, and set it on fire.
- *April 21, 1977:* A man and two women forced their way into the University of Bocconi, Milan, computer center and blew up computer equipment.

Exhibit 3   Terrorists Overpower Security Guard at Data-Montedison

Terrorists attacked the computer center of a multinational company. The computer center was housed in a building in an industrial area separated from other offices of the company. Access was controlled by a uniformed guard and electronically operated doors into the facility. The well-dressed individuals explained to the guard that they had a surprise birthday party planned for one of the computer operators and were carrying a number of large boxes wrapped as gifts. The guard admitted them to the lobby and asked to inspect the contents of the boxes. At that point, the individuals opened the boxes, removed automatic weapons, incapacitated the guard temporarily, and entered the computer center. They forced all of the employees in the computer center at gunpoint into the lobby, where they were temporarily held. The entire computer center, including the tape library and programming office, was drenched with gasoline. A fuse was set at the main entrance. The attackers fled in cars, the employees left the building, and the building exploded and burned, completely destroying its contents [Parker, 1981].

- *June 10, 1977:* A three-woman team broke into the University of Rome computer center and destroyed a Univac 1110. The masked women carried Uzi submachine guns and silencer-equipped handguns. While holding two professors and an assistant hostage, they allowed all other personnel to evacuate the building. They then poured gasoline on the center's computer and set fire to it. Damage to the computer and the premises was estimated at more than $2–4 million [Whiteside, 1978].
- *July 1978:* Seven armed terrorists attacked a computer center in Turin and set it on fire with Molotov cocktails. The employees were locked up but managed to escape.
- *July 15, 1978:* "Red Brigade destroyed a regional computer center in Torrino" [Pollak, 1983].*
- *December 3, 1978:* At 6:00 a.m., the computer center at the Italian Ministry of Transport in Rome (*Motorizzazione Civile*) was bombed and set on fire. Three armed men broke in, with the complicity of one of the employees. They bound and gagged the two operators and poured gasoline over the equipment. The resultant fire destroyed the dual Honeywell Level 66 systems that held the records of all Italian cars, stolen cars, and false license plates. Eugenio Orlandi states in his research paper, *Data Processing Security and Terrorism*:

> When the terrorists concentrated on destroying computers, they tested the high vulnerability of a virtually defenseless society. The bombs and fire did not invest all the disk units and the offices. It was possible to restore the site ... from previous general saves, partially destroyed disks, reports [Orlandi, 1984].

---

* Mr. Pollak is quoting from an internal report produced by the International Operations of Data Security Holdings, Inc.

■ However, this incident destroyed so much data that nearly two years passed before the ministry had any reasonable idea of who in the country owned cars and trucks or had licenses to drive them. A Reuters newswire report stated that "hundreds of thousands of files and micro-films representing more than 20 million documents were destroyed" [Clark, 1980].*

The Red Brigade, also called the Armed Anti-Imperialist Movement, the Anti-Imperialistic Military Movement (MAA), Communist Unity Fighters, the Armed Communist Formation, the Communist Combat Unit, and the Proletarian Patrols, announced their strategies and goals against computer centers in their February 1978 publication entitled *Risoluzione Della Direzione Strategica* (Strategic Direction Resolution). This 80-page publication describes in part the rationale behind the destruction of computer centers.

The Red Brigade have identified multinational corporations (mostly those with ties to the United States, which explains the large number of U.S.-built computers destroyed by the Red Brigade) as their enemy. They have identified computers in a twofold manner: (1) as the foremost instruments of the ability of multinationals to succeed, and (2) as the most dangerous instruments to be used against them in terms of files and cross-referencing. To quote a paragraph from their publication:

> ...we find the organizing of a European computer-filing system centralizing all information on guerrilla groups; on the militant members, on their methods; centralizing all data relative to kidnap-pings, numbers of banknote's series, etc.

The heart of the publication as it concerns computer centers and computer technology is shown in Exhibit 4.

> Of interest is the computer center bombed in Frankfort, Germany. The computer center actually belonged to a U.S. Army intelligence facility. A terrorist group calling itself In the Heart of the Beast took credit, proclaiming, "death to U.S. imperialism" [Bequai, 1987].

The United States is also included when it comes to computer terrorism. In November 1969, five members of an anti-war group calling itself Beaver 55 attacked a chemical company's Hewlett-Packard computer center in Midland, Michigan. One thousand tapes were damaged with small magnets. It was a long and expensive job to recreate the files — damage was estimated at $100,000. Attacking a centralized source of information was a way to both protest and sabotage U.S. involvement in the Vietnam War [Bloombecker, 1985]. The terrorists thought they had destroyed data from research into such areas as nerve gases, napalm, defoliants, and other secret chemical weapons. What they had in fact destroyed were records of the local blood bank, research

---

* Reuters newswire dispatch dated December 3, 1978, as quoted in Clark [1980].

Exhibit 4   Red Brigade Strategic Direction Resolution Directive

We must not underestimate the use of computer technology in the repression of the class war, as the efficiency of computers is supported by the ideology and by the technical-military personnel responsible for their functioning.

Computer systems are the monopoly of the American multinationals and, in addition to ensuring the U.S. hegemony over the world economy (the electronic sector is the strategic sector of advanced capitalism), they also guarantee the exportation of forms of control, of police methods, and they export also the highest levels of repression, ripened in the strongest link of imperialism. In fact, the exportation of these "systems" is not only exportation of advanced technology, it is also a relationship of production, of an ideology. It is the American "filing system" ruling the control structures of all the states of the imperialistic chain. And exactly because of this, it is also the creation of a layer of technicians-policemen in charge of preventive and total espionage of the people. You see, computers are identified as a symbol, the highest profile target. It is important to destroy their mesh, to disrupt these systems, beginning from the technical-military personnel which directs them, instructs them, and makes them functional against the proletariat [Pollak, 1983][a]

---

[a] Mr. Pollak is quoting his source as coming from an internal report belonging to the International Operations of Data Security Holdings, Inc. Mr. Pollak is the Chairman of the Information Security Committee, E.D.P. Auditors Association, Israel.

on air pollution, history of the company's industrial health program, and the chemical test results of a mumps vaccine under development. Again in Michigan, in Eagan this time, saboteurs broke into a Sperry Corporation plant and destroyed military computer equipment that was to be used for nuclear weapons guidance and control systems [Bequai, 1987].

In 1969 and 1970, computer centers were also attacked at Boston University, California's Fresno State College, and the University of Kansas. In March 1976, a Hewlett-Packard electronic circuit manufacturing site in Palo Alto, California, was bombed; and in May 1976, bombs were exploded in two floors of a Kennebec building housing the data processing facilities of Central Maine Power. One Vietnam War protest action inside the Pentagon did involve the bombing of an unoccupied restroom. Water from the damaged plumbing lines reportedly flooded and disabled a nearby classified U.S. Air Force computer center [Menkus, 1983]. Further research revealed that the incident did indeed disable the computer center; the restroom was located directly above the computer center on the next floor.

In 1970, American anti-war activists set off a bomb outside the Army Mathematics Research Center at the University of Wisconsin. The blast killed Robert Fassnacht, a 30-year-old postdoctoral researcher working there after hours. Damage included a Control Data Corporation 3600 system, a Univac 9300 terminal, a Honeywell DDP124 and a Scientific Control Corporation 4700 computer. Three smaller computers belonging to the physics department were also destroyed. The explosion damaged ten buildings (mainly by shattering window glass). What was believed to be the world's finest cryogenic (extremely low temperature) lab was also destroyed and subsequently all projects, including those in the field of superconductivity, were abandoned. It was estimated that the research data represented 1.3 million staff hours of effort built up over 20 years. The loss was estimated at more than $18 million. The complete story of this incident can be read in Tom Bates' *Rads* [Bates, 1992].

On September 28, 1973:

> [A] time bomb demolished four rooms in the Latin American Section of International Telephone and Telegraph (ITT) Corporation head-quarters in New York, but no one was injured. The attack was linked to the radical Weatherman faction of the SDS (Students for a Democratic Society), connected with Al Fatah and PFLP (Arab terrorist organizations), and the IRA (Irish Republican Army). The bombing, which coincided with several bomb blasts elsewhere in the world, was reported to be a protest against ITT's activities in Chile [Rand, 1975].*

In March 1984, a U.S. terrorist group calling themselves United Freedom Front bombed an IBM facility in White Plains, New York. They claimed that the attack was in protest of the company's business operations in South Africa [DRC, 1986]. In a publicly distributed newsletter, the group claimed that "IBM is a death merchant ... The computer is an integral part of the fascist South African government's policies of racist repression and control" [Lamb, 1986]. Another attack on a computer center in South Africa resulted in one fatality (see Exhibit 5).

Canada has also suffered destruction of computers at the hands of terrorists. In February 1969, rioting students burned the computer center at Montreal's Sir George Williams University [Menkus, 1983].

A long battle of terrorist groups against computer centers was also occurring in France. On August 14, 1979, at the Bank de Rothschild in Paris, windows of the keypunching room were blown out and data processing facilities were attacked with Molotov cocktails, causing major damage in the data preparation area [Parker, 1975].

In Toulouse, France, on May 20, 1980, an organized left-wing terrorist group calling itself the *Comite Liquidant ou Detoumant les Ordinateurs* (Committee on the Liquidation or Deterrence of Computers — CLODO. *Clodo* is also French slang for *tramp*) and a terrorist group calling itself the Direct Action Organization of March 27–28 claimed responsibility for the destruction of computer systems and data during an attack on Philips Data Systems. Another report translated CLODO as "Computer Liquidation and Hijacking Committee" [Dobson, 1982]; still another translated CLODO as "Committee for the Liquidation and Misappropriation of Computers" [TLB, 1986]. And still another claims CLODO stands for "Committee for Releasing or Setting Fire to Computers" [Norman, 1985]. *Processed World,* an underground magazine published in the United States, reprinted a rare interview with a representative of CLODO in its tenth issue.

---

* A report prepared for the Department of State by the Defense Advanced Research Projects Agency (DARPA).

Exhibit 5   Attack on Computer Center in South Africa

Durban Oct 2 SAPA — A young computer consultant who recently completed his national service was killed instantly when he opened a parcel bomb at his offices in Durban on Tuesday (2 Oct) morning.

The explosion rocked the premises of PC Plus Consultants, a computer hardware and service company, at 37 Crart Avenue at 9.20 a.m. (0720 GMT).

The bomb box was delivered by a transport company and was thought to have contained a computer in need of repairs. It exploded as Mr. Nic Cruse, aged about 23, opened the parcel, according to the co-owner of PC Plus, Mr. Tam Alexander. Mr. Cruse, who had been employed by PC Plus only since August 1, was killed instantly.

The bomb extensively damaged an office in the residential house converted into business premises. Two front windows and steel burglar bars were blown completely out of the window frame. Police were on the scene almost immediately and the area was cordoned off as detectives combed the area. Residents living across the road said they heard a tremendous explosion followed by a woman's scream.

Mr. Alexander suggested the bombing might have been politically motivated because his company supplied merchandise to "liberal organisations." Recent clients included the ANC [African National Congress], Women for Peaceful Change, the Black Sash, and trade unions. Several of the company's employees were also ANC members, Mr. Alexander said.

Police confirmed the death but said further details were unavailable. Crart Avenue is in a busy residential sector with a nursery school nearby.

Mr. Alexander said the company had experienced "political problems" some time ago, but he had not believed they would result in death. He did not elaborate but said the bomb had come without warning. Another employee, Mr. Gary Pelser, said he had recently clashed with members of a rightwing organisation and had received threatening letters at his home. "I wouldn't put it past them to do something like this," he said [FBIS, 1990][a]

---

[a] FBIS message traffic. Source came from a Johannesburg, South Africa SAPA broadcast in English on October 2, 1990, at 1229 GMT.

Philips specializes in the sale of computers and the storage of bookkeeping data of private companies. The terrorists claimed to have destroyed the equipment and data because, according to them, the equipment and data were being used by the armed forces and the French counterespionage organization.

Members of the two terrorist organizations gathered the computer programs and magnetic data cards and burned them in the toilets of the offices. They also damaged the computers and removed all the personnel files from the firm.

In a statement by CLODO to the left-wing newspaper *Liberation*, it said:

> We are computer workers and therefore well placed to know the present and future dangers of computer systems. Computers are the favorite instrument of the powerful. They are used to classify, to control, and to repress. We do not want to be shut up in ghettos of programs and organizational patterns [Bequai, 1987].

A different translation of the statement was published in another magazine:

> We are workers in the field of data processing and consequently well placed to know the current and future dangers of data processing and telecommunications. The computer is the favorite tool of the dominant. It is used to exploit, to put on file, to control, and to repress [Lamb, 1986].

As if to help the terrorists make their point, the pro-government daily newspaper *Le Figaro* pointed out, "the destruction of a computer could cause far more damage than the murder of a politician" [Dobson, 1982]. Another source states that the newspaper wrote: "...a modern nation is infinitely vulnerable. It is much more effective for those who aim to harm or even paralyze it to put computers out of action than to shoot up ministries or murder policemen" [Lloyd, 1980].

Within four days of the attack on Philips, the computer center for the CII-Honeywell-Bull company in Toulouse was set on fire. Soon after, responsibility was claimed by the same Direct Action Organization group in a telephone call to the French press agency. The caller told the press that a systematic plan to paralyze the operations of computer firms located in France was in operation. Their group was out to destroy computer systems on the grounds that they were weapons in the hands of the government. The other group, CLODO, also claimed responsibility. CLODO had approached both Philips and CII-Honeywell-Bull earlier when it had placed bombs at the computer centers. There was no damage, and CLODO made its involvement public by scrawling slogans on the grounds proclaiming "out with computers."

In June 1980, CLODO terrorists in Toulouse ransacked a hall that had been prepared for an international symposium. The raiders left the message: "Scientist swine. No to capitalist data processing."

Around the same time, another band of French terrorists, picking up CLODO's computer cudgel, fired a bazooka rocket at the buildings that housed the French Ministry of Transportation in Paris. The *Action Directe,* which claimed credit for the attack, wanted to protest the agency's "planned computer projects." Its salvo of protest, however, missed its mark. Instead of landing as planned on the sixth floor computer center, the explosive ended up in the library one floor below. The blast was intended to dramatize the group's doctrine that computers, used as instruments of repression by the government, condemn people to the "ghettos of program and organizational patterns" [Lamb, 1986].

On December 11, 1980, the French magazine *Computer Weekly* reported bomb attacks, as shown in Exhibit 6.

On March 23, 1981, terrorists struck again, this time destroying an IBM computer at the local headquarters of the *Banque Populaire* in Toulouse. They broke into the computer center through a window and actually set off an automatic alarm. However, they still had time to damage the computer, a terminal, and a line-printer before escaping.

In May 1981, another computer center in Toulouse was seriously damaged in a bomb attack. "British Power Kills in Ireland" was scrawled on the walls of the building. None of the residents were hurt in the dawn explosion, but

Exhibit 6   Bomb Attacks on French Centres

French police are bracing themselves for a new wave of fire bomb attacks on computers following the recent blaze at a central Paris office building owned by a major insurance company. Computers housed in the basement of a seven-storey block near the opera house were undamaged by the fire, which spread to the roof where five office workers were rescued by the fire brigade. Police evacuated 600 people from the burning building during the evening rush hour. A few minutes later, an anonymous telephone caller claimed responsibility for the outbreak on behalf of the self-styled "CLODO" movement which was answerable for a long catalogue of attacks on computers.

CLODO, a slang term for "tramp," stands for Comite de Liberation Ou de Detournement des Ordinateurs (Committee for Releasing or Setting Fire to Computers). The organisation first made newspaper headlines last April when it placed bombs at the Toulouse computer centres operated by Philips Informatique and CII-Honeywell-Bull. There was no damage and CLODO made its involvement known by scrawling slogans proclaiming "out with computers."

CLODO emerged again on May 20 when it burned down ICL's shop, again in Toulouse. Computer wreckers returned to the attack in the same city on June 25 when they ransacked a hall that had been prepared for an international symposium. The raiders left behind the message "Scientist swine. No to capitalist data processing."

CII-Honeywell-Bull's centre at Louveciennes, near Paris, was singled out in August for a series of attacks. First, a ten-pound plastic bomb was left outside the wall of the buildings but failed to detonate. Then a security door protecting computers and confidential software was destroyed, police finding next day a one-foot deep hole bored in a wall, apparently for a future explosive charge.

CLODO switched its attention back to Toulouse on September 12, when three fires gutted a computer and electronics goods shop [CW, 1980].

---

stores and equipment were destroyed. Despite the IRA slogan, police believe CLODO was responsible.

The 1983 bombing attack against the West German *Maschinenfabrick Ausburg-Nuernberg* (MAN) computer center was an act committed by terrorists calling themselves *Rote Zellen* in order to protest against the participation of the MAN Company in the production of Pershing and Cruise missiles and transportation systems. Damages to the center exceeded $7 million; however it would have been much more had the backup copies of the data in the computer system also been destroyed (they were located at another site) [Seiber, 1986].* The group warned that additional attacks would follow if the company did not cease manufacturing transport vehicles for the missiles.

In October 1984, a new terrorist group literally exploded onto the European terrorism stage with a series of bombings. These bombings included sites that had been the previous bombing targets of other terrorist organizations. In October 1984, the Combatant Communist Cells (*Cellules Communistes Combattantes,* or CCC), headed by Pierre Carrette, bombed the headquarters of Litton Data Systems in Brussels and severely damaged three buildings and 25 vehicles. Also during October, they bombed the parking lot of the MAN

---

* According to Seiber's own footnote, this case description was based on police and company statements.

Exhibit 7 Bomb Attack on Brussels Research Center

Brussels, October 15 — A bomb seriously damaged a research centre linked with the Liberal Party early today, in the fourth bombing in the Belgium capital in two weeks. First accounts said a man hurled a bomb into the ground floor of the building and escaped in a car. Damage was severe, and windows were shattered in a dozen nearby buildings. The attack was not immediately claimed.

Since October 2 a previously unknown *Communist Combatant Cell* has claimed bomb attacks against three companies involved in projects for the North Atlantic Treaty Organization (NATO) here: Litton, Man, and Honeywell. Belgium's Liberal deputy premier, Jean Gol, was particularly severe in his condemnation of these attacks [FBIS, 1984b][a]

[a] FBIS message traffic quoted from Paris source given in English at 0752 GMT on 15 October 1984.

Corporation, the headquarters of Honeywell-Bull, and the computerized Belgian Liberal Party Research Center, all in the Brussels, Belgium, area (see Exhibit 7).

The Belgium terrorist group CCC is believed to have joined with the West German Red Army Faction (RAF) and the French group Direct Action in forming an Anti-Imperialist Armed Front to conduct attacks to protest the "Americanization of Europe" and to frustrate increased military cooperation among members of NATO [TGP, 1988]. Other destructive efforts took place:

- *November 21, 1984, Brussels, Belgium:* Offices of the U.S. electronics company Motorola are bombed. The Belgium terrorist group Combatant Communist Cells (CCC) claims responsibility. It was reported that the terrorist group left a note that delivered the kind of ultimatum that computer firms and users are beginning to dread: "This is a revolutionary action against the Motorola offices. In the interests of your security, leave the building immediately. It will be destroyed 30 minutes after one of our militants has taken action." While the building was not actually destroyed, it was seriously damaged [Lamb, 1986].
- *November 26, 1984, Liege, Belgium:* Two military communications masts at a NATO base near Liege are destroyed by a bomb. CCC claims responsibility.
- *December 6, 1984, Oudenarde, Belgium:* A bomb explodes at a NATO fuel pumping station in central Belgium. CCC claims responsibility.
- *December 6, 1984, Paris, France:* A bomb explodes at the offices of NATO's Central European Operating Agency, near Versailles outside Paris, which manages the 5900 kilometer NATO pipeline network. CCC claims responsibility, but also states that an unspecified "international communist group in France" assisted.
- *December 11, 1984, Verviers, Belgium:* Six bombs simultaneously explode along NATO's emergency fuel pipeline near Brussels, forcing a temporary shutdown of computerized operations. CCC claims responsibility, stating that it is fighting a "war against NATO."

- *December 30, 1984, Mannheim, FRG:* A U.S. Army communications center is bombed. RAF claims responsibility.
- *January 3, 1985, Heidelberg, FRG:* A bomb explodes at a molecular biology center at Heidelberg University. RAF claims responsibility.
- *January 1985:* The CCC bombs a NATO support facility in suburban Brussels.
- *January 15, 1985, Paris, France:* France's *Action Directe* and the RAF release a five-page statement announcing the start of joint operations targeted at NATO.
- *January 21, 1985, Stuttgart, FRG:* A known RAF sympathizer, Johannes Thimme, is killed and his female companion is seriously injured when a bomb they were wheeling in a baby carriage toward a computer center explodes prematurely.
- *April 30, 1985, Paris, France:* Two telecommunications firms connected with the French arms industry are bombed. *Action Directe* claims responsibility.
- *August 15, 1985, Wuppertal, FRG:* A branch of the U.S.-based Westinghouse Corporation at Wuppertal, north of Cologne, is bombed.
- *November 16, 1985, Heidelberg, FRG:* An IBM computer research center sustains serious damage from a bomb attack [Heather, 1987].

The bombings in late August–early September 1985 were particularly severe.

> Bombs caused nearly $1.5 million in damage to two West German computer companies with military contracts, officials reported. Police said no one was hurt, and there were no immediate claims of responsibility. The affected companies are a subsidiary of the Hoesch Steel firm in Dortmund, which has sold a computer program to the U.S. Army, and Scientific Control Systems in Hamburg, which is owned by British Petroleum [LAT, 1985].

In December 1985, the CCC exploded a bomb at the Bank of America offices, causing major damage to the building, to the computers, and to the surrounding area. In December 1985, Pierre Carrette and three other CCC militants were arrested and no known CCC attacks have occurred since.

Recently, the RAF was blamed for a series of bombings on computer centers, including the Frankfurt, Germany, Stock Exchange (see Exhibit 8).

In an April 1987 example, a bomb exploded and damaged a decoding computer plant in Bavaria (see Exhibit 9). Although the report stated that the company affected "mainly manufactures devices used to decode and analyze handwriting," another report was a bit more specific:

> April 13, 1987, Munich, FRG: A bomb explodes at the Munich office of TST, a computer firm that does business with West German security and intelligence agencies, specializing in cryptographic equipment [Heather, 1987].

Exhibit 8   RAF Blamed for Frankfort Stock Exchange Bomb

Assailants hurled firebombs inside the Frankfurt Stock Exchange and an electronics firm Wednesday [April 12, 1989], and police blamed both attacks on supporters of jailed terrorists staging a hunger strike.

Authorities said the attacks destroyed or damaged several computers and delayed the opening time by a few minutes.

Authorities said the attack caused millions of dollars worth of damage but no injuries.

Earlier, in the northern city of Muenster, unidentified assailants set off a firebomb inside the offices of the AEG electronics firm, a subsidiary of the Daimler-Benz automotive and high-technology conglomerate [AJC, 1989].

Exhibit 9   Bomb Damages Bavarian Decoding Computer Plant

Tutzing, West Germany, April 13 — A bomb exploded Sunday night in the basement of a Bavarian computer plant specializing in the production of decoding devices used by security services, police said Monday. Police estimated the damage to the plant at between six and eight million Deutsche marks (between $3.3–4.4 million). A witness said he saw two young men fleeing from the building on foot shortly after the explosion. Investigators have not ruled out the possibility that the two were wounded in the attack. TST TeleSecurity, based in the neighbouring community of Poecking, has its production plant in this Bavarian town, on the perimeter of Lake Sternberg. It mainly manufactures devices used to decode and analyze handwriting. Bavarian police have not ruled out a political motive behind the bombing, and are offering a reward of 5000 marks ($2800) for information leading to the capture of the criminals. Computer firms with large defence contracts have in the past few years been the targets of several bomb attacks in West Germany [FBIS, 1987][a]

[a] FBIS message traffic quoted from source in Paris in English at 1244 GMT on 13 April 1987.

Even in a quiet part of the world, computers are being destroyed, as evidenced from this article coming from Malta:

> Valletta, Oct 13 1984 — A bomb wrecked a computer used by 19 Maltese government departments today and caused 1.5 million dollars worth of damage, informed sources said here. The explosion was at a government electronics centre at Dingli, 13 kilometers (eight miles) from Valletta, and responsibility has not been claimed. The sources said the bombers cut a hole in wire fencing and slipped past two security guards before placing the device at the window of the room where the computer was kept. The electronics centre was opened three years ago in a building formerly used by the British Navy [FBIS, 1984a].*

---

* FBIS message traffic quoted from source in Paris in English at 1543 GMT on 13 October 1984.

Exhibit 10   Animal Rights Activists Claim Responsibility for Bomb at the University of Bristol

Two animal rights groups in Britain have claimed responsibility for a bomb that caused severe damage to the administration block at the University of Bristol. The activists said that the high-explosive device was intended to be a protest against research using animals being carried out at the university's medical and veterinary schools.

Although militant animal rights groups have, in recent years, admitted responsibility for a number of incendiary devices planted in stores in London and elsewhere, the Bristol University blast is the first time that high explosives have been used in such incidents.

There were no casualties in the explosion, which took place in the early hours of 23 February [1989]. However, the bomb caused severe damage to a bar and dining area used by university teaching and research staff, as well as to the university's computer.

After visiting the scene of the explosion, the British Secretary of State for Education and Science, Kenneth Baker, described it as "an act of terrorism" [Dickson, 1989].

Computers have also been destroyed elsewhere in the world. For example, members of the East Asian Anti-Japan Front made their way into the ninth-floor offices of a Japanese construction company and planted a bomb that seriously damaged the company's computer system. And in England, members of a group calling itself Angry Brigade attempted to bomb police computers in London [Bequai, 1987].

Also in London, animal rights activists are being called terrorists by the British government after the activists claimed responsibility for a bomb that blew up at the University of Bristol and severely damaged the university's computer center (see Exhibit 10).

In the United States, saboteurs made four attempts to damage the computer center at the Wright-Patterson Air Force Base near Dayton, Ohio [Bequai, 1987].

To date, terrorists have bombed hundreds of computer sites around the world [TF, 1988]. These actions are fast replacing kidnapping or assassinations of political and business leaders as a means to have terrorits' demands met or at least publicized. When a terrorist group or other organization has a point of view it wants to receive public attention, it may sabotage a computer instead of kidnapping the head of the company [Bartimo, 1982].

Terrorist propaganda that often accompanies such destruction focuses on the computer as a symbol or as an instrument of capitalistic oppression. August Bequai, a Washington, D.C., attorney and an expert in the field of terrorism, describes the computer as a symbol:

> Computer technology has attracted the ire of terrorists. For example, members of Italy's Red Brigade have bombed computers at a government nuclear facility and research center near Rome; terrorists in West Germany have sabotaged those of private corporations. The computer has come to represent for the politically alienated in many Third World countries the domination of Western civilization. It has become an outlet for their frustrations. The kidnappings and assassinations of business and political officials is giving way to hatred of the machine; few shed tears when computers are attacked. The

economical and political losses, however, can be profound; the attackers understand this very well. The computer, by its very mystique, has become a symbol of all the evils we associate with technology [Bequai, 1987].

Through the use of computers, the possibility exists that terrorist groups could be financed through the manipulation and transfer of large sums of money. No longer would there be bank robbers photographed by the bank's cameras, or a kidnap victim to worry about, or even something as simple as fingerprints. The money would simply be electronically diverted into other accounts and withdrawn. One of the best examples was the fraud perpetrated in South Korea in the early 1970s.

Through manipulation of a U.S. Army supply computing program largely operated by Korean technicians, huge quantities of food, uniforms, vehicles, gasoline, and other American supplies were diverted into the hands of a Korean gang for resale on the black market. The swindle was so effective that the theft of about $18 million worth of equipment a year was being concealed by the misuse of inventory-and-supply computer programs [Whiteside, 1978]. It is easy to believe that profits from such actions could fall into the hands of organizations not sympathetic to the Security Administrator's own causes.

Although terrorists still kidnap and rob banks for their financial needs, the principal danger to Electronic Funds Transfer Systems (EFTS) by terrorists is the destruction of wealth and entire economies in an attempt to achieve certain political goals. This is not science fiction. Terrorists indeed pose a threat to EFTS. Professional terrorists are presently active internationally. Unlike the criminal, the terrorist is activated by ideological fervor. Monetary considerations play a secondary role in the terrorist's activities; what makes the terrorist potentially dangerous is a willingness to sacrifice both himself and others for the cause. EFTS have already attracted the attention of such groups in France, Italy, and other industrialized nations. Open societies pose a special problem for law enforcement; lax security makes them ideal targets for the politically malcontent. The terrorist thus poses a twofold challenge to the cashless society: a threat to the security of its economic institutions, and a threat to its political well-being. The terrorist has both the requisite weaponry and the will to severely damage key EFTS facilities, bringing a nation's financial institutions to their knees. Of greater concern to society, however, should be the terrorist's ability to force the governing authorities to impose dragonian (sic) measures on citizens so as to curtail the terrorist's activities. A technologically advanced society — and one that comes to rely on EFTS for its everyday financial transactions — would find it difficult to preserve its democratic safeguards if its major financial institutions were seriously threatened. The objective of the terrorist is to cause societal havoc, to disrupt a society's political mechanisms. The EFTS is potentially ideally suited for this task [Bequai, 1983].

The 1983 movie *War Games* was an amusing but disturbing glimpse into the world of the computer hacker and the computer and telecommunications network that has become increasingly critical to our way of life. In the movie, a teenaged hacker nearly starts World War III when he breaks into the computer system at the North American Air Defense Command (NORAD) in Colorado Springs, Colorado. Thinking he had hacked his way into a game, he sends a message to the computer that the computer mistakes for a Soviet missile launch. It was widely publicized that the military had taken precautions to see that this particular scenario could never occur. However, it is a little known fact that the movie was loosely based on the case of Steven Rhoades and Kevin Mitnick, teenaged hackers who claim to have broken into NORAD in 1979. They claim that they did not interfere with any defense operations. Rhoades said "We just got in, looked around, and got out" [Johnson, 1989].

Most commercial teleprocessing systems are not nearly as well protected as NORAD. Prominent examples are, as previously mentioned, the EFTS networks that link banks and other financial institutions — the four major networks alone carry the equivalent of the federal budget every two to four hours. These almost incomprehensible sums of money are processed solely between the memories of computers, using communication systems that are seriously vulnerable to physical disruption and technical tampering. The potential for massive computer fraud or theft is self-evident, but even more worrisome is the danger of a deliberate effort to disrupt the U.S. financial structure. The most serious vulnerability of U.S. banks may not be bad loans to Latin American nations, but rather a way of conducting business over networks that these institutions and their investors now take for granted [Wilcox, 1984].

An economy is based on an electronic money system and when ownership of property is based on electronic records rather than on physical possession, the use of computers and data communications invites a different and most effective kind of war. If enough key computers, data communication facilities, and computerized record management centers were destroyed, it would not be any stretch of the imagination to see a society thrown into a deep economic depression and far more easily dominated by the philosophies of terrorist groups.

Access to many systems will present few difficulties to the terrorist, but what is he likely to do once inside? The possibilities are, in fact, considerable. The nationalist/separatist group might access the local police or military computer and extract the names of spies and infiltrators, whom they could then target or feed false information. The group requiring certain materials — explosives, radio-control equipment, etc. — might access the order facility of a supplier's computer, and arrange for items to be delivered to a location in which an ambush or hijack can be made. The establishment of a fictitious company is also a possibility, and this might be done with a view to ordering and paying for items electronically that would otherwise be beyond the group's reach. Bacteria samples, for example, are available on the open market, but only to *bona fide* companies or research or teaching establishments. Few, if any, of these suppliers will check to see if a computer-placed order is from a company that has been around for a year or a week. And very often the computer does the whole process of ordering, shipping, and invoicing automatically. Another possibility is to access intelligence-agency databases and remove the names of wanted persons or to alter important details pertaining to those persons. False and misleading information about politicians or military personnel may be added to a database. When the database is next accessed by operatives, the false data will be accepted as valid and generate serious resource wastage as surveillance and investigative projects are established to confirm or refute implications drawn from the information. Many such intelligence databases are shared by different governments. A computer in Berlin, for example, may be simply accessed by police agents in New York by telephone [Conner, 1987].

Terrorists have also discovered another type of computer destruction. Besides physical destruction, militant activists, hackers, and terrorists have been trained to produce logical damage to a computer and its data. The most popular method of causing logical damage is through a crash program that can erase large amounts of data within a short period of time. Known as *trojan horses,* these computer programs are slipped into existing programs and lie there dormant until someone runs that particular program. Crash programs can be executed at a later date, after the perpetrator has left the company grounds. Through modems, the crash program can even be transmitted to the computer electronically by a phone call from anywhere in the world.

The crash programs that are executed at a later date are appropriately called *time bombs.* The most dangerous modification of these time bombs is the *virus* program. The first computer virus appeared in the United States in 1983. Since 1985, virus programs have been described in detail in European underground newspapers and hacker information sheets [Seiber, 1986].*

Virus programs are self-reproducing programs that copy and implement themselves into other programs and data files to which they have access, spreading through all files, utility programs, operating systems, and shared resources of the computer system. This is extremely dangerous, because virus programs carrying damaging instructions can bring down a system in a very short time. By the time you have discovered the problem, you may be able to find most of the virus programs and destroy them; but if you miss just one, hidden in some forgotten file, that one virus program can begin the problem all over. Now imagine that the virus program contained another program that methodically erased commands, transferred funds, dropped decimal points, etc. You get the picture. The ability to produce logical damage to computer systems, to electronically transfer funds or materials, to crash a system at any time, or to cause statistical and accounting programs to arrive at wrong numbers or conclusions will become the new *modus operandi* of the terrorist. "Sadly, these viruses and other forms of computer-based terrorism are symptoms of our Information Age that are likely to endure" [Culnan, 1989].

Technologies of destruction, originally aimed toward people and hardware, are turning to another vital commodity — information stored in computers. Computer viruses are among the newest means available to terrorists seeking to cripple the infrastructure of an increasingly information-oriented society.

---

* Seiber's own footnote on this mention of underground publications states: "See, for example, *Die Bayerische Hackerpost,* April 1983, pp. 1 et seq."

Exhibit 11   Virus Priority Alert Message

A new type of self-modifying ultra-stealth viruses, called polymorphic viruses, has begun to propagate through the world's computer community. The polymorphic virus scrambles itself using a random number generated by the system clock. By altering every byte of itself when it enters a new environment based on a random number, the newly propagated virus is able to escape detection by most virus scanning programs. The small kernel of code used to unscramble the body of the virus avoids being "fingerprinted" by interspersing DO-NOTHING statements among those that do the unscrambling (e.g., MOVE A TO A). As the virus copies itself to a new destination, it randomly selects and distributes DO-NOTHING statements from a self-contained list into its own code.

The Dark Avenger bulletin board system, which disseminates virus code, has recently published the complete source code for the Dark Avenger mutation engine. The mutation engine is a code kernel that can be attached to an existing or future virus and turn it into a self-encrypting polymorphic virus. The mutation engine uses a meta language-driven algorithm generator that allows it to create completely original encryption algorithms. A varying amount of needless instructions are then inserted into the unique algorithm, resulting in decryption algorithms that range in length from 5 to 200 bytes long [Higgins, undated].

These viruses pose a significant risk to computers in the defense and commercial sectors [Rawles, 1990b].

One of the latest computer viruses to receive a great deal of press coverage was the Michelangelo virus. It got its name when researchers noted that the date it was timed to strike (March 6, 1992) was the birthday of the Italian Renaissance artist, born 517 years earlier. D'Arcy Jenish, author of an in-depth article on this particular computer virus, called it a *terrorist virus* [Jenish, 1992].

The worst virus yet has recently been released into the computer community. An unclassified Priority Alert message was recently released to all members of the Department of Defense (see Exhibit 11).

Eugene Spafford, a computer scientist and authority on viruses at Purdue University in West Lafayette, Indiana, said, "Writing these programs is like dumping cholera in a water supply. I view it as terrorist activity" [Jenish, 1992].*

As virulent as they are now, new generations or "strains" of computer viruses capable of mutating are feared as the next phase of malevolent software. Such viruses would be able to literally evolve and circumvent viral immunization and antidote programs and hardware, because such programs and hardware are designed to check for specific lines of code or specific attributes of viruses. As the mutating computer virus spreads, these virus-detection programs probably would not be able to detect its presence because it has mutated. Herein lies the potential for information devastation from this destructive technology — the virus threat [Rawles, 1990b].

The effective Security Administrator must have a background in computer science, and a definite technical background in programming. The reason becomes clear in the face of a threat such as Tequila, the latest in polymorphic viruses. It is a virus common in Europe (it was written in Switzerland) and is

---

* Eugene Spafford, as quoted by D'Arcy Jenish.

Exhibit 12 Tequila Virus

When the user runs an infected .exe program, the program installs itself on the partition sector of the hard disk using a stealth technique called tunneling. In the case of Tequila, it puts the processor into single-step mode, and calls interrupt 13H to reset the disk. However, on every instruction interrupt 1 is called, and Tequila has reprogrammed that to look at the location in memory from which it is being called. When it finds that it is being called from the firmware, it stores that address and switches off the single stepping. Now, Tequila knows the address of the hard disk controller firmware and any program that is supposed to be blocking attempts to write to the hard disk via the interrupts is easily evaded by doing a far call to the firmware. Tequila then installs itself on the partition sector.

The next time the computer starts up, the partition sector runs before any antivirus software runs and installs the virus into memory. Tequila then "stealths" the partition so that any antivirus software that examines the partition sees only what was there before Tequila came along.

Now Tequila can start infecting files. It has a complex code generator in the body of the virus, so that the decryptor/loader of the rest of the code is very variable. There are a few two-byte strings that one can scan for and some one-byte strings. However, some scanners have difficulty detecting all instances of the virus and some scanners set off false alarms on innocent files.

The virus adds 2468 bytes to each infected file. With the virus in memory, the growth in file size is concealed from programs that ask DOS for this information; thus, the virus is quite difficult to spot and easily gets copied to diskettes and passed on [Solomon, 1992].

just now starting to appear in the United States. The technical maturity of a complex virus such as this is what makes the role of Security Administrator so important. This complex, mutating virus is described in Exhibit 12.

Do you still believe that anything like this could never happen to you because you live in America? Well, there are various pamphlets and books circulating that tend to describe in detail how to attack a computer center and do a massive amount of destructive work in a minimum amount of time. One such publication is called *Ecodefense: A Field Guide to Monkeywrenching*, published by Earth First!. Under the section on Computers, the book has some interesting things to say [EFP, 1992].

The attacks on computer centers in Italy and France described earlier indicate that terrorists understand the vulnerabilities resulting from loss of computer services. Should a Security Administrator prepare to defend his computer center from this type of attack? If so, to what length must the Security Administrator go to provide a reasonable assurance of protection? Terrorists do not share the world view of their victims, however rational it may be. For the terrorist, the ends are held to justify the means. It is quite logical, therefore, to ensure that your computer system is not selected by the terrorist as a means. Terrorism generally requires symbols, and conspicuous computer sites have well appeared to be suitable targets for bombings and other physical destruction.

Computer centers of major corporations are increasingly being seen as targets for terrorist activities, particularly in Europe, where attacks on computer facilities of such companies as Bull, Philips, ICL, Honeywell, and Litton Industries were politically motivated. The reaction to such attacks on computer resources in Europe and elsewhere is a renewed effort to protect the facilities from outside risks and the formulation of comprehensive plans in the event of such an attack. Information assurance staff and terrorism analysts expect the attacks to continue, perhaps in greater numbers as the terrorists have come to realize the importance and vulnerability of corporate databases and data processing centers.

Having analyzed terrorist incidents, it appears that terrorism against computer centers will indeed continue or even increase and that terrorists will continue to engage themselves mostly in physical or electronic forms of attack against computer centers, which entail little risk to themselves. This includes the fairly simple acts of penetrating computer centers and bombing them. One bombing incident occurred in Lima, Peru on May 14, 1992. Six nearly simultaneous explosions were heard in the San Isidro, Miraflores, and La Victoria neighborhoods. At the Government Palace in the Rimac neighborhood, terrorists exploded a 1988 Mitsubishi truck that had been stolen two days before in Huancayo. According to the explosives experts, the car bomb contained 200 to 300 kilograms of dynamite. Four persons were injured, including a policeman who had been working in the computer section. The back wall of the building was totally destroyed and the explosion left debris over a four-block area [FBIS, 1992a].* Later reports identified the computer section as being located at IBM's Peruvian headquarters building [Lamb, 1986].

This was not the first time that IBM offices in South America had been the victim of terrorist bombings. On October 6, 1969, bombs damaged IBM offices in San Miguel de Tucuman, Argentina. Three years later, on November 9, 1972, a powerful bomb exploded and damaged the same IBM offices. On April 29, 1973, an explosion caused extensive damage to IBM corporate offices in San Salvador, El Salvador [Rand, 1975].

It also appears that terrorists will increase their electronic penetrations of computer centers and destroy or steal data because it represents little risk to the terrorist as it is accomplished over the phone lines. The information on phone numbers and how to penetrate computer centers via phone lines; how to penetrate operating systems, such as Unix, once you have gained entry into the computer; and how to penetrate the data security software packages usually residing on mainframes is available through underground hacker sheets, electronic bulletin boards, and terrorist-produced newsletters.

The threat of the "intelligent terrorist" requires diligence in knowing the computer center's risks, threats, vulnerabilities, and existing and planned countermeasures. The intelligent terrorist that recognizes the value of a computer center as it relates to the fabric of society has now arrived. While terrorists have been mostly launching isolated bombing and vandalism attacks on computer centers around the world, one must be warned of the threat to computer-based networks and the compromise, rather than the destruction, of data by terrorists. Stealing data surreptitiously may cause greater harm to the computer center than actually destroying the computer center and its data.

---

* FBIS source was from the Lima Pan-American Television Network (in Spanish) from a 1200 GMT broadcast on 14 May 1992.

In October 1985, Georgetown University's Center for Strategic and International Studies (CSIS), in Washington, D.C., warned of the terrorist threat to computer centers in a report entitled *America's Hidden Vulnerabilities.* The report concluded that computer systems should be safeguarded against acts of terrorist sabotage intended to disrupt or cripple society. The vulnerability of computers to electronic penetration by hackers has increased concerns that terrorists will be following the same logic, but with greater destructiveness.

According to Jay Bloombecker, director of the National Center for Computer Crime Data, sabotage of computers by terrorists is one of the highest potential crimes currently worrying experts in international computer crime.

> It strikes me as unlikely that bombs will be the way to sabotage computers. The motivation to use computer knowledge against the establishment is there. Terrorists will find the computer an attractive target. We have not handled terrorism very well in the past and this will not get any better with the introduction of the computer [Bartimo, 1982].*

When we think about protecting a high-tech resource such as a computer center, most people have a habit of thinking that the threats to a computer center must also be high-tech. But, in fact, a single terrorist with a bomb can do more damage in the shortest amount of time than any high-tech threat could do. Fire is the major problem within a computer environment. Most fires that break out inside computer centers are due to an electrical short circuit or the buildup of deposits of flammable dust or waste. One danger to computers comes from the mass of cables that are found beneath the raised flooring because the covering of the cables burns easily. It is usually hard to locate a fire under the raised flooring because of the heavy concentration of smoke coming from the burning cables. Of course, fire may occur from the result of an exploding bomb.

Even the terrorists' bombs themselves are becoming more sophisticated. Japanese police have reported evidence that shows the bomb planted in a Canadian jet was composed of a timing device constructed with computer chips. Police are also examining the possibility that the same kind of device was used in the terrorist activity that blew a hole in the side of an Air India jet.

The vulnerability of computers to electronic penetration by hackers has increased concerns that terrorists will be following the same logic, but with greater destructiveness. Electronic terrorism is feasible now, and potentially effective against financial institutions, military systems, and research and development labs. The debate over the effectiveness of electronic sabotage has recently escalated with the penetration of computer systems at the Naval Research Labs, U.S. Army in the Pentagon, Lawrence Berkeley Labs, Massachusetts Institute of Technology (MIT), Mitre Corporation, Stanford University, the University of Illinois, and others.

---

* Jay Bloombecker, as quoted by Jim Bartimo.

The Italians, sensitive to the destruction of computer centers by the Red Brigade, are now preparing their computer centers against such destruction and compromise. The Italian Metallurgical Workers Union has recently blamed the Red Brigade for equipment sabotage at the Italtel plant that makes Protel public switching systems. SIP, Italy's National Telecommunications carrier, has decided to invest 3.2 trillion Lira in a five-year plan that will emphasize data switching and networks with backup data sites within the Italian computer center community.

Computers themselves are now being used to counter the terrorists. The most advertised counterterrorist computer is located in Weisbaden, Germany. It is nicknamed "the Komissar." It is controlled by the Federal Criminal Investigation Department (BKA) housed in a cluster of glass and concrete buildings on a hilltop in a suburb of Weisbaden. The staff running the computers and performing the analysis increased from 933 in 1969 to 3122 in 1979, and in the same period the annual budget multiplied ten times, from 22 million to 200 million marks (about $80 million). The heart of the system is an index of information called the PIOS: *Personen, Institutionen, Objekte, Sachen* (Persons, Institutions, Movable and Immovable Objects). It stores every clue: every address and telephone number found in a suspect's possession, the name of every person who writes to him in prison, and information about every object found at the scene of a terrorist attack or in a place where terrorists have been is stored among the computer's ten million data sheets. They include, for example, nearly 200 addresses in London that are in some way, however remotely, connected with West German terrorists [Dobson, 1982].

The computer known as the Octopus at the Langley, Virginia, headquarters of the CIA forms the backbone of the U.S. effort against international terrorism; data from every terrorist movement in the world is fed into the Octopus, along with information detailing the movements and activities of known or suspected terrorists. By assembling and digesting myriad bits and pieces of information, experts ultimately seek to predict terrorist behavior [Livingstone, 1982].

The FBI's National Center for the Analysis of Violent Crime (NCAVC) is developing a threat model for evaluating proposals for combating terrorist attacks on computer systems. This model uses a threat evaluation model developed from research by the U.S. Army [USA, 1983]. The FBI presented this model during a 1989 Defense Advanced Research Projects Agency (DARPA) workshop on responses to computer security incidents [Icove, 1989].

The Reagan administration became very aware of such potential for electronic terrorism. The administration initiated a new policy requiring federal agencies to identify sensitive information stored in government computers. The new policy reflects the administration's view that data communications and government computers must have additional security protection both from foreign adversaries, as well as domestic terrorists.

If there were little to worry about on the terrorist threat, then why has terrorism generated such a market for access control systems? A research firm estimated that the access control systems market is a $10 to 11 billion industry (1996) growing at double-digit rates.

The New Reality of Risk Management

To meet the security needs of connected information systems using an infrastructure not completely under your control, the authors believe that there is a need for a better understanding of information security management as it applies to risks, threats, and vulnerabilities. First, consider examples of what those in the field of information assurance are responsible for:

- Providing the ability to securely pass sensitive or even classified information over public or open communication links or networks to authorized users
- Resisting computer viruses and other malicious software attacks
- Detecting and controlling penetration of networks, systems, applications, and databases by hackers, and even surviving full-scale information warfare or corporate espionage attacks
- Ensuring the authenticity of e-mail and preventing repudiation of their receipt
- Keeping confidentiality and integrity of sensitive but unclassified information such as payroll records
- Protecting the privacy of personnel files and investigative dossiers as required by law
- Providing confidentiality of the identities of personnel in sensitive assignments
- Ensuring integrity in electronic payments to vendors and contractors
- Ensuring the components of the information infrastructure are designed for the rapid detection of malicious activities and for the ready restoration of required services
- Effectively managing and controlling access to information at any protection level on a global basis

Risk Management Policy for Tomorrow

The new policies must be network-oriented, recognizing the need for coordination and cooperation between separate organizations and enclaves connected via the infrastructure. Policies must be sufficiently flexible to cover a wide range of systems and equipment. They must take into account threat, both from the insider and the outsider, and espouse a risk management philosophy in making security decisions; and given the knowledge that unclassified information can be just as important and is even more vulnerable than classified information, the new policies, strategies, and standards must also ensure its protection. Information that has no requirement for confidentiality may still require protection to ensure that it is not illicitly modified or destroyed and is available when needed [JSC, 1994].*

---

* This report was the first significant post-Cold War examination of government security policies and practices. It established a framework and an agenda for reform that is still being slowly and not entirely successfully pursued.

Information Systems Risk Management

Information systems risk management is the integrated process of assessing the risks, threats, vulnerabilities, and the value of the information, and applying cost-effective mechanisms to protect the information. The purpose of risk management is to balance the risk of loss, damage, or disclosure of information against the costs of the protection, and to select a mix that provides adequate protection without excessive cost in dollars or in the efficient flow of information to those who require ready access to it. The use of the risk management process provides a rational, cost-effective framework as the underlying basis for security decision making. Information assurance risk management consists of the following five-step process:

1. Information valuation and judgment about consequence of loss. The step is about the determination of what information needs to be protected and its ultimate value. Remember that an adversary may place a different value on the information than the owner.
2. Identification and characterization of the threats to the information. Assessments must address threats to the information in as much detail as possible based on the needs of the customer.
3. Identification and characterization of any weaknesses in the storage of the information. Vulnerability assessments help identify weaknesses in the information that could be exploited, such as a back door in a database.
4. Identification of protection mechanisms, costs, and trade-offs. There may be a number of different protection schemes available, each with varying costs and effectiveness.
5. Risk assessment. There needs to be a consideration of information valuation, threat analysis, vulnerability assessments, and an acceptable level of risk and any uncertainties to make a judgment of what protection to apply.

Risk Assessment

Experience has shown that a risk assessment will produce the following benefits:

- Objectives of the security program are directly related to the missions of the agency.
- Those charged with selecting specific security measures have quantitative guidance on the amount of resources that it is reasonable to expend on each security measure.
- Long-range planners will have guidance in applying security considerations to such things as site selection, building design, hardware configurations and procurements, software systems, and internal controls.

■ Criteria are generated for designing and evaluating contingency plans for backup operation, recovery from disaster and dealing with emergencies.

■ An explicit security policy can be generated that identifies what is to be protected, which threats are significant, and who will be responsible for execution, review, and reporting of the security program.

For all these reasons, it is recommended that you begin development of the security program with a risk analysis. There are a number of documents relating generally to information systems risk management, risk assessments, and threat and vulnerability analysis that will be helpful to security planners. These, as well as a number of other useful references, are listed links in Appendix C. It is suggested that those responsible for information assurance consult this list in order to take advantage of the extensive font of knowledge they represent.

Chapter 4

Overview of
Systems Engineering

I must Create a System, or be enslaved by another Man's; I will not
Reason and Compare; my business is to Create.

William Blake

This chapter presents a brief background in accepted systems engineering
concepts and methodologies. It is the framework for the rest of the discussion.
We show how a solid systems engineering plan can be adapted to the specific
issues of information architectures, information assurance (IA), interoperability,
and other information technology issues. Before we can launch into a detailed
IA program, we must first ensure that we are all communicating with accepted,
standard terminology and concepts. The conceptual background is presented
here. For the uninitiated, a complete list of acronyms and definitions can be
found in the appendices.

Information systems, like any other system, are constructed of hardware
and software components that come together to perform a particular set of
functions. There are well established methods to address the systems engineering of such complex structures. We will adopt many basic systems engineering constructs to this problem of designing, building, implementing, and
operating large-scale, distributed information systems. So, let us commence
with a brief introduction to systems engineering principles. This is a continuation and refinement of previous work [Curts, 1989a] directed at military
information architecture development.

A Systems Engineering Case Study

This section describes a systems engineering approach to be used in the development and maintenance of any large-scale information architecture. Naval battle force architectures are used here as an example and case study of a very large, diverse, distributed, representative, complex, and dynamic system about which the authors have an intimate familiarity and some measure of understanding. However, the concepts are sufficiently generic to apply to any large-scale system. For reasons of national security, specific equipments (current and planned) are not addressed; only the overall process is examined to the following minimum levels of detail:

- Force
- Platforms (comprising the force)
- Systems (equipments on platforms)

Systems engineering methodologies are described for each step along the way. Though many sources and models include a large number of "elements" or "tasks" in the systems engineering process (Exhibits 1–4), only five basic areas are addressed here [DSMC, 1986]:

- Requirements analysis
- Functional analysis
- Evaluation and decision
- System synthesis
- Documentation

It has been determined, through repeated application of the concepts, that this methodology should result in a more complete, repeatable process for the development, review, maintenance, and update of any organizational architecture. It is intended to provide an architectural recipe that can be followed in the generic case and modified as necessary for particular, individual circumstances. In the context of our case study, it should provide a foundation from which battle forces of the future can be designed.

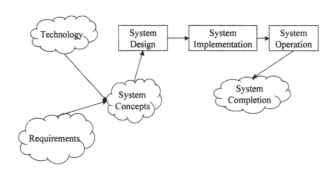

Exhibit 1   Systems Engineering Stages [Ryberg, 1988]

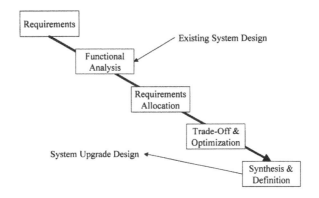

Exhibit 2   Systems Engineering [Pollard, 1988]

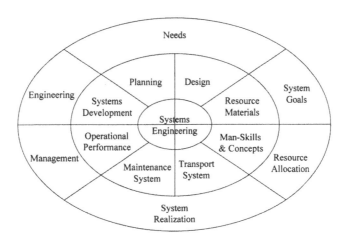

Exhibit 3   Systems Engineering Tasks [Ryberg, 1988]

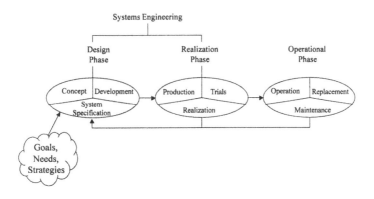

Exhibit 4   Systems Life Cycle and Systems Engineering [Ryberg, 1988]

Additionally, the process, if followed to completion, provides a means of maintaining historical background, as well as detailed documentation about the particulars. This allows each reviewer to retrace the train of thought for himself, and to confirm or disprove the original assumptions, conclusions, and recommendations at each step.

Case Study Background

The U.S. Navy has been in the process of composing "battle force architectures" for many years now. The actual process of "architecting" naval forces has been going on since the inception of navies, and dates back to 1775 in the case of the United States. When the country was young and the Navy small, the process was relatively easily handled by a small staff (in some cases one person) with paper, pen, and a firm grasp of naval tactics and seamanship. As the force grew larger, however, more men, paper, pens, expertise (in both depth and breadth), and time were required to keep track of the current forces, as well as stay abreast of emergent technologies. To compound the problem, the Navy was split into several fleets, and the fleets were further divided into battle forces (BFs), task forces (TFs), task groups (TGs), task units (TUs), and task elements (TEs). It took many years of evolution, but the job eventually became overwhelming and continues to get more and more difficult and complex.

The ultimate goal of any such planning process is, of course, to build a knowledge and experience database on which to formulate decisions toward shaping the future design of naval forces to meet the projected threat. This is more than just managing information. Planners must be able to organize and reorganize the components of a large, complex system (battle force) so that it functions smoothly as an integrated whole. We must be able to manage, manipulate, and study the effort on a conceptual level so that it can be implemented on the physical level.

During the late 1980s and early 1990s, the U.S. Navy was wrestling with the task of developing and maintaining about 59 (the exact number fluctuates) separate battle force "architectures" (Exhibit 5), which are intended to be molded together into a total naval battle force architecture (Exhibit 6). Each was developed by a small group composed mainly of senior engineers with virtually no operational expertise. The process is a two-year cycle, i.e., each architecture was (supposedly) written, assessed, and published, with a review and update every two years thereafter. Unfortunately, the process was very disjointed and unorganized, and took longer than two years to complete.

The Mission

The official mission to be accomplished by the Navy's warfare systems architecture and engineering (WSA&E) process is to transform top-level warfare requirements (TLWRs) into viable warfare system architectures that can meet the following objections [SPAWAR, 1987a]:

Exhibit 5   Architecture Matrix

| WMA | Battle Force | | | | |
	Carrier Battle Force (CVBF)	Battleship Battle Force (BBBF)	Area ASW Force	Amphibious Force (ATF/ARG)	ALOC Protect Force (SPF)
Command (Force, OTC)	X	X	X	X	X
Anti-air warfare (AAW)	X	X	X	X	X
Anti-surface warfare (ASUW)	X	X	X	X	X
Anti-sub warfare (ASW)	X	X	X	X	X
Mine warfare (MIW)	X	X	X	X	X
Strike warfare (STW)	X	X	X	X	
Amphibious warfare (AMW)	X	X	X	X	
Space warfare (SPW)	X	X	X	X	X
Command and Control warfare (C3)	X	X	X	X	X
Intelligence (Intel)	X	X	X	X	X
Electronic warfare (EW)	X	X	X	X	X
Logistics (Log)	X	X	X	X	X
Special warfare (SPCW)			X	X	

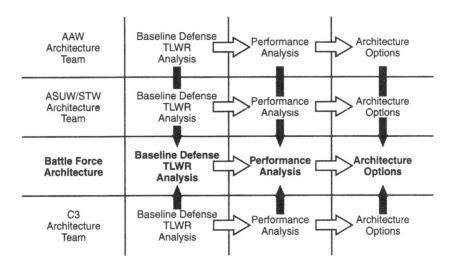

Exhibit 6   Architecture Integration Concept

- Develop requirements from fleet initiatives
- Assist the Chief of Naval Operations (OPNAV) in defining requirements
- Conduct analyses and critical experiments to evaluate the architecture
- Investigate options, trade-offs, and optimization
- Provide element performance and interface specifications
- Invoke design guidance and commonality

All of these considerations fit the types of systems analysis described by Sutherland [1975], Eisner [1987], Yourdon [1989a], Ward [1984, 1985], and others. To be worthwhile, however, this process must be transformed into useful action. It must translate into programs and definitions of critical areas that require funding. Therefore, the process must also:

- Provide guidance to program definition teams in defining systems and programs
- Implement systems engineering and integration to transform require-ments and architecture into top-level system specifications (design guidance)
- Provide more capability for less cost:
  — Optimized top-level systems
  — Integrated/cooperative performance
  — Optimized design and engineering
- Assist in defining requirements:
  — Analyze requirements and develop options
- Provide input to system master plans
- Support interoperability for joint and combined organizations
- Provide top-level system architecture arbitration among systems:
  — Allocation of requirements and capabilities
  — Analysis of performance
- Provide top-level systems engineering across systems:
  — Performance specification and control
  — Interface specification and control
  — Integration
  — Test and evaluation specification
- Provide design guidance to optimize systems:
  — Establish standards

The Goal

Within the bounds of our case study, the finished product was defined as a collection of documents (Exhibit 7) intended to accomplish the following [SPAWAR, 1987a]:

- Collect basic information
- Describe the functional structure of the organization using required operational functions (ROFs)

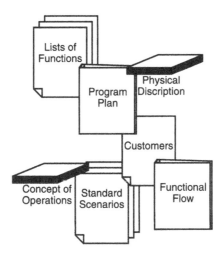

Exhibit 7   Architecture Components

- Describe the physical structure of the organization to the generic platform and major systems levels
- Describe connectivity and organization of the force
- Establish essential performance measures at force, platform, and system levels
- Describe the current performance and capability of the force (organization)
- Compare expected performance to TLWRs and identify shortfalls and overlaps (prioritized)
- Rank options relative to performance, affordability, etc.
- Create a notional acquisition roadmap appropriate to each option
- Identify required technological emphasis
- Relate current performance to TLWRs
- Transfer concepts to implementation support master plan development, program reviews, etc.
- Support the acquisition process:
  — Relate tentative operational requirements (TORs) to the overall force warfare concept
  — Formulate and issue specific guidance tailored for individual Development Options Paper (DOP) formulation
  — Monitor compliance with guidance and standards
  — Maintain oversight of acquisition programs
  — Maintain contact with force critical acquisition programs
  — Participate in major program milestones
  — Respond to program execution disruptions

The end products included:

- Current architecture
- Assessment of current architecture
- Shortfalls and overlaps
- Options

- Assessment of options
- Notional architecture (recommended procurement actions)

Each product will be addressed in a logical, stepwise fashion and discussed in detail.

An Approach Toward a Solution

A proper system, according to John W. Sutherland [1975], is an entity meeting the following criteria:

- When viewed from without, a system constitutes an entity of determinable morphology, i.e., it must be in (or be capable of obtaining) a state of integration sufficient to separate it from its environment (or surroundings).
- A system must encompass two or more morphologically determinable entities, i.e., it must contain multiple, differentiable subsystems where the differentiation may be structured, functional, or spatial.
- A system must exercise (or be capable of exercising) constrained animation among its subsystems, such that their behavior is not entirely autonomous, i.e., at least a portion of the energy available to subsystems must be co-opted by the system for the "larger" mission or for maintenance of the integrity of the whole.

These criteria provide the three dimensions common to all systems. The "ecological" dimension considers the interface properties of a system and the inflow and outflow of forces they regulate. This encompasses the external configuration of the system, the nature of the interchanges with its environment, relations with other systems, and the possible internal reactions resulting from external or exogenous forces. The "domain dimension" deals with the structural aspects of the system involving the broad, static patterns of internal behavior. The "dynamic dimension" is concerned with the nonstatic, process-related properties of the system, and involves the origin or evolution of any structural changes that can be identified within the system. This includes the nature of the work performed by the system and alterations in patterns of interaction among the various components or between the components and the system as a whole [Sutherland, 1975].

Any force can be thought of as a very large, complex "system." In the case of a naval force, this system (force) is composed of a collection of platforms (ships, aircraft, etc.), each with specific capabilities, functions, and requirements.

Each platform can be further divided into a list of equipments or systems. These systems also have specific requirements, capabilities, and functions. Equipments can then be broken down into components or subsystems. The process continues to the level of detail required; to the most minute component if necessary or desired. Exhibit 8 presents a small portion of the battle force breakdown as an example.

Except during periods of major conventional war, ships and aircraft typically last for 20 to 40 years with modifications. This is generally attributable to less

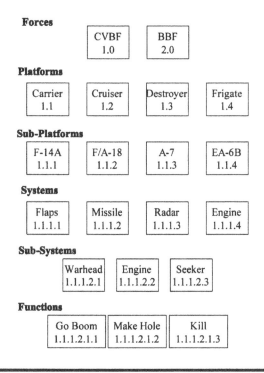

Exhibit 8   Battle Force Breakdown

wear and tear on the equipment, an artificially (bureaucratically) drawn-out procurement process that results in 10 to 15 year procurement cycles for new equipment (from identification of need to initial operational capability [IOC]), as well as a historically austere funding atmosphere, and a false sense of well-being during peaceful periods. Because the information contained in a battle force architecture is, therefore, relatively nonperishable, the process could benefit immensely from a structured systems engineering approach captured in a generic requirements database for continued use. The physical and functional breakdown of forces could and should be stored for future update. The development of architectures, thus, can be viewed as a step in the systems engineering approach to defining, designing, and procuring a naval force or, more generically, any large, complex system.

The process must provide for continuing prediction and demonstration of the anticipated or actual achievement of the primary technical objectives of the system, and must be responsive to change. The impact of changes to system and program requirements must be traceable to the lowest level of related documentation in a timely manner. The process is always iterative [DSMC, 1986].

CASE Tools: A Means of Managing Architectural Information

Architectures lend themselves quite nicely to systems engineering methodologies including functional analysis (FA), data flow diagrams (DFDs), entity-relationship diagrams (ERDs), structure charts, process specifications, context diagrams, event lists, etc. Many CASE (computer-aided systems engineering) tools prompt the user to input the appropriate information, and provide much of the documentation automatically.

- A CASE product supports requirements definition by providing capture and indexing of (text-based) requirements documents, cross-references between requirements documents, and later development models.
- A CASE product supports analysis specification by providing languages and analysis routines for: processing/input/output/control; information modeling; data composition modeling; process description modeling cross-references between analysis/specification models and later envelopment models.
- A CASE product supports design by providing languages and analysis routines for processing, input, output, and control; data composition modeling; process description modeling; structure chart modeling; translation from the analysis/specification model to the design model; cross-references between the design model and the end product.
- CASE also supports project management with:

  — *Deliverable document production:* The ability to merge portions of graphic models with text into an output document; the ability to print intermodel cross-reference information in the form of tracing tables; the ability to capture and store requirements information and interrelate it to other information; the ability to produce exception reporting showing unmet requirements and model segments not matched to requirements
  — *Configuration management:* Multiple releases with additions of functionality in later releases, multiple versions for different target environments, complex integration testing with changes being made simultaneously by many developers, determine the differences between two versions
  — *Model query/reporting capabilities:* Collect data on "who did what to which part of the model, when?," provide standard reports on current model contents and changes to the model since a given point in time, provide query facilities to allow *ad hoc* reporting on the model
  — *Cost analysis/cost estimation* [DCI, 1988]

Microcomputer- and workstation-based CASE tools seem to be a means of automating the process, while meeting many of the specific requirements. There are a variety of commercial off-the-shelf tools (COTS) on the market that would certainly do the job. The difficulty is in choosing one that is flexible enough to handle a large volume and variety of modifications, fill the functional requirements of the process, and is also available for use by the vast majority of small groups or individuals working each portion of the project. These groups, in general, do not have access to sophisticated workstations required to run many of the available software packages. Instead, offices abound with a proliferation of IBM PC clones, Macs, and a variety of other, generally incompatible equipment.

Additionally, many individuals are basically computer illiterate and reticent about operating sophisticated workstations. Though this situation is improving due to the widespread use of microcomputers, it is important to choose a tool that is easy and, if possible, fun (or at least not onerous) to operate, with maximum use of graphic interfaces to increase understanding and effectiveness (a picture is truly worth a thousand words). Further, graphic presentations in the final product are significantly easier to interpret and use than reams of textual data.

Another key issue is life expectancy of the data after it has been entered into the tool. Building a database is very costly in terms of time, money, and staffing, and, therefore, it should be useful beyond the confines of any specific tool. If the developers of the original tool fail to keep up with customer needs or technology, if a better database management system or CASE product becomes available, or if, for any reason, a different tool is to be implemented, the current database must be salvageable, preferably without the requirement to write a proliferation of complex data, schema, view, report, or interface conversions routines. Additionally, the data should be transportable to and interoperable with other systems. Models and simulations, for example, all require many of the same data items. This information should not have to be re-keyed, as is often the case today, nor should the organization be required to incur the expense of acquiring a translation routine. Many tools plan for this contingency by using "industry standard" formats for their internal data and directly access databases using standard formats and languages such as SQL. The trick, then, appears to be finding a user-friendly tool that will operate on existing equipment and meet the technical requirements of the process.

While general qualities, characteristics, and capabilities of database management systems, CASE, and other tools will be discussed later, specific tools will not be analyzed. It is not within the scope of this work to investigate specific software packages. In addition, the relative speed with which the software industry is advancing renders any such discussion outdated within a very short period of time.

The Current Process

The primary "fighting unit" of the Navy is the multiple-carrier battle force, which serves as the principal example for what is meant by a "force." The collection of units that comprise the force cannot remain rigid. Each force can be described in terms of its elements and their tactical groupings (Exhibit 9) and the warfare tasks (mission areas) it must accomplish (Exhibit 10).

Warfare mission areas are broken down into two distinct groups: (1) fundamental or primary tasks, and (2) supporting tasks. They are used as a logical and convenient division of requirements, forces, tactics, etc. The architectural effort is, therefore, similarly divided into warfare mission areas

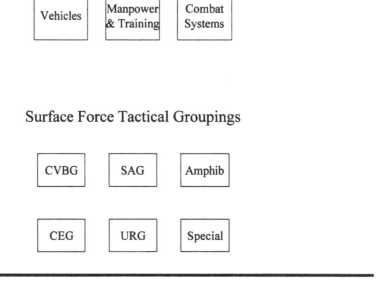

Surface Force Tactical Groupings

Exhibit 9   Basic Elements of Tactical Units [Wiersma, 1987]

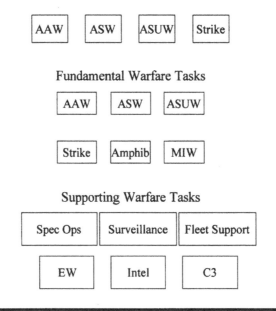

Exhibit 10   Warfare Mission Areas [Wiersma, 1987]

(WMAs), each of which is produced by a separate team of individuals. The most notable of these WMAs are anti-air warfare (AAW), anti-sub warfare (ASW), anti-surface warfare (ASUW), STRIKE, EW, C3, INTEL, and SPACE, with the first four referred to as primary warfare mission areas (PWMAs), and the rest as "support" areas. Primary warfare mission areas are defined as those areas responsible for a specific major phase or portion of naval warfare. At the time of the original study, support mission areas (SMAs) included such

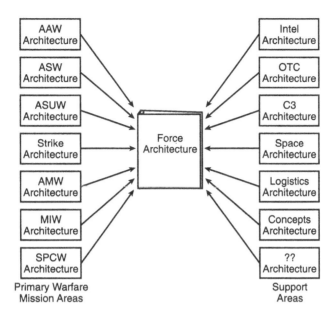

Exhibit 11   Architecture Integration

things as logistics; electronic warfare (EW); Intelligence (INTEL); and Command, Control, and Communications (C3), which provide support that crosses the boundaries of many PWMAs. More recently, C3, Intelligence, and EW have been combined to form a new primary mission area: Command, Control, Communications, Computers, Intelligence, Surveillance, and Reconnaissance (C4ISR).

As defined for warfare systems architecture and engineering (WSA&E), battle force architecture follows the process outlined below. Products in each mission area are produced by a separate group in virtual isolation, with the final product consolidated, as shown in Exhibit 11. Exhibit 12 is a graphical representation of the process flow.

Maritime Strategy

The Maritime Strategy considers the required naval role in the national context (usually delineated in the National Strategy), and states that role in terms of broad objectives. For the research, development, and acquisition (RDA) process, the Maritime Strategy is the entry point for requirements definition. This is analogous to high-level corporate strategies or visions that are then divided into segments, sectors, divisions, groups, teams, or other organizational structures peculiar to the corporate entity in question to determine long term organizational goals.

The Maritime Strategy outlines the naval objectives for sea control, maritime power projection, and control and protection of shipping compared with identifiable trends in the future threat. The theme of the Maritime Strategy is to maintain the strategic initiative and ensure that the terms of war are favorable

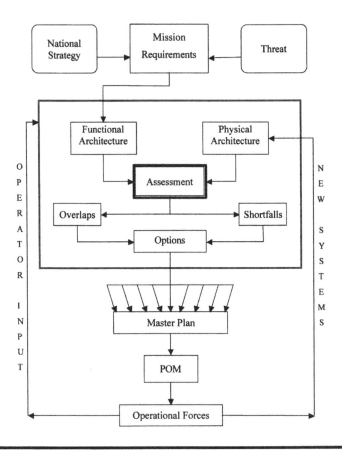

Exhibit 12   Architecture Process

to the United States and its allies [Wiersma, 1987]. The maritime strategy originates at the Joint Chiefs of Staff (JCS) level with links to the political arena where national policies and objectives are formulated.

Establishing requirements for the RDA process involves assignment of priorities and war-fighting values, which cross platforms and mission area boundaries. Existing processes are utilized to the maximum extent possible to develop such a requirements base. The National Policy and Objectives, together with the Commanders-in-Chief (CINC) War Plans, form a solid foundation for the Maritime Strategy.

The Threat

The threat is a major driving factor in the design of military forces (Exhibit 12) and is discussed in more detail later. However, for our current discussion we can see that the architectural process starts with the perceived threat as defined, in this case, by the Naval Technical Intelligence Center (NTIC). The threat receives a good deal of attention and is a composite of many pieces of intelligence from a variety of sources. Each is investigated, analyzed, correlated, categorized, and cross-checked for corroboration. Extensive laboratory analysis is performed on captured, simulated, or emulated enemy equipment. In short, the estimated threat is as rigorously derived as possible, and is, in essence, Red Force (adversary) architecture, consisting of the platforms, systems, and functions of our opponents. In any case, it is so deeply enmeshed in the cloak-and-dagger secrecy of the Intelligence world that further discussion here is both inappropriate and futile. Threat information is accepted as accurate and reliably given.

Top-Level Warfare Requirements

Naval warfare requirements are founded on the Maritime Strategy and expressed in TLWRs (top-level warfare requirements). TLWRs are written for 10 to 15 years in the future and are constrained by estimates of available resources and technology. They are much less rigorously derived than the threat. In some cases, many small models are used to provide a semirigorous analysis. Unfortunately, these models are very limited in scope, each addressing only a small portion of the battle force problem and usually ignoring all too significant connections with the rest of the real world. Additionally, it must be kept in mind that the models themselves are not precisely formulated. Though TLWRs are generally laced with the requirement to perform a required function within a specific, designated probability of success, that requirement is more a consensus of expert opinion than mathematically derived. This is so, largely because the threat can only be estimated based on what we think we know of our opponent's military strength, technology, strategy, tactics, intentions, and national interests. Strangely, our own Blue Force estimates are sometimes equally inaccurate. In many cases, it is not known to any great detail how well Blue equipment will function in a variety of environmental situations, nor what, if any, interference problems will emerge when an attempt is made to integrate certain systems on a platform or within the force. Parallels exist in every major corporation or large organization with which the authors are familiar.

CASE and other automated tools can help alleviate this problem by allowing "what if" or "sensitivity" analyses of the current system. Substitutions can be made to see what, if any, incompatibilities arise. This is, of course, at a very high level and the information is only as good as the information available (data flow, entity relationships, system interconnectivity, etc.). Still, some relevant, legitimate analysis is better than the current void.

Architecture: A System Description

The baseline architecture is defined as a complete list and description of equipment that can be found "at the pier" today. It exists and is very loosely maintained as a conglomeration of platform descriptions, system specifications, and operational and maintenance data in the form of publications, computer databases, and test results. Each piece of this puzzle is compiled and maintained by separate agencies for their own use in whatever format appealed to the original drafter. Even if a piece of information is known to exist, locating the cognizant office and obtaining a current copy may be difficult. Additionally, certain information is available from more than one source, many of which disagree on pertinent details.

Because each WMA working group has its own preferred source of information, the composition of the battle force itself also varies from architecture to architecture, depending on where the information originated and for what purpose. The architectural database, therefore, is incomplete, fragmented, inconsistent, and confusing.

The WSA&E methodology calls for each group to develop its own small piece of the architecture in virtual isolation and then merge the products, as suggested by Exhibit 11. Unfortunately, the end result of the previously mentioned inconsistencies is a large group of independent architecture "chapters" or "sections" that do not lend themselves easily to consolidation without a considerable amount of modification.

Assessment: How Well Does it Fulfill Requirements?

After all the data is compiled, the architecture is then assessed to determine how well it can perform the established requirements in light of the perceived threat. As with requirements definition, this assessment is not rigorously performed. Extensive, complete, complex, total battle force models simply do not exist. Though some small simulations are used to assess segments of the architecture, most of the information is determined simply by expert opinion. Even when models are used, most of the initial parameters, equations, and algorithms used by the model are empirically derived. Performance of certain systems can be specified mathematically with some rigor using test results, etc., but for the most part there is no precise information available to indicate how a friendly system might fare against any given threat system in a realistically intense environment.

Shortfalls and Overlaps: Identifying Strengths and Weaknesses

As might be expected, there are areas of the architecture where capabilities are better than needed to counter the existing threat, as well as other areas where there is simply not enough capability. These are referred to as overlaps and shortfalls, respectively. This is a pivotal checkpoint in the entire exercise. If the process up to this point has been followed faithfully, it is now obvious where our attention must be placed in the future. Unfortunately, due to the imperfections stated previously, these shortfalls and overlaps are very subjectively derived and stated at a macro level. The detail required for precise option development simply does not exist.

Architectural Options: Making the Right Choices

The next and final step is the development of options to successfully fill the gaps and eliminate unnecessary duplications uncovered in the previous step. This supposedly presents the Warfare Requirements Board (WRB) with a list of options from which to choose, resulting in a consolidated Navy battle force strategy for the formation of future fleets.

The Proposed Process

The process as outlined in this case study leaves much to be desired and is not atypical. There are large inconsistencies at every step along the way. The Navy, at least, has worked the problem and continues to address architecture and systems engineering issues. Many other large organizations, both within and outside of government, have failed to recognize the issues or have chosen to ignore them.

The following argument assumes that official, standard data items can be found and agreed upon by all of the players. In fact, within the Department of Defense, several programs are under way that could help alleviate some of this difficulty. There are several governmental agencies that are responsible for the maintenance of large, "official" databases. These agencies are located in the four corners of the continental United States and some even reside overseas in Hawaii and Europe. The current concept is to standardize the database schema, and then connect these agencies via a network. The resultant distributed database is to be accepted and used by any and all official activities, and will provide a standard source of information from which to draw. In the following discussion, we will attempt to outline a more-rigorous architectural process utilizing the five basic phases proposed at the beginning of this chapter. The Naval Force case study will be utilized to draw parallels with the previous discussion.

Architecture Development

If we assume that the likelihood of global conventional war is minimal, the fleet of tomorrow (within 15 to 30 years) will not differ significantly from that of today for several reasons. First, platforms generally have an actual service life of 20 to 40 years or longer (despite the service life advertised at procurement). Although they may be modified with newer equipment from time to time, the basic platform with most of its original systems will remain intact. Second, the current Department of Defense procurement cycle, for all but the most simple, inexpensive, and mundane of systems, is on the order of 10 to 15 years. Barring a major technological breakthrough (reminiscent of the atomic bomb), that could seriously tip the balance of power; it is virtually impossible to propose any significant improvements and expect them to be in place in a shorter timeframe. Existing platforms and systems thus form a base upon which to build. The following architectures are defined and established for reference:

■ *Baseline architecture:* The hardware that is actually operational today. This category includes all deployed sites, platforms, and systems and their associated functions, and is identical in content to the baseline architecture discussed previously. The baseline is the generic architecture that forms a basis for the development of all future architectures.

■ *Current architecture:* At any one time, there are several approved, funded, "viable" equipments in varying stages of the development and procurement cycle. By virtue of the fact that these systems have already been approved through a lengthy chain of endorsers from the individual program office, up through the Secretary of the Navy (SecNav) and Congress, they are virtually impossible to impact significantly. Though most are not rigorously integrated into the overall architecture, they can be shown to be answering a threat that already exists. Except in very extreme cases, interference with these programs is counterproductive, and quite possibly (politically) pointless. Each has associated with it a target date for initial operational capability (IOC), i.e., the date by which the first unit is expected to be installed, tested, certified, and deployed on an operational platform. All such equipments whose IOC falls within the timeframe defined by the Five Year Defense Program (FYDP) are added to the baseline with appropriate removal of replaced, obsolete equipments, and the result is titled current architecture. This document is the basis for establishing current force performance assessments.

■ *Current-plus architecture:* As one might suspect, not all approved, funded, "viable" procurements are scheduled to IOC within the next five years. Though these may be important systems with significant impact on the war-fighting capability of the fleet, they are also at the mercy of Congress and budget cycles for a prolonged period of time, and their prognosis for successful completion, therefore, is less rosy. Though their eventual procurement is not sufficiently reliable to count on, the capabilities of these systems are deemed indispensable, and their inclusion in the architecture mandatory. To cover this class of system, the current-plus architecture is established to include these systems superimposed on the current architecture previously described, and is intended as a point of departure for the notional system.

■ *Notional architecture:* The final product, the ultimate goal for the entire process is the development of a notional fleet architecture for some future date. As previously explained, that date is generally 15 to 20 years in the future. For purposes of further discussion, it will be assumed that one such document is to be produced, although several alternative notional architectures could (and probably should) be developed to give decision makers an alternative.

Similar "architectures" or categorizations of systems can be defined for any organization. The names and definitions will, of course, change to fit the context, but within any organization, it is important to establish the current state of the organization, the goal state of the organization, and possibly one or two intermediate states. Each of these must be well defined and named so that they can be referenced and discussed without confusion.

Warfare systems architecture consists of establishing the overall structure of platforms, sensors, weapon systems, and communication links required to fulfill the needs of naval forces. It includes the macro-assignment of functions to platforms and systems, and the categorization of like functions together for purposes of commonality, as well as addressing the needs of individual platforms to operate both autonomously and within the context of the battle force. It is a systematic, structured approach to determining the composition of hardware and software systems for naval forces.

The systems architectures, then, are developed by segmenting the force into platforms, platforms into systems, and functional systems into semiautonomous sections (subsystems). Each segment is allocated specific functions and is configured to fit together with other segments along well-defined boundaries (interfaces) in order to perform the functions of the total system. Exhibit 13 depicts the elements of an architecture; Exhibits 14 and 15 are examples of how an architecture might be represented.

Accurate, logical segmentation at the outset is probably the most-important single element of the system design. Failure to do well is seldom correctable and, at best, extremely expensive.

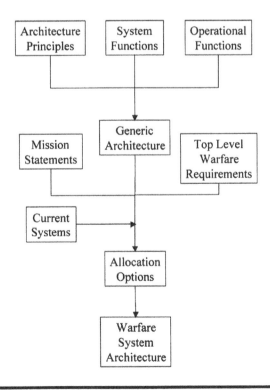

Exhibit 13   Architecture Elements [Wiersma, 1987]

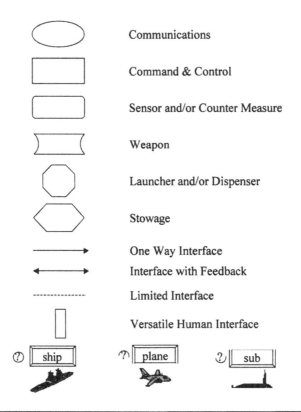

Exhibit 14   Architecture Symbols

Architectural Principles

Architectures should possess a variety of attributes (see Exhibit 16), such as the system attributes discussed in Chapter 2, the most notable of which, according to Ray Wiersma, are presented here [Wiersma, 1987]. Though explained in military terms to coincide with the current discussion, the concepts apply to any large-scale system architecture.

- *Simplicity:* The simplest correct structure is the most desirable. Simplicity must be retained throughout implementation, use, modification, expansion, and reconfiguration of the battle force "system." If a system is not simple at the highest levels, it cannot be expected to reduce to simplicity as the process continues.
- *Economy:* The architecture must allow achievement of the required battle force performance (as derived from the TLWR) within projected constraints of financial, material, and personnel resources.
- *Correspondence:* The systems structure must be in accordance with the steady-state, functional responsibilities of the user command structure. As such, it must be complete in its correspondence to all levels of hierarchy, including those compartmented by security constraints.

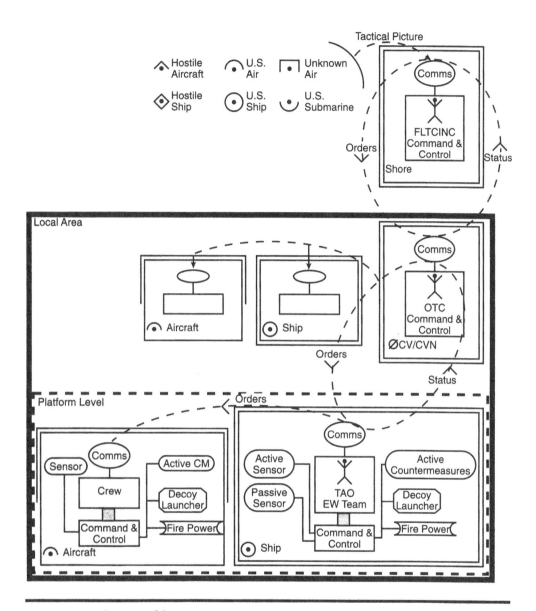

Exhibit 15   Tier 1 Architecture

- *Layering:* Battle force systems functions must be allocated hierarchically in the command structure to support primary and alternative missions in both coordinated and autonomous modes of operation. Functions must be distributed so that there are multiple ways to achieve an equivalent result, to retain unity of command, and to adapt to changes in threat protocol.
- *Continuity:* There must be continuity of information across battle force elements so that any appropriate aggregation of information presented to a user at any level in the hierarchy is consistent with any other aggregation presented to any other user.

Exhibit 16   Principles of Architecture [Pollard, 1988]

• Modularity	Loosely coupled federation
• Connectivity	Only essential communications between elements
• Simplicity	Best for operation and acquisition
• Economy	People, material, and funding
• Correspondence	Best match to structure, mission, and operations
• Continuity	Consistent information, decision rules
• Layering	Support hierarchy
• Sustainability	Maintain capability, survival, and readiness
• Compatibility	Constructive to existing systems
• Security	Must be designed in

■ *Sustainability:* The battle force systems must include provisions that contribute to survival and readiness, through embedded self-test, on-line training, physical protection, and logistics support.

■ *Connectivity:* The systems must provide essential communication services between battle force elements with minimal exploitable electronic exposure.

■ *Compatibility:* Changes or additions to the battle force systems must be constructively operational with the existing system.

■ *Modularity:* The system should be designed to operate as a federation of modules that perform independent functions, require minimum coupling or interaction, and whose internal processes are not apparent to connected modules.

Note that it is not the intent here to imply that systems should function autonomously. On the contrary, it is extremely important that systems interact continually, sharing information and providing for centralized command and control at both the platform and the force levels. It is equally imperative, however, that all systems have the capability of autonomous operation if the necessity arises either by design or through the fortunes of war.

Mission Requirements Analysis

The first phase in the development of a notional architecture is the definition and analysis of mission requirements. In the context of the Navy battle force, that translates into top-level warfare requirements (TLWRs). TLWRs are developed and written for the Chief of Naval Operations (CNO) by his staff. Each of these staff (OPNAV) organizations are responsible for developing a section of the total force TLWR in their specific areas of expertise and responsibility (WMA). Referring to Exhibit 17, for example, it can be seen that the OPNAV code 76 staff office (OP-76) is responsible for the areas of electronic warfare, C3I, and space. Similarly, OP-75 handles AAW, etc.

Requirements are formalized through a series of engineering studies and trade-offs including [DSMC, 1988]:

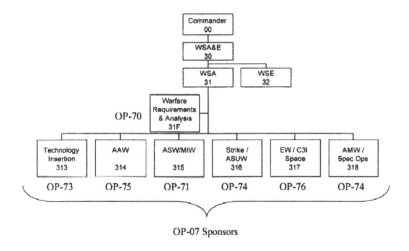

OP-07 Sponsors

Exhibit 17   WSA Organization: This accurately represents a small portion of the OPNAV organization at the time of the study. However, due to several reorganizations, the structure presented here may no longer apply.

- *Requirements analysis:* The overall system requirements, including constraints, should be examined to identify the factors that drive requirements. These factors may include system interfaces, interoperability, communication functions, personnel functions, the anticipated level and urgency of change, and requirements for reliability and responsive support.
- *Operational concept analysis:* The operational concept is analyzed in order to determine the role of resources. Particular attention is paid to requirements for mission preparation, operator interface, control functions, and mission analysis.
- *Trade-off and optimization:* The effects of system constraints such as the operations concept, the support concept, performance requirements, logistics, availability and maturity of technology, and limitations on cost, schedule, and resources are determined. Alternative approaches are studied to:
  — Meet operational, interoperability, and support requirements
  — Determine how the system requirements for reliability and maintainability will be satisfied
  — Determine how requirements for system security will be met
- *Risk:* For each approach, the associated risks are evaluated. Typical risk areas include system maturity, availability and maturity of the support tools, loosely defined or incomplete interface definitions, and lack of adequate throughput capability.

Upon completion of the individual warfare mission area TLWRs, these documents are combined to form the total force TLWR. As an example, Exhibit 18 shows primary warfare mission area TLWRs, each of which has, in

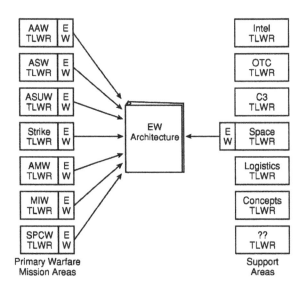

Exhibit 18   TLWR Integration

this case, an annex for the support mission area of EW. All of these EW annexes can be combined to form a consolidated EW TLWR. The primary warfare mission area TLWRs can be combined into the battle force TLWR similar to the architecture combination depicted in Exhibit 11. Some, as you can see in Exhibit 18, do not! A complete discussion of TLWR development parallels architecture development in scope and content (Exhibits 11 and 18). For purposes of this paper, requirements are considered to be a given.

Functional Analysis

As previously mentioned, time, monetary, and political considerations preclude the design and development of a totally new battle force from scratch. It must evolve from existing parts. The challenge is in guiding that evolution so that it results in an efficient, effective, affordable overall system. Therefore, no realistic analysis of required functions can take place without some consideration of existing equipment and the functions they perform.

Analysis of required functions, as well as those currently performed by the force, can be accomplished in parallel if examined by separate, distinct groups. If, as is more likely the case, the same persons are to complete both, it is best to perform the breakdown of required functions first. In this way, the imagination can be given free reign without being constrained into predetermined concepts, influenced by reality, or forced into the artificial limitations of established, discrete (and possibly wrong) compartments. In any case, the processes described in this section must be completed for both the existing force (current architecture) and also in the abstract for the notional architecture of the future.

Tasks:

- Decompose the requirement objectives into functions and develop functional flow diagrams.
- Develop an arrangement of those functions that define a preliminary packaging concept or architecture.

Functions are derived from requirements and successively decomposed into tiers. Each tier completely describes a process. Lower tiers provide greater levels of detail. Each function must have inputs and outputs. Equipment, computer programs, and people are part of the system. Functional allocation is based on similarity, data flow, and design considerations.

Operational Functions

Operational functions are the processes that must be accomplished by any particular force in order to carry out its assigned missions, and therefore to successfully support the Maritime Strategy and its role in the national context through CINC War Plans. Operational functions are generally a higher level definition of battle force functional requirements.

System Functions

System functions are the processes that are embedded in the design of physical system elements, mechanized in equipment design, or written into computer programs. The relationship between system functions and operational functions is best expressed by cross-correlating the two sets of functions. Ray Wiersma delineates a representative list of top-level system functions as follows [Wiersma, 1987]:

- *Sensing:* The creation of signals and the processing of received signals to create manageable data and information.
- *Dynamic data management:* Those functions required to create and maintain the database of track files, navigation data, environmental data, and other dynamic sensor data as required by the system.
- *Static data management:* Those functions required to create and maintain the database of unit and system characteristics, orders of battle, and other relatively static information.
- *Man–machine interaction:* Those processes which assist the operator/commander to perceive, understand, manipulate, and interpret the available tactical information, and to direct action to be taken by the system. This function includes the information display and man–machine dialog.
- *Decision support:* Those tools used to process data to collect information relevant to a tactical decision, present alternatives to courses of action, project effectiveness of tactical decision, or assess the effectiveness of a tactical action that has been taken.

■ *Weapon/sensor control:* The process of gathering and providing to a weapon, weapon system, sensor, or supporting system those commands which are intended to guide the movements and activities associated with the engagement of targets.

■ *Communications processing and distribution:* Those functions required to prepare data for transfer across platforms and to effect the distribution of transferred messages.

Requirements Allocation

Requirements allocation is the further decomposition of system-level functional requirements to the point where a specific hardware item or software routine can fulfill the performance requirements. It is the logical extension of the initial functional identification. Because architectures are not intended to be detailed, hardware-specific, procurement documents requirements are allocated on a macro level to subsystems, systems, and platforms. A more-detailed discussion of this area can be found in DSMC [1986].

Assessment of the Current Architecture

In order to develop an appreciation for the magnitude of the problem in both depth and breadth, it is necessary to consider how well the current fleet (architecture) meets the existing threat, and then extrapolate both the threat and technology advances 15 to 20 years hence. To this end, an evaluation is made of how well the current architecture (existing equipment) satisfies the established requirements in light of the current known (or presumed) threat.

This assessment can be completed on a number of levels. Initially (and currently) the assessment is simply the opinion of notable experts. Ideally, this provides a combination of operational, engineering, and technical expertise. As models and simulations are developed and perfected, their results can be inserted, thus making the assessment progressively more quantitative. If CASE tools were in widespread use, the large database used by the tool could be easily cloned as necessary for the models.

Identification of Shortfalls and Overlaps

The assessment process must be done as rigorously as possible, utilizing accepted methods; approved, "official" threat data; and actual hardware configurations (actual, operationally derived performance vs. advertised performance). This assessment then yields a succinct list of overlaps (areas in which there may be too much capability) and shortfalls (areas where improvement in capability is necessary or desirable). Care must be taken to document and weigh the interplay between entities, because one will most likely have side effects on one or more of the others. Again, automated tools would help ensure that these interconnects are duly considered.

Development of Architectural Options

The next step is the development of several alternative ways to approach and rectify the problems that surfaced in the previous step. There are numerous remedies to any situation and, again, each will impact on the others. This should be viewed as a brain-storming or think-tank type of exercise. All possible options should at least be considered (including the null option). In this step, many nontactical and strategic issues will, of necessity, be addressed. These issues can be grouped into several major categories:

- *Risk:* Can it be done?
  - *Technologic:* Is it within the realm of possibility?
  - *Political:* Is it supportable?
  - *Administrative:* Can it survive the lengthy bureaucratic paper mill?
  - *Legal:* Are there legal barriers to funding, procurement, international partnerships, etc.?
  - *Sociological:* Will it cause problems in society at large?
- *Cost:* Is it affordable?
- *Schedule:* Can it be completed in the timeframe required?

In the development of options, each of these areas must be addressed in detail and documented for decision makers. This "reality check" will tend to eschew and narrow the choices available.

Assessment of Options

After the full range of options has been explored and documented, it then becomes a task of assessing the proposed options, using the same methodology employed in the assessment of the architecture for consistency. This process should narrow the field to a select group that represents the most cost-effective, efficient method of meeting the threat, in light of existing equipment and national policy.

Proposed New (Notional) Architecture

This is the optimization step in our process. The few selected options are folded back into the current architecture as replacements or new capabilities, and the results are checked for consistency and operability. This notional architecture can then be translated into a procurement strategy for the battle force of the future.

System Synthesis

The synthesis step of the system engineering process will result in a design that is complete at a given level of detail, from a total system element viewpoint (hardware, facilities, personnel, computer software, and procedural data). Synthesis is the documentation of the resulting configuration [DSMC, 1986].

The performance, configuration, and arrangement of a chosen system and its elements, and the technique for their test, support, and operation will be portrayed in a suitable form such as a set of schematic diagrams, physical and mathematical models, computer simulations, layouts, detailed drawings, and similar engineering graphics. These portrayals will illustrate intra- and intersystem and item interfaces, permit traceability between the elements at various levels of system detail, and provide the means for complete and comprehensive change control. This portrayal will be the basic source of data for developing, updating, and completing:

- The system, configuration item, and critical element specifications
- Interface control documentation
- Consolidated facility requirements
- Content of procedural handbooks, placards, and similar forms of instructional data
- Task loading of personnel
- Operational computer programs
- Specification trees
- Dependent elements of work breakdown structures [Mil499A, 1974]

The Need for Maintaining Up-To-Date Documentation

Documentation is of ultimate importance throughout this or any systems engineering process. It is imperative that the documentation capture the flavor, tone, and mood of the analysis, as well as the hard core data that results. The thought processes must be repeatable to be truly useful to those that follow. In any organization, personnel come and go; in this regard, a military organization is probably worse than most. Also, in any group a small subset (occasionally as small as one person) accomplishes much of the actual work. If (when) key people move, those that follow must be able to read the documentation in virtual isolation, glean the substance of the effort, and quickly grasp the method, techniques, assumptions, prejudices, decisions, and conclusions of their predecessors. The corporate memory must be maintained.

The documentation can either assume a standard format used by most system engineering applications, or it can be modified to better suit the needs of the user. The precise format is not as important as content, traceability, and consistency. In the specific case of battle force architecture, current formats closely parallel standard data flow diagrams (DFDs), entity relationship diagrams (ERDs), and data dictionaries. There is also a good deal of information that is simply presented in tabular or textual form. Minor format modifications would result in an excellent, user friendly, easily interpretable product.

For this case study, one such useful modification might be a switch to standard Navy Tactical Data System (NTDS) symbols in the DFDs rather than the more familiar bubbles. This modification allows for immediate graphic recognition of platforms by general type. Samples were was presented in Exhibits 14–18. The following is a list of just a few of the components normally included in a documentation package. Architectural documentation normally includes:

- Systems Engineering Management Plan (SEMP)
- Configuration Item Specification
- Interface Control Documents
- Trade Study Reports
- Risk Analysis Management Plan
- Survivability/Hardness Plan
- Design Review
- Mission Analysis Reports
- Functional Analyses
- Reliability Plan
- Maintainability Plan
- Safety/Hazard Analysis Plan
- Human Engineering Plan
- Integrated Logistics Support Plan (ILSP)
- Electromagnetic Compatibility
- Test and Evaluation Master Plan (TEMP)
- Mission Support Plan
- Production Engineering Plan
- Others as required

Summary

Though limited in scope, this chapter has attempted to illustrate a structured, systematic approach to systems engineering and architecture development. With a system as large as a carrier battle force or any large, complex system — government or commercial — it is especially important that a rigorous, systematic, structured approach be taken. Each step must be fully and clearly documented, and the process must be maintainable and repeatable. The current system (used by many large organizations) of manual manipulation of data items, connectivities, relationships, flow diagrams, and other textual information is clearly inadequate to deal with such vast quantities of information. Additionally, it is very costly in terms of time, money, and manpower. Though the second and subsequent iterations should be easier, they are still very manpower intensive and prone to human error. Automation through CASE tools, databases, or similar technologies could provide significant improvement in speed, accuracy, maintainability, and flexibility. Although initial implementation of such a tool suite is bound to be at least as costly as the current process, the end results are clearly worth the investment, which will, no doubt, be recouped very quickly.

Architectures, indeed all large systems engineering projects, are iterative. Because this approach has never been followed to completion for large-scale information systems such as described here, there are bound to be perturbations and deviations in the first and most probably in every application. In any given scenario, however, this approach will provide a solid foundation upon which to build. The system in general should provide a systematic, repeatable method for producing large-scale system architectures.

There is a plethora of issues in the development of architectures, many of which have been briefly addressed here. Time and space limitations, however, precluded the in-depth, detailed investigation and discussion that these issues deserve. A more-rigorous investigation of the requirements for architectural description must be completed before an appropriate toolset can be selected; then comes careful definition of the data structure, data entry, and design of desired output products.

For the interested reader, a number of good systems engineering documents exist, including DSMC [1986], Eisner [1987, 1997], and Sutherland [1975]. These and more are cited in the reference list. Now that we have established the basics, we move on to the application of these concepts to IA.

Chapter 5

Information Assurance Task Force

Plans get you into things but you have to work your way out.

Gen. Merrill McPeak, USAF (Ret.)

This chapter discusses the Information Assurance Task Force (IATF) that is basically considered the Information Assurance Systems Engineering Program Management Team. In reality, the IATF is responsible for the systems engineering, systems acquisition, risk management, certification and accreditation, and total life-cycle support processes for the systems engineering of an information system. The purpose of this chapter is to put the system engineering process of the previous chapter in the context of information systems, and to describe the skill required to successfully complete the process. This chapter provides the background for tailoring the basic systems engineering concept of Chapter 4 and applying it to IA systems, as discussed in subsequent chapters.

Systems engineering methodologies are described in painstaking detail in various publications for each step along the way. Many sources and models include a large number of "elements" or "tasks" in the systems engineering process; however, in the interest of brevity, only five basic areas were addressed in the previous chapter:

1. Requirements analysis
2. Functional analysis
3. Evaluation and decision
4. System synthesis
5. Documentation

However, before any of these processes can be realized, we must first build a Systems Engineering Team or collect a group of experts who are especially suited to analyze information requirements, design, build, deploy, and document an information system. We call this our Information Assurance Task Force (IATF) or, more specifically, the Information Assurance Systems Engineering Program Management Team (IASEPMT)

The IATF is responsible for designing and implementing the system engineering processes as they apply to information systems, bringing a focus to information assurance needs in parallel with other systems engineering concerns. The IATF will need to be formed to support the evolution, verification, and validation of an integrated and life-cycle balanced set of system product and process solutions that satisfy customer information assurance needs. Taking the same five basic areas of systems engineering and applying them to information assurance systems engineering, we have the following:

- *Requirements analysis:* This initial phase undertaken by the IATF is comprised of the research needed to discover information assurance needs by talking to the users, and deriving mission information assurance needs from that research. At this phase, the IATF will need to identify threats to information management and consider all existing information assurance policies and procedures. The IATF will define the information assurance system and state the IA objectives, define system context and its operating environment, and compile and derive from all that information a set of information assurance requirements. While there are feedback loops to each phase, this is the most important as it builds the foundation for the system and the rest of the phases.
- *Functional analysis:* The IATF will need to use systems engineering tools to understand the functioning and allocation of functions to various information assurance components.
- *Evaluation and decision:* The IATF will become involved in preliminary and detailed information assurance design reviews at this phase.
- *System synthesis:* The IATF will need to actually implement the IA system at this phase.
- *Documentation:* The IATF will have been writing various documents along the phases, including a Mission Essential Needs Statement, Preliminary and Critical Design Reviews, etc. The procurement, build, and test phases will rely on such documentation.

The IATF will need to focus on identifying, understanding, containing, and optimizing information assurance risks. Throughout all these phases, IATF activities will be directed toward:

- Describing information system/information assurance needs
- Generating information system/IA requirements based on needs early in the systems engineering process

- Satisfying the requirements at an acceptable level of information protection risk
- Building a functional information assurance architecture based on requirements
- Allocating information assurance functions to a physical and logical architecture
- Designing the Information Assurance Center (IAC) to implement the information assurance architecture
- Balancing information assurance risk management and other IATF systems engineering considerations within the overall context of cost, schedule, and operational suitability and effectiveness
- Participating in trade-off studies with other information assurance and system engineering disciplines
- Integrating IA concerns with standard systems engineering and acquisition processes
- Testing the various systems to verify information assurance design and validate information protection requirements
- Supporting the customers after deployment and tailoring the overall process to their needs

Activities performed by the IATF should begin alongside the system engineering activities to ensure that information assurance is built into the overall IT system. Considering information assurance objectives, requirements, functions, architecture, design, testing, and implementation simultaneously with the corresponding system engineering analogues allows information assurance to be optimized based on the technical and nontechnical considerations of the particular system.

Requirements Analysis

Discovering Information Assurance Needs

The IATF will begin with a review of the user's mission needs, relevant policies, regulations, standards, and threats with respect to information in the user environment that was defined by the system engineers. The IATF then identifies the users of the information systems and information, the nature of their interaction with the information systems and information, and their roles, responsibilities, and authorities in each stage of the information assurance system life-cycle. The information assurance needs should come from the user's perspective and not overly constrain the design or implementation of the IAC.

In an Information Assurance Policy and Procedures Manual or the Security Concept of Operations (CONOPS), the IATF should describe, in the user's language, how information assurance supports successfully achieving the mission or desired market capability in the overall IAC environment. When the information assurance needs of the IAC are discovered and described during this activity, the information assurance processes surrounding the IAC will develop as an integral part of the overall system development process.

Mission Information Assurance Needs

The role of information and information systems in the larger mission and functions of the IAC must be considered. The IATF must consider the impact to the mission of organizational elements — people and systems — losing the use of the IAC, the information systems or information that they depend on; specifically, the loss of confidentiality, integrity, availability, nonrepudiation, or any combination thereof. At this point, the IATF has begun to elicit information assurance needs from the user.

Users know best the importance of their information, but usually need help in discovering their protection needs and priorities. Discovering the customer needs leads to the information assurance needs in terms of what information could be used to harm the mission if it were disclosed, modified, or lost. The IATF should be able to:

- Assist customers in modeling their information management process
- Assist customers in defining information threats
- Assist customers in prioritizing protection needs
- Prepare information assurance policies
- Achieve customer agreement

Identifying needs is a customer interface activity performed by the IATF to ensure that the mission/business needs include information assurance needs and that the system functionality includes the information assurance functionality. The IATF brings together security disciplines, technology, and mechanisms, and applies them to satisfy the protection needs of the customer. The result is an IAC that includes the information assurance architecture and mechanisms that best meet the protection needs within the cost, performance, and schedule allowed by the customer.

The IATF must adhere to the customers' priorities in designing protection for the IAC, for the information systems, and for the information that the systems perform functions on, based on an assessment of the information and systems' value to the mission. The role of information and information systems in supporting the mission should be described in terms of:

- What kind of information records are being viewed, updated, deleted, initiated, or processed (classified, financial, proprietary, personal, private, etc.)?
- Who or what is authorized to view, update, delete, initiate, or process information records?
- How do authorized users use the information to perform their duties?
- What tools (paper, hardware, software, firmware, and procedures) are authorized users using to perform their duties?
- How important is it to know with certainty that a particular individual sent or received a message or file?

The IATF and the users will have to work together on the nature of the role of information systems in furthering the users' mission. An IATF making these decisions without user input is not likely to satisfy the users' needs.

Threats to Information Management

In terms of what the IATF must address, the technical system context must identify the functions and interfaces of the IAC's information system that interacts with elements outside of the system boundaries. The context should address physical and logical boundaries and the general nature of the inputs and the outputs to the information system. Included in the context is a description of the bidirectional flow of the information carried on signals, energy, and material between the system and the environment or other systems. Both intended and unintended interfaces with the environment and other systems must be considered. Part of describing unintended interfaces is describing the threat environment to information and information systems. A threat is defined as the potential for circumstances in which some agent might take some action, which could cause some event, having a consequence that could result in a harmful impact. The threat context will be described in terms of:

- Types of information
- Legitimate users and uses of information
- Threat agent considerations
- Capability
- Intent
- Willingness
- Motivation
- Damage to mission

Information Assurance Policy Considerations

The IATF must consider all the existing information assurance policies, regulations, and standards that are binding on the organization and develop a system information assurance policy. The most important issues an information assurance policy must define are:

- Why protection is needed and
- What protection is needed, not how protection is achieved

Just as in the systems engineering process, the IATF must consider all the existing policies, regulations, and standards that are binding on the organization. For example, national, executive level, Department of Defense, and Navy policies may bind a U.S. Navy base. These all must be considered as inputs to the formulation of a local information assurance policy for a particular base.

Two examples of existing policies that prevail throughout the federal government information assurance field is the Office of Management and Budget Circular A-130 [OMB A-130, 1996] and Public Law 100–235 [PL 100–235]. Both delineate requirements to protect all U.S. government information systems to the level commensurate with the risk, to define roles and responsibilities of individuals authorized to have the information, and to develop and implement appropriate security plans that address continual administrative support throughout the system life-cycle. The same wording could be used in industry.

The most important issues an organizational security policy must define are:

- The resources and assets the organization has determined are critical or need protection
- The roles and responsibilities of individuals that will need to interface with those assets (as part of their operational mission needs definition)
- The appropriate way (authorizations) authorized individuals may use those assets (security requirements)

A multidisciplined IATF team of systems engineers, information assurance system engineers, users' representatives, accreditation authorities, and design specialists is needed to develop an effective organizational information assurance policy. The IATF needs to work together to ensure that the various inputs to the policy are correctly and completely articulated, and that the resultant policy is correctly stated and consistent.

Senior management must issue the organizational information assurance policy. It needs to be decisive and set a direction to enable lower-level decisions to be made. The policy must be available to, and easily understood by, the entire workforce, even if that workforce is global in nature. There must be a procedure to ensure the policy is enforced throughout the organization, and the workforce must understand the organizational and personnel consequences if the policy is not enforced. Although the organizational information assurance policy must be updated as conditions warrant, a high-level policy should be relatively constant. For specific guidelines, see the following:

- DoD Directive 5200.28, Security Requirements for Automated Information Systems (AIS) [DoD5200, 1988]
- Director of Central Intelligence Directive 1/16, Security Policy on Intelligence Information in Automated Systems and Networks [DCID 1/16, 1988]
- Internet Security Policy: A Technical Guide, and Introduction to the Internet and Internet Security, both located at http://csrc.nist.gov/

Define the Information Assurance System

In this phase of the information assurance system engineering life-cycle, the user's description of information assurance needs and the information system environment are translated into objectives, requirements, and functions. This activity defines what the information assurance system is going to do, how well the information assurance system must perform its functions, and the internal and external interfaces for the information assurance system.

Information Assurance Objectives

Information assurance objectives have the same properties as system objectives. Each will be unambiguous, measurable, verifiable, and traceable to an information assurance need. The rationale for each objective should explain:

- The mission objectives supported by the information assurance objective
- The mission-related threat driving the information assurance objective
- The consequences of not implementing the objective
- Information assurance guidance or policy supporting the objective

System Context/Environment

The technical system context identifies the functions and interfaces of the system that interact with elements outside of the system boundaries. In the case of the information assurance system, the mission objectives, nature of the information, mission information processing system, threats, information assurance policies, and facilities strongly affect the system context. The context of the information assurance system should address physical and logical boundaries between it and the mission information processing system, other systems, and the environment. Included in the context is a description of the bidirectional flow of information inputs and the outputs, signals, and energy between the system and the environment or other systems.

Information Assurance Requirements

The IATF will need to perform a requirements analysis that includes review and update of prior analyses (mission, threat, objectives, and system context/ environment) conducted as part of the systems engineering process. As the information assurance requirements evolve from the user needs to more-refined system specifications, they must be sufficiently defined to permit system architecture concepts to be developed within the integrated concurrent systems engineering process. The IATF will examine, with other information assurance system stakeholders, the set of information assurance requirements for correctness, completeness, coherence, interdependence, conflicts, and testability. The information assurance functional, performance, interface, interoperability, and derived requirements, as well as design constraints, will go into the Operational Requirements Document (ORD) of the system.

Functional Analysis

Functional Analysis

The IATF will use many of the systems engineering tools to understand the functioning and allocation of functions to various information assurance components. The IATF must understand how the information assurance subsystem is part of and supports the overall system.

Design the Information Assurance System

In this activity, the IATF will need to build the system architecture and specify the design solution for the information assurance system. As the IATF proceeds through this activity, it will continue to:

- Refine, validate, and examine technical rationale for requirements and threat assessments
- Ensure that the set of lower-level requirements satisfy system-level requirements
- Support system-level architecture, component, and interface definition
- Support long lead-time and early procurement decisions
- Define information assurance verification and validation procedures and strategies
- Consider information assurance operations and life-cycle support issues
- Continue tracking and refining information assurance relevant acquisition and engineering management plans and strategies
- Continue system-specific information assurance risk reviews and assessments
- Support the certification and accreditation processes
- Participate in the systems engineering process

Functional Allocation

As the system functions are assigned to people, hardware, software, and firmware, information assurance functions are also assigned to these system elements. As functions are allocated to components, the components become responsible for satisfying the corresponding functional and performance requirements as well as a subset of the overall system constraints in the problem space. Various information assurance system architectures will be examined, and the IATF will negotiate an agreement on the information assurance system architecture with system stakeholders that are both conceptually and physically feasible.

Preliminary Information Assurance Design

The entry conditions to this phase are, at a minimum, stable agreement on information assurance requirements and stable information assurance system architecture under Configuration Management. Once the architecture is defined and baselined, system and IATF engineers will generate specifications that detail what is to be built, down to the component level. Production and review of the higher-level specifications occur before the Preliminary Design Review (PDR). IATF activities for this activity include:

- Reviewing and refining Needs and System Definition activities' work products, especially definition of the component-level and interface specifications
- Surveying existing solutions for a match to component-level requirements
- Examining rationales for proposed PDR-level (of abstraction) solutions
- Verification that component specifications meet higher-level information assurance requirements
- Supporting the certification and accreditation processes
- Supporting information assurance operations development and life-cycle management decisions
- Participating in the system engineering process
- The PDR results in an Allocated System Baseline Configuration.

Evaluation and Decision

Detailed Information Assurance Design

Detailed information assurance design results in lower-level product specifications that either complete the design of components that are under development or specify and justify the selection of components that are being bought. This activity will conclude with the Component-Completed Design Review (C-CDR), a review of each detailed component specification for completeness, conflicts, compatibility (with interfacing systems), verifiability, information assurance risks, integration risks, and traceability to (and satisfaction of) requirements. IATF activities for the detailed information assurance system design include:

- Reviewing and refining previous Preliminary Design work products
- Supporting system- and component-level design by providing input on feasible information assurance solutions and review of detailed design materials
- Examining technical rationales for CDR-level solutions
- Supporting, generating, and verifying information assurance test and evaluation requirements and procedures
- Tracking and applying information assurance mechanisms
- Verifying component designs meet higher-level information assurance requirements
- Completing most inputs to the life-cycle security support approach, including providing information assurance inputs to training and emergency training materials

- Reviewing and updating information assurance risk and threat projections, as well as any changes to the requirements set
- Supporting the certification and accreditation processes
- Participating in the system engineering process

System Synthesis

Implement Information Assurance System

The objective of this activity is to build, buy, integrate, verify, and validate the set of components that will compose the information assurance subsystem against the full set of information assurance requirements. The processes in this activity include those previously identified in the system engineering process. There are, however, a number of additional functions that the IATF will need to perform in the implementation and testing of the information assurance system. These include:

- Updates to the system information assurance threat assessment, as projected, to the system's operational existence
- Verification of system information assurance requirements and constraints against implemented information assurance solutions, and associated system verification and validation mechanisms and findings
- Tracking or participation in application of information assurance mechanisms related to system implementation and testing practices
- Further inputs to and review of evolving system operational procedure and life-cycle support plans including, for example, Communication Security (COMSEC) key distribution or releasability control issues within logistics support and IA-relevant elements within system operational and maintenance training materials
- A formal information assurance assessment in preparation for the Security Verification Review
- Inputs to Certification and Accreditation (C&A) process activities as required
- Participation in the collective, multidisciplinary examination of all system issues

These efforts and the information each produces support the Security Verification Review. Security accreditation approval would typically occur shortly after conclusion of the Security Verification Review.

Documentation

Procurement

Normally, the decision to procure or produce system components is based on a hierarchy of preferred outcomes, ranging from a strong preference for commercial-off-the-shelf (COTS) hardware, software, and firmware products, to a lesser preference for government-off-the-shelf (GOTS) items.

Among the various documents required, a trade-off analysis on new development is needed for a procurement and production decision. The IATF team must ensure that the total analysis includes the relevant security factors to ensure the best overall architecture based on a balance of operation, performance, cost, schedule, and risk. In support of the decision to procure or produce system components, the IATF team should survey the existing documentation of products to determine if there are products that satisfy the requirements for the system component. Wherever feasible, a set of potentially viable options should be identified, rather than a single source. In addition, where appropriate, the IATF team should consider new technologies and products in ensuring the system, when implemented, will continue to be viable.

Build

The system designed by the system engineers needs to be translated into an information assurance system by the IATF. The purpose of this activity is to ensure that the necessary protection mechanisms have been designed, documented, and implemented into the system. The information assurance system, like most systems, is subjected to variables that can either enhance or degrade its effectiveness. In an information assurance system, these variables must be documented and will play a crucial role in determining the system's suitability for information assurance. Some of these variables that must be documented include:

- *Physical integrity:* Have the components that are used in the production been properly safeguarded against tampering?
- *Personnel integrity:* Are the people assigned to construct or assemble the system knowledgeable in proper assembly procedures, and are they trusted to the proper level necessary to ensure system trustworthiness?

As stated previously, the completion of this activity will significantly affect the remaining activities and the proper level of attention must be afforded when system assembly commences.

Test

The IATF will need to develop IA-related test plans and procedures. The IATF may also have to develop test cases, tools, hardware, and software to adequately exercise the system. IATF activities include:

- Reviewing and refining Design Information Assurance System work products
- Verifying system- and component-level information assurance requirements and constraints against implemented solutions and associated system verification and validation mechanisms and findings

- Tracking and applying information assurance mechanisms related to system implementation and testing practices
- Providing inputs to and review of the evolving life-cycle security support plans, including logistics, maintenance, and training
- Continuing risk management activities
- Supporting the certification and accreditation processes
- Participating in the systems engineering process

Assess Effectiveness

The IATF will need to focus on the effectiveness of the information assurance system. The IATF's emphasis will pertain to the system's ability to review documentation that is stipulating that the necessary levels of confidentiality, integrity, availability, and nonrepudiation to the information can be processed by the IAC and is still required for mission success. If the information assurance system cannot adequately meet these documented requirements, the success of the mission may be placed in jeopardy. This focus includes:

- *Interoperability:* Does the system transfer and protect information correctly across external interfaces?
- *Availability:* Is the system available to users to protect information and information assets?
- *Training:* What degree of instruction is required for users to qualify to operate and maintain the information assurance system?
- *Human/Machine Interface:* Does the human/machine interface contribute to users making mistakes or compromising information assurance mechanisms?
- *Cost:* Is it financially feasible to construct and maintain the information assurance system?

Concluding Remarks

The Information Assurance Task Force (IATF) is an Acquisition/Program Management Team responsible for designing and implementing the system engineering process and focusing on the information assurance needs within that process. The process that the IATF will need to perform must focus on identifying, understanding, containing, and optimizing information assurance risks. IATF activities are covered in this book, as shown in Exhibit 1.

The following chapter describes how an organization takes the user's IA needs and turns them into IA requirements.

Exhibit 1 IATF Activities Covered

Chapter	Title	IATF Activities
1	Introduction to Information Assurance	Describing information assurance needs
2	Basic Concepts	Describing information assurance needs
3	Risk, Threat, and Vulnerability Assessments	Satisfying the requirements at an acceptable level of information protection risk
4	Overview of Systems Engineering	Generating information assurance requirements based on needs early in the systems engineering process Allocating information assurance functions to a physical and logical architecture Participating in trade-off studies with other information assurance and system engineering disciplines
5	IA Task Force	
6	Requirements	Building a functional information assurance architecture based on requirements
7	Conceptual Design	Designing the organization to implement the information assurance architecture
8	Implementation and Testing	Integrating the IATF process with the systems engineering and acquisition processes Testing the various systems to verify information assurance design and validate information protection requirements.
9	Life Cycle Support and Operational Considerations	Balancing information assurance risk management and other IATF considerations within the overall context of cost, schedule, and operational suitability and effectiveness
10	Information Assurance Center	Supporting the customers after deployment and tailoring the overall process to their needs.
11	Automated Tools	Testing the various systems to verify information assurance design and validate information protection requirements.

Chapter 6

Requirements

Example isn't another way to teach, it is the only way to teach.

Albert Einstein

As we discussed in Chapter 4, the first and probably most important step in any systems engineering development project is the identification, collection, analysis, and allocation of requirements. Much research has surrounded knowledge extraction, data mining, Computer Aided Systems Engineering (CASE) tools, and other methods of arriving at a complete list of requirements for any given system. Yet, despite years of effort on the part of large organizations in both commercial and government sectors, we still seem to have a great deal of difficulty capturing those requirements in any form of automated system. Perhaps this is due, at least in part, to the nonexistence of a single, standard method for identifying and capturing requirements. In this chapter, we address this issue and propose a solution.

Historically, requirements for information systems have been captured as natural language statements in textual documents. In the 1980s, thanks to the work of Howard Eisner [1987] and others, CASE tools became popular for capturing and storing requirements. However, these tools were mostly applied to hardware and software systems or system components at the micro engineering level of detail. High-level, macro requirements do not seem to fit these tools all that well. So, the only form of automation used for system descriptions (macro requirements) was a typewriter, word processor, or other such document production aid. Simply because nothing else existed and because the Department of Defense (DoD) was a major procurer of systems, the standard format for such documentation became the U.S. DoD Standard 2167A [DoD2167A, 1988] by default. Despite the fact that this standard was cancelled in 1994, it seems to remain the commonly accepted format for many system descriptions — again, simply because nothing else exists. 2167A called for a very large and structured set of documents that describe the system, system modules or components, and the requirements of each. Unfortunately, the result is typically a mountain of paper that, although dutifully and meticulously produced, sits on a shelf and goes largely unread except, perhaps, by the authors. These documents usually represent good descriptions of the systems in question, but are difficult reading and even more cumbersome as reference documents. Their authors, no doubt, spent considerable time and effort collecting requirements and categorizing and carefully articulating them in this documentation. Unfortunately, in order to extract the necessary information to actually develop and produce a system, someone else must read every line very carefully and extract each requirement individually — a time-consuming and tedious process at best. We have been personally involved in requirements collection and the production of such documentation on a number of large-scale, global systems on many occasions. Early in the process we concluded that there must be a better way.

Beginnings

In the early 1990s, while engaged in the development of Naval Force architectures, and thus the generation of literally thousands of requirements along with the accompanying, obligatory documentation, we began investigating automated methods as an alternative. The first step was the production of a simple relational database. Using commercially available products, data tables were created to store the pertinent facts pertaining to requirements without the usual, excess verbiage. We quickly found that we could actually store more useful "information" in a smaller space than previously accomplished in document form. Moreover, the information thus captured was readily available for sort, search, and retrieval, a concept totally unavailable in document format. For the first time in this environment, requirements could be sorted, searched, compared, analyzed, weighted, scored, and other wise manipulated quickly and easily without the necessity to convene what was affectionately known as a BOGSAT (bunch of guys sitting around a table). Previously, such analysis would quite literally take weeks of debate among technical experts convened into a group for just such a purpose. Quite often, answers were required in a much shortened timeframe.

Though the database concept was widely accepted and proved useful in a number of situations, it still produced row upon row of technical details. Even with the sorting and summary capabilities inherent in database management systems, a good deal of manual manipulating is still required before a human being could actually understand the overall implications of the interaction of multiple requirements, functions, and systems in a plethora of scenarios. Visualization was still a problem.

Building on this success, the next step seemed to be some method of using the data we had collected to conceptualize the resultant environment or situation. In the early 1990s, the Space and Naval Warfare Systems Command

(SPAWAR) funded a software development project to produce a visual "front end" to the database. The resultant tool "Architect" was used successfully to help planners understand the interactions of all the requirements, conduct "what if" and "sensitivity" analyses, cost–benefit analyses (CBA), hierarchical descriptions, and other useful functions. Architect will be discussed in more detail in Chapter 11. Interestingly, although many were concerned with the costs of developing such software, the cost of software development and maintenance proved to be significantly less expensive than data collection. The tool became quite popular and was used for many years by a number of DoD agencies. Unfortunately, following personnel turnovers, major reorganizations, and change of focus, the requirements collection process, which in this case was tied to the warfare systems architecture and engineering (WSA&E) effort mentioned in Chapter 2, took a back seat to other priorities and the process, data, and tools received less and less attention.

Still, requirements for the purpose of designing interoperable system architectures remain an issue, and capturing a very diverse set of requirements in some logical, usable, understandable form remained elusive — until the late 1990s.

While engaged in numerous efforts, the authors helped develop a new concept for capturing the most detailed requirements and using them to build segments, components, systems, and organizational entities. This work centered around Object-Oriented (OO) technology and Object-Oriented Database Management Systems (OODBMS). In order to understand the concepts that evolved, it is first necessary to understand the basics of the OO paradigm.

The Object-Oriented Paradigm

Object-oriented (OO) concepts have evolved from three distinct disciplines: (1) artificial intelligence, (2) conventional programming languages, and (3) database technology. The object-oriented paradigm first surfaced in the late 1960s with the introduction of the SIMULA programming language. Developed years later, the Smalltalk programming language was, until recently, the best known and most popular example of object-oriented languages. In recent years, C++, Java, and other OO or OO-like languages have become widespread.

The following events have probably had the most influence over object-oriented development:

- Advances in computer architecture, including more-capable systems and hardware support for operating systems
- Advances in programming languages
- Advances in programming methods

An object-oriented data model would be implemented in Level 1 (the foundation of our cognitive hierarchy, Chapter 2) where we would manipulate objects instead of records or relational database tuples. The basic goal of this object-oriented database would be to model a real-world entity or object with a corresponding object in the database. Object-oriented databases are better at storing complex information and real-world data than are previous constructs. Much has been written on the OO paradigm. The interested reader can find complete and detailed discussions in several of the references cited. David A. Taylor [1997] provides a very readable synopsis, while Peter Coad and Edward Yourdon [Coad, 1990] and Derek Coleman et al. [1994], among others, take a more in-depth look. What follows here is a very brief, high-level overview.

The Concept

An OO system has a single type of entity, the object. An object is an entity whose behavior is characterized by the actions performed on and by it. "An object is an abstract mechanism that defines a protocol through which users of the object may interact" [Zaniolo, 1986]. Objects represent entities and concepts from the application domain being modeled and can be thought of as an identifier or type. Simply put, an object is an abstraction of a set of real-world things such that all of the real-world things in a set (the instances) have the same characteristics, and all instances are subject to and conform to the same rules [Exhibit 1; Zdonik, 1990].

Most OO systems make a distinction between the description of an object and the object itself. In a pure OO language or system, all conceptual entities are modeled as objects, described by attributes, and behave as encapsulated in methods.

An attribute is an abstraction of a single characteristic possessed by all the entities that were, themselves, abstracted as objects; simply put, attributes describe objects. Attributes generally fall into three categories.

1. *Descriptive attributes* are the intrinsic characteristics of an object. They provide facts indigenous to each instance of the object. Descriptive attributes of a building, for example, may be length, width, height, type, intended uses, facilities, capacity, etc.
2. *Naming attributes* provide facts about the arbitrary labels and names carried by each instance of an object, such as name or identification number.

Exhibit 1   What Is an Object? [Zdonik, 1990]

- An object is an abstract mechanism that defines a protocol through which users of the object may interact.
- Objects represent entities and concepts from the application domain being modeled.
- An object can be thought of as an identifier, type, or value.
- Simply put, an object is an abstraction of a set of real-world *things*.

---

3. *Referential attributes* capture the facts that tie an instance of one object to an instance of another object. In the building case, the type of building might be used as a referential attribute between class of buildings and the type of facilities installed in that class of building.

An identifier is a set of one or more attributes that uniquely distinguishes each instance of an object. An object may have several identifiers, any of which can be used as a key.

A method is a function, capability, algorithm, formula, or process that an object is capable of performing. A method has five properties [Kim, 1989]:

1. The generic function that it specializes
2. Its applicability condition
3. Any qualifiers that identify the method's role
4. A parameter list that receives the arguments
5. The body executed when the method is called

All of the action in OO systems comes from sending messages between objects. Message sending is a form of indirect procedure call. A message must be sent to an object in order to find out anything about it.

Object-Oriented Design (OOD) is the process of decomposing a program or system into objects and establishing the relations between them. It is neither a function nor a data decomposition process; instead, it seeks to identify those objects in the real world that must be manipulated to effect a decision by the user.

An Object-Oriented Database Management System (OODBMS) is a system that provides database-like support for objects (i.e., encapsulation and operations). It is a persistent, shareable repository, and manager of an object-oriented database. The database itself is a collection of objects defined by an object-oriented data model (objects that capture the semantics of objects supported in object-oriented programming) [Kim, 1990]. While semantic models are oriented toward structural abstraction and data representation, object-oriented models are concerned with behavioral abstraction and data manipulation.

An OODBMS attempts to extend flexibility to "unconventional" data and associated processing tasks (including text, graphics, and voice data) that cannot be handled and integrated by conventional database systems. Great strides have been made with OODBMS, but at this writing, few commercial products neither possess all the desirable features nor have they fully implemented the OO paradigm. Still, well-designed, functional, usable, commercial systems exist today and they are getting better all the time.

The basic idea of an object-oriented database is to represent an item in the real world with a corresponding item in the database. Coupling an object-oriented database with an object-oriented programming style results in the virtual elimination of the semantic gap between a program and the supporting data. Three levels of "object orientation" have been defined by Klaus Dittrich [1986] and Frank Manola [1987]:

1. *Structurally object-oriented:* The data model allows definitions of data structures to represent entities of any complexity (complex objects).
2. *Operationally object-oriented:* The data model includes generic operators to deal with complex objects in their entirety.
3. *Behaviorally object-oriented:* The data model incorporates features to define arbitrarily complex object types together with a set of specific operators (abstract data types). Instances can only be used to call these operators, and their internal structure may be exploited by the operator implementations only.

Key features of systems that truly support the object-oriented philosophy as described by Brad Cox [1986, 1987] include:

- *Inheritance:* Instance variables, class variables, and methods are passed down from a superclass to its subclasses. A technique that allows new classes to be built on top of older, less-specialized classes instead of being rewritten from scratch.
- *Information hiding:* The state of a software module is contained in private variables, visible only from within the scope of the module. Important for ensuring reliability and modifiability of software systems by reducing interdependencies between components.
- *Dynamic binding:* The responsibility for executing an action on an object resides within the object itself. The same message can elicit a different response, depending on the receiver.
- *Encapsulation:* A technique for minimizing interdependencies among separately written modules by defining strict external interfaces. The user no longer applies operators to operands, while taking care that the two are type compatible.
- *Data abstraction:* The behavior of an abstract data object is fully defined by a set of abstract operations defined in the object. Objects in most object-oriented languages are abstract data objects. Can be considered a way of using information hiding.
- *Object identity:* Each object has a unique identifier independent of the values of properties.

Related notions currently associated with the object-oriented approach include messages, overloading, late binding, and interactive interfaces with windows, menus, and mice [Zaniolo, 1986].

OO Advantages

Object-oriented programming and database management systems offer a number of important advantages over traditional control- or data-oriented techniques, including [King, 1986; Manola, 1987; Thomas, 1990]:

- The modeling of all conceptual entities with a single concept, the object
- The notion of a class hierarchy and inheritance of properties along the hierarchy

■ The inheritance mechanism of object-oriented languages, which allows code to be reused in a convenient manner

■ Facilitates the construction of software components that loosely parallel the application domain

■ Encourages the use of modular design

■ Provides a simple and expressive model for the relationship of various parts of the system's definition and assists in making components reusable or extensible

■ Views a database as a collection of abstract objects rather than a set of flat (though possibly interrelated) tables

■ Captures integrity constraints more easily

■ Offers a unifying paradigm in the database, programming language, and artificial intelligence domains

■ The ability to represent and reference objects of complex structures resulting in increased semantic content of databases

■ Provides a more-flexible modeling tool

■ Allows protection and security mechanisms to be based on the notion of an object, a more-natural unit of access control

■ Can provide version control functions

■ Incorporation of software engineering principles such as data abstraction and information hiding

OO Disadvantages

Despite its many advantages, the object-oriented view is not perfect. However, though there are several drawbacks to OO systems listed here, most are a direct result of its relative infancy and lack of development. Most of these problems are expected to be resolved as the model matures, as expressed by Timothy Andrews [1990], Kyung-Chang Kim [1990] and Frank Manola [1987]. These drawbacks include:

■ The object-oriented paradigm lacks a coherent data model. There is currently no established standard for object-oriented design, methodology, language facilities, etc.

■ Research into structures for efficient object storage is in the early stages of development.

■ Use of an object-oriented database from a conventional data processing language is difficult because of the semantic gap.

■ In current environments, the run-time cost of using object-oriented languages is high.

■ Object-oriented database management systems provide only limited support for integrating data in existing, possibly heterogeneous databases.

■ Typical OODBMSs do not integrate existing database application code with the object methods maintained by the system. This is similar to the previous point, but concerns procedures rather than data.

■ Many object-oriented database systems do not support the strict notion of metaclass.

■ Some OODBMSs do not emphasize the efficient processing of set-oriented queries, although most of the commercial OODBMSs provide some form of query facility.
■ Object-Oriented Programming/Processing (OOP) can be very memory intensive.
■ There is no adequate, accepted, standard query language based on the OO view of data.

Many of these issues are well on their way to resolution. For example, the Unified Modeling Language (UML) seems to be emerging as a standard [Fowler, 1997], filling the gap for a consistent, unified model mentioned in the first bullet in this list. The OO concept has already made great strides. As the paradigm matures, most, if not all, of these issues are expected to be resolved.

Object-Oriented Architecture

Architecture is a planning process or tool. The ultimate goal of any such process is, of course, to build a knowledge- and experience-base upon which to formulate decisions toward shaping the future. To this end, planners must be able to capture the necessary data to be able to organize and reorganize the components of a large, complex system so that it functions smoothly as an integrated whole. The decision maker must be able to quickly manage, manipulate, and study the effort on a conceptual level so that it can be implemented on the physical level in some preplanned, logically structured fashion.

The ability to gracefully accommodate dynamic evolution, such as that needed in shortening the OODA Loop (Chapter 2), is an important research issue in database technology. Databases use several concepts, methodologies, and programming paradigms to accurately document the "view of the world" and to assist the decision maker in drawing conclusions from that data. In many cases, the conclusions arrived at by the decision maker were not explicitly programmed into the model. In recent experience, these projects are more frequently being implemented in the form of object-oriented systems. This dynamic evolution begins just like the evolution of any living creature — from a set of common building blocks (Exhibit 2).

So, how would we go about building this architectural definition with the OO paradigm? Just like the children who play with these blocks, we:

■ Do not know what they are
■ Do not understand where they come from
■ Do not know how to make one
■ Do not know what to do with them
■ Do not know how they fit together

So, we will start by defining what they are in an architectural context.

Exhibit 2   Building Blocks

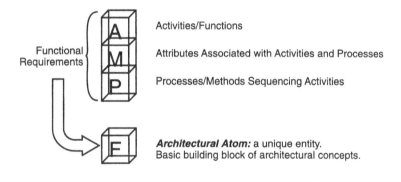

Exhibit 3   Basic Building Blocks

Building Blocks

As we have mentioned already, there is a need for a common description for architectures. Architectures are typically developed from the functional requirements (in the case of notional architectures) or functional capabilities (in the case of physical, existing architectures) that we consider essential to system development and operation. These requirements have been expressed in many forms and at varying levels of granularity. However, if we adopt the concept of functional requirements* as the building blocks of our architectural description, we have the opportunity to conduct direct comparisons of effectiveness, interoperability, and a large variety of other descriptors that are of interest to us (Exhibit 3).

---

* The term *functional requirements* will be used henceforth to include both the functions that we wish to perform (requirements) and the functions that existing systems actually do perform (capabilities).

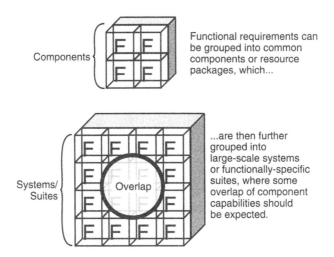

Exhibit 4   Functions and Components

Functional requirements lend themselves quite nicely to the OO approach previously described. First, they can be represented as objects where each function or activity has a name; there are attributes associated with that function; and processes, methods, or activities are performed by that function.

By this definition, functional requirement objects become "architectural atoms," the building blocks from which any and all architecture components can be constructed. This is not the first time that building components from functions has been attempted. However, to our knowledge, it is the first viable implementation that has been proposed.

The components thus constructed become systems, and systems in turn form a system of systems, or suite (Exhibit 4). From an architectural perspective, these "architecture atoms" also allow us to readily identify shortfalls (gaps in our functional capabilities) and functional redundancies (overlapping capabilities from multiple suites, systems, or components) for further analysis. Shortfalls usually require attention, while redundancies are often intentional and required as in the case of military systems. Some redundancies, however, may be targeted for elimination in the name of efficiency and cost effectiveness.

Thus, from a functional perspective, the entire architecture can be described using combinations of functional requirements (Exhibit 5).

Object-oriented architectural components, when assembled, might resemble a Rubik's Cube (Exhibit 6). Each module represents a unique unit, system, or capability that can be combined with others in a virtually limitless number of ways. In addition to this physical flexibility, once assembled, the architecture can be viewed from multiple perspectives (also nearly limitless) to satisfy the requirements of the viewer.

This is one of the major disappointments with architectures today and a primary reason that our systems are still not interoperable despite more than ten years identifying the issues. Numerous studies have shown that many useful architectures and architectural constructs exist. Unfortunately, they were all developed by different organizations, for different purposes, using similar

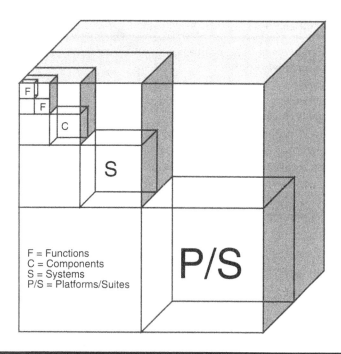

F = Functions
C = Components
S = Systems
P/S = Platforms/Suites

Exhibit 5   Building Block Architecture

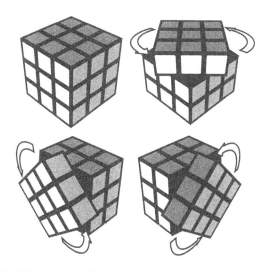

Exhibit 6   Rubik's Cube Architecture

but differing data, at varying levels of detail. Most were captured as documents (text and graphics) rather than as manipulable data. Although undoubtedly useful to the owners and developers, they cannot be directly combined nor compared in any meaningful way. By definition, if we have more than one architecture, in effect we have no architecture (Exhibit 7). Decision makers come from many and varied backgrounds with very different perspectives and interests in different and sometimes conflicting areas. All decision makers

Exhibit 7   Architecture Views

- There can be many *views* of an architecture, but there must be *one and only one* architecture for any given entity
  - Operational view
  - Organizational view
  - System (physical) view
  - Technical view (standards)
  - Functional view (requirements/capabilities)
  - Mission (or task) capabilities package view
- Operations are carried out by *organizations* and resourced by *systems* that combine *functional capabilities* into *Capability Packages*

should have the capability to view the architecture in any fashion that is required. However, it is critically important that they all view the same architecture founded on the same data. Information assurance (IA) has been a significant driver in both government and industry recently. However, IA cannot be accomplished without interoperability, and we are not likely to achieve interoperability without a solid architectural foundation [Curts, 1999, 2000].

Traditional database systems are limited in their data abstraction and representation power, and they fall short of providing important information management capabilities required by certain applications such as office information systems, personal databases, design engineering databases, and artificial intelligence systems. The use of object-oriented methodologies to support the decision maker at various levels of abstraction is an important emergent area where great strides can be made.

Summary

How does this concept of object-oriented architecture help us progress to a higher level within the cognitive hierarchy, and what will that do for the speed and precision with which we navigate the OODA Loop?

All things start with raw data elements, just as every living creature is composed of thousands of deoxyribonucleic acid (DNA) molecules. Whether strands of DNA or strings of "ones and zeros," each helps shape the individual, and each controls the way that individual functions. In the case of architectures, that data equates to functional capabilities or functional requirements; in other words, our "architectural atoms." Alone, they are not much more than small bits of information built from well-structured data points. By combining these atoms into components, we begin to climb the cognitive hierarchy — collecting more and more information about our systems and situation. This leads, in turn, to a better understanding and awareness upon which to base our decisions. In addition, it provides a common, base dataset that can be used by all systems so that all architectural views depict the same basic information (i.e., everyone operates from the same sheet of music). The simple action of standardizing, centralizing, and utilizing one common dataset solves many of the problems that we have discussed here and many more that were only alluded to. In synopsis, if we are to be successful in the design, description, and integration of systems and architectures, we must:

1. Establish one standard method of representing and storing architectural data.
2. Collect all architectural data into a single central, distributed, or federated repository to ensure that everyone is working with the same "big picture," all singing from the same sheet of music.
3. Ensure that the architectural data in centralized, standardized, common, and available to all that need it, which makes for great strides toward solving the interoperability issue. Ensure someone is paying close attention to the interfaces so that apples can at least be compared to apples.
4. Allow for a more-efficient analysis of capabilities across multiple services, battle forces, platforms, systems, and organizations so that we can make more informed, efficient, and effective acquisition decisions.
5. Collect, organize, and mature these data so that we can begin to climb the cognitive hierarchy, learning more and more about ourselves, our systems, and our capabilities. If we apply the same rigor to risk, threat, and vulnerability data, we can easily produce a better understanding of our antagonists, their systems, and our relative standing in any conflict or engagement.
6. This higher understanding leads to a heightened level of awareness that allows us to navigate that all-important OODA loop more quickly and efficiently than our adversaries.

Thus, by attacking and resolving the lowest-level problem (the architectural atom), we can achieve a significant impact on our system capability, while maximizing the bang from our acquisitions buck.

Implementation of the paradigm described here is nontrivial. There are a number of hurdles to overcome:

- *Organizational:* Some centralized, honest broker organization must be charged with collection, storage, retrieval, manipulation, comparison, maintenance, and management of the data.
- *Technical:* The data standards and database schema must be carefully designed to provide maximum flexibility and expandability.
- *Operational:* The data must be readily available to whomever needs it.
- *Collection:* Very large quantities of data must be collected, verified, catalogued, sorted, stored, and maintained.

Of these tasks, the first and last tasks mentioned probably present the biggest challenges. Although both government and industry are getting much better at multicomponent organizations and operations, we continue to have political difficulty assigning such widespread, global responsibility to any single organizational entity. We must be careful to resist the urge to take the easy way out by allowing each component to design, develop, and maintain its own separate architectural data and data structures, even if we can successfully prescribe a standard format. This is precisely the problem that we have today. While a data steward should, no doubt, be assigned responsibility for the accuracy and completeness of a particular class of data (possibly by service or functional organization), it is important to ensure that data elements, format, schema, etc. are standard across all architectural data. This can most easily be accomplished in a single, centralized data repository, but a distributed or federated system will fulfill the same goal if properly implemented.

The biggest and most costly challenge will likely remain the collection of the huge amounts of data required to drive such a concept. However, if we consider the large amounts of money that are spent today by a very large variety of offices collecting redundant and often inconsistent data, we might find that we will end up with significantly more information for less expenditure than we currently experience. Costs notwithstanding, what we have shown in this chapter is that it is quite possible for a decision maker to be able to compare or otherwise manipulate large amounts of data in order to "observe, orient, decide, and act" without achieving information overload through an object-oriented, Rubik's Cube "view of the world."

Chapter 7

Design

Any sufficiently advanced technology is indistinguishable from magic.

Arthur C. Clarke

In this chapter, the authors identify the need for an Information Assurance Program (IAP) — one that will enhance the ability of an organization to achieve its operational, technological, and business continuity objectives. The conceptual design phase determines the appropriate IAP solution, defines the basic goals of the program, and defines a high-level project work plan. The Information Assurance Master Planning Process reflects the first steps of the conceptual design phase. Organizations will identify the need for specific IA programs by analyzing the business needs and goals of the organization.

The program plan outlines the scope, policies, procedures, philosophies, responsibilities, guidelines, major milestones, assumptions, and constraints. The resulting plan provides the blueprint for implementing a successful, cost-effective, overarching IA program.

This chapter establishes the links between the IA objectives of the organization, the design of IA around the organization, and the proposed systems engineering solution. We begin with the high-level conceptual architecture design principles surrounding these linkages.*

---

* Many thanks to the State of Connecticut's Department of Information Technology with respect to information available from their Internet server at http://www.state.ct.us.

Conceptual Architecture Design Principles

The Conceptual Architecture Design Principles (CADPs) are the core business and high-level technical philosophies upon which the systems architecture is based. These principles guide the global life-cycle implementation of technology to meet the requirements of the users. They are also the standards and recommended practices that guide investment strategies and influence design decision making to maximize business benefit and the adaptability of the organization to the IT environment. The CADPs must be incorporated into the organization's IT planning and solution design activities and must include the organization's supporting IT contractors.

Guided by government and industry Best Practices, the principles have been provided in basic business language so that they can be understood by all those involved in the decision-making process of the organization. The authors identify twenty-three Conceptual Architecture Design Principles and organize them into three basic sets of design considerations: (1) operational, (2) technology, and (3) business continuity. The three categories are explained in additional detail later in this chapter.

Operational Design Considerations

1. Information is power. Information in and of itself is valued as an asset, which must be shared to enhance and accelerate decision making and at the same time protected from those who do not have a "need to know."
2. The planning and management of a corporatewide architecture emanating from the organization must be unified and have a planned evolution that is governed across the organization.
3. Architecture support and review structures must be used to ensure that the integrity of the architecture is maintained as systems and infrastructure are acquired, developed, and enhanced (see Exhibit 1).
4. Data warehouses must be secured and at the same time leveraged to facilitate the sharing of existing information to accelerate and improve decision making at all levels.

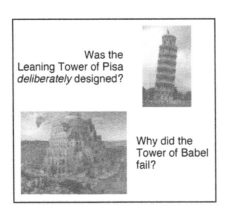

Exhibit 1   Poor Technical Designs

5. The organization and its IT systems must be designed and implemented in adherence to all security, confidentiality, and privacy policies, as well as applicable international, federal, state, and local statutes.
6. The architecture must reduce integration complexity to the greatest extent possible.
7. The reuse of existing applications, systems, and infrastructure must be considered before investing in new solutions. Only those applications or systems that provide clear business advantages and demonstrable cost savings will be built.
8. Systems must be designed, acquired, developed, or enhanced such that data and processes can be shared and integrated across the global reach of the organization and with other corporate or government partners.
9. New information systems must be implemented after business processes have been analyzed, simplified, or otherwise redesigned, as appropriate.
10. A total cost of ownership model for applications and technologies must be adopted, and it must balance the costs of development, support, disaster recovery, and retirement against the costs of flexibility, scalability, ease of use, and reduction of integration complexity.
11. A small number of consistent configurations for deployment across the organization must be created.
12. A standardized set of basic information services (e.g., e-mail, voice mail, user training) must be provided to all employees.

Technology Design Considerations

13. Applications, systems, and infrastructure will employ reusable components across the organization, using an n-tier model.
14. The logical design of application systems and databases should be highly partitioned. These partitions must have logical boundaries established, and the logical boundaries must not be violated.
15. The interfaces between separate application systems must be message-based; this applies to both internal and external systems.
16. Application systems that are driven by business events must be the only systems deployed.
17. Online transaction processing (OLTP) must be separated from data warehouse and other end-user computing.
18. The organization shall adopt and employ consistent software engineering practices and methods based on accepted government and industry standards (see Exhibit 2).

Business Continuity Design Considerations

19. IT solutions will use government- and industry-proven mainstream technologies.
20. Priority will be given to products adhering to industry standards and open architecture.

Exhibit 2   Poor Operational Design

21. An assessment of business recovery requirements is mandatory when acquiring, developing, enhancing, or outsourcing systems. Based on that assessment, appropriate disaster recovery and business continuity planning, design, and testing must take place.
22. A corporatewide, secure backbone network that provides a virtual, companywide intra-network must be implemented.
23. The underlying technology infrastructure and applications must be scalable in size, capacity, and functionality to meet changing business and technical requirements.

Operational Design Considerations

Information Is Power

Principle 1

Information is power. Information in and of itself is valued as an asset, which must be shared to enhance and accelerate decision making and at the same time protected from those who do not have a "need-to-know."

- *Rationale:* In the global information assurance program, decision making requires information beyond the traditional borders of a system or company or even government agency. The efficiency and effectiveness of the delivery services must be enhanced, enabling new systemwide, companywide or agencywide solutions across multiple systems, companies, or government agencies. Today, most information is in isolated pockets such that the value of information is not always recognized. However, treating the information as a business asset increases its integrity and the relevance of the information.
- *Conceptual design:* Policies pertaining to information ownership must be developed. The value of the information must be identified, authenticated, and leveraged. To do so will require a unified information management approach. There will also be an ancillary requirement to establish supporting policies for security, privacy, confidentiality, and information sharing. Finally, data needs to be structured for easy access and management.

Architecture Process

Principle 2

The planning and management of a corporatewide architecture emanating from the organization must be unified and have a planned evolution that is governed across the organization.

- *Rationale:* Without a unified approach, there will be multiple and possibly conflicting architectures. Common sense tells us that good change requires collaboration and collective planning. Any architecture must be well thought out, and governance over the architecture must be simplified.
- *Conceptual design:* A unified approach will require a change in cultural attributes. Normal evolution will require prioritization and reprioritization across all organizational and IT initiatives. While dependencies must be maintained, the architecture must be continually reexamined and refreshed. Short-term results vs. long-term impact must be constantly considered and everyone needs to understand that establishing the architecture takes time and involves a considerable amount of change.

Architecture Compliance

Principle 3

Architecture support and review structures must be employed to ensure that the integrity of the architecture is maintained as systems and infrastructure are acquired, developed, and enhanced.

- *Rationale:* To realize the benefits of a standards-based architecture, all IT investments must ensure compliance with the established IT architecture. For maximum impact, the review of standards should begin as early in the solution planning process as possible.
- *Conceptual design:* A structured project-level review process will be needed to ensure that information systems comply with the IT architecture and related standards. Processes incorporating the principles of this architecture must be developed for all application procurement, development, design, and management activities. This compliance process must allow for the introduction of new technology and standards, and conceptual architecture principles should be used as evaluation criteria for purchasing as well as developing software.

Leverage Global Data Warehouses

Principle 4

Data warehouses must be secured and at the same time leveraged to facilitate the sharing of existing information to accelerate and improve decision making at all levels.

- *Rationale:* Data can be replicated and combined from multiple systems, companies or government agencies without changing the originating systems or developing new systems. Lately, reduced business cycle times have led to a need for faster access to ever-increasing quantities of information. There is a significant burden on programmers to generate reports, data queries, and statistical information on the data itself. Data warehouses and their associated end-user tools make it possible to relieve this burden by placing the responsibility on end users. Therefore, warehouses fulfill the need for internally consistent data.

- *Conceptual design:* Data warehousing must become a core competency of IT. Data warehouses become types of configuration standards that need to be developed and maintained. End-user tools must be provided and the users themselves will have to become more knowledgeable about information and the tools that they use to access and analyze it. The processes and procedures for data extraction, "cleansing," and the loading of warehouses will require high levels of reliability and integrity.

Ensure Security, Confidentiality, and Privacy

Principle 5

The organization and its IT systems must be designed and implemented in strict adherence to all security, confidentiality, and privacy policies, as well as applicable international, federal, state, and local statutes.

- *Rationale:* Adhering to such statutes helps safeguard confidential and proprietary information that, in turn, enhances public trust. This also establishes the proper ownership of public information and helps to ensure the integrity of the information.

- *Conceptual design:* Applicable policies must be identified, published, and kept current and at the same time monitored for compliance. The requirements for security, confidentiality, and privacy must be made clear to everyone. Education on issues of privacy and confidentiality must become a routine part of normal business processes.

Reduce Integration Complexity

Principle 6

The architecture must reduce integration complexity to the greatest extent possible.

- *Rationale:* Reducing integration complexity increases the ability of the company or agency to adapt and change while also minimizing product and support costs.

- *Conceptual design:* Such reduction will decrease the proliferation of vendors, products, and configurations in any given organizational environment, although some vendor-supplied components will be required segments of the system. The organization must maintain configuration discipline despite the fact that doing so will, no doubt, sacrifice performance and functionality in some instances. The organization must also make a determination of the wording "to the greatest extent possible" in this principle to determine if it includes consideration of how reducing complexity can negatively impact providing critical client services.

Reuse Before Buying, Buy Before Building

Principle 7

The reuse of existing applications, systems, and infrastructure must be considered before investing in new solutions. Only those applications or systems that provide clear business advantages and demonstrable cost savings will be built.

- *Rationale:* The use and availability of effective packaged solutions is increasing. Using tested solutions reduces risks and the total cost of ownership.
- *Conceptual design:* Software license agreements and system development contracts should be written to allow for reuse across systems, even at the global level, barring encryption problems. The definition of "reusable" will include solutions available from other industry and government entities (e.g., other corporations, states, federal government agencies, etc.). Areas that provide clear advantages and business case cost savings are likely to require quick adaptation. Each organization must identify the areas in which it is seeking to distinguish itself.

Integration

Principle 8

Systems must be designed, acquired, developed, or enhanced such that data and processes can be shared and integrated across the global reach of the organization and with other corporate or government partners.

- *Rationale:* There is always a need to increase efficiency while better serving customers (e.g., the public, agencies, etc.). Although redundant systems cause higher support costs, we are assured of more accurate information, with a more-familiar look and feel. The bottom line is that integration leads to better decision making and accountability.
- *Conceptual design:* The IT staff will need to consider the impacts on their wide-scale systems when designing applications. They will require new tools and training for their proper use. They will certainly need a method for identifying data and processes to be integrated, when integration should take place, which processes should have access to the data, and cost justification for integration. An overall "architect" will be needed who can maintain and arbitrate a common set of domain tables,

data definitions, and processes across the organization. At the same time, apply the KISS principle (keep it simple, stupid), i.e., over-integration can lead to difficult data management and inefficient processes.

Reengineer First

Principle 9

New information systems must be implemented after business processes have been analyzed, simplified, or otherwise redesigned, as appropriate.

- ■ *Rationale:* There is no real "value" in applying technology to old, inefficient legacy processes. Work processes will need to be more streamlined, efficient, and cost effective, and as such, work processes, activities, and associated business rules must be well understood and documented. This reduces the total cost of ownership.
- ■ *Conceptual design:* The organization must establish an agreed upon business reengineering process and new technology must be applied in conjunction with the business process reviews. It will be understood by all participants that business processes must be optimized to align with business drivers and additional time and resources will have to be invested in analysis early in the system's life cycle. Organizational change may be required to implement reengineered work processes due to regulatory or legislative change.

Total Cost of Ownership

Principle 10

A total cost of ownership (TCO) model for applications and technologies must be adopted, and it must balance the costs of development, support, disaster recovery, and retirement against the costs of flexibility, scalability, ease of use, and reduction of integration complexity.

- ■ *Rationale:* Consideration of all costs associated with a system over its entire life span will result in significantly more cost-effective system choices. This effort enables improved planning and budget decision making, reduces the IT skills required for support of obsolete systems or old standards, simplifies the IT environment, and leads to higher-quality solutions.
- ■ *Conceptual design:* The organization's budget process needs to accommodate TCO of a system over a longer timeframe than current budgeting models allow. Unfortunately, this does not work well within the annual budget cycles of the U.S. government and many large corporations. Accommodating TCO will require looking closely at technical and user training costs, especially when making platform or major software upgrades during the lifetime of the system. This effort requires designers and developers to take a systems engineering approach that may

include selectively suboptimizing individual IT components, developing a TCO model, and ensuring the coordinated retirements of systems.

Minimize Platform Configurations

Principle 11

A small number of consistent configurations for deployment across the organization must be created.

- *Rationale:* Reducing uniqueness in product selection and standardization of installed components reduces support and maintenance costs, and simplifies training and skills transfer.
- *Conceptual design:* Initial capital investment will increase and must be planned. The applications must be deployed on uniformly configured servers. The organization must also plan to replace multiple, nonstandard configurations with a small number of consistent configurations, as well as plan for the regular replacement of platform components to ensure the retirement of obsolete and unique configurations.

Basic Information Services

Principle 12

A standardized set of basic information services (e.g., e-mail, voice mail, user training) must be provided to all employees.

- *Rationale:* Providing basic information services increases productivity; reduces costs of maintenance; provides the basis for international, state, local, or regional business initiatives; and provides for organizationwide access to information.
- *Conceptual design:* The "Basic Services" definition must to be created and regularly reviewed. This may increase "one-time" costs to upgrade to the minimum service level and to provide training to all users of basic services, but should reduce overall cost and complexity in the long haul.

Technology Design Considerations

Shared Components Using an n-tier Model

Principle 13

Applications, systems, and infrastructure will employ reusable components across the organization, using an n-tier model. The term *n-tier* refers to the various levels of responsibility in a system's design; the "n" can be any number from two and up. For example, a very common design is the three-tier model in which the application is divided into three distinct tiers of responsibility:

the user interface, the business logic, and the database. Each of these tiers can be implemented using one or more objects that are dedicated to the responsibilities of that tier.

- *User interface:* The user interface tier would contain all of the visual aspects of the system. This tier handles anything that involves interaction with the system user. All dialogs, message boxes, forms, reports, and other user-interaction components resides in the user-interface tier of the system.
- *Business logic:* The business logic layer fills the responsibility of determining where the data comes from and how it should be formatted for the user interface. It also applies any constraint rules on the data coming from the user interface before posting the data to the system database. The business logic tier does not have user-interface components as it has no responsibility to interact with the user. Problems sensed with the data should be communicated to the user interface layer through return values from methods or procedures while the user interface tier displays these messages to the user.
- *Database management:* The database is responsible for handling the domain constraints on the data and for updating and retrieving the data in the tables. The rules in the database should be restricted to only those that are a direct implementation of the domain constraints. "Business rules" are not part of the database rules; instead they are enforced in the business logic tier.

Three-tier is not the only n-tier design, although many practitioners and theorists advocate it. Andrew P. Sage used the same three-tiered concept to explain Decision Support Systems (DSS) and labeled them Dialogue Generation and Management System (DGMS) (the user interface), Model Base Management System (MBMS) (business logic), and Data Base Management System (DBMS) (data management) [Sage, 1995]. Some of the things that might be considered for additional tiers are operating system interface, network interface, and multiple levels of business logic tiers. For example, one might design a system for a bank where the business logic object for an account needs to have various different formats, depending on which department of the bank is using the data. In this case, we may have one business logic object for "account" that is generic across the entire bank, and others that are specific to particular departments, each using the generic account object and adding or restricting features based on the department's requirements.

The advantages of n-tier system design include:

- The business logic, or any other tier for that matter, may be modified without making changes to either the user interface or the database or any other tier.
- If built correctly, the business logic object can be used by multiple user interfaces and databases.
- It isolates the knowledge, processes, and procedures required in any given tier to that tier.

Some of the disadvantages include:

- The system design may be more complex.
- The memory footprint of the application is likely to increase.

With these disadvantages, why would someone want to build an n-tier system? The answer is a single word: scalability (see Principle 23). The n-tier design can scale up to extremely large systems without compromise. By "large," we are referring to the number of users, the number of differing user-interface and business-logic components, the size of the database, the structure of the network, and a variety of other size and complexity issues.

Using the n-tier design, one can design a system that will handle multiple divergent user interfaces without requiring a rewrite of the business logic for each interface built. The business logic can be shared by multiple user interfaces. Through subclassing, the business logic classes can be customized to handle different database servers. While n-tier design is not right for every project, it is an extremely powerful design approach.

- *Rationale:* Changes can be made to a component of a system, such as changing from a Windows client to a Web browser client, without changing the rest of the system. This enables simplification of the environment and geographical independence of servers. N-tier design takes advantage of modular off-the-shelf components and the life-cycle approach in reuse will show lower costs and lower maintenance efforts. This allows for leveraging skills across the organization.
- *Conceptual design:* Component management must become a core competency. This requires developing a culture of modularity and reuse and at the same time ensures that reusable components are platform independent. The Information Analysis Center will need to understand that physical configuration standards must be established, and with that, design reviews become crucial. Application systems must be highly modularized without making components too small or too simple to do useful "work."

Logical Partitioning and Boundaries

Principle 14

The logical design of application systems and databases should be highly partitioned. These partitions must have logical boundaries established, and the logical boundaries must not be violated.

- *Rationale:* A change in a database or application can potentially affect many large programs if they are not highly partitioned. The organization cannot separate the components in a system from each other without creating logical boundaries. One will need to understand that recoding leads to time-consuming retesting, and that partitioning isolates and minimizes change impact. Partitioned code is more adaptive to changes in internal logic, platforms, and structures.

- *Conceptual design:* Applications need to be divided into coded entities or modules (e.g., presentation, process, and data access). For databases, there will be a need to develop competency in partitioning horizontally and vertically that will result in more but simpler tables. This may require sacrificing data normalization for simplicity and optimization. Design reviews must ensure logical boundaries are kept intact.

Message-Based Interfaces

Principle 15

The interfaces between separate application systems must be message-based; this applies to both internal and external systems.

- *Rationale:* The use of messaging is important for enforcing the architecture principle of logical partitioning and boundaries. This enables rapid response in maintenance and enhancement activities as required by changes in business processes. Messaging technology simplifies integration efforts and allows for transparency in locations, databases, and data structures.
- *Conceptual design:* The implementation of a messaging infrastructure will be necessary. In designing the roles and responsibilities of the organization's staff, one will find that trust, or letting go of control, is often the most difficult aspect among IT staff when messaging is introduced into the IT culture. During this process, common messaging formats, IDs, and standards must be established and developers must learn how to use messaging. Overall, the organization will also notice an increase in network traffic.

Event-Driven Systems

Principle 16

Application systems that are driven by business events must be the only systems deployed.

- *Rationale:* Deploying only event-driven systems enables applications to adapt quickly to changes in business processes by changing only the application component related to the changed business event. This strengthens linkages to the business by mirroring the actual business environment. It is easier to realign IT when change occurs.
- *Conceptual design:* This will require systemic thinking as event-based processing crosses traditional system boundaries. The business processes need to be optimized to obtain full benefits, and the organization will need to retrain developers to incorporate business concepts in software development methods.

Physical Partitioning of Processing

Principle 17

Online transaction processing (OLTP) must be separated from data warehouse and other end-user computing.

■ *Rationale:* Separating end-user requests and OLTP maximizes the efficiency of both environments. When growth in OLTP is incremental, the requirements become predictable; but when the growth in data warehouses and end-user computing has been nonlinear, the requirements are very difficult to forecast. Separating such processes also fosters the concept of data ownership.

■ *Conceptual design:* Data warehousing brings about types of configuration standards that need to be developed and maintained. Data warehousing must become a core competency of IT and business, and IT must agree on the purpose and objective of the data warehouses. Business users must justify the cost of compiling and maintaining the data (warehouse).

Formal Software Engineering

Principle 18

The organization shall adopt and employ consistent software engineering practices and methods based on accepted government and industry standards.

■ *Rationale:* Formal software engineering reduces training costs, leads to benchmarks for measurement, enables improved quality assurance, and facilitates the reuse of programming modules and code.

■ *Conceptual design:* The organization will need to agree on practices and methods. This requires training in the practices and methods, and requires monitoring for compliance. All linked organizations and third-party developers will employ the organization's software engineering practices and methods, which means that the organization will need to employ software engineers.

Business Continuity Design Considerations

Mainstream Technologies

Principle 19

IT solutions should use government- and industry-proven mainstream technologies.

■ *Rationale:* By using mainstream technologies, the organization avoids dependence on weak vendors, reduces risk, ensures robust product support, and enables greater use of commercial-off-the-shelf solutions.

- *Conceptual design:* The organization will need to establish criteria for vendor selection and performance measurement. The organization will also need to establish criteria to identify weak vendors and poor technology solutions. This effort requires migration away from existing weak products in the adopted technology portfolio.

Industry Standards

Principle 20

Priority will be given to products adhering to industry standards and open architecture.

- *Rationale:* Adherence to industry standards avoids dependence on weak vendors, reduces risks, ensures robust product support, enables greater use of commercial-off-the-shelf solutions, and allows for flexibility and adaptability in product replacement.
- *Conceptual design:* Demanding such adherence, unfortunately, requires a culture shift in thinking. The organization will need to establish criteria to identify standards and the products using them, and to determine how it will transition to this mode.

Disaster Recovery/Business Continuity

Principle 21

An assessment of business recovery requirements is mandatory when acquiring, developing, enhancing, or outsourcing systems. Based on that assessment, appropriate disaster recovery and business continuity planning, design, and testing must take place.

- *Rationale:* Due to factors such as the explosion of Internet usage by hackers, upsurge in virus attacks, the Year 2000 (Y2K) problem, and recent terrorist activities, customers and partners have a heightened awareness of systems availability. The pressure to maintain availability will increase in importance. Any significant visible loss of system stability could negatively impact the organization's image. The continuation of any business activities without the use of IT is becoming nearly impossible. Application systems and data are becoming increasingly valuable assets that must be protected.
- *Conceptual design:* Systems will need to be categorized according to business recovery needs (e.g., business critical, noncritical, not required). Alternate computing capabilities need to be in place and systems should be designed with fault tolerance and recovery in mind. Plans for work site recovery will need to be in place, which makes organizational costs higher.

Corporatewide Network as Virtual LAN

Principle 22

A corporatewide, secure backbone network that provides a virtual, company-wide intra-network must be implemented.

- *Rationale:* Networks are the essential enabling technology for client/server, Internet, and collaborative computing. This is the basis of the anywhere-anytime, seamless access that is a major goal of the organization. There is an increasing need for access to information across the global network, and the lack of a robust network architecture will impact the success of distributed applications. This expands the vision of the organization by reaching out to customers and suppliers.
- *Conceptual design:* The organization will need to implement a robust, unified directory services capability. This requires higher-speed and higher-bandwidth networks and an interconnection of distributed LANs. The organization will also need to create connections from legacy systems to client/server and Internet applications.

Scalability

Principle 23

The underlying technology infrastructure and applications must be scalable in size, capacity, and functionality to meet changing business and technical requirements.

- *Rationale:* Scalability reduces total cost of ownership by reducing the amount of application and platform changes needed to respond to increasing or decreasing demand on the system. It also encourages reuse and leverages the continuing decline in hardware costs.
- *Conceptual design:* Scalability must be reviewed for both "top down" and "bottom up" capability. This may increase initial costs of development and deployment and will reduce some solution choices, but will pay substantial dividends as the system matures and grows.

Concluding Remarks

Can this multitude of Conceptual Architecture Design Principles be further reduced to an acceptable level of globally interoperable constructs? The authors believe so. There are five overall recommendations that can be proposed:

1. *Compile and use a common lexicon/taxonomy.* This does not sound like a particularly difficult task, but it is. Organizations can lay claim to having their own (officially or unofficially), but they all use slightly

different terminologies with varying connotations. The interoperability problem is tough enough if we *can* communicate; it is nearly impossible if everyone is speaking a different language.

2. *Define architecture development, definition, maintenance, and interface standards.* This includes a myriad of efforts such as unifying guidance, terms of reference, common models and simulations, hardware interfaces, software interfaces, data standards, representation standards, etc.

3. *Standardize a well-defined, automated architecture process to simplify the evolution of architectures while adding a certain amount of rigor, reproducibility, and confidence to the process.* We have constructed a high-level example. Congress and the President dictate the National Strategy based on their national goals and objectives, national interests, and some perceived threats. For the military and intelligence agencies, this translates into a set of missions and mission requirements. Mission requirements, in turn, drive the functional requirements or the functional architecture of our fighting forces and members of the various intelligence agencies. This same construct can be standardized in the commercial world as well. Unfortunately, commercial organizations cannot afford to start from scratch. All existing organizations have a physical set of legacy systems that forms the basis upon which they must build. If the functional capabilities of the physical systems that exist today are compared with where the organization wants to be functionally, the organization will, no doubt, find some areas where it has an overabundance of capabilities and others where it is lacking. From these shortfalls and overlaps, an organization can formulate several options that will get it where it wants to go. Then an organization will pick one (based on some set of criteria such as cost, schedule, importance, etc.). The courses that each organization chooses get folded into its long-range plan. The plan is used to generate Program Objectives that eventually provide new systems or enhanced capabilities to the operational side of the business. These new systems then become part of the physical architecture and the cycle starts over. Do not forget that each organization needs the user's input from the very beginning and throughout the process.

4. *A commitment to interoperability on the part of organizations and individuals, backed up by accountability through a strong report card for compliance, is needed as part of the existing performance evaluation system.* Acquisition Managers/Acquisition Authorities must be evaluated on meeting all of their requirements including interoperability and information assurance. It appears that these measures are beginning to be graded at the operational level and they are receiving more attention than ever before, but it is an important issue that bears emphasis.

5. *An overall architect must be assigned at the very highest levels of the organization and embodied with the responsibility and authority that ensures compliance with the organization's architecture concepts.* However, this assumes that an organization has a concept. Interoperability

must be a design requirement that is not easily ignored. Although it has been a key recommendation of many studies, committees, and reports, and although most major organizations have established an office of Chief Information Officer (CIO), it seems that it is very difficult to exercise sufficient control in all of the necessary areas. Clearly, many organizations continue to need a different paradigm.

Chapter 8

Implementation and Testing

What goes up must come down. Ask any system administrator.

Anonymous

America's increasingly computerized society will become vulnerable to attacks by criminals and high-tech terrorists unless new computer-security precautions are taken, a National Research Committee (NRC) announced today [SPT, 1990].

Take your ordinary, garden-variety terrorist. Add a tempting, unprotected corporate target that contains one of the organization's most vital strategic assets, — a target that, if knocked out, could lead to major disruptions of service or even to corporate bankruptcy. What you've got is a recipe for disaster — the soft underbelly of the Information Age — and it's time to shake off some of the dangerous complacency that now exists at corporate and governmental computer data centers across America [Beadsmoore, 1986].

In this chapter, you will learn that the implementation phase is more than simply testing the information assurance (IA) program to ensure it meets requirements. This phase includes preparing the program for implementation, user acceptance, and the actual implementation of the new program. We have written this chapter in a way that gives you the ability to actually build an Information Assurance Center (IAC). The exact size and scope of the center should, of course, be appropriate for the size, type, and scope of the project. When the program is completely tested and accepted, the actual implementation can take place. The objective of this phase is to first ensure the IA program satisfies the stated requirements, and then provide an environment that will ensure the program's continued success. Review of program objectives, requirements, plans, and user acceptance and sign-off are stressed as crucial throughout the implementation phase.

Whether the threat is the bombing of your computer resources by a terrorist or an electronic attack by an intelligent hacker bent on destroying your data, there are protection schemes that can be taken to reduce the threat, and tests available to see if the protections in place are working.

We feel that the following are the mandatory minimum requirements that should be in place in an IAC to protect against a physical or electronic attack.

Our own Information Assurance Test Plan (IATP) describes the events, actions, organizational and personnel responsibilities, constraints, and assumptions required to conduct such a test for your computer system environment within your IAC. The goals of this IATP are to assist the IA team in understanding why an IATP is needed; to specify management's scope of involvement; to show the contents of the IATP in detail, and to describe how a computer security "Tiger Team" would proceed in analyzing, testing, and evaluating the IAC's protections already in place. Conclusions and recommendations for additional protection, if any, would be provided in an "after-actions" report at the conclusion of the testing.

There are several different methods and procedures concerning the design and implementation of IATPs — each of which, in part, are adequate when used for the specific tests intended by a "Tiger Team." The methods and procedures described in this IATP represent an integration of those found in:

- DoD 5200.28-STD, "DoD Trusted Computer System Evaluation Criteria" (the TCSEC or "Orange Book") [DoD5200, 1985]
- DoD 5200.28-M, "Techniques and Procedures for Implementing, Deactivating, Testing, and Evaluating Secure Resource Sharing ADP Systems" [DoD5200, 1979]
- Various FIPS publications

The underlying premise was to establish a valid test against the criteria outlined in the TCSEC at our modified C2 level. In addition, NCSC-TG-005, "Trusted Network Interpretation" (the "Red Book") [NCSC005, 1987], was also used at that level.

The intended audiences of this IATP are IAC managers, IA administrators, and others within a data processing community who are specifically responsible for automated data processing (ADP) resources and who have a genuine need to know. Although many similarities exist among ADP facilities, the disparities in equipment, operating systems, criticality of functions, types of customers, geographic locations, and other factors tend to make each IAC unique. This uniqueness not only precludes the use of one organization's IATP for another, but makes each IATP unique to the specific computer center it was placed against. Each IATP will list all protective measures in place meant to ward off possible threats.

IATP Defined

Our Information Assurance Test Plan (IATP) is an examination and analysis of the security features of the ADP system within the IAC (that is, as applied in an operational environment) to determine the security posture of the system against an attack. Prior to preparing an IATP, the IA administrator should perform a risk assessment of the IAC in order to weigh the threats and weaknesses of the center. This risk assessment should include an analysis of existing and planned protective schemes for dealing with threats to a sensitive processing environment. With the protections identified, the risks would then be weighed, weaknesses anticipated, and strategies for coping with realized threats established. The next logical step would be the testing and evaluating of these protective measures. This is where the IA administrator would implement the IATP. Implementing the IATP would include analyzing the possibility of sensitive data inadvertently or deliberately being taken from the IAC (in clear-text form) and other such major computer security violations. It should be noted that it is the rising vulnerability of society to terrorist sabotage of information systems that is threatening to be a major issue, and controls to protect against this risk are rarely in place [Baskerville, 1988]. This is the reason this IATP should be seriously considered.

Requirement for an IATP

The growing dependence during the past 40 years of virtually all large organizational entities on computer resources continues today at an unprecedented rate. Every IAC reflects this dependency within its user community. Included in the growing scope of computer user support is the requirement to provide access to and processing capabilities for "unclassified but sensitive" data — corporate records, payroll, medical records, etc.

IAC managers consider that the computer is a tool for doing work or providing services that, in practical terms, cannot be done without the computer. Reverting to processing and providing access to limited amounts of data, due to a successful attack, is simply not practical and certainly is not desirable. A significant threat to the continued success of an IAC would be the loss of processing. This IATP offers the IA administrator adequate assurance that the protective measures planned and those already in place will provide the required protection to ensure the surety of continued processing capability and the continuance of the IAC's mission.

Management's Role

The key ingredient in a successful IATP is support of the plan by both ADP operations management and senior project management. The fact that support by ADP operations management is necessary is apparent — because ADP operations is the primary participant in the evaluation and testing. The requirement for senior project management support, though perhaps not immediately obvious, is also absolutely essential. The primary reason is that everyone within the IAC, including ADP operations, must understand the importance of the IATP and receive a mandate to cooperate to the fullest. In summary, IAC management should:

- Be aware of, understand, and support the IATP
- Direct that all affected elements of the organization cooperate with the execution of the IATP, including computer room contractors
- Direct the periodic comprehensive testing of the IATP and revision(s) as necessary

The overall responsibility for preparing, testing, evaluating, and maintaining the IATP belongs to the IA administrator.

Disruption of Service Caused by IATP Implementation

The "Tiger Team" will implement, test, and evaluate the IAC's protective measures during normal working hours and, if necessary, after hours and weekends. Testing of certain protections should occur more than once to ensure knowledge of those protections across the board by main computer room and site personnel.

Simulating "a loss of power to a server while processing sensitive data" should not occur while demand for the intranet is high; rather, this simulation should occur during "slack" hours. However, testing personnel procedures should be done during working hours when additional personnel are working.

Items covered in detail later in this IATP include consideration of the hardware, software, data, environmental, managerial, sensitive processing procedures, and human resources protective measures.

Many functions now thought of as belonging to computer security have traditionally been categorized as a part of good management. An IATP evaluation of protective measures at an IAC located on a foreign shore is certainly one of these — as prudent managers have always been aware of the nature of sensitive data and what could happen to them and others if the data were compromised. Unfortunately, however, the ever-increasing growth of sensitive material being processed on computers has not been matched by a corresponding growth in awareness of the need to preserve the sensitive data. Actions and events occurring today, including the penetration of computer systems by hackers, make it increasingly important to recognize sensitive processing for what it is, i.e., a vital element of the organization needing support. In recognition of the importance of sensitive data processing and the need to provide a secure environment, this IATP was created as part of our ongoing information assurance, computer security, and counter-terrorism programs.

IATP Development

Two activities are essential for the implementation and testing of an adequate, cost-effective and workable IATP. First, the functions supported by the IAC that are critical to processing must be identified. Second, the resources essential to the accomplishment of these specific functions must also be identified. Both should be accomplished by performance of a risk assessment and the assignment of protective measures. This done, the IATP can begin in a logical and systematic manner, determining the critical elements to be included in the IATP and their interrelationships.

Critical Elements of the IATP

It is difficult to categorize any one section of the IATP as being more important than another. Essentially, each section of the IATP is critical and has to be accomplished and tested with equal diligence for the program to be successful. Essentially, the IATP follows the criteria established in the Orange Book at the C2 level, with some additional criteria at the B1 level included, and additional criteria outside the scope of the Orange Book also included. Specifically, the IATP tracks with the Orange Book at the C2 level on the following items:

- *Audit:* Must be able to create, maintain, and protect from modification or unauthorized access or destruction an audit trail of accesses into the computer system.
- *Design Documentation:* Documentation must exist that provides a description of the philosophy of protection and how this philosophy is translated into the computer system.
- *Security Features Users' Guide:* Documentation must exist that describes the protections in place and guidelines on using the computer system.
- *Security Testing:* Testing will be performed to assure that there are no obvious ways for an unauthorized user to bypass or defeat the current protection mechanisms.
- *Discretionary Access Controls:* Must allow users on the computer system (through default or explicit user action) to protect files, etc., from unauthorized access from other computer system users.
- *Identification and Authentication:* The computer system must require users to identify themselves before being able to perform any actions (passwords, etc.). In addition, the computer system must be able to uniquely identify each individual user (userid).
- *Object Reuse:* All authorizations in accessing a specific file are negated once the user with those authorizations leaves the file. The next user accessing the same file can only access it based on specific authorizations.
- *System Architecture:* Computer system resources must be protected so that they can be subjected to access control and auditing requirements.

- *System Integrity:* Hardware and software must be provided to periodically validate the correct operations of the computer system.
- *Test Documentation:* A document needs to be provided that describes the test plan, test procedures, and results of the testing.
- *Trusted Facility Manual:* A manual must be provided that will be addressed to the security administrator about functions and accesses that should be controlled by him.

The following are additional items not required at the C2 level, but are nonetheless required for additional protection:

- Trusted Distribution
- Trusted Facility Management
- Trusted Path
- Trusted Recovery
- Mandatory Access Control
- Labels
- Device Labels
- Label Integrity
- Subject Sensitivity Labels
- Labeling Human-Readable Output
- Exportation of Labeled Information
- Exportation to Multilevel Devices
- Exportation to Single-Level Devices
- Design Specification and Verification
- Covert Channel Analysis
- Configuration Management

Of those items originally required, all exist within the Orange Book at higher levels, such as the B1 level. The five most important items will be discussed in this book:

1. Labels
2. Label Integrity
3. Labeling Human-Readable Output
4. Exportation of Labeled Information
5. Configuration Management

Many items are also included that did not exist within the constraints of the Orange Book, yet were necessary inclusions to the IATP:

- *Disaster Recovery Plan:* Documentation needs to be evaluated that provides for recovery from various scenarios (fire, water flooding, electrical outages, system crashes, etc.). Documentation also addresses availability of backup facilities.
- *Disaster Recovery Test and Evaluation:* Procedures in place to respond to emergencies need to be evaluated, with later testing resulting in

fine-tuning the existing procedures. Backup site should also be evaluated and later tested.

■ *Certification:* Someone in authority needs to certify that the computer system meets all applicable federal policies, regulations, and standards, and that the results of the security testing demonstrate that the installed security safeguards are adequate for the applications (in response to OMB Circular A-130 [OMB A130, 1996]).

■ *Periodic Reviews and Recertification:* Security is an ongoing function. Audits and security tests and evaluations need to be continuously conducted at the computer site.

■ *Microcomputer Security:* Security at the micro level needs to be evaluated as more and more terminals with internal hard drives reside on those desks that also access sensitive data.

■ *Security Awareness and Training:* A security awareness program needs to be evaluated in response to the Computer Security Act of 1987 [PL 100–235] for all having access to computer system: management, operations, programmers, and users.

Preliminary Planning: Test Requirements

Implementation of the IATP will require that the system and all its protective measures be challenged (tested) to determine if the system and its protections react properly to various actions (e.g., bombing, fire, unscheduled loss of power). Expected results of these tests are usually included in IATPs. The procedures that the IAC, other sites, and associated personnel use must also be tested and challenged, in some cases, without the knowledge of site personnel.

Scope

The IATP as defined and detailed in this chapter will apply to a site encompassing a mainframe, peripheral automated data processing equipment (ADPE) inside the main IAC, microcomputers outside the main IAC but attached to the mainframe, the storage areas holding media or material affecting the use of ADPE inside the IAC, the areas and offices around and above the IAC (there will be no offices, crawl spaces or other open areas beneath the IAC), and the personnel who operate the mainframe or are involved in handling sensitive media before, during, and after processing. The IATP will be structured to accomplish three distinct security activities:

1. Determine whether the necessary protective measures are in place to counteract the various threats
2. Test and evaluate these specific protective measures using a formal methodology
3. Observe, in an informal manner, any computer security improprieties not necessarily covered under specific protective measures (e.g., observing someone looking in a wallet or purse for their password)

Expected Results

It is anticipated that all protective measures in place will be adequate in reducing the overall risks of operating a sensitive-processing computer room and a remote site operating in an online mode. It is also expected that any protective measures that still need to be put in place will be minor in nature and will not affect the data processing (e.g., the posting by the nearest telephone of instructions on "How to Handle a Bomb Threat").

Methods Used

Individual test methodologies are listed by their areas of consideration and by specific protective measures in "Preparatory Actions" of this IATP.

Assumptions

The major assumptions, which will affect the outcome of the IATP, concern the availability of key personnel to participate in the conduct of the IATP and the accessibility of the IATP team to the computer environment (i.e., the total system). IATP team members will require broad access to the system in order to test and evaluate all of the protective measures. This availability of and accessibility to the IAC and its systems will also require availability of key ADP operations personnel for escort, to respond to questions, to react to loss or impairment of protective measures, and to assist in making the IATP a smooth-flowing and unrestricted operation. It is further assumed that the IA administrator and appropriate security personnel will spend the required time observing and assisting in the implementation of the IATP.

It is also assumed that information derived from the testing and evaluating of protective measures will be treated in a sensitive manner to allow for the tracking back of any discovered inadequacies to the responsible individual or procedure. It is assumed that certain personnel-related protective measures will be tested and evaluated, including contractors involved in the processing and handling of sensitive data on the computer system.

Test Team

This section describes the "Tiger Team" — its members and their responsibilities, their access capabilities, special permissions, limitations, and testing and evaluation strategies.

Team Members

For this hypothetical IATP, a "Tiger Team" would test and evaluate the terrorist-protective measures in place, assuring that sensitive data is securely processed in an interactive, online mode. Rather than relying on individual efforts, this team should remain together and assist one another in implementing each formal protective measure scenario. Informal observations will be individually made and recorded and later reviewed by the team for inclusion in the IATP report. The team should be identified at this point.

The combined experience of the team should cover the entire realm of protective measures being tested and evaluated for this particular IATP. Any additional assistance, outside that of the IA administrator and participating ADP operations personnel, would be nonproductive.

Special Permissions

The IATP team should test and evaluate protective measures (some more than once) over a period of days, including weekend and evening tests of certain protective measures if necessary. Protective measure testing should encompass a variety of security areas, including physical, environmental, hardware, and software. As a result, the IATP team should accrue an amount of information on the IAC's weaknesses not usually gained by individual users, programmers, or possibly even the IA administrator. Therefore, the responsibility of the "Tiger Team" is to bring management's attention to the entire spectrum of knowledge gained from the implementation of the IATP. To successfully accomplish this task, the IATP team needs to be equipped with a blanket, need-to-know policy, allowing the IATP team full access to hardware, software, data, etc. This permission needs to be instigated by management and circulated among those staff participating in the IATP during normal working hours and during the evening and weekend shifts.

In turn, the IATP team should execute the IATP in a timely manner, creating as little disruption as possible to IAC personnel and operations. There is no need for the IA administrator to be physically present during all testing and evaluating. However, the IA administrator should be accessible if needed during the testing period. A limitation to be considered is the needed presence of the IA administrator during evening and weekend countermeasure testing. Access by the IATP team to the system site or to IAC personnel should not be prevented or denied at any time.

Preparatory Actions: Test Methodology

The IATP is an examination and analysis of the security features in an IAC, applied in its operational environment. The IATP will be the final determining factor on which accreditation is based. Basically, the IATP is designed to accomplish two major objectives:

1. To determine whether the necessary protective measures, as chosen in the risk assessment, have been installed
2. To determine whether the installed protective measures are working effectively

A five-step approach should be used to determine the extent to which the objectives are met:

1. Identify qualified individuals capable of evaluating and reporting on the installed protective measures. (the "Tiger Team" would meet this requirement).
2. Review the risk assessment for currency and accuracy, identifying and analyzing the nature of the threats, IAC weaknesses, and their respective protective measures.
3. Develop the IATP. This plan describes how each protective measure will be tested to determine its effectiveness. Because a "Tiger Team" will be attempting to defeat certain system protections, information on these attempts will be found in this plan. Simple scenarios, walk-through inspections, documentation reviews, and procedural reviews will be utilized and will also be found in this plan. This plan will be modified during the actual IATP if unanticipated situations arise.
4. Execute the IATP. Conduct the protective measure tests and evaluations indicated in the following paragraphs. Document the IATP activities as the implementation proceeds, identifying discrepancies and problem areas, if any, so that recommendations can be made for inclusion in the IATP report to the IA administrator.
5. IATP Documentation. This final step documents the results of the IATP. This report will include a recommendation to the IA administrator to accredit or not accredit the system based on the level of risk identified by the IATP team. If nonaccreditation is recommended, the IATP report will contain the appropriate recommendations regarding security deficiencies and their resolution.

The fourth step of the five-step approach warrants elaboration of the component areas, discussed by protection measure area (i.e., software, hardware, administration procedures, physical, environmental, personnel, and management) and within each protection measure area by a detailed listing of how the testing and evaluation will be conducted. The IATP methodologies are contained in the following sections.

Audit

The IAC should be able to create, maintain, and protect from modification or unauthorized access or destruction an audit trail of accesses to the objects it protects. The audit data should be protected by the computer system so that read-access is limited to those who are authorized for audit data. The IAC should be able to record the following types of events: use of identification and authentication mechanisms, introduction of objects into a user's address space (e.g., file open, program initiation), deletion of objects, actions taken by computer operators and IA administrators and system security officers, and other security-relevant events. For each recorded event, the audit record should identify date and time of event, user, type of event, and success or failure of the event. For identification and authentication events, the origin of request (e.g., terminal ID) should be included in the audit record. For events that introduce an object into a user's address space and for object-deletion events, the audit record should include the name of the object. The IA administrator should be able to selectively audit the actions of any one or more users based on individual identity.

While the authentication and identification areas referenced here are better responded to in the section on Identification and Authentication, the following audit capabilities and audit-related areas can be addressed in this section.

Residue Control

After completion of any data processing within the IAC, the operating system may allow a portion of the data to remain in some resource-sharing storage. Electronic terrorists who may succeed in a direct attempt to access your information may then compromise this data. Failure to clear memory can contribute to accidental disclosure of the data and could also contribute to the success of probing attempts.

Purging or erasing all resource-sharing accessible storage areas significantly reduces the risk of allowing data to remain in memory or online storage. This purging or erasing must be accomplished before memory and the IA administrator or system operator releases online storage-device locations. Software areas may be purged or erased by either a software program or a hardware clear switch.

Password Protection from Visual Observation

Log-on attempts, unique passwords, and the authentication process require testing for the system and are detailed in later sections of this chapter. This accountability of protecting your own password includes those cleared users inside the computer sites, especially the system operator. If a password of an authorized user of the sensitive processing system is displayed on the terminal screen or on hardcopy, the password may be compromised.

To prevent this, the IATP team should check that the current sensitive processing system is providing some mechanism to protect passwords from being displayed on the terminal screen or on any print-outs observed. For those that are displaying the password on the monitor screen or on hard-copy print-outs, software is available that will either suppress printing of the password when entered or present a strikeover field on which the terminal operator can enter a password. Such mechanisms should be in place for sensitive processing.

Tape Storage and Data Encryption

The sensitive tapes being run should be physically removed from the IAC and secured after the processing period. Floppy disks containing sensitive data should also be secured in an appropriate manner. Because of the newest threats of HERF (High-Energy Radio Frequency) guns and EMP-T (Electromagnetic Pulse Transformer) bombs, it is wise to keep your tapes in another area of the building or even off site.

While various levels of protection may exist for different but sensitive media (e.g., Privacy Act, agency-sensitive, For Official Use Only, etc.), these sensitive data files could be encrypted to reduce the possibility of compromise through disclosure. Encryption provides a protective measure that protects the files as offline media. However, this provides no protection while files are being processed as clear text. Responsibility within the sensitive processing system for the removal of sensitive tapes from the computer room and assuring adequate security should belong to the IA administrator.

Inspections of Software

Software may have intentionally placed "trap doors," or may be retaining access availability known only to the person or vendor who created or supplied the software or to former computer room operators. To conduct periodic inspections of the sensitive processing site's software, the IATP team should implement one or more of the following:

- Make visual inspections of program listings and files to detect unusual instances of data or software differences.
- Perform automated code matches. A program can be developed to compare files for exact matches. These files can contain software or data.
- Verify the current date or modification-level identifier of the configuration item that is assigned whenever a file is modified. Compare this date or identifier against the approved configuration item date or identifier (e.g., when the file was modified for authorized purposes). This requires that the system is able to maintain the last date of access to a file or maintain configuration management procedures used to control the application programs.
- Compute and securely store checksums for software and data files. Then, periodically checksum each file and compare the result to the stored checksum. A checksum is computed based on a portion of the data in each record.

Changes to mission-specific software (systems and application programs) should be under software configuration control, employing recognized software configuration management procedures and software identification techniques. To be effective against maliciously or accidentally entered faults, such checks and the governing software algorithm may normally be stored under restricted access conditions. As applied against error accident, the check and its algorithm serve best when continuously accessible by the system and employed as part of the diagnostic process.

Controlled Use of Assembly Language Coding

Assembly language software provides the most-direct access to hardware and software features that may be manipulated. The IATP team should check each of the following alternatives to see which can effectively minimize the risk of penetration to the operating system:

- Physically remove the assembler language processor from the sensitive processing system.
- Control access to the assembler language processor through the use of passwords. Limit the issuance of these special passwords to programmers who have a valid requirement to use assembler language.
- Place the assembler language processor on an offline storage medium so that it cannot be used without the active cooperation of the computer console operators or the site security officer who will have to mount the offline storage medium to the computer.

There are those who may choose to attack a computer center by planting malicious "bugs" resembling programming errors in computer software, thereby making computers malfunction:

> Like mines in naval warfare, all software warfare bugs are carefully designed to be small, hidden, and leave few telltale traces even after being activated, with devastating effects, such as causing repeated crashes of a major computer system [Boorman, 1987].

Security Editing and Accounting

Deficient input and output procedures may damage the integrity of operational files. This could result in decisions being made based on invalid and inaccurate data. The IATP team should check that strong edit and transaction accounting features are in place to ensure data integrity. Some controls that the security administrator should have in place are:

- Controls on input, such as transaction counts, batch totals, and machine-readable document input; types of input validation checks include:
  - Character checks, such as testing for numeric, alphabetic, or specific character groups, blanks, field separators or special characters, and the proper or valid arithmetic sign
  - Field checks such, as testing for limits, ranges, valid item, consistency, and sequence
- Controls on processing, such as transaction counts, batch control totals, validation by file reference, consistency checks, and control on rounding errors
- Controls on output, such as item counts, control totals, trailer labels on data sets, control records, or serial numbers on documents (e.g., social security number)

Example of an input/output control group's typical responsibilities include the following:

- Log of jobs received for processing from user departments
- Check document counts and control totals of work received
- Notify user department that the work has been received and indicate whether the counts and totals are correct
- Note any work that was due but not received
- Note and initiate action on any improper preparation by the user departments, such as failure to provide counts or totals
- Submit documents to be entered

EDP Auditor

To prevent inadequacy of system controls, the IA administrator should acquire professional electronic data processing (EDP) audit expertise. Considering the growth of typical IACs, a full-time, internal ADP audit specialist should be available to carry out EDP audits of the system. With an EDP auditor, the IA administrator should feel that management can be assured about the adequacy of information assurance and can be notified on a timely basis of any realized threats or additional weaknesses on the system.

Requirements and Participation of an EDP Auditor

EDP auditors, along with the IA administrator, should participate in the development of security requirements for important applications systems to ensure that the information assurance requirements are adequate and that adequate controls have been specified. A list of certified EDP auditors is available from the Association of EDP Auditors; these auditors are required to sign off on all formalized application system requirements and specifications. The auditability and security of application systems is strengthened and can reduce the cost of both internal and external security audits.

The IATP team should recommend that the IA administrator periodically review EDP auditor participation and ensure that all significant application systems receive audit attention.

Computer User Trouble Call Logging

All calls from users and staff regarding problems with a computer and communications system should be logged, detailing the caller's name, the time and date, and the nature of the problem. A brief disposition report should then be prepared for each problem report.

The IATP team should recommend that the IA administrator review each of the problem disposition reports to determine that a problem was satisfactorily resolved and also to determine that there were no adverse impacts of the solutions provided (e.g., a correction of the operating system may have some side effect with a security or privacy implication). This practice forces user and staff liaison people to justify their actions and to document each correctional action that they have taken. The log can then be analyzed by performance monitoring and by the EDP auditor or software or system development people for possible improvements of the current operating environment.

Independent Control of Audit Tools

Audit programs, documentation, and test materials need to be kept in secure areas by the site security officer. Also, audit programs should not remain in the data center tape library. The audit programs should not be kept on disk or in any other way kept on the system where they might be subject to tampering.

Computer Systems Activity Records

Most computer systems produce a number of auditable system activity logs, journals, and exception reports. Such recordings should be periodically and selectively examined both manually and through automated means by the site security officer, looking for key indications of possible unauthorized activities. Such recordings on tape, disk, and sometimes paper listings should be archived for a reasonable period of time, and records should be kept to ensure that no reports âre missing. For example, printed console logs should be on continuous forms. Any breaks in the forms should require signatures indicating integrity of operation and no missing pages. In one IAC, the console logs are examined on a sample basis monthly. All logs should be dated and timed with an indication of operational personnel on duty at the time the logs were produced. It may be necessary to keep manually written logs of some computer operation activities, especially at some overseas sites, to compare with or complete the automatic logging of system activity. The IATP team should evaluate such records and see if they are adequate.

Employee Identification on Work Products

All IAC computer operators and other employees should have standard identification in the form of official names, numbers, and passwords. This identification is to be entered into all records, data input, and activity logs and journals to identify workers associated with all work products. Identification can be accomplished by manual signatures or keying of identification into equipment keyboards. Data entry clerks should be required to initial all batch control forms used for data entry and enter identification into computer input data. Computer operators should sign computer console printer listings or enter their codes through console keyboards indicating the starting and ending of work periods. Print-outs should also have the requestor's name or identification on the cover sheet.

Design Documentation

Documentation should be available that provides a description of the manufacturer's philosophy and an explanation of how this philosophy is translated into the computer system. If the computer system is composed of distinct modules, the interfaces between these modules should be described.

This design documentation is formally called the Network Security Architecture and Design Report. The Network Security Architecture section of the report must address the security-relevant policies, objectives, and protocols. The Network Security Design portion of the report must specify the interfaces and services that must be incorporated into the network so that it can be evaluated as a trusted entity.

Security Features Users' Guide

A single summary, chapter, or manual in user documentation should describe the protection mechanisms provided by the computer system, guidelines on their use, and how they interact with one another. This users' guide needs to describe user-visible protection mechanisms at the global (networked) level and at the user-interface level of each component (and the interaction between them).

Security Testing

The security mechanisms of the ADP system should be tested and found to work as claimed in the system documentation. Testing should be done to assure that there are no obvious ways for an unauthorized user to bypass or otherwise defeat the security protection mechanisms of the computer system. Testing should also include a search for obvious flaws that would allow violation of resource isolation, or that would permit unauthorized access to the audit or authentication data.

Backup Personnel Control

The loss of one person whose corporate knowledge of the system is lost with him, such as the loss of the IA administrator, should have minimal impact on the continuing operation and testing of the sensitive processing system. Such persons should have an assistant at all times so that the loss of the person primarily responsible, whether planned or unplanned, would allow the assistant to step in and continue operating.

Testing and Debugging

The procedures for testing and debugging software may be inadequate. If there is a software failure during sensitive program testing or debugging, it may be difficult to determine the state of the computer and ensure the integrity of data that was online or otherwise readily accessible. In the period of system instability during a software failure, normal system safeguards may not be in effect.

The IATP team should suggest that the IA administrator look at one system program and one application program. The IA administrator should ensure that the testing and debugging of both programs are done during the appropriate time in a controlled environment. Specifically, in systems software, the testing and debugging should be performed initially during dedicated time in a controlled environment. If operational user files are required for testing, copies of these files should be used. Operational testing may be carried out when quality assurance personnel are satisfied that the programs are operating reliably.

In application programs, the testing and debugging may be permitted during nondedicated times, but again, only copies of data files should be used.

Discretionary Access Controls

The computer system should define and control access between named users and named objects (e.g., files and programs) in the ADP system. The enforcement mechanism (e.g., self/group/public controls, access control lists) should allow users to specify and control sharing of those objects by named individuals, or defined groups of individuals, or by both, and should provide controls to limit propagation of access rights. The discretionary access control mechanisms shall, either by explicit user action or by default, provide that objects are protected from unauthorized access. These access controls should be capable of including or excluding access to the granularity of a single user. Access permission to an object by users not already possessing access permission should only be assigned by authorized users.

Password File Encryption

The file access control mechanism in the operating system may not prevent a skilled penetrator or "hacker" from obtaining the online password file. This may lead to a further penetration of the computer system and the disclosure of sensitive information; also, the data security software package may not be able to encrypt data.

The IATP team should suggest that a password encryption algorithm is employed, resulting in storage of passwords in encrypted form only. Alternately, the file containing the passwords used to log-on to the system can be encrypted. Such a scheme will prevent an online password file from being readily intelligible if the file is disclosed. The password file is stored in encrypted form using a one-way or irreversible algorithm. The encrypted passwords cannot be inverted to obtain the original clear text passwords. In operation, user supplied passwords are encrypted and compared against the encrypted passwords in the file. A match indicates that a valid password was supplied. Presumably, if anyone is able to gain access to this file, then the other access control authentication mechanisms could also be bypassed. Encrypting the password file is an effective measure against disclosure and casual browsing.

Clearances and Identification of Personnel

All sensitive processing system users should be cleared to the level of data classification they are allowed to access. Although an individual may be cleared to corporate sensitive, the individual user should also have a need-to-know status to be established by management.

The IATP team should verify the existence of up-to-date clearances of those involved with sensitive data processing, including contractor personnel. The IATP team should also verify the procedures used in gathering and storing such information. For example, because all federal government employees undergo a National Agency Check (NAC) up to and including secret on them before being hired, it is recommended that managers are aware of what those background checks revealed before allowing recent hires access to sensitive data on the system. The ability to pass an NAC may not be a clear indication that the person should still be allowed onto the system; access should be permitted on a case-by-case basis by management only after careful inspection of the investigation.

Participation of Personnel during Sensitive Processing

System users, including those providing input data and using output reports, should supply explicit control requirements to systems analysts and programmers who are designing and developing application systems. Users should also be required to explicitly agree that necessary controls have been implemented and continue to function during production use of the sensitive processing system and programming maintenance.

Users' understanding of their own applications is enhanced significantly when control specifications are required from them. Users are placed in a position where they can make better decisions regarding the appropriate controls in some aspects of applications and determine recovery time requirements. Users become knowledgeable of and sensitive to the needs for computer security and privacy. Sharing the responsibility of accountability for control is enhanced. Separation of duties is also enhanced. Completeness and consistency of controls is facilitated.

Library Access Control

Computer program libraries containing listings of programs under development and in production and associated documentation should be protected from unauthorized access. In large organizations, a full-time or part-time librarian may be used to control access, logging in and logging out all documents. Barriers from other activities should physically separate the program library. Documents should be distributed only to authorized users. It may be necessary to enforce strict access control to programmers' offices as a means of protecting programs and documentation. Programmers should have lockable file cabinets in which they can store materials currently in use. A clean desk policy at the end of each working day may be justified as an extreme measure. Program and documentation control is particularly important when using or developing licensed software packages because of the strict contractual limitations and liabilities.

This demonstrates the importance of computer program assets to the organization. It provides separation of duty among programmers to ensure that programmers have access only to the documentation and programs within their areas of responsibility.

Identification and Authentication

The computer system should require users to identify themselves to it before beginning to perform any other actions that the computer system is expected to mediate. Furthermore, the computer system should use a protected mechanism (e.g., passwords) to authenticate the user's identity. The computer system should protect authentication data so that any unauthorized user cannot access it. The computer system should be able to enforce individual accountability by providing the capability to uniquely identify each individual ADP system user. The computer system should also provide the capability of associating this identity with all auditable actions taken by that individual.

Separation and Accountability of ADP Functions

Holding managers accountable for the security in the areas they manage requires that these areas are clearly and explicitly defined so that there is no overlap or gaps in the managerial control of ADP functions. ADP functions should be broken down into as many discrete, self-contained activities as is practical and cost-effective. Besides being a good general management principle to maintain high performance, identifying specific functions also provides the necessary explicit structure for assignment of controls, responsibility for them, accountability, and a means of measuring the completeness and consistency of adequately meeting all vulnerabilities. Separate, well-defined ADP functions also facilitate the separation of duties among managers, as is required in separation of duties of employees. This reduces the level of trust needed for each manager. The functions of authorization, custody of assets, and accountability should be separated to the extent possible.

Separation reduces the possibility of accidental or intentional acts resulting in losses. More-efficient ADP functions are created and the possible loss of control is inhibited from migrating from one function to another. However, increased complexity of ADP functions could result from excessive separation of functions, making the application of individual controls more difficult.

Terminal User's Agreement

A terminal user should be required to read and comply with a list of items initially brought up on the terminal screen when the user first enters the system. On transfer, the user is also required to read and comply with the terms ending his use on the system. It is recommended, for at least legal implications, that these forms are created and signed as appropriate. It is not enough to give employees handling sensitive data a packet of "dos and don'ts"; a legally binding form where they agree not to divulge sensitive data, etc., should be incorporated.

Employees are the weakest link in computer security; little if anything stops them from walking in and out of their computer center with floppy disks, modems, print-outs, etc., except warning them that they had better not get caught.

Terminal Identification

The IA administrator's computer system may have improper or insufficient authentication of hardware. This can lead to a situation where the operating system cannot properly identify a terminal before responding to a request for data. There is then the possibility that data will be rerouted to a terminal whose location is not secure enough to support the display or storage of the data.

A hardware feature in synchronization with the operating system should individually identify each remote terminal i.e., the communications port should always communicate with the same terminal unless physically switched by an authorized person.

Object Reuse

All authorizations to the information contained within a storage object should be revoked prior to initial assignment, allocation, or reallocation to a subject from the computer system's pool of unused storage objects. No information, including encrypted representations of information, produced by a prior subject's actions is to be available to any subject that obtains access to an object that has been released back to the system.

The IATP team should find this to be true. Allowing someone to continue processing from a terminal in which someone else failed to log-off may result in the next user observing data the new user may not have seen under their own log-on user identification and password. Employees traditionally tend to walk away from their terminals and leave them on; this would allow anyone else to use that terminal, with the consequence that if anything went wrong, the person who had previously logged in would get blamed for it.

System Architecture

The computer system should maintain a domain for its own executions that protects it from external interference or tampering (e.g., by modification of its code or data structures). Resources controlled by the computer system may be a defined subset of the subjects and objects in the ADP system. The computer system should isolate the resources to be protected so that they are subject to the access control and auditing requirements.

Redundant Equipment

In some situations, even short periods of downtime due to equipment failure may pose a serious threat of denial-of-service if there is no backup hardware or contingency plan.

While the criticality of operating the current sensitive processing system is fairly low at this time (uptime requirements only), it is anticipated that as the number of terminal sites increase and the amount of sensitive data increases, the reliance and thus the criticality of uptime requirements will also increase.

Enough redundant equipment should be available from vendors, contractors, and support organizations to carry on the minimum critical functions in the event of an equipment failure in the main configuration.

Concerning tape backups, in many sites daily or weekly backups are kept in the same room as the computer equipment; they should be kept in the same building, but not in the same room. It is also true that secondary backups are often kept off site at an employee's home; notwithstanding the allegiance of the employee, they should be kept in a more-secure place.

Concerning backup sites, there should be one. If an IAC goes up in flames because of a terrorist attack or is destroyed by a natural disaster, the IAC loses its ability to process data. No commercial backup company may be capable of handling the current configuration; many IACs have one-of-a-kind equipment, equipment so old that they are not even held in vendor warehouses anymore, and special communications configurations. These configurations make these sites so unique that no matter how much money is thrown at the problem after the site is destroyed, an IAC could not be up and running for many months.

Interruption-Resistant Power

The power supply for the sensitive processing system may be inadequate to meet the IAC's future performance requirements. The IATP team should evaluate various solutions to ensure that there is no weakness. For example, the IATP team should inspect these items:

- The installation of a voltage regulator transformer to correct for minor power-line fluctuations (transients). This regulator will provide protection against minor transients and brown-outs
- The use of a motor alternator with an energy storage flywheel to protect against short-term power failure
- The use of batteries to protect against long-term power failures
- The use of a backup generator to supply electricity to the system during a graceful shutdown

Access to Sensitive Processing Computer Sites

The physical aspects of the IAC may make it difficult in some ways to control access to the facility. Appropriate physical security controls, employed to safeguard the equipment, apply not only to the computer equipment itself and terminals, but also to such removable items as listings, magnetic tapes, etc. The point is to protect not only the user's data and programs, but other components of the system configuration as well. Because parts of the computer system (e.g., magnetic disks, tape files, or copies of machine listings) contain sensitive data, it may be necessary to separate them physically and to control access to them independently. This applies to the environmental facilities required to provide reliable operation of the system. One solution is to install an access system to prevent unauthorized persons from entering the IAC. The following systems provide protection by requiring the entrant to unlock a door and may be used singly or in combination: conventional key and lock set, electronic key system, mechanical combination locks, and electronic combination locks.

One example seen at various processing sites is the air intakes that draw outside air into the building. These are sometimes at ground level, rather than being on the roof or otherwise protected. The introduction of noxious or caustic agents or fumes at the intakes, such as hydrochloric acid, would cause damage to computers and other equipment. The introduction of carbon monoxide (e.g., an exhaust pipe of a car next to the air intake), would not be noticed and could injure site personnel. The environmental support system for the computer site buildings should be separate from the environmental support system for the computer room.

The IATP team also finds that some IACs plainly advertise themselves as an ADP facility; the IATP team would suggest not advertising your building as one that holds ADP equipment. The IATP team also finds that access to many of the computer sites by vehicles is possible right up to the physical building. There are usually no protections to stop that. The IATP team would then suggest placing a perimeter fence around the buildings if possible and installing card readers for entry behind the fence. As a minimum, the team would suggest that large concrete planters be placed at the entrances so that vehicles could not run up onto the curb and through glass doors into the lobby. One IAC had such concrete barriers, but the planters were spaced too far apart to stop a car or even a truck from going between them.

Physical Layout

The physical layout inside the IAC and other sites networked into the IAC may make it difficult to control the movement of persons within the ADP facility. The IATP team should ensure that procedures exist to minimize access to the IAC on a need-to-know basis. Visitors, cleaning personnel, maintenance personnel, and customer engineers should be required to provide identification, a valid reason for access, and should always be escorted.

Fire Protection

Fire protection may be inadequate, making the IAC vulnerable to loss or damage by terrorist actions and a resulting fire.

The IATP team should look at the following appropriate protections:

- *Installation of a fire/smoke detection system:* Place additional fire/smoke detectors above false ceilings, below raised floors, and in air conditioning ducts. Install a control panel that can identify the location of the detector that has identified the fire or smoke. At some IACs, an IATP team can usually find neither smoke detectors nor overhead water sprinklers in the entire building, much less the computer room. One IATP team found asbestos in the ceiling on every floor, making the cost of putting in an overhead water pipe system for fire suppression very expensive because the asbestos needed to be removed. In case of a fire, the asbestos will keep the firefighters away from the scene, as asbestos-laden smoke is carcinogenic. At one IAC, an IATP team found that if a fire alarm was pulled from anywhere inside the building, someone then had to manually call the fire department. The alarm should automatically ring at the fire department, because people will tend to forget to make that call if there is a real fire. At another IAC, there was no water drain under the raised floor in the IAC, probably because there was no overhead water sprinkler installed; however, any water introduced into the room to fight fire would add increased weight to the IAC floor and may buckle it. Worse, the floor could fail. Smoke alarms should also be placed in air return ducts.
- *Make fire extinguishers available in accessible locations:* Mark each extinguisher according to the type of fire for which it is to be used. For example, Class A extinguishers should only be used on paper, wood, or other material that would leave ashes (unlike electrical or cleaning fluids [fuel] fires).
- *Provide a means of extinguishing or controlling a fire in the IAC by installing an automatic fire extinguishing system:* Three types of fire extinguishment systems are (1) a water sprinkler system, (2) a carbon dioxide system, and (3) a HALON-1301 deluxe system. Install alarms to alert personnel if the system has been activated. A water flow alarm can be used for sprinkler systems, and a pressure sensor alarm can be used for gaseous systems.
- *Provide a fire protection plan to reduce the cause of fire and to extinguish a fire quickly:* Develop the fire plan with the aid of the local fire station. Conduct frequent inspections to identify and eliminate potential fire hazards.
- *Make plastic sheeting available to cover equipment to protect against water damage:* Store magnetic tapes and removable disk packs in fireproof or fire-resistant containers or rooms.
- *Look at the use of Emergency Power Off (EPO) switches in and around the IACs:* At one IAC, EPO plungers were only located at exits in the rear of the computer room, none at the two main entrances into and out of the IAC. The IATP team suggested EPO switches be placed at those exits. At another site, there was no EPO switch in the computer room at all to disable electricity to computers in case of electrical fire.

There was no Uninterruptible Power Supply (UPS) at that site either, so loss of electricity would crash the tape heads. At this particular site, the building's backup generator kicks in 4 to 5 seconds after loss of main power, too long a lapse for computers to remain running.

Environmental Control System

The environmental support systems (air conditioning, heating, and humidity controls) may be inadequate to meet ever-increasing performance requirements. The IATP team should research and report on at least three appropriate protections:

1. Installation of multiple units to protect against the failure of the Air Handling Unit (AHU). For example, use three 20-ton AHUs in place of one 50-ton AHU. There should be enough capacity to maintain the environment with one unit out of service. The AHUs circulate the air inside the IAC, provide temperature and humidity control, and filter the air.
2. If the environmental control system fails, the capability to use outside air may be beneficial. Depending on location and weather, the use of direct outside air via vents and fans may be sufficient to maintain the temperature and humidity of the facility.
3. Install the AHU designed to use and recirculate inside air in the event that outside air becomes unusable. The outside air may contain high amounts of noxious fumes or may be of such poor quality that the filtration system would not be useful. Even a rumor of toxic germs released in a ventilating system (remember the Legionnaires' disease in Philadelphia) could keep occupants outside of a building for days, shutting down any computer and communication centers inside as effectively as if they had been physically damaged [Wilcox, 1984].

The IATP team would suggest that the IA administrator test for the following areas:

- Loss of air conditioning
- Loss of humidity control
- Loss of heating

Discarded Document Destruction

Input/output documents, including any human-readable documents or non-erasable computer media, should be reviewed for potential loss sensitivity and appropriately destroyed when no longer needed. Appropriate protection of materials awaiting final disposition should be used. Logging of all actions to ensure an audit trail and adherence to rules is essential. Strict assignments of tasks and accountability are essential. Documents such as obsolete system development materials, test data, and manuals should be considered. This provides complete accounting for all documents, reduces exposure to loss in facilities and trash, makes facilities less cluttered, reduces fire hazards, and reduces cost of storage.

Physical Security

The physical perimeter within which security is to be maintained and outside of which little or no control is maintained should be clearly established. All vital functions should be identified and included within the security perimeter. Physical access control and prevention of damage immediately outside security perimeters should be carefully considered. For example, physical barriers should extend to the base floor and to the base ceiling around sensitive areas. Areas beneath false floors and above false ceilings should be controlled consistent with the control of working areas between them. Important equipment (such as electrical power switching and communications equipment and circuits) should be made secure and included within the security perimeter. Employees and on-site vendors should be made aware of perimeters on a least-privilege basis. The perimeter should be easily discernible, simple, uncluttered, and sufficiently secure relative to the value of assets inside the perimeter. Drawings and specifications of the perimeter should be available and used for planning any facilities changes. Additional barriers between areas with different security requirements within the exterior barrier also should be established.

Emergency Preparedness

Emergency procedures should be documented and periodically reviewed with occupants of areas requiring emergency action. Adequate automatic fire and water detection and suppression capabilities are assumed to be present. After a physical attack, reduction of human injury is the first priority, followed by saving other important assets. Emergency drills that enact the documented procedures should be held periodically. It should be assumed that occupants of an area in which an emergency occurs do not have time to read emergency procedures documents before action. Procedures should include activation of manual alarms and power shut-off switches, evacuation routes, reporting of conditions, safe areas for regrouping, accounting for all occupants, use of equipment such as fire extinguishers to aid safe evacuation, and actions following complete evacuation. A hierarchy of emergency commands should be established with backup assignments. Emergency drills should be organized to minimize loss of critical activities such as computer operation. Close supervision of drills by managers, who are aware of practice drills or real emergencies, is necessary. Large, clearly visible signs providing basic directions are required. For example, locations of fire extinguishers, portable lights, and emergency switches should clearly be identified with signs that can be read from the most likely workstations.

Unattended Periods

Many IACs are staffed at least eight hours a day. There may occur unforeseen events that cause the IAC to be unstaffed for various lengths of time. The IAC and other sensitive sites are sensitive areas that, during unattended times, should be made physically secure with locked doors, significant barriers, and automatic detection devices for movement or natural disaster losses. Periodic inspection by guards is also important. In addition, sensitive areas, not generally visible to others, should never be occupied by a lone employee for reasons of safety and prevention of malicious acts. Adequate control of unattended periods will ensure consistency of security.

Smoking, Eating, and Drinking Prohibitions

Smoking, eating, and drinking are not permitted in computer equipment areas. Prevention requires signs, written policy, enforcement, and the rigorous application of penalties. In addition, personal grooming and dress codes should be voluntarily practiced to avoid interference with moving parts of peripheral equipment and personal injury. In addition to obvious benefits, these rules would also prevent the remote chance of a smoke detection or water detection alarm being triggered unnecessarily. If an IATP team encounters evidence of smoking, eating, or drinking within a computer room environment, they can be assured that the protective measures against terrorist actions or hackers are also lax.

Traffic Minimization

Access authorization should be granted on a privileged basis. Three access levels can be granted: general, limited, and by exception. General access is granted to those whose workstations are in a restricted area. In one IAC, this included computer operators, maintenance staff, and first-level supervisors. Limited access is granted for specified periods of time to those responsible for performing specified preplanned assignments, such as auditors, security personnel, and repair or construction crews. Finally, exceptions can be made in emergencies as long as those having access are escorted and, after which, extraordinary measures are taken to ensure integrity of the area. Application programmers no longer need access to the IAC except on an emergency basis. Systems programmers need access on a limited basis. Visitors would be restricted entirely from IACs unless by exception and are accompanied by a high-level manager, who explicitly accepts responsibility for the visitor. Other sensitive areas, such as programmers' offices, job set-up areas, and data entry work areas, should be similarly restricted to authorized access. Signs identifying limited access areas should be posted, and rules should be strictly enforced. Also, computer peripheral equipment requiring human operation should be in rooms separate from computer equipment requiring little human attention. Unauthorized physical access is one of the greatest security vulnerabilities and is effectively reduced by careful placement of computing activities.

Alternate Power Supply

A power supply independent of the original source for uninterrupted service should be provided by batteries charged from original power, providing a few minutes of independent power or by an independent power source, such as a diesel generator for longer durations. An alternative source of energy, such as a diesel generator without batteries but with adequate power quality regulators, can be used when uninterrupted service is not important, but long durations of outage are harmful. This control is needed only where power is sufficiently unreliable relative to the seriousness of computer failure or unavailability. The location, environment control, and access security are important to ensure integrity of the alternative power equipment and fuel. Periodic full tests are important for maintenance.

Materials Storage and Access

Equipment such as telephone-switching panels and cables, utilities, power and air conditioners, computer devices, and supplies (e.g., paper, tapes, and disks) should be placed or stored to ensure their protection from damage and to minimize the adverse effects they may have on other items. Dust, vibration, chemical effects, fire hazards, and electrical interference could be introduced into the IAC environment. Items requiring special safeguards should be isolated to reduce the extent of required safeguard coverage. In multifloor buildings, vertical as well as horizontal proximity should be considered.

Separation of ADP Equipment

Different types of computer equipment (central processors, disk drives, tape drives, communications equipment, printers, power supplies, tape libraries, terminals, consoles) require different environments for optimum operation, and different numbers and types of operations personnel. Therefore, they should be placed in different rooms with appropriate separation walls, distances, and accesses. For example, printers create dust and vibration from paper movement and should be separate from disk and tape drives that are sensitive to air quality and vibration. Again, if the IA administrator is allowing these situations to occur, then the protective measures against terrorist actions are also probably lax.

Magnetic Media Library

A simple physical security survey is usually performed by the IATP team on the Magnetic Media Library (MML). Items surveyed include the use of battery-operated emergency lighting to facilitate the safe exit of personnel from the library in the event of a power failure; deadbolt locking device to secure the room when it is not occupied; the placement of an automatic door closer so that the door does not remain ajar; two-hour fire ratings of the walls; doors and door frames should be of metal, not wood; installation of a smoke/fire detection device, especially in ductwork; and installation of a fire suppression system.

Inspection of Incoming/Outgoing Materials

Certain materials and containers are inspected, and entry or departure is restricted. Within constraints of all applicable laws and personal privacy, any computer operator should prevent movement of materials and inspect contents of closed containers into and out of the computer room. Mail bombs have been delivered to computer centers with devastating results. Materials may include tapes, disks, listings, equipment, recorders, food and beverages, chemicals, and containers such as lunch boxes and briefcases. Unneeded materials should be stored outside for later retrieval by owners. Authorization forms may be used to control movement. Spot checks and posted signs rather than continuous inspection may be sufficient.

Flooding/Water Protection

The IATP team would inspect the computer room and other sites for overhead water pipes, and inspect the adjacent rooms, including the floor above, for water pipes. If an overhead water sprinkler system exists, the type (reaction or pre-action) will be brought to the IA administrator's attention. If water pipes do exist in or near a sensitive computer, the flooding drill should be tested by the IA administrator. Restrooms have been bombed by terrorist groups with the resulting flow of water running onto computers and flooding computer centers.

System Integrity

Hardware and software features should be provided that can be used to periodically validate the correct operations of the online hardware and firmware elements of the computer system.

Software Engineering Tools

The failure of software to perform according to specified requirements has the potential to compromise security. Software failure may, for example, destroy the integrity of a particular database or allow inventory shortages to go unnoticed. The IATP team should conduct a preliminary overview of the software engineering tools available to those whose software will be running in the sensitive batch processing mode. These tools aid the development process and provide an increased confidence that software will perform reliably and in accordance with stated requirements. The IATP team should look at what currently exists or is being used, including:

- Research in Secure Operating Systems (RISOS) tools developed to analyze assembly language programs. Analytical tools available in RISOS include a program that counts occurrences of a specified symbol, a program that identifies the control flow and flags specified items, and a program that locates instruction patterns. These are some of the software engineering tools developed specifically for security.

- Software quality measures are computer programs that examine a program to generate a quantifiable measure of the program's quality. This allows testers to reject programs with quality measures that are outside a certain range, on the assumption that program reliability decreases as quality decreases.

- Self-metric software examines the source code of a computer program and inserts software measurement probes. Data gathered from such probes might indicate the number of times a loop is executed, entry and exit values, and the test stimuli provided. This data helps testers estimate the extent to which a program has been tested.

- Test data generators are computer programs that generate test cases to be used in software testing. These programs range from utility-type programs that generate sequences of alphanumeric or numeric data based on parametric inputs, to entire systems that interpretively examine the flow through a program and attempt to generate appropriate sequences of test cases.

- Audit programs ensure that programs conform to a given set of programming standards. Programs that deviate significantly may be more difficult to understand and may have flaws that could affect security.

- Trace programs record data such as program variables or events that can assist in program debugging and validation.

Suppression of Incomplete and Obsolete Data

The dissemination and use of incomplete and obsolete data should be prevented or restricted. The suppression of incomplete and obsolete data will prevent decisions from being based on such invalid information. This also prevents the privacy of a data subject from being violated. It allows databases to be updated (old and irrelevant information may be deleted), thus reducing operating costs and potentially increasing performance.

The IATP team would verbally review dissemination policies and procedures for reasonableness and compliance with regulatory, statutory, and civil requirements; review procedures to block dissemination of certain types of information; and review procedures to expunge records from certain databases. The reviews would be made with IA administrators who were found to be adequately aware of such compliance and who were also aware that obsolete and incomplete data were handled in the same manner as the more-active online sensitive data.

Personal Data Inspection

Many IACs belong to organizations that receive and disseminate data files from and to outside sources. As such, the organization should have an input/output control group. This group checks the data files when they are received and disseminated. It checks for the inclusion of improper data fields, such as individual names and social security numbers; also, more-sophisticated checking of the relational aspects of the data field is done to determine whether individuals can be identified by combining information from multiple fields. The group screens all files to be received and investigates anomalies. A log should be kept of all activity.

In this manner, potentially sensitive privacy and confidentiality problems are caught early before data are made available to outsiders. This group should also examine data to see that the organization's standards are met with respect to items such as format, content, and value.

Human Subjects Review

Besides handling the sensitive-level data, the computer system may also handle Privacy Act data. The manner in which individual privacy (data confidentiality) is handled is a key issue and would be further inspected by the IATP team. The IATP team should investigate three main areas:

1. Sensitivity of system operators to issues of privacy
2. Personal values associated with the handling of Privacy Act data
3. General competence and ability to cope with unforeseen situations in which Privacy Act data is compromised

Input Data Validation

Validation of all input to a sensitive processing computer system should be performed in both applications and computer operating systems to assist in the assurance of correct and appropriate data. Validation should include examination for out-of-range values of data, invalid characters in data fields, exceeding upper and lower limits of data volume, and unauthorized or inconsistent control data. Program errors, dependent on the content or meaning of the data, should also be checked.

The IATP team would suggest that the IA administrator review systems design documentation to determine that input data controls are appropriately designed into the system. Run tests, using erroneous data to check on the functioning of validation controls, should also be performed.

Also, if essential data are still missing beyond a certain time limit, steps should be taken to obtain the appropriate data. This procedure acts as an error correction/detection control, identifying records for which important information is still missing after a certain period of time (the update could have been misplaced, processed incorrectly, inadvertently omitted, etc.). Such a procedure preserves personal privacy, ensuring that incomplete records, which could cause misleading decisions, are reduced. The control also helps keep records up-to-date.

Protection State Variables

If the mainframe does not employ two or more protection-state variables, both the user and the operating system should operate in the same state. As a result, a hacker could be able to perform hardware functions without restriction.

The IATP team should ensure that the processor has at least two protection-state variables (e.g., privileged mode and user mode), in which certain instructions are illegal except in privileged mode. Examples of privileged instructions include input/output, memory management, and context switching. Modification of the protection-state variables should be contained by the operating system and hardware so that a program in user mode cannot switch itself into privileged mode.

Memory Protection Mechanisms

The architecture of the mainframe may not include mechanisms to restrict main memory access by user software programs. Lack of memory protection mechanisms also makes it possible for user software programs to interface either inadvertently or maliciously with other user software or with the operating system itself.

The mainframe should support the use of memory protection mechanisms. These mechanisms are designed to isolate users from each other and from the operating system. The hardware checks each fetch and store instruction for proper access. Examples of hardware protection mechanisms include memory bounds registers, storage locks and keys, segmentation, paging, rings, capabilities, tagged architecture, and descriptor-based protection.

Hardware Error and Tampering Detection

Undetected hardware errors or hardware tampering may compromise security. The IATP team should check to see if the mainframe and microcomputers have been provided with facilities to detect and expose internal hardware malfunctions. Modern hardware normally has error detection capabilities, such as parity error detection. Hardware components should cause an interrupt to occur whenever there is a change in their status. Software can then be developed to intercept the interrupt for possible tampering or change in hardware configuration. Software may also be developed to detect unusual error or interrupt patterns.

Data Accountability Assignments to Personnel

Users should be aware and formally assigned the responsibility for the accuracy, safekeeping, and dissemination of the sensitive data they handle. If the data processing department does not handle data properly, then it is up to the users to require corrections. Organizationally, users provide a data processing department with the resources to assist them with their functions. In terms of controls, users should be able to tell data processing what is required in terms of data accuracy, relevance, timeliness, handling procedures, etc.

The IATP team realizes that this may run contrary to many current organizational structures where data processing, in some sense, controls the users. However, the team should review organizational assignment of responsibilities for computer security matters, and discuss with users and data processing management their mutual responsibilities regarding computer security and privacy. The IATP team should also review procedures in which users correct records, control the dissemination of records, and otherwise actively participate in the enforcement and design of computer security controls.

Protection of Data Used in System Testing

Application and test programmers usually need test data to develop, debug, and test programs under development. In some cases, small amounts of fictitious test data can be generated independent of users and production data. However, many application programs require significant amounts of test data that are exact copies of a full range of production data. Test data are frequently obtained as samples of entire files of production input data currently being used or recently used for the application being replaced or as output from other preprocessing computer programs. There is sometimes significant exposure by providing current production data to programmers. Often data can be obtained from obsolete production input data files, but in some cases even these data may be confidential. Customers for whom production programs are being developed should be made aware of the exposure problem, and should obtain advice and assistance for producing test data in the least-confidential but most-expedient manner. Sensitive test data should be treated with the same care as equivalent production data. In any case, development and test programmers should not be given access to real production files in a production computer system, except in the case of emergency and then under highly controlled conditions.

This control can greatly reduce the exposure of an organization to a wide range of errors, omissions, and intentional acts. It also imposes a beneficial discipline on development and test computer programmers.

Production Program Authorized Version Validation

The authorized versions or copies of production programs, according to identifiers, are checked with a list of authorized copies and changes made to the production programs to determine that the version of a production program to be run is authorized. Update of the list is part of the ordinary maintenance process of production programs. Separate test and production program libraries are maintained.

This prevents unauthorized versions of the production programs from being executed when used in conjunction with other related controls. Accidentally running a test version or an old version of a production program can be prevented and detected using this technique. Unauthorized versions of production programs can be similarly detected and prevented from being run.

The IATP team would suggest that the IA administrator examine, where feasible, the logs showing all exceptions (compile dates that do not match).

The IA administrator should follow up on instances where a match between the list of authorized versions does not match the identifiers.

Computer Programs Change Logs

All changes to computer programs should be logged into a permanent written document. The log can be used as a means of ensuring formal approval of changes. This enables review of the purpose, time, type, and individuals who made changes. This control aids in researching problems that occur; utility programs that maintain program libraries in the computer are useful as they can automatically log change activity.

Exceptions Reporting

Exceptions reporting on a timely basis should be built into the computer operating system, utility programs, and application systems to report on any deviation from normal activity that may indicate errors or unauthorized acts. For example, if a user defines a data file that allows anyone access to it, a message should be printed out warning the user and possibly the operations staff that the file is not protected. Exceptions reporting should occur when a specific control is violated, or the exception report may constitute a warning of a possible undesirable event. Exceptions reports should be recorded in a recoverable form within the system and when necessary for timely action displayed to the computer operator, or in case of online terminal use, displayed to the terminal user.

Technical Review of Operating System Changes

Whenever any change is to be made to the computer operating system programs, a review of the change is made. The intent is to make sure that the new changes are valuable and will not compromise controls and integrity, have an unanticipated impact on some other part of the system, or interfere excessively with vendor updates. The IATP team would suggest that the IA administrator review the logs of system changes and compare them with the actual changes.

Evaluation Documentation

The system developer should provide to the evaluators a document that describes the test plan, test procedures that show how the security mechanisms were tested, and results of the security mechanisms' functional testing. This security test documentation should establish a plan to examine, analyze, test, and evaluate each protection in place on the system. Each protection is "challenged" to determine if, and how well, it reacts to various adverse conditions. The test documentation reflects the evaluation findings, conclusions, and recommendations made by the IATP team.

Trusted Facility Manual

A manual needs to be addressed to the ADP system administrator that should present cautions about functions and privileges that should be controlled when running a secure facility. The procedures for examining and maintaining the audit files as well as the detailed audit record structure for each type of audit event should be given.

Security Administrator Functions

Security is a full-time job, and the IA administrator should have adequate authority to manage an appropriate security program. The position or function of the IA administrator, including duties and responsibilities, should be established in writing. The IA administrator should be located within the ADP facility organizational structure so that the IA administrator reports directly to the appropriate authority on matters concerning security of the sensitive processing system. Functions of the IA administrator should include:

- Serve as the single-point-of-contact for ADP security at the respective ADP facility
- Analyze or assist in analyzing the ADP environment and identify weaknesses, assess threats, and apply protections when needed
- Develop, maintain, and document security requirements and operating procedures
- Ensure that all personnel who install, operate, maintain, or use the ADP system know system security requirements and their responsibilities
- Establish methods for detecting, reporting, investigating, and resolving ADP security incidents
- Establish procedures for controlling changes to system hardware, software, applications, passwords, and central facility and terminal access
- Conduct or assist in conducting periodic audits of security procedures and controls

The IATP team should check that the IA administrator has been granted the appropriate authority and has the appropriate training to carry out the responsibilities.

Software Development Procedures

Software development procedures at the IAC may be inadequate to ensure that software is developed and controlled according to standards. Management should establish and publish a Configuration Management Plan that describes software development procedures and change procedures, and places explicit controls on the development and change processes. The plan should cover the areas of program design, coding, and documentation. Program design should include:

- Audit trails to establish a historical record of processing
- A thorough and comprehensive plan for program testing
- Controls on the accuracy of data, such as input verification, matching against legal values, control fields, and self-checking digits
- Quantitative controls, such as transaction counts, batch control totals, controls on rounding errors, reasonableness checks, and error suspense files

Program coding should include:

- Programmers organized in teams, making sure that no single programmer is responsible for an entire sensitive application system
- Structured naming conventions so that all references to a data element within an application are called by the same name
- Use of comments explaining accompanying code segments; these comments ease the task of program maintenance and help provide documentation
- Use of standardized indentation of source code to improve both readability and maintainability
- Use of a second programmer/analyst to inspect every program before it is compiled to ensure it conforms to standards, does not use restricted functions, and is logically complete

Program documentation should be standardized within the computer center and should contain:

- A functional description of the program written in a narrative form describing the initial definition of the program and any subsequent changes
- A program or subprogram section that contains information about the hardware environment, design elements, and interfaces
- A program specification section that describes the program inputs, outputs, functions performed, interdependences, and exception conditions
- A program manual section with flowcharts, source listings, cross-reference listings, test data used, and operating instructions; these standards may have to be adapted to individual facility needs

Software Maintenance Procedures

The procedures governing the maintenance of production computer software may have weaknesses that lead to a compromise of security. Management should establish and publish a Configuration Management Plan that describes the software maintenance procedures that place explicit controls on the maintenance process. Controls on the software maintenance procedures should include:

- An approved "Request for Change" required to initiate changes in production programs
- Program changes should be coded, tested, and documented in accordance with software development and acceptance procedures; these controls may have to be adapted to individual needs
- New software releases should be advertised in advance and properly identified by version or modification identifiers

Processing Procedures

The IAC may have inadequate procedures for the acceptance and release of data. Input/output procedures should be established that place explicit controls on the submission of input and receipt of output. The input/output procedures should:

- Require the system to log job requests when users request a sensitive production run
- Identify persons authorized to submit and pick up work from the sensitive processing computer facility
- Control housekeeping activities to maintain the flow of work through the ADP facility
- Provide all users with instructions for obtaining and returning tapes and disks to the magnetic media library
- Provide instructions to cover the signing of receipts on receiving sensitive material and obtaining a receipt for sensitive output

Access Procedures

Inadequate procedures for controlling access to the sensitive processing facility or site, media library, and supplies area may lead to disclosure, theft, fraud, modification, or destruction. Procedures should be established for controlling access to the sensitive processing facility, supply storage area, and other associated sites, such as remote terminal areas and backup sites. Methods for controlling access to the ADP facility may include:

- Access lists
- Escort procedures
- Identification badges
- Guards
- Mechanical or electronic door locks
- Prompt removal of transferred or terminated employees from access lists and the mandatory surrender of any facility identification or access keys or cards

Periodic inventories should be conducted of computer equipment and related supplies.

Waste Procedures

Existing procedures at the IAC may be inadequate for disposal of ADP waste material. Procedures should be established that clearly define the ADP waste materials that are to be disposed of in a secure manner and that provide the sensitive processing computer room with site(s) for secure disposal. These procedures should identify and provide destruction facilities for:

- Paper and paper products, including carbon paper
- Printer ribbons
- Magnetic tapes, disks, drums, memory, etc.
- Microfilm and microfiche.

Destruction facilities include incinerator, shredders, disintegrators, pulp machines, magnets, and tape degaussers.

Emergency Procedures

Security procedures for emergency situations may be inadequate, absent, or unenforceable at the IAC. Well-conceived and technically feasible emergency procedures should be established and tested periodically. Sources of advice for the development of these procedures include:

- Local fire and police department
- Local National Weather Service
- Buildings and grounds manager
- Overall ADP security manager

These procedures will normally:

- Provide for off-site storage of duplicate records and files
- Arrange for processing critical applications at other ADP facilities
- Identify materials to be evacuated or destroyed
- Designate a single-point-of-contact for developing emergency procedures
- Provide transportation in the case of emergency evacuation

Operating Procedures

The operating procedures may be inadequate and lead to disclosure, destruction, or modification of data, or a denial-of-service. Operating procedures should be established that clearly and explicitly state how the sensitive processing system will function on a day-to-day basis. Some of the points that these procedures should cover include:

- System start-up, shut down, and crashes
- Priority scheduling of production runs

- Computer operations personnel interface with users and programmers
- Separation of duties
- Rotation of duties

Personnel Controls

Poor management controls and policy can lead to lapses in security. The controls listed below provide various solutions, depending on the vulnerability:

- To prevent lapses in security, management should actively comply with security regulations and control procedures, and make sure that employees do the same. Training and indoctrination courses should be given regularly to employees.
- To prevent misuse or damage to the sensitive processing facility, screen all potential civilian and military employees for personal integrity, stability, and conscientiousness. Maintain close and effective communication with the staff to prevent employee dissatisfaction or to deal with complaints as they arise.
- To improve safety and security, periodically observe the work environment and work habits of employees. Observation will detect poor housekeeping habits that may increase the possibility of physical losses, such as magnetic paper clips or magnetic screwdrivers left near or set on tapes and disks, trash left in computer room, or coffee cups and soft drink cans left in computer rooms. Observation will also detect poor work habits that may compromise security, such as listings left unattended or files left open for unauthorized browsing.

Personnel Compromise

All personnel having system access (e.g., Development Office staff, users, contractors, and visitors) can represent a degree of weakness that could be exploited by a hacker or terrorist to compromise security. To reduce the weakness of a compromise of sensitive information, all personnel with unescorted access to the ADP facility should be required to have a security clearance. The level of clearance should be at least as high as the level of information being processed. Authorized persons should escort uncleared personnel, and sensitive information should be protected.

To reduce the risk of inadvertent damage by personnel, employ competent and well-trained personnel. Make clear the duties and obligations of employees.

Assets Accountability

Specific data producers, computer users, and computer center staff are assigned explicit ownership or custodial accountability and usage rights for all data, data handling and processing capability, controls, and computer programs. This can be done by establishing policy; establishing meaning of ownership, usage, and custodianship; and requiring that forms be completed and logs kept, designating and recording such accountability for data and programs, and copies of them in all locations and for specified times. For example, one organization has a set of booklets for each data activity area stating ownership, usage, custodial, and control requirements. Another organization has this information as part of its policy manual. Accountability for assets is basic to the organization's security. Accountability assignments also make clear who is responsible and accountable for each control and its effectiveness and overall adequacy of protection.

Classification of Data File and Program Name

Names for data files and computer programs are necessary for computer program development and documentation. They are also necessary for job setup and, in some cases, for computer operation. However, those people who are in a transaction relationship with the computer system and not concerned with programming of computer applications need not know file and program names. Therefore, a different set of terminology and naming of entities should be developed for documentation of users manuals and for transaction activities, especially those of a sensitive nature. The least-privilege or need-to-know principle significantly reduces the exposure of sensitive assets. Separation of duties should also include the separation of information.

Compliance with Laws and Regulations

A statement regarding the new or modified system's compliance with relevant laws and regulations should be provided in requirements and specifications. Direct quotes from laws and regulations regarding ADP security and privacy applying within a legal jurisdiction, or those that may apply, should be included. This provides management with increased assurance that an application system is in compliance with relevant laws and regulations, thereby reducing the chances that management liability and other sanctions might be applied. However, unless reviewed by a lawyer or some other knowledgeable person and assured by audit, control can become merely a perfunctory piece of paperwork where the blanks are filled in regardless of compliance with laws and regulations.

Labels

Sensitivity labels associated with each subject and storage object under its control (e.g., process, file, segment, device) should be maintained by the computer system. These labels should be used as the basis for mandatory access control decisions. In order to import nonlabeled data, the computer system should request and receive from an authorized user the security level of the data, and all such actions should be auditable by the computer system.

Classification Printed on Media

Sensitive and valuable documents have a classification (e.g., secret, confidential, For Official Use Only, Privacy Act, etc.) or an explicit warning indicating that the information is the property of a certain organization, that it should be handled according to special criteria, that it is not to be used for certain purposes, etc. One IAC chose to print "CONFIDENTIAL" in the middle of the page; although this made reading a bit more difficult, it prevented people from cropping and photocopying the record, removing any indication that it was confidential. Another approach is to have the computer print appropriate words on only sensitive output. This has the advantage of warning display terminal users that the information should be specially treated. Policies and procedures should also be written.

This control reduces ambiguity associated with the use and dissemination of sensitive information, provides concrete evidence that steps were taken to control information, and can be used to control use of proprietary software. Likelihood of privacy violation can to some extent be avoided or lessened. Use of copyright or trademark laws may reduce unauthorized distribution and usage of sensitive information.

Labeling Human-Readable Output

The ADP system administrator should be able to specify the printable label names associated with exported sensitivity labels. The computer system should mark the beginning and end of all human-readable, paged, hard copy output (e.g., line-printer output) with human-readable sensitivity labels that properly represent the overall sensitivity of the output or that properly represent the sensitivity of the information on that page. The computer system shall, by default and in an appropriate manner, mark other forms of human-readable output (e.g., maps, charts, graphics) with human-readable sensitivity labels that properly represent the sensitivity of the output. Any override of these marking defaults should be auditable by the computer system.

Data Classification Levels

Data may be sensitive at different security levels to produce cost savings and effectiveness of applying controls consistent with various levels of data sensitivity. Some organizations maintain the same level of security for all data, believing that making exceptions is too costly. Other organizations may have only small amounts of data of a highly sensitive nature and find that applying special controls to the small amount of data is cost-effective. When data are sensitive, they may be identified in two or more levels, often referred to as general information, confidential information, secret information, and other higher levels of classification named according to the functional use of the data, such as trade secret data, unreported financial performance, etc.

Separate security treatment of data at different levels of security can result in control cost savings when the volume and concentration of sensitive data warrant special treatment. Otherwise, savings can be achieved by reducing control exceptions.

Keeping Security Reports Confidential

Computer security requires the use and filing of numerous reports, including results of security reviews, audits, exception reports, documentation of loss incidence, documentation of controls, control installation and maintenance, and personnel information. These reports are extremely sensitive and should be protected to the same degree as the highest level of information classification within the organization. A clean desk policy should be maintained in the security and audit offices. All security documents should be physically locked in sturdy cabinets. Computer-readable files should be secured separately from other physically stored files and should have high-level access protection when stored in a computer. The security function in an organization sets an example for the rest of the organization by appropriately caring for confidential information.

Exportation of Labeled Information

The computer system should designate each communication channel and I/O device as either single- or multilevel. Any change in this designation should be done manually and should be auditable by the computer system. The computer system should maintain and be able to audit any change in the security level or levels associated with a communication channel or I/O device.

Courier Trustworthiness and Identification

Couriers are frequently used to distribute computer output reports to computer users. Couriers should be especially trustworthy, have a background investigation similar to that for computer operators, and be bonded. A new courier should be personally introduced to all those persons to whom he or she will be delivering computer output and to all persons from whom he will be receiving materials for delivery. Couriers should be required to use signed receipts for all transported reports. Couriers should be required to keep all reports in their personal possession in properly locked or controlled containers. All users should be informed immediately on the termination of any couriers delivering or picking up reports. Couriers should carry special identification to show that they are authorized to function in claimed capacities. Telephone calls in advance of delivery of highly sensitive reports should be made to recipients of those reports.

The IATP team would suggest that the IA administrator follow anyone picking up a sensitive batch run tape from the computer room. Their activities should be compared to receipt of tape at both pick-up and drop-off sites. In lieu of a contracted courier service, this procedure would also apply to employees from other organizations carrying a sensitive tape between sites.

Configuration Management

During development and maintenance of the computer system, a configuration management system should be in place that maintains control of changes to the descriptive top-level specifications, other design data, implementation documentation, source code, the running version of the object code, test fixtures, and documentation. The configuration management system should assure a consistent mapping among all documentation and code associated with the current version of the computer system. Tools should be provided for generation of a new version of the computer system from source code; also available should be tools for comparing a newly generated version with the previous version in order to ascertain that only the intended changes have been made in the code that will actually be used as a new version of the computer system.

Configuration Control

Poor security procedures may permit the system to be configured improperly. This could lead to the unintentional storing of sensitive data on nonsensitive devices or the sending of sensitive data to a remote terminal that should have been disconnected. Both hardware and software configuration management is necessary to permit reasonable and continual verification that the computer system functions as intended. Modular design provides a means of isolating the security features to a large extent, thus minimizing the number of interactions between them and other operations. Establishing a system of configuration control affords the methodology for thorough analysis and testing of any system changes before implementation, which is advisable to protect against undesirable effects on the system's security. After the system is operational, configuration control of both hardware and software serves to verify that undetected changes have not taken place.

The IATP team would suggest that the IA administrator check to see that a configuration control checklist has been established. This checklist should contain detailed procedures for connecting the individual sensitive processing system components together into the specific system configuration to be employed during each period. These procedures include setting all hardware switches, powering up and down of each device, loading the standard software and firmware for the configuration system, system operating procedures, and shut-down and restart procedures. Strict adherence to the established procedures is essential for overall system security. To ensure that the procedures are followed, it is desirable that two people verify the new configuration.

The cost of developing a configuration control checklist is principally administrative. The cost of following this checklist is the time for the console operator and another person to verify the actual configuration against the checklist.

Computer Program Quality Assurance

A testing or quality control group should independently test and examine computer programs and related documentation to ensure the integrity of program products before production use. This activity is best authorized by software development management or by the quality assurance or test department. Excessively formal program development standards should be avoided. Basic life-cycle procedures should be established before more elaborate practices are required. However, compliance with the established standards and procedures should be strongly enforced. A consistent compliance with good controls design offsets computer programmers' resistance to independent observation of their work. The IATP team would suggest that the IA administrator independently test and examine computer programs and related documentation to ensure their integrity.

Responsibilities for Application Program Controls

The inclusion of controls in application programs should be explicitly ensured and documented, beginning with design requirements and continuing through specifications development, production, and maintenance stages. The responsibility for adequacy and types of controls should be shared among EDP auditors, systems analysts, computer programmers, users, and data owners. Explicit documentation of controls is essential to ensure completion of their implementation and testing. Operational procedures should be developed to carry out the intent of the controls, and to ensure their integrity during system change and maintenance.

It is difficult to explicitly document all application program controls. However, establishing procedures to ensure that controls are adequate and included in applications provides assurance that applications will be adequately controlled.

The IA administrator should monitor auditors' participation in design requirements and post-implementation testing for compliance with specifications.

Vendor-Supplied Program Integrity

To the greatest extent possible and practical, vendor-supplied computer programs should be used without modification. Many new vendor-supplied computer programs have been developed with controls and integrity built into them. Any modifications to these programs could compromise the built-in capabilities. Desired changes to the programs should be obtained from the vendor as standard program updates. This control is a means of preserving the security and integrity built into vendor-supplied computer programs. It is also a means of holding vendors responsible for any deficiencies in the programs.

The IATP team would suggest that the IA administrator check to see if this control will reduce the frequency of changes to computer programs, facilitating direct code comparison of production programs with master backup copies. This should be done periodically to ensure that management policy is followed in restricting modification of vendor-supplied computer programs.

Confirmation of Receipt of Media

The confirmation process consists of verification of receipt of documents. Confirmations of delivery can be made by obtaining master files of names of input/output documents and their addressees, performing a selection of a sample of addressees by running the master file on a computer separate from the production computer or at least at a time different from normal production work. Confirmation notices and copies of the documents are then sent to the addressees to confirm that the documents are correct and that they received the documents as expected. Confirmation of smaller volumes of documents can be easily done on a manual basis. Receipt forms are used by recipients of particularly sensitive documents and returned to the sender to confirm correct report distribution and encourage accountability.

This control is used as an audit tool. The IATP team would suggest that the IA administrator review the number and nature of confirmation-related activities for cost and benefits. The IA administrator should also sample receipts and sensitive report deliveries to confirm correct procedures.

Correction and Maintenance of Production Run

In spite of implementation and strict enforcement of security controls and good maintenance of application and systems programs, emergencies arise that require violation or overriding of many of these controls and practices. Occasionally, production programs will fail during production runs on the computer. This may happen on second and third shift, during periods of heavy production computer activity. If a failure occurs in a critical application production run, it is frequently necessary to call on knowledgeable programmers to discover the problem, make a change in the production computer program, make changes in input data, or make decisions about alternative solutions (e.g., reruns using previous versions of the production program). When such emergency events occur, all necessary and expedient measures should be taken, including physical access of programmers to computer and production areas, access by such programmers to data files and production programs, correction of production programs, and *ad hoc* instructions to operations staff.

During any of these activities, it is necessary for a trusted individual in computer application production work to record all of the events as they occur or shortly thereafter. Following the termination of the emergency, programmers should be required to make the necessary permanent changes that may have been made on a temporary basis during the emergency and document the emergency actions. This usually requires updating and testing production programs and the normal process of introducing tested and updated programs for production use.

After an emergency and before permanent corrections have been made, the production application program should be treated in a "suspicious" mode of operation, requiring increased levels of observance by users, production staff managers, and possibly ADP auditors. These extra efforts should continue until confidence has been built up in the production activities through acceptable experience.

The IATP team would suggest that the IA administrator create a theoretical situation in which an emergency override will take place. The IA administrator should oversee the emergency procedures and production work that should take place in patching a sensitive computer program.

Limited Use of System Utility Programs

Most computer installations have one or more system utility programs capable of overriding all or most computer system and application controls. In some IACs, one such computer program used is called Superzap. In one large IAC previously studied by the authors, five such utility programs were found. These programs should be controlled by password or kept physically removed from the computer system and the program library, and physically controlled so that they are available only to a limited number of authorized users.

Occasionally, if the programs are made available online, they can be protected by special passwords required for their use. Changing the name or password frequently is another way to better safeguard these online programs. Limitations of availability of system utility programs forces programmers to use more-accepted means of accomplishing their purposes that can be safely done under the controls of the system.

Tape and Disk Management

A tape and disk management system can be used to keep track of all tapes and disks using a serial number appearing on the tape reel or disk. Serial numbers may contain storage rack location information as well as an identification number. Operators handling the tapes or disks do not know the contents of the tapes, because the identity of the data set owner, creation and update dates, data set names, and similar information is recorded only on internal (machine-readable) labels. The software package for managing tapes and disks contains an index of serial numbers and the corresponding label information. An up-to-date copy of the index, relating serial numbers and tape and disk information, is maintained at an off-site storage location.

This control provides operators with no more information than is necessary to do their jobs, thus preventing potential abusive acts that were made possible because these data were available to the operators. Operators are presented only with a request to mount or dismount certain tapes based on provided serial numbers. Disks should always be secured. A tape and disk management system can be used to monitor operator performance as well as to control the tape library. Persons in the tape library or machine room cannot learn the nature of the data on a tape simply by examining the reel. Disks can be kept in off-site storage using proper security methodology.

The IATP team would suggest that the IA administrator trace the steps taken to obtain a tape from the Magnetic Media Library, mount and dismount the tape reel, etc., from initiation of a request to actual performance of the operator to return of the tape to Magnetic Media Library. The IA administrator should also examine the data available to the operator to determine if confidentiality is not lessened by unwarranted exposure. The IA administrator should also inspect the storage of disks at the sites.

Contingency Recovery Equipment Replacement

Sensitive processing commitments should be obtained in writing from computer equipment and supplies vendors to replace critical equipment and supplies within a specified period of time following a contingency loss. Some vendors will commit to replacement of their products within a reasonable period of time and will specify that period of time as a commitment. For example, in one computer installation a vendor agreed to replace a central processor within five days and a second processor, if necessary, within ten days. The paper-forms supplier agreed to deliver a two-week supply of all special forms in the same timeframe. In contrast, other vendors would not guarantee replacement times, but would only indicate that best efforts would be provided. This usually means that the next-available equipment within the vendor company inventory would be provided with a priority over other normal product deliveries. Emergency ordering procedures should be established as part of a contingency recovery plan. Vendor commitments provide a means of planning alternative data processing until equipment and new computing capabilities have been restored.

The IATP team would suggest that the IA administrator confirm the validity of agreements to be sure that they are still in effect. Commitment periods should be checked relative to disaster recovery plans with regional offices, etc.

Minimizing Copies of Sensitive Data Files and Reports

The number of copies of sensitive tape, disk, or paper files should be minimized. Destruction dates should be specified and instructions followed. It may be advisable to destroy most paper copies of files on the basis that the information can be retrieved and reprinted from computer media when necessary. This is based on the concept that files stored in computer systems and computer media are generally more secure than on paper. Normal backup procedures often require that several copies of computer media files be made and stored at different sites. However, some files may be so sensitive that numerous copies in different locations may contribute to their exposure. As many as 20 to 30 copies of computer-stored files may be produced in a single year in a large computer installation. The organization primarily accountable for highly sensitive information should have control and logs of all copies and their locations. Adequate backup should be balanced with the exposure danger of multiple copies and backup procedures.

The IATP team would suggest that the IA administrator make a selective examination of storage areas, looking for sensitive records and comparing them to others for possible duplication.

Automation of Computer Operations

Computer operations should be made as automatic as possible, using such capabilities as production, program and test program libraries, automatic tape library management, and computer operator activity logging. This reduction of manual procedures generally results in improved control of computer operations activities. Reduction of staff reduces exposure to accidental or intentionally caused loss, and provides motivation to use automated operations packages beyond other considerations of cost effectiveness.

Disaster Recovery Planning, Testing and Evaluating

Contingency and Recovery Funds

The IAC should be assured of readily available emergency funds for contingencies and recovery from terrorist or hacker attacks. Leasing equipment, which will be replaced by the vendor if damaged or otherwise lost, may not be the only solution. The IATP team would suggest that the IA administrator determine what funds can be made available if needed and what equipment hardware, software, etc., is owned rather than leased by the IA administrator's organization.

Data File and Program Backup

The current form of every data file that may be needed in the future should be copied at the time of its creation, and the copy should be stored at a remote, safe location for operational recovery purposes. It may be advisable to store several copies, one immediately available in the computer center, another available some short distance away, and a third archived at some remote distance for longer-term storage. Periodically updated data files should be cycled from the immediate site to the local site to the remote site by data file generations (father, grandfather, etc.). In addition, copies of the computer programs necessary to process the backed-up data files, documentation of the programs, computer operation instructions, and a supply of special printed forms necessary for production running of the programs should also be stored at a remote, safe location. This hierarchical arrangement of backup data files provides for convenient restarting of production runs in case of damaged or missing files; more serious problems that could result in loss of local backup data files can be resolved by using copies of remote backup data files. When a backup file is returned to the computer center for use, there should be assurance that it is also backed up safely with another copy.

Defensive depth of backup provides significant increase in assurance of recovery that addresses small as well as large contingencies. Recovery from backup files is commonly done under abnormal conditions that usually accompany recovery efforts. These conditions increase the likelihood of loss of the backup files. Therefore, it is important to have at least secondary backup in addition to primary backup files. The IATP team would suggest that the IA administrator insist on an actual demonstration of recovery from the backup level. Inspection of backup sites should also be conducted to ensure their secure status.

Disaster Recovery

The IAC and remote sensitive processing sites should have a written disaster recovery plan and a recovery management team. Primary and backup managers should be assigned specific responsibilities for each aspect of recovery from all types of partial or complete disasters. Each aspect of the disaster recovery plan should have assigned a specific individual responsible for its execution. Separate individuals should be assigned to coordination, systems support, hardware recovery, facilities, administration, scheduling, communications, documentation and supplies, backup data files and security recovery funding, personnel, historical, and recording of events. Priority processing needs of all time-dependent applications to be recovered after a disaster should be identified. This requires that all computer users (or someone acting on behalf of the users) specify the importance of their computer applications, processing requirements, alternative means of processing, and consequences of failure to process. Data processing management is responsible for meeting the critical needs of computer users in the best interests of the organization. Priorities will assist in the scheduling of processing when it is restored.

A designated person should provide liaison with users, informing them of special needs and the status of processing of their work. A detailed history of the recovery process should be documented and recovery activity verbally reported during the recovery process. After recovery, the historical documentation should be analyzed to determine how future contingencies might be better handled and to handle insurance claims recovery and any litigation that may follow a disaster. Every job function should be analyzed relative to its performance during and prior to a disaster. Measures of criticality and priority of functions should be determined and documented in the plan.

Flexibility in plans facilitates meeting a wide range of contingencies. A documented recovery plan provides for a means of practicing and testing all recovery procedures. Potential hacker or terrorist threats that can provide a means of adding controls to reduce risk may be identified. Prioritizing applications provides users with perspective on the importance of better applications recovery needs. Application of limited data processing resources can be more effectively planned. Communication among recovery managers helps ensure smooth and minimum cost recovery. Documentation of recovery activities encourages responsibilities and accountability among managers and workers. Job function analysis facilitates management's quick mobilization of critical personnel and resources in the event of a disaster. Management can more easily and effectively assign work to employees during recovery. A disaster plan reduces the likelihood of confusion. Use of a disaster recovery contact list provides for speedy notification of vendors, suppliers, and customers who can take appropriate action to assist or reduce loss.

The IATP team would suggest that the IA administrator study all organizational disaster recovery plans to ensure that they are current. Proof of testing plans should be documented and reported. Scenarios of possible terrorist and hacker actions should be generated and theoretically played against the disaster recovery plans to ensure their adequacy. Application priorities should be verified through the IA administrator for the audit of specific functions of an organization dependent on computer services. Examination of historical documentation recovery experience should be performed to note any changes necessary in disaster recovery planning for the future.

Electrical Equipment Protection

Every item of computing equipment that is separately powered should have a separate circuit breaker in the electrical supply for that equipment. Alternatively, equipment may be supplied with other protective mechanisms from power failures or other electrical anomalies. Circuit breakers should be clearly labeled for manual activation. The locations of all circuit breakers should be documented and available in disaster and recovery plans.

Individual devices can fail and be switched off without having to cut power to other devices. Failures can be localized as well as more readily detected. Device configurations can be changed more readily, avoiding excessive time in diagnosing electrical problems and reconfiguring electrical systems to suit new equipment setups.

Electrical Power Shut Down and Recovery

Emergency master power-off switches should be located next to each emergency exit doors. The switches should be clearly identified, and easily read signs should be posted, giving instructions for use of the switches. Activation of any of these switches should be followed with reports documenting the circumstances and persons responsible for their use. Alternative power supplies should be available when data processing needs justify continuous operations, and they should be tested on a periodic basis. The power supply should be used during the test for a sufficiently long period of time to ensure sustained operation under emergency conditions.

Easily identified power-off switches are valuable for firemen, rescue workers, and others in the event of emergencies. Testing facilitates preventive maintenance work and familiarizes staff with emergency procedures. Redundancies in alternative power supplies increase assurance of emergency recoveries.

Security Awareness and Training

Security Training

Security training is of the utmost importance if only to remind personnel that they are handling sensitive data, etc. In compliance with the Computer Security

Act of 1987 [PL 100–235], the IATP team may well find that the IAC has provided the required mandatory security awareness and training, covering technical, administrative, personnel, and physical security areas.

Security Administrator

An organization has sufficient computer security resources to justify an individual as a full-time IA administrator. The IA administrator should ideally report to the overall security department covering the entire organization. This provides proper scope of responsibility for information and its movement throughout the organization. For practical purposes, the IA administrator often functions within the computer department. Job descriptions are highly variable; examples may be obtained from many organizations with established computer security officers. An IA administrator provides a focus for the formal development of a computer security program.

Communications Security

Communication Lines and Links

It is possible to tap or monitor surreptitiously a data communications line or link. Any data passed along the communications lines or links are susceptible to hostile interception or manipulation. Transmissions and communications lines and links between components of the system should be secured at a level appropriate for the material to be transmitted. In the case of sensitive material, the protections for secure communications lines or links can be found as guides published by the Department of Defense. One such publication is DoD Military Handbook #232 on Red/Black criteria of communications lines and links. Approved cryptography can also be used to protect information against a variety of threats. For secure electrical transmission of unencrypted information, when relatively short distances and controlled areas are involved, a Protected Distribution System (PDS) may be used as an alternative to cryptography. For sensitive information or Privacy Act data, secure transmission is not mandated. However, some form of security should be provided during transmission, especially for sensitive business data.

Microcomputer Security

Hardware Concerns

The IATP team, before reviewing the data and software security issues surrounding microcomputers and terminals linked to networks, should review the hardware concerns of physical access, potential for theft, environmental damage, lack of magnetic media protection, and the lack of built-in security mechanisms common with the microcomputer environment.

The IATP team may find that access to microcomputers is normally limited to authorized users. While evidence will probably exist that untrained individuals or malicious acts may have damaged a small percentage of terminals, the necessary precautions should be in force.

The IATP team will probably find some high-value computer items to be unaccountable. While short of inspecting everything that leaves the building, it is suggested that rooms are secured at the end of the working day and that lock-down devices are installed to secure the terminals to a table or desk.

Microcomputers are handled more than the automated equipment in the IAC and are thus more susceptible to damage. They are sensitive to the quality of electrical power and it is suggested that surge protectors are used; also, while a site may not know the electrical line configuration in the building, it is recommended that microcomputers are not plugged into the same electrical box that is also providing power to the coffee maker, refrigerator, or other heavy electrical-use appliances.

The other potential for environmental damage is static electricity. It is suggested that an antistatic spray is used to minimize this danger.

Particular attention should be given to the protection of magnetic media, whether floppy disks or internal rigid disks. The IA administrator should post a sign or otherwise publicize the fact that disks need to be handled with care, always stored in their protective jackets, protected from bending, stored within an acceptable temperature range, etc.

Finally, a major security weakness of microcomputers is that they lack built-in hardware security mechanisms, such as memory protection features, multiple processor states, or privileged instructions. It is virtually impossible to prevent users from accessing the operating system, thereby circumventing any intended security mechanisms. For example, any user could reformat the hard disk on the C drive by mistake. It is suggested that certain functions be removed from the operating system and that these functions be delegated to a central point within the organization.

Data Concerns

The information processed and stored at the microcomputer level is more easily accessed (potentially by unauthorized users) than that found on larger systems. The IATP team should look at labeling, the security of data media, data corruption, and data transmission.

Sensitive data resources must be clearly labeled. Sensitive data, especially those that could qualify for the agency-sensitive or Privacy Act label, should not be allowed to reside on the hard disk. All floppy disks should be labeled to indicate the sensitivity of the data on the disk. These floppy disks should be placed in a secure container or locking desk (if the user has the only key to the desk lock). Locking the disks in a diskette box is of no value as the entire box can be removed from the area; also important is the daily use of backups of all important and sensitive data and their storage.

Because of the lack of hardware security features, the IATP team should insist that microcomputers cannot be trusted to prevent the corruption of data. For example, while in a sensitive Word document you decide to "Copy and Paste" a sensitive paragraph within the file; you then save that document and bring up another Word file that is not sensitive in nature. By using the Paste command again, you can duplicate the sensitive data left in memory from the previous file. Your nonsensitive file is now corrupted and now actually contains sensitive data. You may wish to delete that file from the floppy or hard disk; however, few users realize that deleting the file only removes the file name pointer and not the data. By using a software utilities package such as Norton Utilities, you can recall the file by just following the menu in the program.

Finally, transferring data to or from a mainframe environment should be carefully controlled and monitored. The microcomputer user must be held accountable for ensuring that sensitive data is transferred only to other computers designated to receive sensitive data. For example, a sensitive report can be sent to everyone on the message handling address database if the person sending the file does not know how to send the message. If there is a question, the user should not proceed.

Software Concerns

Operating systems cannot be trusted because certain functions do not work as reasonably expected. For example, as mentioned earlier, certain commands do not actually erase files; they merely release the file space, leaving the data intact. The IATP team would suggest that some type of user identification is used and that the IA administrator make users aware of potential damage to their system due to software attacks, such as trap doors, Trojan horses, worms, and viruses.

Certification

It would always be highly suggested by the IATP team that a certification process begin and continue to be maintained by those ultimately responsible for the handling and security of the sensitive data. The certification begins when an ADP Security Handbook has been published and distributed. Included in the certification process is a workable disaster recovery plan, an up-to-date risk assessment of the sites handling sensitive data, and other security items of interest (follow NIST Special Publication 800–18 [NIST, 1998]).

Computer Security Management Committee

A high-level management committee should be organized to develop security policies and oversee all security of information-handling activities. The committee should be composed of management representatives from each part of the organization concerned with information processing. The committee would be responsible for coordinating computer security matters, reviewing the state of system security, ensuring the visibility of management's support of computer security throughout the organization, approving computer security reviews, receiving and accepting computer security review reports, and ensuring proper control interfaces among organization functions. Computer security reviews and recommendations for major controls should be made to and approved by this committee.

The committee ensures that privacy and security are part of the overall information-handling plan. The steering committee may be part of a larger activity within an organization having responsibility for the function of information resource management. For example, in one research and development organization an oversight council was established, made up of representatives from organizations that send and receive databases to and from the R&D organization. The council was charged with oversight responsibilities for the conduct and control of the R&D organization relative to the exchange of databases. Especially important are questions of individual privacy concerning the content of the databases. The objective is to prevent the loss of security support that could result from ineffective handling of sensitive information.

A steering committee visibly shows top management's dedication and support for security issues to the entire organization. Security activity is organized on a top-down basis. A committee that crosses organizational lines can better ensure the consistency of security across the interfaces and the consistency of attention to security in all information-processing related functions. The steering committee can consider security and privacy within the context of other issues confronting the organization. Policies and procedures can be more effectively enforced. The committee approach can avoid the control of computer security by technologists who tend to be limited to technical solutions to security problems.

Concluding Remarks

Plan the tests and test the plans. The IATP needs to identify those functions critical to processing and the resources that are needed to accomplish those functions. The IATP must allocate sufficient time to assess, protect, validate, train, monitor, manage and test — in essence, implement a service-oriented life-cycle approach to protecting the data. This life-cycle approach is introduced in the next chapter. Above all, remain dynamic and flexible.

Chapter 9

Information Assurance Life-Cycle Support and Operational Considerations

Anything that can go wrong will go wrong at the worst possible moment.

Murphy's Law

The purpose of this chapter is to acknowledge that the development and implementation of an information assurance (IA) life-cycle methodology can be the most demonstrable indicator of support toward an aggressive, proactive approach to secure critical information and infrastructure. By incorporating "Best Practices" from industry and global government initiatives, the IA life-cycle methodology becomes a complete solution. A comprehensive life-cycle strategy should accommodate a full range of information systems security needs — assessment, protection (implementation), validation, training, and monitoring and management. We believe that a life-cycle, service-oriented approach that is supported by the best security technologies available is the proper approach to protecting critical information and infrastructures.

The fundamental principle of the IA life-cycle methodology requires that security measures must be implemented with the intent of providing long-term, continuous protection. The logic is simple: even if an organization's infrastructure is secure today, it may not be tomorrow. New risks and vulnerabilities are introduced at an alarming rate, and new technologies are being developed and implemented just as fast. New hardware and software platforms are constantly being installed; new business features, functions, and capabilities are being created, etc. More ominously, the skill, sophistication, and motivation of system hackers seem to be increasing proportionally. The critical challenge, then, is to keep IT configurations current and to do it on a continuing basis.

The IA life cycle is a framework best represented by a series of five basic operational phases that protect critical assets. The protection is accomplished by establishing a defensive perimeter around them. Each phase is a precursor to or continuation of every other phase in the life cycle, forming a secure barrier that offers uninterrupted protection as systems grow and evolve.

At the core of this protective perimeter is the security architecture, surrounded closely by security policies and procedures, and any other security measures that make up an actual security posture. Therein lies the critical data that the IA staff becomes responsible for protecting.

The Information Assurance Life-Cycle Methodology

Phase 1: Assess

Assessing an organization's current security posture is generally the first phase in resolving the myriad complex information assurance issues facing it today. The question, put bluntly, is not whether information system resources and business-critical assets will be compromised, but when. Far too many organizations have little notion of the risks their information infrastructures face, the value of the information systems themselves, or the value of their intellectual capital and data. Most organizations confront these issues only when sifting through the debris left behind following a disastrous breach in what was supposed to be a secure system, or following the misappropriation of critical assets.

Information assurance assessment establishes the baseline that is the current state of information assurance within an organization. Using this baseline as a starting point, the IA staff can help its organization develop strategic and tactical security objectives that evolve along with the organization. The assessment process evaluates the security of an organization (both physical and logical), identifies assets to be protected and security vulnerabilities, and then recommends protective options for eliminating or mitigating security risks.

The complex information assurance issues in open networks (e.g., the Internet) and wide area networks (WANs), as well as on closed corporate and enterprise networks, is a reality in today's IT environment. Under such conditions, the IA staff becomes responsible for meeting the information assurance needs in communications, protecting intellectual property, safeguarding financial transactions, and having reliable business-to-business activity.

The optimal life-cycle strategy begins with an assessment from multiple perspectives, ranging from physical security, to the configuration of the firewalls, to the reliability of personnel. Information assurance remains cohesive throughout the life cycle. It takes a system perspective to ensure that any new partial solutions remain compatible with the remainder of the system. Clients, servers, databases, infrastructure protocols and links, router and firewall configurations, policies, and procedures all have their individual issues, as well as an impact on the overall level of trust placed on information assurance.

Assessing the risks inherent in each must be done in the context of the information assurance policy and objectives. Topics typically covered in an assessment include:

- Physical network architecture
- Onsite review of operations and physical security
- Network description (functions, topology, and components)
- Network services and protocols
- Audit trails logging, alarms, and intrusion detection
- Firewall, clients, servers, routers, bridges
- Internal and external connections
- Information security standards, procedures, and policies
- Procedures, responsibilities, tasks, and authorizations
- Management network infrastructure
- Management access
- Management functions (e.g., change control, problem, security)

Phase 2: Protect

Once the risks and the protective measures for mitigating them have been identified, the natural second phase is to implement the mechanisms needed to secure at-risk information assets in an organization's information infrastructure.

With 62 percent of Americans believing that not enough is being done to protect Internet consumers against cyber crime,* winning customer confidence becomes one of the keys to a successful E-business implementation. Organizations must clearly demonstrate their efforts to protect their information systems environment from a breakdown in accountability, privacy, confidentiality, availability, and data integrity.

Preventing unauthorized access to information assets, protecting against intentional or accidental damage (especially as the use of information technology grows among nontechnical users), creating systems that are easy to use, and maintaining a protective shield around those systems requires a sure, methodical approach that addresses forward-thinking strategies, as well as current goals. Information assurance protection provides enhanced levels of total system security by implementing advanced security technologies using field-proven secure system engineering methodology. Public key infrastructure (PKI) technologies identify and authenticate users over the Internet, intranets, or extranets. Privacy and data integrity are achieved using encryption technologies and hashing algorithms. Digital signatures (now as binding in court as inked ones) provide the basis for nonrepudiation. Access control allows only trusted users to view confidential data. Smart cards, tokens, and biometrics facilitate the positive identification of users so they can be quickly and automatically routed to the information they require.

---

* Results from a nationwide poll released in July 2000 by the Information Technology Association of America (ITAA) and EDS, Inc.

The principal task accomplished during this phase of the life cycle is the implementation of solid architectures, plans, and policies for integrating robust security practices enterprisewide that ensure maximum levels of security and productivity.

Phase 3: Validate

The third phase in securing an organization's information systems and infrastructure is to validate that the security mechanisms put in place during the protection phase do indeed adequately address security policy and the risks and vulnerabilities identified during the assessment phase. How? By comparing the results of the protection phase against the original requirements, exposures, and vulnerabilities identified in the assessment phase, as well as against any intervening changes in requirements or in the IT environment.

Validation should always be done following the implementation of any new protective measure, whether the measure is as simple as the installation of a new firewall or as complicated as developing and testing a new organizational security policy. Indeed, continual reverification of an organization's security posture is one of the requirements for reaccreditation if you need industry or government security-level certifications.

Information assurance validation consists of a set of standardized capabilities and processes that help determine the suitability of a system for a given operational environment. These capabilities help reduce fraud, mission failures, and embarrassing information and data leaks while increasing overall information system assurance. The defined processes provide standardization for the acquisitions, operations, and sustainability of IT systems that collect, store, transmit, or process information.

It is essential for organizations to look at information systems validation as a business necessity — a tool for ensuring customer, vendor, and employee confidence. Information assurance validation provides a high degree of certainty that the IT systems will operate within an acceptable risk environment. As appropriate, the information systems infrastructure is periodically retested to determine how well products, applications, policies, and procedures are functioning in accordance with a given standard — defined at the government, industry, or corporation level — and reassessed to determine the impact of any new threats.

These validations target existing technologies, as well as emerging ones. System, plan, and procedure reviews are conducted to verify that all components are operating within established parameters and that contingencies are addressed and newly implemented technologies are appropriately configured.

Phase 4: Train

An information assurance security program is only as effective as the people implementing, managing, and using it. It is essential that an organization have a clear and concise understanding of the relationships between specific protection requirements, people, and their roles and responsibilities. The overall success of the tactical and strategic programs that protect critical information assets is, in the end, dependent on the knowledge, skill, and responsiveness of employees.

Information assurance training, the fourth phase in this life-cycle model, ensures that organizational support personnel are appropriately trained and skilled in all IA service areas. In short, that they have acquired the precise technical expertise necessary for an organization's protective security measures to achieve optimum results. The training phase also provides more-generalized security awareness training for employees and management to help them understand the importance of maintaining a rigorous defensive perimeter, as well as more advanced and more difficult-to-find training for IA professionals. Industry-recognized certifications are offered through the following information assurance programs.

Certified Information Systems Security Professional (CISSP)

The certification is from the International Information Systems Security Certification Consortium, or (ISC)² (www.isc2.org). In effect, the CISSP designation is to security people what CPA is to accountants. CISSP certification is achieved by passing a CISSP examination composed of 250 multiple-choice questions. The (ISC)² bases the exam questions on what they term the CBK (common body of knowledge). It is the opinion of (ISC)² that an accomplished and experienced security professional should have a foundation in all 10 areas of the CBK:

1. Access Control Systems and Methodology
2. Telecommunications and Networking Security
3. Security Management Practices
4. Application and Systems Development Security
5. Cryptography
6. Security Architecture and Models
7. Operations Security
8. Business Continuity and Disaster Recovery Planning
9. Law, Investigation, and Ethics
10. Physical Security

The test is not easy. In no more than six hours, you have to achieve no less than 70 percent of the questions correct. It costs $395. But that is not the end of the certification process. (ISC)² requires those who have successfully received certification to recertify at intermittent intervals through continuing education and practical career experience. A CISSP can only maintain certification by earning 120 CPE (Continuing Professional Education) credits over a three-year recertification period. Two thirds (80 CPEs) must be earned in activities directly related to the information systems security profession and up to one third (40 CPEs) may be earned in other educational activities that enhance the CISSP's overall professional skills, knowledge, and competency. For those who do not want to or cannot obtain the 120 CPEs, they must retake and pass the exam every three years. Moreover, to become a CISSP, you must subscribe to the (ISC)² Code of Ethics, and have three years of direct work experience in the field.

Certified Protection Professional

For years, the world has recognized a need for competent professionals who can effectively manage complex security issues that threaten people and the assets of corporations, governments, and public and private institutions. As the emphasis on protecting people, property, and information increases, it has strengthened the demand for professional managers. To meet these needs, the American Society for Industrial Security (www.asisonline.org) administers the Certified Protection Professional (CPP) program. More than 9,000 professionals have earned the designation of CPP. This group of professionals has demonstrated its competency in the areas of security solutions and best business practices through an intensive qualification and testing program. As a result, these men and women have been awarded the coveted designation of CPP, and are recognized as proven leaders in their profession.

Certified Information Systems Auditor

With more than 23,000 members in 100+ countries, the Information Systems Audit and Control Association (www.isaca.org) is a recognized global leader in IT governance, control, and assurance. Founded in 1969, ISACA sponsors international conferences, administers the globally respected CISA (Certified Information Systems Auditor) designation earned by more than 26,000 professionals worldwide, and develops globally applicable information systems auditing and control standards. An affiliated foundation undertakes the leading-edge research in support of the profession. The IT Governance Institute, established by the association and foundation in 1998, offers symposia, original research, and presentations at both ISACA and non-ISACA conferences, and electronic resources to assist enterprise leaders in their responsibility to make IT successful in supporting the enterprise's mission and goals. To earn and retain the CISA designation, CISAs are required to:

- Successfully complete the CISA examination
- Adhere to the Information Systems Audit and Control Association's Code of Professional Ethics
- Submit evidence of a minimum of five years of professional information systems auditing, control, or security work experience (substitution and waivers of such experience applies)
- Adhere to a continuing education program

Business Continuity Professional Certifications

DRI International's (DRII) world-renowned professional certification program acknowledges an individual's effort to achieve a professional level of competence in the industry. Designed to be rigorous, well controlled, and free of bias, the program is centered on the "Professional Practices for Business Continuity Planners," the international industry standard.

Certified Business Continuity Professional

DRII's Certified Business Continuity Professional (CBCP) certification is reserved for individuals who have demonstrated their knowledge and experience in the business continuity/disaster recovery industry. The CBCP level is designed for an individual with a minimum of two years of experience as a business continuity/disaster recovery planner.

Associate Business Continuity Planner

The Associate Business Continuity Planner (ABCP) or Associate level is for individuals with at least a specified minimum level of knowledge in business continuity/disaster recovery planning, but who have not yet attained the two years of experience required for CBCP. Individuals can also qualify if they work in positions related to but not actually in business continuity/disaster recovery planning.

Master Business Continuity Professional

The Master Business Continuity Professional (MBCP) or Master level, targets an individual with a minimum of five years of experience as a business continuity/disaster recovery planner. In addition, the MBCP must attain a higher score on the CBCP examination, and either successfully complete a case-study examination or complete a directed research project and paper.

An additional prerequisite for the CBCP and MBCP certification levels is the demonstration of proficiency in a specific number of subject areas of the Professional Practices for Business Continuity Planners. For more information, see the Disaster Recovery Institute International Web site at http://www.dr.org.

Phase 5: Monitor and Manage

The fifth phase in the information assurance life cycle addresses the need for constant, active vigilance at the defensive perimeter, including security policies, practices, procedures, and processes, as well as disaster recovery and business continuity plans.

The broad adoption of the new communications media, new ways of doing business, the Internet, and E-commerce presents both traditional brick-and-mortar and new click-away enterprises with some thorny challenges. Never before have business opportunities grown so quickly, offering so many rich services to such a broad market. Government, finance, transportation, education, health care — virtually every sector in the global business community is heavily influenced by the possibilities of worldwide distribution and dissemination of information. Organizations with high-volume/high-value, business-critical E-commerce requirements and an Internet presence are faced with the very real possibility of lost revenue, lost opportunity, and ultimately, lost customers if they cannot ensure the availability, performance, privacy, confidentiality, and integrity of their new globally visible Web-based infrastructures and applications.

Information assurance monitoring and management services facilitates continued, secure electronic business over the Internet, intranets, extranets, and virtual private networks. It provides a layered, defense-in-depth strategy to adequately secure, monitor, protect, and manage an organization's critical business environment, including intrusion detection and response. The capabilities within this service assist in controlling the major security threats faced by today's digital enterprises, providing proactive as well as reactive network operations center services 24 hours a day, 365 days a year.

Concluding Remarks: The Information Assurance Life-Cycle Methodology

Cycling just once through the five-step life cycle model, though, isn't enough. Change is happening at a rapid rate — in any organization, in technology, in the economy — and with each new change comes a new set of security challenges that must be assessed, protected against, validated, trained for, and monitored. The life-cycle approach must be rigorous, repeatable, and measurable. The IA staff must be able to get the continual assurance it needs that the business applications, systems, and critical data are secure when accessed or deployed any time, anywhere.

The IA staff may also be responsible for building security into IT solutions based on a system life-cycle methodology that integrates security requirements into each phase of the system's development life cycle. Integrating security into the development and maintenance of business applications is more than just another good business strategy. It becomes an imperative. Integrated security mechanisms result in a higher level of cost-effective security. One must realize that the right amount of security must be integrated into business applications from the outset. This further reduces costs typically associated with "grafting" security features onto an existing business system after the fact.

Unlike many niche solutions, a rigorous, repeatable, and measurable process such as an information assurance life-cycle process would be standardized and far-reaching, embracing a wide variety of security products, systems, and mechanisms. A comprehensive life-cycle information assurance solution must be based on proven, industry-leading processes.

While the opportunities and rewards are great, potential security hazards lurk at every juncture, every interface, every portal. Establishing and maintaining effective policies that address the security, integrity, availability, confidentiality, and privacy of critical information system assets is crucial to business survival.

Organizations must put into operation and institutionalize a set of security measures (hardware, software, and data), along with their controlling policies, practices, and procedures. These must address the full range of exposures, vulnerabilities, threats, and risks created by the new E-business model. To that end, a truly robust set of security services, implemented in accordance with an information assurance life-cycle methodology, is the surest way to mitigate risk now and in the future.

An effective life-cycle methodology will provide the full range of security services required to protect the enterprise on an ongoing basis:

- Security assessments to assess the organization's current security posture and recommend the appropriate security policies, processes, and procedures
- Development and implementation of protective measures, including security policies, plans, and architectures that address the identified exposures
- Validation of the organization's information systems infrastructure, following the implementation of security measures
- Personnel training to ensure the continued security of the organization's information systems
- Procedures to continuously monitor the security status of systems and to manage and administer the organization's security policies, processes, procedures, and security technologies

The information assurance life-cycle methodology delivers the skills, tools, and resources needed to keep business-critical data secure and to protect physical and intellectual capital from assault and compromise. End-to-end, the life-cycle methodology helps organizations gain control over user access, simplify security management and administration processes, improve accountability and data integrity, ensure privacy and confidentiality, and guard against costly security breaches across platforms, over the Internet, and around the world.

Operational Considerations

The purpose of this section is to acknowledge what can be done to assist the decision maker to Observe, Orient, Decide, and Act (the OODA Loop), i.e., to achieve the level of knowledge required to ensure the quality and quantity of information while avoiding, or at least reducing, information overload. Decision makers become "intelligent" enough to make decisions by the mental manipulation of data, information, or knowledge (levels of the cognitive hierarchy explained later in this chapter). We will show how a decision maker would be able to consider operating an information assurance system by comparing or otherwise manipulating large amounts of data to "Observe, Orient, Decide, and Act" without achieving information overload. This can best be accomplished through an object-oriented "view of the world."

As introduced in Chapter 2, the dilemma of the decision maker within the OODA Loop is largely a problem of data collection, storage, retrieval, manipulation, and comparison. Some sort of sophisticated set of algorithms, expert systems, or neural nets may eventually be required to fulfill the comparison portion of the decision-making process. For now, an object-oriented approach to data definition, storage, and manipulation would most certainly satisfy the decision maker's need for a common dataset without resulting in information overload.

To begin, the use of an overall object-oriented architecture is needed as a planning process or tool. The ultimate goal of any such process is, of course, to build the knowledge base and experience base upon which to help decision makers to better "Observe, Orient, Decide, and Act." To this end, we conclude our research by acknowledging that planners must be able to organize and reorganize the components of a large, complex information assurance system so that it functions smoothly as an integrated whole.

The OODA Loop

Based on Boyd's observations, his OODA Loop model of air-to-air combat was useful to the Air Force. His model also worked its way into the U.S. Army through the maneuver warfare writings of William F. Lind [Bateman, 1998]. Lind, in his writings on ground combat and the role of maneuver in ground combat, reoriented Boyd's OODA cycle and used it as a tool to describe how U.S. forces might be able to more efficiently prosecute ground combat. The OODA Loop thus became the method used to describe the process by which ground combat formations might be able to fight the enemy more efficiently by moving more quickly through the OODA Loop. Both Boyd and Lind postulated that if U.S. ground commanders could see, think, and then act faster than their adversaries, they could hit their adversaries before they were ready, or place them in a position that they were not prepared to accept. It appears appropriate to assume that the OODA Loop model could indeed be reoriented and used as a tool in information assurance and knowledge superiority.

In its most basic form, one can see that today's fighter pilots and ground troops are not the only ones who can perform the functions of "Observe, Orient, Decide, and Act" to prosecute operations. History shows that even Alexander the Great was better at analyzing, deciding, and controlling his engagements — and he prevailed in nearly every conflict. To master the OODA Loop in today's environment, decision makers need the help of technology to obtain more or better information. Technology has the ability to mature the concept of the OODA Loop far beyond what Boyd had ever envisioned (see Exhibit 1). But this technology now forces us to solve two fundamental challenges if we expect our information assurance system to succeed. First, the proliferation of unintegrated architectures gives the decision makers potentially conflicting perspectives of the information needed to make decisions and thus introduces an exploitable vulnerability. Second, the explosion of available data creates an environment within the cognitive hierarchy that leads to information overload and hence to flawed decision making.

Exhibit 1   Obituary: Colonel John Boyd

9 MAR 1997 — WEST PALM BEACH, FLORIDA — Col. John R. Boyd, an Air Force fighter pilot whose belief that quicker is better than faster became the basis of a theory that revolutionized military strategy, died of cancer today. He was 70.

Boyd flew only a few combat missions in Korea. But after wondering why the comparatively slow U.S. F-86s almost totally dominated the superior MiG-15 fighter, he figured out the F-86's advantages: better visibility and a faster roll rate.

Boyd theorized that the key to victory was not a plane that could climb faster or higher, but one that could begin climbing or change course quicker.

From 1954 to 1960, Boyd, who helped establish the Fighter Weapons School at Nellis Air Force Base in Nevada, had a standing offer to pilots: take a position on his tail, and after 40 seconds of twists and turns he would have the challenger in his sights or pay $40. He never lost the bet.

He was assigned to the Pentagon in 1964. Boyd's design ideas helped give the F-15 a big, high-visibility canopy. But his major triumph was the F-16, which is far more agile and costs half as much.

Though his writings on the subject of decision cycles and OODA Loops were seminal and prolific, the majority of his works were never published.

Regarding the first challenge, the large number of specialized, and often noninteroperable, architectures makes the integration of information to support overall coordination and control more important and more difficult. The second challenge is to harness that information explosion, thus improving decision making. Recent tests reveal an alarming number of unread messages, e-mail and other such communications because of information overload. As the quantity of data rises, the difficulty of preparing, disseminating, digesting, interpreting, and acting upon it grows. Traditionally, many have attempted to solve this problem by increasing the number of communications nodes. These past solutions only injected additional inputs and information without improving decision-making capability. The optimum solution must integrate the functions within the OODA Loop and give the decision maker the correct dataset filtered through the cognitive hierarchy.

To gain advantage over someone else's OODA Loop (e.g., a competitor going after the same market with a similar product), the decision maker is faced with the problem of shortening the life cycle of the decision-making process without increasing the failure rate of the decisions being made, i.e., the decision maker needs to secure an objective knowledge of the environment before his adversary does. This "perceptual" input will come from many sources and will begin to form a picture in the mind of the decision maker. The object-oriented picture that is forming (data) will then be used to obtain information (people, systems, strategies, etc.), and analysis of that information will then be used to gain knowledge (e.g., market placement), understanding (competitor's intent), and awareness (which direction will the market shift to next).

One can sense that the OODA Loop would be affected by a growing deluge of data that are insignificant or not applicable to the task at hand. The

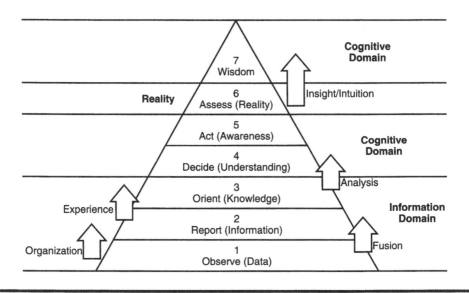

Exhibit 2   Cognitive Hierarchy

difficulty lies in being able to percolate up through the cognitive hierarchy the exact bits and bytes of data that are useful. This filtering process can be pictured as a pyramid with the wealth of "data" laying the broad foundation for what will eventually reach the top — the wisdom that comes from having filtered the right data. Unfortunately, most decision makers possess limited time (driven by the OODA Loop) to perform specific tasks and issue orders. This is especially evident during most operations. Further, as increased volumes of data are input into the base of the pyramid or as the rate of input increases, natural defense mechanisms try to protect the decision maker from information overload [McKitrick, 1995]. A key method is a "bounded rationality" [Simon, 1976] that allows decision makers to screen out inputs prior to being over-loaded or inundated so that they can continue to focus on a particular task. One danger lies in the decision maker screening out "golden nuggets" because they are focused elsewhere. A second danger lies in failing to recognize when new data should dictate a refocus or reorientation. As mentioned earlier, recent tests revealed an alarming number of unread messages, e-mail, and other such communications that might have guided that recognition. A quick review of a "cognitive hierarchy" is shown in Exhibit 2.

- *Level 1 — Data:* Raw data is collected, and thus observed, from one or more sources. These data can eventually be augmented by rules embedded in an expert system, or through population of large, sepa-rately maintained data structures. To reach the next level, the data would have to be organized into information. In other words, data correlated becomes information.
- *Level 2 — Information:* Data organized into some form that is useful to a human operator. Must be reported in a meaningful, recognizable form. To attain the next level, one must be able to fuse/integrate

multiple information sources to form knowledge. In other words, fused information from multiple sources becomes knowledge.

- *Level 3 — Knowledge:* Information integrated from multiple sources. To attain the next level, one must add common, environmental, real-world experience to arrive at understanding. In other words, specific knowledge orients the decision maker in real-world settings and is used to predict the consequences of actions. This leads to understanding.

- *Level 4 — Understanding:* Knowledge as personalized for the decision maker and the situation, allowing the formulation of sound decisions. To attain the next level, analysis, cognitive agility, and feedback from others yields awareness.

- *Level 5 — Awareness:* The decision maker's perception of reality, based on forming a picture in the mind (sometimes referred to as "having the big picture"). This "big picture" is a balance between one's own personal "view of the world" and the perceptions and inputs of those having close contact with the decision maker (e.g., analysts and strategists). This is where the decision maker takes action.

- *Level 6 — Reality:* This is the "real world." The closer that the decision maker's "big picture" matches when overlaid onto the picture of the real world, the better the decision making. Insight progresses from reality to wisdom. Reality, of course, includes the world of those not in close contact with the decision maker (e.g., corporate management) and information about which he may not be aware. At this point, we are back in the observation mode to determine the results of our actions and to see how well our awareness matches the reality. "Lessons learned" are usually derived at this point in the Loop.

- *Level 7 — Wisdom:* This encompasses a deeper understanding of real-world constructs coupled with intellect, instinct, and intuition. The decision-making events at this level become textbook cases in how to master the shortening of the OODA Loop to overcome any competitor.

Technology can integrate functions within the OODA Loop and speed up the cycle. It does this by creating decision support tools to alleviate the doubtful situation that exists when crucial nuggets of information are omitted from the individual's OODA Loop. The tools aid in managing information to fit how decision makers actually form a picture in their minds, assess situations, and then issue orders [McGinnis, 1994]. The decision support tools can deal with inputs from a large variety of different, sometimes contradictory, ambiguous or incremental sources.

Chapter 10

The Information Assurance Center

Any community's arm of force — military, police, security — needs people in it who can do necessary evil, and yet not be made evil by it. To do only the necessary and no more.

Lois McMaster Bujold, *Barrayar,* **1991**

In this chapter, readers learn that the implementation phase is more than simply testing the IA program to ensure it meets their requirements. This phase includes preparing the program for implementation, user acceptance, and the actual implementation of the new program. We have written this chapter in a way that gives the reader the ability to develop a successful Information Assurance Center (IAC). The exact size and scope of the IAC would, of course, be appropriate for the size, type, and scope of the organization. After the IAC concept is completely tested and accepted, the actual implementation can take place. The objective of this phase is to first ensure that the IAC satisfies the stated requirements, and then provide an environment that will ensure the IAC's continued success. Review of IAC program objectives, requirements, plans, and user acceptance and sign-off are stressed as crucial throughout the implementation phase.

The underlying premise of this chapter is the hypothesis that benefits could accrue if a more-flexible and responsive methodology could be applied to how information assurance (IA) is managed within any organization. In many organizations, the words *safety* and *security* are often used in the same sentence; it is our contention that information assurance functionalities could be successfully modeled along the same lines as safety functionalities. In this chapter, we discuss one of the premier safety organizations in the world — the U.S. Naval Aviation Safety Center (NASC) Program — to see how its efforts became so successful. The purpose of the original research on this subject was to determine what areas within this Navy program could serve as templates or analogies to strengthen the manner in which information assurance could be applied within any organization.

This chapter ends with a recommendation for an IAC that could provide monitoring and assistance, and be responsible for a standard lexicon (a common language) and taxonomy (a common framework), standards (common interfaces), Best Practices (common processes and procedures), commitment (a common attitude), accountability (a common report card), and an architecture (a common blueprint).

Introduction

Fifty years ago, the U.S. Naval Safety Center (NSC), which includes its Aviation Safety Program, began its tenure neither liked nor respected. Many Naval and Marine Corps officers in charge of aviation squadrons, ships, or organizations ashore felt that safety requirements were a "tax" on their operational goals. They did not see a real value in safety inspections, and consequently did not wholeheartedly support the effort. The basic belief was that low marks on a safety inspection would have a significant, long-term, and ultimately negative impact on their military careers.

The same could be said about the various IA programs over the years. No Naval or Marine Corps officer in charge of a command wanted to sign off on a computer security accreditation package. The basic belief was that if something ever went wrong, such as an unauthorized entry into a secure network, the responsibility would have to fall back to the accrediting authority. Even the conduct of a friendlier vulnerability assessment to test the systems was often met with reluctant cooperation.

Today, the U.S. Naval Aviation Safety Program is a completely operational program in which the key responsibilities are vested in operational units, with program support and advice from staff organizations such the NSC and the Safety School at the Naval Postgraduate School in Monterey, California. Today, those same officers in charge of their squadrons, ships, and organizations ashore are responsible for all safety issues and they have the authority and accountability that goes with such responsibility. The Safety Program continues to provide a source of expert advice for both proactive and reactive safety issues. How did this come about?

The degree to which safety has been accepted by the senior officers responsible was seen as the key to this original research. The thought was that the roles and responsibilities of those working in the safety arena had to have evolved to facilitate the Safety Program, and information had to flow regularly throughout the Navy for the purpose of increasing safety.

Similarly, the criticality of information and the degree to which information assurance must be accepted by organizations must also rise dramatically.

However, the roles of those in the IA community have failed to take into account the systems-level approach to a successful information assurance program. Our original research identified several proven management techniques that the IA community could adapt from the Naval Aviation Safety Program.

We conclude this chapter with the thought that there are significant benefits to any organization wanting to build a successful IAC to base its approach on the success for the Naval Aviation Safety Program. In our original research, it became clear that the Naval Aviation Safety community had clearly defined its goals, adapted a helpful attitude of providing service to its customers, and were willing to have its successes and setbacks held up for all to see and evaluate. As a result, the safety community has continued to receive the necessary support to manage its programs. We feel that the same success stories could be applied toward information assurance programs within any organization.

Overview of the Naval Aviation Safety Program

The Naval Aviation Safety Program is an operational program with key responsibilities vested in operational units, or the "fleet," and with program support from the safety staff. The operational units are supported by the Naval Safety Center (NSC), headquartered in Norfolk, Virginia, and the Safety School at the Naval Postgraduate School (NPS) located in Monterey, California.

The operational component of the program is managed by the Navy's Air Warfare Division. The safety component is led by the staff of the Vice Chief of Naval Operations, as the Special Assistant for Safety Matters. This dual functionality is carried downward directly to the key department heads at the squadron level: the Squadron Operations Officer, the Maintenance Officer, and the Safety Department Head. The Squadron Operations Officer is responsible for flight operations and scheduling; the Maintenance Officer is responsible for aircraft maintenance and ground operations; and the Safety Department Head manages the Aviation Safety Program, including the Naval Air Training and Operating Procedures Standardization (NATOPS) and ground safety programs. All three report directly to the Squadron Commanding Officer (CO), who has the ultimate responsibility for squadron operations and safety.

At the squadron level, each squadron has a dedicated Safety Officer who manages the squadron safety program under the direction of the squadron's CO. The NSC provides support as discussed later; the Safety School provides the required education for all prospective squadron CO's and Safety Officers.

Although it is difficult to state precisely which changes caused which improvements, it is correct to state that overall safety has improved significantly as a result of the focus provided by the Safety Program. It became clear that some of the lessons learned and the techniques developed by the Safety Program could be used to strengthen an organization's IA program, which is now required to mature in a much shorter period of time.

The Safety Program itself is a completely operational program in which the key responsibilities are vested in operational units with program support and advice from staff organizations such as the NSC and the Safety School at the Naval Postgraduate School. The fleet is responsible for all safety issues and has the authority and accountability that goes with such responsibility. The support organizations assist in the management of the Safety Program and provide a source of expert advice for both proactive and reactive safety issues.

The degree to which safety has been accepted by the operational units can be seen in the key roles that have evolved to facilitate the program, as well as in the information that flows regularly throughout the Navy to increase safety.

The cause-and-effect of a Naval Safety Center having an influence in reducing both the loss of aircraft and the loss of life is unknown. However, it is important to see that the naval aviation mishap rate (mishaps per 100,000 flight hours) has been dropping overall since the early 1950s, when angled flight decks on aircraft carriers and the Naval Safety Center came into existence. Various actions have taken place that may have directly or indirectly influenced the continuing reduction of such mishaps. These actions include:

- Angled decks on aircraft carriers
- Establishment of the NSC in 1953
- Establishment of the Naval Aviation Maintenance Program in 1959
- Initiation of the Replacement Air Group (RAG) concept in 1959
- Initiation of the NATOPS Program in 1961
- Initiation of the Squadron Safety Program in 1978
- System Safety Designated Aircraft in 1981
- Initiation of Aircrew Coordination Training (ACT) in 1991

"White Hat" Approach

It is extremely important to note that the NSC plays a "White Hat" role in all areas regarding safety. The term *white hat* is synonymous with those who provide advice and assistance in the management of the Safety Program. The NSC does not assign blame nor are they responsible for directly ensuring safety throughout the fleet. The NSC performs safety visits, with the safety teams spending six months a year on the road performing such visits. These are nonattribution visits in that the team comes in, audits safety, reports its findings to the Safety Officer and CO, and then "burns the notes."

Whenever the NSC participates in a mishap investigation, its only purpose is to determine the actual cause, regardless of any personnel actions proceeding in parallel by other organizations, such as those performed by the Judge Advocate General's (JAG) office. To that end, the NSC has the authority to keep specific information confidential if so requested by an individual. Over the years, this authority has been consistently upheld at the highest levels of the Navy and by the U.S. Supreme Court. Consequently, all personnel know that they can speak freely to NSC investigators so that critical safety-related information can be acquired without fear of retribution. According to those interviewed for this chapter [including personnel from the Space and Naval Warfare Systems Command (SPAWAR), the Naval Safety Center's Aviation Safety Program, and the Naval Air Systems Command (NAVAIR) Aviation Safety Team)], this is one of the most critical aspects of NSC's role and is probably the most significant reason for its success over the years in determining the true cause of safety problems.

The importance of obtaining accurate mishap information cannot be over-stated. Mishap reports, when initially submitted, may not provide a complete picture of the incident. Trained, expert investigators from the NSC help to clarify the key issues and to determine the most likely cause. As such, when the mishap report is completed and added to the NSC's database, it represents an extremely valuable piece of information for further study, which in the future may help predict potential problems.

Based on the degree to which the NSC has been accepted into the day-to-day activities of the fleet, as demonstrated by the following, it is evident that the NSC has successfully staved off the image of "safety cop" and is now truly "trusted" by the fleet.

Naval Safety Center Mission and Functions

Mission

The mission of the NSC is: "to enhance the war-fighting capability of the Navy and Marine Corps by arming our Sailors, Marines, and civilians with the knowledge they need to save lives and preserve resources." Of interest here is that the NSC has as its mission to "enhance the war-fighting capability" using "knowledge" as its only armament. The same could be said about information assurance in that it is the increased knowledge that must flow to and from the IAC that will save lives and preserve resources.

Functions

From the NSC perspective, "knowledge" takes many shapes. The NSC assists the Chief of Naval Operations (CNO) in managing all aviation safety programs, both for the ships at sea and their support organizations on land. This is accomplished by the following:

- *Supporting many and varied program areas:* Aviation, surface ships, submarines, diving, occupational safety and health, motor vehicles, explosives and weapons, fire protection, environmental, recreational, off duty, and high-risk training safety.
- *Collecting and providing safety data:* The NSC is the repository for all collected safety data, and performs analysis on such data and responds to requests for such data.

- *Participating in safety visits:* The NSC participates in safety surveys, safety stand-downs, and maintenance malpractice and mishap investigations; assists the Inspector General; and holds a seat on several boards and committees.
- *Hazard awareness products:* The NSC produces and distributes the bimonthly *Approach* magazine and various safety-related newsletters; attends and participates in conferences and seminars; and publishes checklists, bulletins, and messages.

Goals

The NSC has defined 15 goals; exactly how each goal is to be achieved is under constant scrutiny by the NSC, pending availability of resources, but the conscious act of writing them down is a step in the right direction. These 15 goals are as follows:

1. Develop a sense of ownership for our mission, vision, and strategic plan.
2. Improve our methods of collecting and analyzing data.
3. Standardize the quality of safety programs in the aviation, shore, and afloat directorates.
4. Ensure our staff is well-trained.
5. Improve communications with our customers.
6. Increase the NSC's participation in policy-setting groups.
7. Pursue new ideas.
8. Market risk management as a part of everyday life.
9. Exploit the use of all media. Identify our target customers.
10. Better manage our resources.
11. Foster trust and openness in our relationships with our customers.
12. Establish the most effective NSC organization that best enhances our ability to anticipate and respond to customer needs and improve the safety process.
13. Have the Commander, NSC, designated Director of Naval Safety.
14. Pursue a new marketing strategy.
15. Make our customers more knowledgeable.

Guiding Principles

The NSC team exists to assist the naval forces (identified as their "customers"). In their dealings with these customers, the NSC is guided by the following principles:

- Be honest and cooperative and treat all customers with dignity and respect.
- Make sure our customers and their needs come first.
- Continuously improve.
- Serve as consultants and advisors, enabling our customers to recognize hazards and manage risks.

To ensure that these guiding principles are met, the NSC supports its own personnel by:

- Allowing them to exercise authority at the lowest level
- Promoting open communications
- Encouraging teamwork
- Stimulating and supporting professional development

Safety Awareness

The Safety Awareness Program is the key NSC program. The Awareness program includes:

- A bimonthly safety magazine, *Approach,* directed toward the aircrews
- Quarterly reviews by aircraft type
- Monthly messages
- Mishap reports to collective addresses
- Squadron safety stand-down support
- The Director of the NSC speaks to every command class (one-week safety class for aviation CO's and the CO class for ships)

Process Improvement

The NSC has a Process Action Team (PAT) that is reviewing the way the NSC manages the Safety Program. The NSC is moving toward the use of "trip wires," which serve as alerts when certain events occur, similar to Indications & Warnings (I&W) within an IA program.

Training

The key safety training is performed by the School of Aviation Safety at the Naval Postgraduate School. The mission of the School of Aviation Safety is

> ...to educate aviation officers at all levels; to identify and eliminate hazards, to manage safety information, and to develop and administer command safety programs; to foster and conduct safety-related research; and to provide assistance in support of the Naval Aviation Safety Program; thereby enhancing combat readiness through the preservation of assets, both human and material.

Command Level Course

The five-day Aviation Safety Command (ASC) course is offered eight times each year at the Naval Postgraduate School in Monterey, California. The ASC course is offered to Navy and Marine commanding officers, executive officers, officers in charge of aviation detachments, officers screened for command,

and staff officers in the rank of Lieutenant Commander, Major, and above. This course is designed to provide information that will assist commanding officers in conducting an aggressive mishap-prevention program and to prepare the graduate for the duties of Senior Member of a Mishap Board. The course consists of approximately 35 classroom and laboratory hours over five instructional days, addressing subjects including safety programs, safety psychology and human factors, aviation law, aircraft systems, mishap investigation techniques, mishap and incident reports and endorsements, and aerospace medicine.

Safety Officer Course

The 28-day Aviation Safety Officer (ASO) course is offered seven times each year for those commands needing an Aviation Safety Officer (ASO). This course prepares the graduate to assist the commanding officer in conducting an aggressive mishap-prevention program. When the ASO completes the course, he or she is able to organize and administer a mishap-prevention program at the squadron level as defined in one of the Navy Instructions, OPNAVINST 3750.6 [OPNAV, 1989]. This course consists of approximately 160 classroom and laboratory hours. Subjects addressed include safety programs, risk assessment and mishap prevention techniques, operational aerodynamics and aero-structures, mishap investigation and reporting, psychology, human factors, safety law, and aeromedical support. Designated naval aviators and naval flight officers of the Navy and Marine Corps in the rank of Lieutenant (USN), Captain (USMC), and above are eligible to attend.

Additional Courses

Aviation squadron staff receive safety training at many levels. The airman is introduced to safety training in many stages as he or she prepares for the first assignment. The aviator has safety training emphasized at each stage of training from preflight to completion of aircraft-specific training. By the time a replacement arrives in a squadron, the trainee has a firm foundation of safety training.

Squadron CO Perspective

There are training tools and benefits present which clearly demonstrate that naval aviation safety has become ingrained in the career development/career enhancement of every naval aviator from Airman to Admiral. The perspective can be seen at the Squadron CO level in the formal training available to the CO and staff. Commanding Officers also have a myriad of tools available at their disposal. Every CO understands the benefits to the squadron from the use of such tools and in participating in the Safety Program. The formal training, discussed previously, is supplemented by the squadron-level programs and the NATOPS program in the squadron. There are frequent reviews and check flights for the aircrew and inspections or reviews for the squadron.

If COs feel the need for additional assistance, they can request a visit from the NSC.

Squadron safety records are viewed as critical information in the evaluation of the squadron CO. A weak or poor safety record is not career enhancing. Conversely, the periodic squadron safety competition and awards are strong motivators for all members of the unit.

Findings

The purpose of this chapter is to determine those areas of the U.S. Naval Aviation Safety Program that may serve as templates or analogies for strengthening an organization's Information Assurance Program. Over time, we have felt that the analogies have held true. Thus, we make some high-level observations about the Safety Program's success and draw some tentative relationships to the success of an organization's IAC.

The success of the Safety Program appears to stem from the following fundamental characteristics:

- More than 50 years of evolution
- Clear assignment of responsibility, authority, and accountability to operational commanders
- Free flow of incident and preventative information to all organizations that have a vested interest in that information
- "White Hat" approach to gathering information and assisting with reviews, both proactive and reactive
- Existence of a database of all safety-related reports, maintained by safety experts and used for a wide range of purposes
- Coordinated training across all ranks and specializations

As indicated in the first bullet, success has not come quickly or easily. The Safety Program has continually evolved a role that works effectively to assist operational commanders, without usurping their authority. Whereas the information and focus lies with the Safety Center, the responsibility and authority still lies with the senior Navy and Marine Corps officers responsible for their commands. Meanwhile, information assurance programs are in their infancy, relatively speaking, and they would be well served by developing a similar role with senior managers in charge.

An information assurance program that views its senior-level managers as "customers" may be the only program that can hope to achieve the same level of acceptance that has been attained by the Naval Aviation Safety Program.

Visibility and Access

Without high-level visibility and access, the NSC would not be able to gather the necessary information, or provide advice to those who can make a difference. To that end, the Safety Center reports directly to the CNO. Similarly, at the squadron level, the Safety Officer reports directly to the CO.

If a similar chain of command were implemented by an organization's IAC, the same level of visibility and access would probably result. This would provide those IA programs with the necessary relationships to gather and disseminate information, and to help build the level of "trust" that the Safety Program has attained. It is possible that an organization's IAC will never achieve the same level of trust, because it may not be possible to convince the average employee that information assurance is a "life-threatening" issue. However, without high-level visibility and access, it is almost certain that the IAC will not be accepted by others within the organization.

How did the safety issue get elevated to its current importance? First, the Safety Program had to gain respect within the different communities. Initially, there was little visibility and the underlying thought was probably that safety was counterproductive. That is no longer true. Safety is now perceived as an important "operational" issue by senior officers, because it helps preserve assets.

The increase in safety importance and acceptability came about during the mid-1970s and 1980s. The Safety Officer was elevated to a Department Head level, giving him direct access to the Commanding Officer. Although not considered a "key" career-enhancing billet, it is a department head billet all the same.

Safety also became a public issue during and after the Vietnam War. The NSC kept track of and documented losses of assets. From those statistics, the NSC was able to recommend solutions to make things and people more safe. The NSC was able to identify the problem and advise operational commanders how to fix the problem. After a sustained period of benefits was shown, the Safety Program was finally recognized as a valuable source for such information, and authority soon followed.

An organization's IAC must emulate this approach of showing positive, tangible benefits to its customers. Then, slowly but surely, the IAC will be able to make a significant impact on the overall security of the organization, and will gain the respect that is needed to ensure acceptance by the organization.

The major difference between aviation safety and information assurance is that aviation safety has the visibility — the "smoking hole" after an aircraft accident. The "smoking hole" clearly displays a quantifiable level of destruction with possible deadly results. Within the IAC, there may not even be an audit log available to prove that an unauthorized user had entered a computer system, or that there had been any intentional or unintentional corruption of data. Similarly, it is well understood that the most-significant threat to most automated information systems is authorized users, not the more publicized hackers. These authorized users could glean information and disclose this information to unauthorized sources for years before they are detected.

An organization's IAC would need to focus its attention on the severity of the problem and the potential or real losses that can occur. Once senior-level managers within an organization are convinced that the loss or compromise of their information-intensive systems could result in the loss of their career, then the IA program may have achieved the desired visibility needed.

Elevating the visibility of information assurance and the IAC within an organization to a level comparable to that of Safety could provide the necessary access.

Advisory Role

The NSC role is informational, not authoritative. The NSC is responsible for writing and maintaining the Navy Instruction called OPNAVINST 3750.6, or the Naval Aviation Safety Program [OPNAV, 1989]. The NATOPS program is a fleet-run program that is supported by the NSC. The NSC recognizes the need to standardize, and has assigned a NATOPS representative for each aircraft type. However, the fleet owns the NATOPS manual and, as such, they are allowed to rewrite it. The Naval Air Systems Command (NAVAIR) controls information related to the aircraft performance envelope, but the procedures (that is, the different ways to operate inside the engineering data box) can be changed by the fleet operators. These changes are coordinated on an annual basis at NATOPS conferences. All this is done with NSC working with NAVAIR and treating the fleet as the customer.

Foster a Role of Assistance Rather Than of Enforcement

This "White Hat" approach should definitely be given serious consideration by any organization building its IAC. For example, an Information Assurance Support Team, or IAST, (similar to military "Red Teams" that perform security tests and evaluations) should be viewed by others within the organization as a group that can help them in meeting their own security responsibilities, instead of being viewed as another inspection team created to cast blame. The IAST reports should be delivered and held in confidence in a manner similar to that of the NSC assistance visits. The organization's IAC will need to make its expertise available without dictating solutions to other elements within the organization. If security is truly beneficial and if the IAC truly provides a net benefit, then the senior-level managers within an organization will find a way to make use of the IAC's services.

Accurate and Timely Information

The NSC collects and analyzes all safety data (850 different attributes), even classified data, but sanitizes and publishes everything as open source. The NSC is proactive in releasing everything it finds back out into the community, with the hope that the information (e.g., what caused a major mishap) would assist everyone else in the Navy by preventing similar incidents from happening to them. In the information assurance community, it seems that incidents (e.g., insider incidents, or hackers successfully entering a network, etc.), are held in confidence and only released to a minimum number of people. Information assurance seems to be a closed environment, and is not operating in a way that would help others prevent the same failure from happening to them. For example, threat and vulnerability information generated by the Department of Defense is routinely labeled "No Contractor," yet it is expected that the DoD integration contractors will build systems that will be resilient, resist penetration, and support the Navy's needs.

The database maintained by NSC for mishap and hazard reports is a critical piece of the "scientific approach" pursued by the Safety Program. Mishap reports represent the final word on "what actually happened" during an incident, and form the basis for both reactive and proactive responses. On the other hand, hazard reports (HAZREPs) represent "this happened to us, watch out." In either case, all reports are disseminated widely so that everyone can benefit from the information contained therein. For example, a HAZREP could include information about different Very High Frequency Omnidirectional Range (VOR) sites in Europe.

This open approach is taken because, more likely than not, the information contained in one report will trigger a proactive response by someone in the fleet. Whereas the experts at the NSC analyze information for a wide range of reasons, individuals throughout the fleet are attuned to their unique situation and needs. Sometimes, a problem reported in one area can spark the concern of one of these front-line individuals, who may then be able to avert a potential problem. Here again, it is extremely difficult to prove that a given piece of information prevented a future problem, but the continuous improvement in safety speaks for itself.

This aspect of the Safety Program is perhaps the most controversial with regard to information assurance. Historically, security information was "held close to the chest," because many felt that it would lead to increased exploitation. In recent years, security experts have reached the conclusion that if the incident information were more widely disseminated, then fewer exploitations would occur, because many problems are the result of previously known vulnerabilities. This debate will continue for some time in the information assurance community, but someone needs to start forming appropriate information flows now in order to gain benefit from that information in the future. In many respects, it is easier to lock down the information flows later, if the data contained therein is too sensitive, then to create the information flows in the first place.

Regardless of who actually sees what information, it is extremely important to note the mechanisms used by the Safety Program to disseminate information, which is based primarily on the type of equipment being used and the mission of a given squadron. By substituting "computer type" for "airframe type," and "system administrator" for "maintenance officer," it is clear that the operational chain of command for computer systems is roughly equivalent to that for aviation equipment. To that end, it seems plausible that the IAC could disseminate security information along those lines, in the same way safety information is disseminated.

Availability of accurate and timely information assurance reports could help an organization's IAC in the achievement of its goals.

Nonattribution Analysis

The official interest of the Mishap Board lies in what needs to be done so that a mishap would not happen again, no matter who was at fault. The information gathering process, as well as the reports themselves, represent a scientific approach, which gives everyone more respect for the process. The same could be considered for "Lessons Learned" after, for example, a virus attack.

It is important to remember that accurate safety information is gathered only because of the respect afforded the NSC and its "White Hat" approach; determining the actual cause of the incident is its only goal. If an organization's IAC can develop the same focus, it should also be able to develop an accurate, and therefore valuable database of security information against which scientific approaches can be used to increase overall security.

The Navy defines three different categories of mishaps based on factors such as dollars or personnel injury. Mishap reports are the most objective of the three, while hazard reports are more subjective and include "close calls." There are also nonhazard reports that are written, collected, and submitted, such as those that document deficiencies (loss tool reports, equipment improvement reports, etc.) and are usually written up by logistics or mainte-nance personnel. If necessary, and if resources are available, one could collect all these reports to research new procedures or trends, study the reliability of tools, the provider of tools, etc.

From an organization's IAC viewpoint, one could establish and collect data points on all IA reports coming in, and suggest the best answer to reduce or eliminate future mishaps such as a successful penetration of a sensitive site. Suggestions may range from upgrading the hardware to providing the most cost-effective software protection, to procedural training.

The IAC needs to conduct rigorous, nonattribution analysis of significant incidents and provide responsive feedback to the employees.

Recommendations

The premise of this chapter is the hypothesis of similarities between manage-ment of the U.S. Navy's Naval Aviation Safety Program and its NATOPS programs, and an organization's IAC. During the course of the original research, we interviewed experts from the Naval Aviation Safety and NATOPS commu-nities and reviewed documentation describing those programs. In addition to the Safety Center's general management approach, we were searching for procedures related to management goal setting, measurement of progress, and the use of metrics.

During the research we discovered a number of areas where the Naval Aviation Safety and NATOPS communities differ from the information assurance community. In particular, the Safety and NATOPS programs have comple-mented each other to have a significant impact on the Naval Aviation man-agement, operational and procedural. The result has been a sharp reduction in aviation incidents since the start of these programs. These communities are continuing to look for ways to get to the next level with their Process Action Team (PAT) and risk management processes.

The following recommendations are provided to assist in the identification of specific actions that could be successfully "ported" to an organization's IAC.

Each recommendation may require some additional research and analysis to determine the best way to adapt those features for an IAC.

Goals

Develop goals for the IAC similar to those of the NSC. Examine the NSC's 15 goals and adapt the strategies and desired outcomes to correspond with an organization's IAC goals and strategies.

Visibility and Access

Elevate the internal visibility of an organization's IAC to a level comparable to that of Safety. If the IAC is to attain the same degree of success as the Safety Program, then the IAC must have the same visibility and access. However, such a high-level position can only be effective if senior-level managers truly accept the responsibility for implementing "their own" IA program, with the assistance of an IAC support organization. With this elevation in visibility, an awards program should be considered. Awards help to increase the visibility of any initiative among the rank and file. Like a Safety Award competition, an IA Award competition could be implemented.

Strength through Knowledge

- Collect and analyze metrics on IA incidents
- Develop a collection and reporting structure similar to that of the safety community
- Provide prompt feedback to the organization with equipment similar to that involved in the incident
- Invest in an effective public relations campaign

The perspective of using "knowledge" to increase the war-fighting capability of the Navy and Marine Corps could be subtly assumed by an organization's IAC. Some IAC staff members could concentrate on collecting and being the repository for all collected IA data.

Of primary interest is the collection of accurate security incident reports, similar to the mishap and hazard reports used in the Safety Program. A formal report should be generated once a given loss threshold is exceeded. An informal report could be generated by anyone who wants to report something "unusual" or potentially dangerous. Any current incident-reporting program should be examined to determine if it is effective and could support a structure similar to that of safety-incident reporting.

The information gathered could also include security metrics and would include data collected from network monitoring devices, firewalls, routers, system operators, systems administrators, AIS security officers, etc. Such information would be invaluable, not only for security purposes, but to assist senior-level managers in the management of their own resources. Senior-level managers could determine for themselves how much effort is "typical" for their employees and could act accordingly, without the fear of being "ranked" against some metric defined by a support organization. In short, the information database should contain whatever the senior-level managers think is necessary for them to be responsible for their own security efforts within their own part of the organization.

NSC is on the Internet as part of its public affairs efforts. A search of the Internet has found many information assurance documents placed there by academia, government, and the public. There should be no reason to hide the efforts of an organization's IAC. Rather, the organization should become proactive in getting the word out as to what it does and what it plans to do. An organization's IAC could:

- Produce and distribute various IA items of interest, from posters warning the employee not to bring in a personal floppy disk without having it first checked for viruses, to more formal newsletters
- Attend and participate in conferences and seminars
- Publish checklists, bulletins, and messages

As an aside, a responsibility of a military Public Affairs Office is to track and report on the history of the organization it serves. Similarly, events that were meant to reduce AIS attacks should be tracked by the IAC for at least historical purposes.

Provide Expert Advice

- Establish a functional equivalent to the NSC within an IAC
- Adopt a similar role as the Safety Center, providing assistance to support the employee

Given a central focus for such information, similar to the Safety Center building in Norfolk, Virginia, a cadre of technical and system management experts could be brought together to assist in the analysis and dissemination of the security information to those organizational elements to which it applies. The IAC should be provided the support necessary to ensure that information assurance becomes a well-established functional responsibility within each department or division in which it is located.

The NSC uses statistics to measure and verify trends. It is currently evaluating the use of trends to provide "trip wires" to warn of impending problems. The most-common metric used at the NSC is the number of Class A mishaps (loss of aircraft/loss of life) per 100,000 flight hours. The NSC's statistical database contains 850 attributes drawn from all the reportable data required in OPNAVINST 3750.5. From that, trends and statistically significant events can be tracked and reported. Similar analysis could be possible for security-related information. The Naval Safety Center collects data on about 850 attributes, whereas only small amounts of metrics and statistics are collected by various information assurance communities. The majority of these statistics are on virus hits, virus types, etc. There should be a requirement by an organization's IAC to capture relevant statistics on the performance of computer systems throughout the organization. Network monitoring tools may be used to capture pertinent data (e.g., before and after firewalls are put in place). What is important is not only the collection, but the storage of such statistics so that historical trends can be measured as additional statistics are collected. Also, organizations like the Defense Information Systems Agency (DISA) or the Navy Computer Incident Response Team (NAVCIRT) cannot assist anyone with the actual software patch code to fix software security problems. Not only should an organization's IAC consider participating in evaluating such incidents, but should consider being the acquisition agent for supplying the corrected code to others.

An organization's IAC could also develop the elements of a full-blown investigative "Red Team" that would operate on both a formal and *ad hoc* basis, and participate in contingency-plan or disaster-recovery exercises, stand-downs (e.g., a polymorphic virus hits an organization's computer network, and immediate action is required), malpractice (when network monitoring shows events occurring outside the normal operating parameters), and investigations (system crashes, etc.).

Recognize Success

Establish an award system similar to the Navy Aviation Safety Awards. A key tenet of naval operations is the recognition of the squadrons and commanders who are successful beyond the norm. The "E" for excellence is awarded for operational excellence in many areas. Senior officers and staff recognize the importance safety plays in this award. Information assurance excellence could be recognized as a significant portion of an organization's existing awards, or a separate award or trophy could be given to outstanding security personnel or departments.

Coordinated Training

Redouble the efforts in bringing everyone involved in automated information systems (system administrators, CSSOs, etc.) up to speed on their role in information assurance. Security, like safety, depends on the actions of every employee. Accordingly, the IAC could develop a training program similar to that evolved by the Safety Program. If resources are constrained, it may be possible to train a small number of IAC staff who could serve as the ombudsmen for security throughout the rest of the organization. There are significant costs associated with training, but an organization will need to accept this as a part of the cost of doing business. The proper training of system administrators, etc., should be addressed the same way.

Currently, no overall standardized training similar to the program at the Safety School in Monterey exists in the field of information assurance. If such courses do exist, they are scattered about in various training curricula, and are neither standardized nor evaluated by independent third-party information assurance professionals.

Proper safety training ensures that aviation commands have people who are trained and ready to respond to a mishap. They are trained to ensure that the mishap is properly investigated (i.e., that evidence is collected and preserved, etc.). A properly trained Aviation Safety Officer has a good chance of answering the question, "What caused the mishap?" On the information assurance side of the house, the IAC should have employees trained well enough to work in the area of information assurance. While this may sound more like common sense, it is more often than not a realization. The person in charge of the IAC should be trained well enough to initiate immediate action procedures in case of natural disaster, hacker attack, etc.

An organization's IAC needs to identify all of the IA training currently being provided by the organization, and determine if the sysops, system administrators, and CSSO/AISSOs are being properly trained to handle their roles in IA. In an Air Force online survey study [USAF, 1996], the following findings were discovered in the area of security education, training, and awareness:

- System administrators indicated a limited awareness of security. Assessment teams concluded that the training received was insufficient, incomplete, or ineffective.
- Only 52 percent of the system administrators had received any kind of security training.
- The majority perception from the system administrators (93 percent) was that their users are aware of their security responsibilities; results discovered in the field disputed this perception.

It should be of considerable interest to an IAC if this Air Force Vulnerability Assessment could be repeated using an organization's assets and resources to ascertain if such vulnerabilities exist within its own organization.

Risk Management Program

Develop an effective risk management program for information assurance that will consider the impact of local risk management decisions on the enterprise-wide infrastructure. The Naval Aviation Safety community, as well as the Nuclear Regulatory Commission, the National Institute for Occupational Safety and Health, the aerospace industry, and many civilian companies have embraced the risk management concept to improve their success in dealing with risk. A Navy Instruction, OPNAVINST 3500, entitled "Operational Risk Management" establishes safety operational risk management as integral in naval operations, training, and planning to optimize operational capability and readiness. The Operational Risk Management process is a decision-making tool used by people at all levels to increase operational effectiveness by anticipating hazards and reducing the potential for loss, thereby increasing the probability of a successful mission.

One concern about the use of operational risk management within an organization's IAC is the inherently subjective nature of risk management. Prudence, experience, judgment, intuition, and situational awareness are all part of an effective risk management program. Without a long-term commitment and proper foundation in IA, there may be no one capable within the IAC of determining or managing such risk.

However, an organization's IAC should still consider implementing some form of an operational risk management technique. It must be understood that no automated information network can be 100 percent "hacker-free." There is risk within IA and it does need to be managed. There must be some realistic goal, which must be addressed by all concerned. We cannot encrypt everything, and we must believe in the trustworthiness of our systems.

There must be a balance between the role that information assurance measures play and the availability of the network to legitimate users. Much like the different levels of security put into place at an airport, based on the actual or perceived threats to the airport resources (e.g., airport, aircraft, the flying public), IA must be capable of operating within minimum and maximum levels of risk. An example of this risk envelope could be the operating levels set on a firewall. During periods of perceived low risk, anyone should be allowed to attach files to an e-mail and send them via the network. As risks increase, there should be a smaller number of users allowed to perform this function; as risks further increase, the byte size of the outgoing files could be kept to a certain level; and, as risks increase still further, all attachments to e-mail could be stopped. Risks increase when the number of packets hitting the firewall from the outside increase beyond an acceptable level. Proper training of sysops, system administrators, and AISSOs would give them the knowledge needed to set the acceptable levels. Proper training using the operational risk management process would increase their ability to make informed decisions by providing the best baseline of knowledge and experience available.

It has been said that the amount of risk we will take in war is much greater than what we should be willing to take in peace. Applying the operational risk management process has reduced mishaps, lowered costs, and provided for more-efficient use of resources. Further research into some form of operational risk management established within an organization's IAC is warranted. It may be feasible to look at combining the risk assessment methodologies used in the naval computer security regulation OPNAVINST 5239 with that of OPNAVINST 3500.

Conclusions

We have concluded that there is significant learning potential for an IA in the analysis of the U.S. Naval Aviation Safety and NATOPS programs. The recommendations identified specific areas where additional study is merited. It was clear to us that the Naval Aviation Safety and NATOPS communities have clearly defined their goals, adapted a helpful attitude of providing service to their customers, and were willing to have their successes and setbacks held up for all to see and evaluate. As a result, the safety community has continued to receive the necessary support to manage its programs.

Our study suggests that there is a real role for the establishment of an organization's IAC.

Our idea is that an organization should have a "one-stop shopping center" that would cover a wide range of IA activities, such as providing outsourcing guidance to others. We looked at many examples and determined that the following general guidelines are pertinent for an IAC:

- Establish at a high level within an organization, with subordinate "shadow" organizations within each department.
- Function as an "honest broker" or "trusted agent" for all customer organizations.
- Be informative, collect and maintain a data/knowledge warehouse (statistics compilation, trends analysis, etc.), and publish this information.
- Provide for training in IA concepts, policies, guidelines, and operational procedures. Ensure that IA training materials are available and provided to users.
- Ensure that a variety of IA awareness materials (e.g., posters, magazines, pamphlets, etc.) are designed and published on a regular basis.
- Establish and control an IA certification process.
- Provide guidance to include operational processes, procedures, checklists, etc.
- Provide a pre-inspection survey support to customers as needed/ requested (i.e., help identify and rectify deficiencies before formal inspection process).
- Consist of a permanent core team of personnel, including procurement and legal personnel with experience in contracting with others. As needed, the IAC could be augmented with outside contractor support to provide a standing and readily available pool of subject matter experts.
- Manage the outsourcing of IA functions to others in accordance with approved rules, regulations, and procedures.
- Identify problem areas, and work with customers and other areas of the organization to develop and implement corrective actions.

An organization should adopt an IAC concept based on the business practices formed by the Naval Safety Center and its Naval Aviation Safety Program and similar to the Information Assurance Center (IAC) depicted in Exhibit 1.

The National Defense Industrial Association IAC Concept: A Closing Note

Early in 1998, we participated in a study conducted by the National Defense Industrial Association (NDIA) to investigate IA issues on behalf of the Office

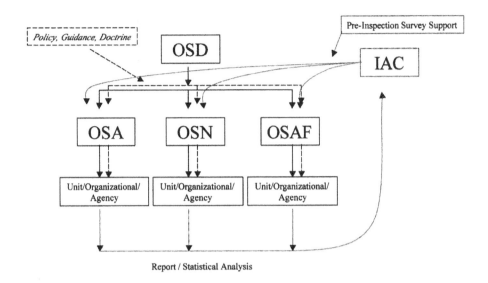

Exhibit 1   Information Assurance Center Concept

of the Assistant Secretary of Defense for Command, Control, Communications, and Intelligence (OASD(C3I)) [NDIA, 1999]. The basic IAC concepts put forth in this study were developed by the authors and adapted to this study. Exhibit 1 was taken from that study. Although developed as a potential solution to the IA problem, the study concluded that we would not be able to solve the IA problem without first solving the interoperability issue.

There was a good deal of concern in the IA study group about the ability of operational commanders to get the help they needed without highlighting deficiencies up through the chain-of-command, and thus potentially jeopardizing their careers. This concern mirrored those found by the Naval Aviation Safety Program. We presented an information security analogy to that paradigm to SPAWAR in 1997 [Campbell, 1997]. It was subsequently updated and elaborated in the NDIA study and in this chapter.

The consensus of the group was to set up an independent, high-level, informative agency modeled after the Safety Center paradigm to assist, monitor, and track IA issues.

Organizational Processes

Introduction/Current Processes

The NDIA study began with an extensive literature search, a plethora of interviews and seminars attended by numerous industry experts in the areas of information warfare, C4ISR, InfoSec, information defense, and related fields. Early in this effort, it became evident that no repeatable, accepted, organized processes, procedures, or infrastructure exist within DoD, nor any of its components, to address the issues associated with IA. Current policies, processes, and procedures related to IA are formulated by numerous commands at various levels within the DoD infrastructure.

Additionally, many such constructs are applicable only to one command, system, agency, or some other relatively small segment of the information infrastructure. Though high-level policies and procedures do exist within the DoD, a recent Government Accounting Office (GAO) report [GAO, 1998a] concluded that many decision makers are not even aware of their existence. Clearly, a better model is required. This absence of a central organizational structure and institutionalized processes was considered a major deficiency. Consequently, the study group set about to define just what such an organization might look like.

In late 1996, a study was conducted for SPAWAR to

> ...examine the procedures and metrics in managing the Naval Aviation Safety, Naval Air Training and Operating Procedures Standards (NATOPS), and the Navy Reliability and Maintainability (R&M) programs to then determine their crossover or relevant applicability to the Navy's Information Systems Security (InfoSec) and Information Warfare-Defense (IWD) programs [Campbell, 1997].

The report concluded that these existing programs had direct transferability to the information assurance problem and that

> a Security Program that views the operational commanders as "customers" is the only program that can hope to achieve the same level of acceptance that has been attained by the Safety program.

That study (summarized in this chapter) and its authors were consulted by this study group as a basis on which to build an overall Information Assurance Center (IAC) concept (see Exhibit 2).

Although the details of these and other functional areas remain to be worked out, there is little doubt that the concept can provide a missing dimension to the IA infrastructure that, as proven by the NSC, can result in substantial benefits (see Exhibit 3).

A high-level, centralized IAC, patterned after the highly successful Naval Aviation Safety Center's Aviation Safety Program, could provide significant benefits to the supporting organization at large.

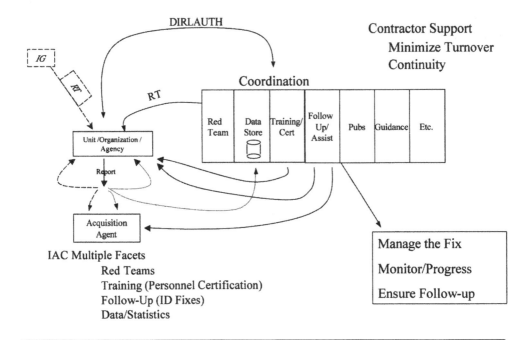

Exhibit 2   Information Assurance Center Organization

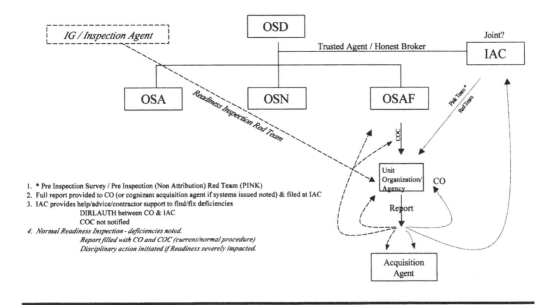

Exhibit 3   Information Assurance Center Process

Chapter 11

Automated Tools

Our Age of Anxiety is, in great part, the result of trying to do today's jobs with yesterday's tools.

Marshall McLuhan

In this chapter, you will learn to recognize the value and limitations of automated information assurance tools. This chapter discusses the automated tools that can be used to protect your information, and the tools that attackers use to attempt to access and compromise your automated information.*

A variety of weaknesses can leave information vulnerable to compromise. For example, information is vulnerable when (1) inexperienced or untrained users accidentally violate good security practices by, for example, inadvertently publicizing their passwords, (2) weak passwords are chosen which can be easily guessed, or (3) identified security weaknesses go uncorrected. Malicious threats can be intentionally designed to unleash computer viruses, trigger future attacks, or install software programs that compromise or damage information and systems.

Attackers use a variety of methods to exploit numerous computer system vulnerabilities. The three primary methods described below account for most of the successful attacks.

1. *Sendmail:* A common type of electronic mail used over the Internet. An attacker can install malicious code in an electronic mail message and mail it to a networked machine. Sendmail will scan the message and look for its address, but also execute the attacker's code. Because

---

* Special thanks to Stephen Quinn at the National Institute of Standards and Technology.

Sendmail is executing at the system's root level, it has all system privileges and can, for example, enter a new password into the system's password file that gives the attacker total system privileges.

2. *Password cracking:* Password cracking and theft is a technique in which attackers try to guess or steal passwords to obtain access to computer systems. Attackers have automated this technique. Rather than attackers trying to guess legitimate users' passwords, computers can very efficiently and systematically do the guessing. For example, if the password is a dictionary word, a computer can quickly look up all possibilities to find a match. Complex passwords comprised of alphanumeric characters are more difficult to crack. However, even with complex passwords, powerful computers can use brute force to compare all possible combinations of characters until a match is found. Of course, if attackers can create their own passwords in a system, as in the Sendmail example in item #1, they do not need to guess a legitimate one.

3. *Packet sniffing:* Packet sniffing is a technique in which attackers surreptitiously insert a software program at remote network switches or host computers. The program monitors information packets as they are sent through networks and sends a copy of the information retrieved to the hacker. By picking up the first 125 keystrokes of a connection, attackers can learn passwords and user identifications, which they can use to break into systems.

Once they have gained access, attackers use the computer systems as though they were legitimate users. They steal information, both from the systems compromised as well as the systems connected to them. Attackers also deny service to authorized users, often by flooding the computer system with messages or processes generated to absorb system resources, leaving little available for authorized use.

Attackers have varied motives in penetrating systems. Some are merely looking for amusement: they break in to obtain interesting data, for the challenge of using someone else's computers, or to compete with other attackers. They are curious, but not actively malicious, although at times they inadvertently cause damage. Others are out to cause harm to particular organizations, and in doing so, attempt to ensure that their adversary knows about the attack. Finally, some attackers are professional thieves and spies who aim to break in, copy data, and leave without damage. Because of the sophistication of the tools they use their attacks often go undetected. Sensitive corporate information (salaries, medical records, cost proposals, etc.) is an especially attractive target to this type of attacker, because, for example, it develops and works with advanced research data and other information interesting to foreign adversaries or commercial competitors.

Attackers use a variety of tools and techniques to identify and exploit system vulnerabilities and to collect information passing through networks, including valid passwords and user names for local systems as well as remote systems that local users can access. As technology has advanced over the past two decades, so have the tools and techniques of those who attempt to break into systems. Some of the computer attack tools, such as SATAN, are now so user friendly that very little computer experience or knowledge is required to launch automated attacks on systems.

Informal hacker groups, such as the 2600 Club, the Legions of Doom, and Phrackers Inc., openly share information on the Internet about how to break into computer systems. This open sharing of information combined with the availability of user friendly and powerful attack tools makes it relatively easy for anyone to learn how to attack systems or to refine their attack techniques [GAO, 1996].

In many organizations, too much emphasis is placed on the use of buzz-word security fixes such as firewalls, virtual private networks, and intrusion detection. Often, the use of freeware or shareware tools is the only software keeping attackers away from sensitive information. These low-level software packages are often equated with total security, which is certainly not the case. While security tools are vital, they need to be part of a comprehensive security program and must be configured to match the organization's security policies.

The following is a brief description of the automated tools that can be used to protect your information, and a brief description of tools that attackers use in attempting to gain access to your information.

Internal Vulnerability Scanning/Auditing Tools

- *Asmodeus (Web Trends Corporation):* This freeware product does not have fancy features, but it is one of the only products that has vulnerability checks such as banner, registry permission, and OS checks. It also includes an Ethernet sniffer and vulnerability scripting capability. It offers no host or port ranges (full domains only), no random scanning, and only modest scanning speeds.
- *Ballista.* See CyberCop.
- *CheckXusers:* This script checks for people logged on to a local machine from insecure X servers. It is intended for system administrators to check up on whether users are exposing the system to unacceptable risks. Like many commands, such as finger(1), CheckXusers could potentially be used for less-honorable purposes. CheckXusers should be run from an ordinary user account, not root. It uses kill, which is pretty dangerous for a superuser. It assumes that the netstat command is somewhere in the path.
- *Chkacct:* Designed to complement tools such as COPS and Tiger. Instead of checking for configuration problems in the entire system, it is designed to check the settings and security of the current user's account. It then prints explanatory messages to the user about how to fix the problems. It may be preferable to have a security administrator ask problem users to run Chkacct rather than directly alter files in their home directories.

- *COPS (The Computer Oracle and Password System package from Purdue University):* Examines a system for a number of known weaknesses and alerts the system administrator to them; in some cases it can automatically correct these problems.

- *Crashme:* The purpose of the Crashme program is to cause instruction faults that would otherwise be only rarely seen in the normal operation of a system. Normal includes conditions of user programs with bugs in them and also includes executable code corruption due to memory, disk, and network problems.

- *CyberCop:* Formerly SNI's Ballista, now Network Associates/PGP Security CyberCop. CyberCop suite is a set of products for intrusion detection and risk assessments. The suite contains CyberCop Scanner, CyberCop Monitor, and CyberCop Sting.

- *DOC (Domain Obscenity Control):* DOC is a program that diagnoses misbehaving domains by sending queries to the appropriate DNS name servers and performing simple analysis on the responses. DOC verifies a domain's proper configuration and that it is functioning correctly. The only required parameter is the valid domain name. *Important:* DOC requires Version 2.0 of the DNS query tool DIG (domain Internet groper).

- *eTrust Intrusion Detection (Computer Associates):* eTrust Intrusion Detection delivers network protection against distributed denial-of-service (DDoS) attacks, malicious and unauthorized use of Internet facilities, and other network misuse events. eTrust includes an integrated URL scanning engine. This auto-updating solution allows administrators to view and check the content of all TCP/IP sessions in real-time to monitor compliance with a company's acceptable usage policy (AUP). All incoming and outgoing traffic is checked against a categorized list of websites to ensure compliance. It is then checked for content, malicious codes, and viruses. If a violation occurs, the sensor will notify the administrator of offending payloads.

- *Internet Maniac:* Internet Maniac is a freeware utility by Sumit Birla. This utility is more than a port scanner; it includes name lookups, traceroute, ping, raw connect, finger, Whois, POP3 check, and a port listener. The scanner does allow for target host ranges and tends to be very fast.

- *IP Prober:* A freeware utility offered by Access Informatics. IP Prober is the simplest of scanners because it does only one thing: scan a single IP address with a range of port numbers.

- *ISS (Internet Security Scanner):* A multilevel security scanner that checks a UNIX system for a number of known security holes, such as problems with Sendmail, improperly configured NFS file sharing, etc. The ISS RealSecure Intrusion Detection suite is an Internet security system (ISS) product for intrusion detections. The suite contains RealSecure Manager, RealSecure Network, RealSecure OS, and RealSecure Server. ISS System Scanner searches deep into online operation to provide a host-based security assessment that targets security weaknesses undetectable through network scanning.

- *Kane Security Monitor* (Intrusion Detection, Inc.): KSM continuously reviews and analyzes NT security event logs on hundreds of NT servers and workstations. Using artificial intelligence, the KSM spots obvious violations such as multiple log-in failures, and can also determine more-subtle irregularities in user behavior that can indicate a masquerading user or other potential troublemaker. The KSM alerts the security administrator in real-time via audible alarm, e-mail, pager, or other interactive technology.
- Netective.
- *OmniGuard/ITA* (Axent Technologies, Inc.): OmniGuard/ITA is a potent weapon for guarding against network attacks by employees, effectively detecting and blocking hack attempts in real-time. It analyzes internal audit logs for signs of danger, correlates seemingly unrelated events, and takes action to thwart malicious actions, such as password guessing, Trojan horse programs, unauthorized file manipulations, audit file disabling, and others.
- *Perl Cops:* This is a Perl version of the Kuang program, which was originally written as shell scripts and C programs. Features including caches passwd/group file entries in an associative array for faster lookups. This is particularly helpful on insecure systems using YP where password and group lookups are slow and frequent. User can specify target (uid or gid) on command line. User can use -l option to generate PAT for a goal. User can use -f to preload file owner, group, and mode info, which is helpful in terms of speed and avoiding file system "shadows."
- *Ping:* One of the most commonly used UNIX commands, this program allows a user to ping another network IP address. This can help determine if the network is able to communicate with the other network.
- *Port Scanner:* Port Scanner is a shareware utility offered by Blue Globe Software. The product offers a range of IP addresses for scanning and port numbers from a maintained list (which provides some degree of randomness). Port Scanner also provides name resolution, target ranges, and list scanning (pseudo-random).
- *Sam Spade:* Sam Spade is freeware written by Blighty Design. Sam is much more than a scanner. It can perform zone transfers, Whois, lookups, ping, DNS, traceroute, DIG, finger, SMTP VRFY/EXPN, and more. It does offer name resolution, target ranges, and list scanning (pseudo-random), and it is very fast.
- *Scanssh:* Scanssh scans networks for SSH servers and returns the connection string provided by the server. From the connection string, you can determine what version of SSHD is running, which SSH Protocol (1 or 2) is implemented, and if SSH Protocol 2 servers can drop back to Protocol 1 in the event that an SSH client cannot handle Protocol 2. Scanssh was developed by Niels Provos at the University of Michigan. The code is multithreaded and scans subnets very fast. Built and tested on OpenBSD and Linux, but it should also run with other UNIX-like operating systems.
- *Secure_Sun:* This program checks for 14 common SunOS configuration security loopholes. It has been tested only on SunOS4.0.3 on Sun4,

Sun3, and Sun386i machines. Each test reports its findings, and offers to fix any discovered problems. The program must be run as root to fix any of the problems, but it can be run from any account by replying \'n\' to any fix requests.

- *SessionWall-3* (AbirNet part of MEMCO): See *eTrust Intrusion Detection* (Computer Associates).
- *SPI (Security Profile Inspector):* SPI provides a suite of security inspections for most UNIX systems at the touch of a button. The SPI software product is available free of charge to all DOE and DoD organizations. Sponsoring agencies may define redistribution policies within their own respective user communities.
- *STAT (Security Test and Analysis Tool)* (Harris Corporation): STAT performs a complete security analysis of Windows NT/2000/XP and Sun Solaris UNIX/RedHat Linux resources. It enables users to accurately identify and eliminate network security deficiencies that can allow hacker intrusion. STAT uses both a Windows vulnerability database and an extensive UNIX database, and automatically detects over 1200 vulnerabilities and corrects a large percentage of them with the exclusive AutoFix feature. Reporting capabilities range from high-level consolidated management reports to detailed reports used by network administrators.
- *Tiger:* Tiger is a package of system monitoring scripts. Similar to COPS in what they do, but significantly more up-to-date and easier to configure and use.
- *Trojan.pl:* Trojan.pl is a Trojan horse checking program. It examines the search path and looks at all of the executables in the search path for people who can create a Trojan horse that root can execute.

Patches and Replacements

- *BSD-tftp:* A hacked copy of the BSD 4.3-tahoe tftpd program.
- *Fingerd:* This is a new, more-functional version of Fingerd. This version offers logging, access control lists for restricting finger requests to certain hosts and certain users, and a message of the day file.
- *Fix kits for Sendmail, WU-ftpd, TCP Wrappers, etc.:* Introduction to the fix-kits archive. Residing in this archive are patches to various popular packages in common use around the Internet. These patches are designed to increase security and robustness. This archive was brought into existence due to a desire to set up server machines, plug them into the Internet, and have them be reasonably secure on their own without hiding behind firewalls. In some cases, these servers would be part of a firewall system.
- *Gated:* A network routing daemon that understands the BGP, EGP, RIP RIP II, OSPF, and HELLO protocols. This version of Gated is more configurable than the routed program that comes with most UNIX systems and can be useful when constructing firewalls.

- *Mountd for Solaris 2.3:* This Mountd for Solaris 2.3 does reserved port checking. As an added feature, it also logs denied mount requests.
- *Msystem.tar.Z:* The file Msystem.c contains a version of system(3), popen(3), and pclose(3) that provide considerably more security than the standard C functions. They are named msystem, mpopen, and mpclose, respectively. While the author does not guarantee them to be *perfectly* secure, they do constrain the environment of the child quite tightly or at least enough to close the obvious holes.
- *OSH (Operator Shell):* A setuid root, security-enhanced, restricted shell for providing fine-grain distribution of system privileges for a wide range of usages and requirements.
- *Patches for Sun machines:* Crucial fixes from Sun Microsystems. These are mirrored from a Sun site. These patches should be checked first.
- *PortMap_3:* This is the third enhanced Portmapper release. The code compiles fine with SunOS 4.1.x, Ultrix 4.x, and ESIX System V release 4.0, but it will work with many other UNIX flavors. Tested with SunOS 4.1.1; an earlier version was also tested with Ultrix 3.0. SysV.4 uses a different program than the Portmapper, however; rpcbind is the name, and it can do much more than the old Portmapper. This is a Portmapper replacement with access control in the style of the TCP wrapper (log_tcp) package. It provides a simple mechanism to discourage access to the NIS (YP), NFS, and other services registered with the Portmapper. In some cases, better or equivalent alternatives are available. The SunOS Portmap that is provided with patch id100482–02 should close the same security holes. In addition, it provides NIS daemons with their own access control lists. This is better than just Portmapper access control. The "securelib" shared library (eecs.nwu.edu:/pub/securelib.tar) implements access control for all kinds of (RPC) services, not just the Portmapper. Reportedly, Irix 4.0.x already has a secured Portmapper. However, many vendors still ship Portmap implementations that allow anyone to read or modify its tables and that will happily forward any request so that it appears to come from the local system.
- *Rpcbind:* This is an rpcbind replacement with access control in the style of the TCP/IP daemon wrapper (log_tcp) package. It provides a simple mechanism to discourage remote access to the NIS (YP), NFS, and other RPC services. It also has host access control on IP addresses. Note that the local host is considered authorized and host access control requires the libwrap.a library that comes with recent TCP/IP daemon wrapper (log_tcp) implementations. If a port requests that are forwarded by the rpcbind process will be forwarded through an unprivileged port. In addition, the rpcbind process refuses to forward requests to RPC daemons that do, or should, verify the origin of the request at present. The list includes most of the calls to the NFS mountd/nfsd daemons and the NIS daemons.
- *Securelib:* Provides a replacement shared library from SunOS 4.1.x systems that offers new versions of accept, recvfrom, and recvmsg

networking system calls. These calls are compatible with the originals, except that they check the address of the machine initiating the connection to make sure it is allowed to connect, based on the contents of a configuration file. Can be installed without recompiling any software.

- *Sendmail:* The Sendmail program by Eric Allman. This version is a successor to the version from O'Reilly and Associates, and is much newer than the version shipped by most UNIX vendors. In addition to a number of improvements and bug fixes, this version has all known Sendmail security holes fixed. It is likely that this version of Sendmail is more secure than the versions shipped by any UNIX vendor.
- *Sfingerd:* Sfingerd is a secure replacement for the standard UNIX finger daemon. The goal is to have the smallest and safest code.
- *SRA (Secure RPC Authentication for TELNET and FTP):* This package provides drop-in replacements for telnet and FTP client/server programs, which use Secure RPC code to provide encrypted authentication across the network, so that plaintext passwords are not used. These programs require no external keyserver or ticket server and work equally well for local or Internet-wide connections.
- *Tftpd:* This version of Tftpd is hacked from the 4.3 Reno Tftpd. The author modified original source code because all of the versions that did a chroot() were unable to then syslog who got what file because of a rather obnoxious subtlety in the way 4.3 syslog works. This version has several improvements: (1) chroot() to a restricted subdirectory; (2) syslog() logs all accesses (and failures) to include the accessor, the file, and the access type; and (3) likely to have the ability to control which files or subdirectories of the tftp directory were accessible to which clients based on the incoming IP address.
- *Ftpd Washington University:* This version is designed for use by large FTP sites, and provides a number of features not found in vendor versions, including increased security. This is the ftpd used by most major FTP sites, including wuarchive.wustl.edu, ftp.uu.net, and oak.oakland.edu. *Note:* Releases of wu-ftpd prior to Version 2.4 have a serious security hole in them, and should be replaced as soon as possible with the latest version.
- *Xinetd:* A replacement for inetd, the Internet services daemon. It supports access control based on the address of the remote host and the time of success. It also provides extensive logging capabilities including server start time, remote host address, remote username, server run time, and actions requested.

Password Enhancing Tools/Authentication and System Security Tools

- *Anlpasswd:* The Anlpasswd program (formerly Perl-passwd) from Argonne National Laboratory. A proactive password checker that refuses to let users choose "bad" passwords.

- *Chalace:* Chalace is an intercept-proof password authentication system that can be used over normal communications channels. Chalace is very, very portable, being for the most part pure ANSI-C. However, it will not run on a terminal or calculator alone. You must have secure access to a local machine in order to run the response client. In an ideal world, everyone would be running something like Kerberos; however Kerberos is not very portable or exportable, and runs only over TCP/IP-style connections. Chalace is useful under many circumstances and not at all useful under others. Chalace is useful for connecting from a local or considered secure machine to a remote machine over a possibly insecure communications line, without giving any intercepting agents access to your account authentication information (password) and thus your account itself. Chalace is not useful for protecting the data that is actually transferred from the remote machine or connection from a dumb terminal, etc., where no computer is nearby to run the Chalace client. http://csrc.nist.gov/tools/
- *Crack* (program by Alex Muffett): A password-cracking program with a configuration language, allowing the user to program the types of guesses attempted.
- *Cracklib* (distribution by Alex Muffett): Cracklib is a proactive password sanity library containing C function that may be used in a "passwd"-like program. The idea is simple: try to prevent users from choosing passwords that could be guessed by "Crack" by filtering them out at the source. CrackLib is an offshoot of the Version 5 "Crack" software and contains a considerable number of ideas nicked from the new software. http://csrc.nist.gov/tools/
- *FakeDoS:* FakeDoS is a PC password system that, when executed from the autoexec.bat file, will present the user with an apparently normal DOS prompt on bootup. However, the system is actually waiting for the correct password to be typed in.
- *LOCK'M-UP:* A utility that requires a password before users are permitted to exit to DOS.
- *Login.* The Login utility allows the creation of authorized usernames and their associated passwords. A user must type the correct password before being given access to the system.
- *NAVYPASS:* The NAVYPASS program, when loaded as the first program in autoexec.bat, allows normal execution only when the user has provided the correct password. It may also be used to "lock" the computer while unattended.
- *Npasswd:* Replacement for existing password program that eliminates the choosing of poor passwords. Includes support for System V Release 3 password aging and Sun's Network Information Service (NIS). http://csrc.nist.gov/tools/
- *Obvious:* This function depends on a subtle property of English. Less than one third of the possible triples, sequences of three letters, are used in English words. This property makes it possible to distinguish random letter strings from strings that look like English words. The

idea is to reject passwords that look like English words. http://csrc.nist.gov/tools/

- *OPIE (One Time Passwords in Everything):* An S/Key derivative (the name was changed to avoid trademark infringement) developed at the U.S. Naval Research Laboratory (NRL) over the past few years. OPIE implements the IETF One-Time Passwords (OTP) standard per RFC 1938 and runs out of the box on most versions of UNIX. OPIE supports MD5 in addition to MD4 and has a number of other security enhancements when compared with the original Bellcore S/Key.

- *Passwd+ (by Matt Bishop):* A proactive password checker that is driven by a configuration file to determine what types of passwords are and are not allowed. The configuration file allows the use of regular expression, the comparison of passwords against the contents of files (e.g., dictionaries), and the calling of external programs to examine the password. http://csrc.nist.gov/tools/

- *Passwdd:* This package consists of two parts. One server based passwd/chsh/chfn replacement and a server based/etc/group editor which gives each and every user the ability to privately manage one group on his own. http://csrc.nist.gov/tools/

- *Passwddet (aka obvious-pw):* The passwddet.c is a function developed by John Nagle, which is known as "obvious password detector." This function depends on a subtle property of English. Less than one third of the possible "triples," sequences of three letters, are used in English words. This property makes it possible to distinguish random letter strings from strings that look like English words. The idea is to reject passwords that "look like" English words.

- *PASSWORD.SYS:* A config.sys device driver that prompts for a password when the system is booted. It will prevent system access until the correct password is entered.

- *PASSWRD5.ASM:* Used to produce a device driver (passwrd.sys) that may be included in the config.sys file. On machine startup, this driver will ask the user to provide a password. The user is repeatedly asked for the password until the correct one is given.

- *Personal Computer Lock:* Personal Computer Lock will password protect the PC hard drive.

- *Pidentd (the pident daemon by Peter Eriksson):* Implements RFC 1413 identification server that can be used to query a remote host for the identification of the user making a TCP connection request.

- *Pwdiff:* Pwdiff takes multiple password files and compares them in an intelligent way. For instance, it will report on different names with the same uid, but let pass the same name with the same uid. http://csrc.nist.gov/tools/

- *pw.exe:* Prompts a user for a password. The user password will be validated against the password file specified in the execution command line. pw.exe disables the Control-C and Control-Break key sequences. A valid password must be entered or the program will not continue.

■ *pw.sys:* A device driver to include in config.sys. It will ask the user for a password each time the machine is booted or a calling program (lock.com) is run. It allows three attempts and then locks up the machine if the incorrect password is given.

■ *S/Key:* The S/Key one-time password system from Bellcore. Implements one-time passwords for UNIX systems. Includes one-time password generator programs for PCs and Macs. Be sure to check out OPIE for a better replacement for S/Key with additional security enhancements.

■ *Shadow (program by John F. Haugh, III):* A replacement for login and passwd that can enable any system to use shadow password files. Shadow is concerned with keeping its user data, as well as the integrity of the network, private and secure. As with all forms of security, this is done with the loss of some convenience. Incoming telnet from hosts on the Internet is blocked, barring presence of the host in an access control file. Incoming FTP to real accounts is blocked as well. This is done because Shadow does not have physical control over all of the routers on the Internet, and thus cannot guarantee the security of incoming connections. It is for this reason that services that require the transmittal of a cleartext password are not normally allowed, because the password can be sniffed with a packet sniffer. http://csrc.nist.gov/tools/

■ *SRA:* Part of the TAMU tool set. SRA provides secure RPC authentication for FTP and telnet.

■ *Station Lock:* Allows users to temporarily lock a computer with a password. http://csrc.nist.gov/tools/

■ *Yppapasswd:* Yppapasswd is designed to do proactive password checking based on the passwd program given in the O'Reilly book on Perl (ISBN 0–937175–64–1). This program has a subroutine called "goodenough" that can easily be extended to perform any type of password checks that are not already being done. Yppapasswd extends this program to be used with Network Information System (NIS). To accomplish this, there is a daemon, yppapasswdd, that runs on the NIS master in replacement of yppasswdd. Yppapasswd supports -f and -s options that change finger and shell information. This also works across the NIS domain so that changes do not have to be on the NIS master server to change passwd info.

Password Breaking Tools

■ *CBW.tar.Z:* The Code Breaker's Workbench, breaks crypt(1) encrypted files. http://csrc.nist.gov/tools/

■ *Crack:* High-speed, dictionary-based password cracking tool with a configuration language, allowing the user to program the types of guesses used. http://csrc.nist.gov/tools/

■ *Password Checking Routine:* This is a password checking program that the author wrote after the infamous Internet Worm. He used the password-cracking algorithm the worm used in order to check the obviousness of a password. http://csrc.nist.gov/tools/

- *UFC-crypt:* This crypt implementation plug-in compatible with crypt(3)/fcrypt is extremely high performance when used for password cracking. Portable to most 32-bit machines, startup time/mixed salt performance not critical, but is 25–45 times faster than crypt(3) when invoked repeated times with the same salt and varying passwords. With alternating salts, performance is only about 4 times that of crypt(3). Tested on 68000, 386, SPARC, MIPS, HP-PA, and RS/6000 systems, it requires 280 kb for tables. http://csrc.nist.gov/tools/

Access Control Tools

- *Deslogin:* This package provides a network log-in service with more secure authentication than telnet or rlogin. Also, all data transmitted to and from the remote host is encrypted using the DES. Thus, this package allows you to use a remote host across untrusted networks without fear of network snooping. This package is not available in NIST's archive due to ITAR restrictions. See the file/pub/tools/UNIX/deslogin/deslogin.readme for details. http://csrc.nist.gov/tools/
- *Drawbridge 1.1:* The drawbridge-1.1.tar.Z package is the Drawbridge base package without DES support. The drawbridge-1.1-des.tar.Z package is a supplemental package that contains the DES support. This package is installed in addition to the drawbridge-1.1.tar.Z package. Simply extract it on top of the regular package. This will add a few source files and new makefiles to the filter and fm directories. Note that the DES package is not required to operate drawbridge; it only allows drawbridge management in a secure manner. http://csrc.nist.gov/tools/
- *Kerberos:* Kerberos is a network authentication system for use on physically insecure networks, based on the key distribution model presented by Needham and Schroeder. It allows entities communicating over networks to prove their identity to each other while preventing eavesdropping or replay attacks. It also provides for data-stream integrity by detection of modification, and secrecy by preventing unauthorized reading, using cryptography systems such as DES. http://csrc.nist.gov/tools/
- *MD5:* A new message-digest algorithm. http://csrc.nist.gov/tools/
- *Permissions:* In a basic BSD environment, only three utilities let people onto a machine: login, rshd, and ftpd. These three programs are modified to check a YP map called "permissions," which determines whether a person is allowed to log in. Control over log in is given, based on four parameters: hostname, ttyname, login, and groups. http://csrc.nist.gov/tools/

- *S/key:* The S/key one-time password system provides authentication over networks that are subject to eavesdropping or replay attacks. http://csrc.nist.gov/tools/
- *Snefru 2.5:* This is an implementation of Snefru. Snefru is a one-way hash function that provides authentication. It does not provide secrecy. http://csrc.nist.gov/tools/

Logging Tools

- *Authd (Authentication Server Daemon):* Authd is an implementation of RFC 931, the Authentication Server under BSD. RFC 931 provides the name of the user owning a TCP connection. This helps network security, unless TCP itself is compromised; it is impossible to forge mail or news between computers supporting RFC 931. Authd also becomes much easier to trace attackers than in the current, largely anonymous network. Authd requires no changes to the current code. The functions connect() and accept() are authenticated automatically, with no loss of efficiency. http://csrc.nist.gov/tools/
- *Dump_lastlog:* Under most versions of UNIX, there is a "lastlog" file that records the time and sometimes the terminal of the last log-in for each user. This is then printed as part of the next log-in as information. Some systems also include information on the number of invalid attempts on the account since the last valid log-in. This Perl program dumps the file for SunOS/Solaris systems, as it works on both. If your lastlog format is different, simply modify this logging format. One may need to adjust the path to the lastlog file. http://csrc.nist.gov/tools/
- *Logdaemon:* Provides modified versions of rshd, rlogind, ftpd, rexecd, login, and telnetd that log significantly more information than the standard vendor versions. This enables better auditing of problems via the logfiles. http://csrc.nist.gov/tools/
- *Logging fingerd in PERL:* This finger daemon is written in Perl to do additional logging into a file called/var/log/trap/fingerd. It contains additional information, such as who is at the other end of the connect (via RFC 931 : read authuser), who does he finger, and any other information that is sent through the finger port. It is programmed to deny chain fingering and stop immediately if it detects special symbols like "|≳.." in the input stream. It can easily be modified to filter out information, deny fingering of a certain person, deny fingering from certain hosts, and filter finger information, etc., without the trouble of recompilation because it is written in Perl. http://csrc.nist.gov/tools/
- *Loginlog.c.Z:* A small program that tails the wtmp file and reports all log-ins to the syslogd. http://csrc.nist.gov/tools/
- *LogTime:* The LogTime program logs the current time into a file, maintaining the last 170 entries stored. This can be useful when placed in autoexec.bat as a method of tracking the use of a computer.

- *Netlog:* Netlog is a C library that can be linked into an existing network application to provide some instrumentation of network performance. It replaces standard UNIX socket calls with its own wrappers, which log the call. Output is either to a local file or via a socket to a client such as Viznet. http://csrc.nist.gov/tools/
- *Spar:* The spar program is used for showing process accounting records. Much more flexible and powerful than the standard UNIX utilities, such as lastcomm. http://csrc.nist.gov/tools/
- *surrogate-syslog:* For systems that have no syslog library. This version logs directly to a file (default usr/spool/mqueue/syslog). The fake syslog that comes with nntp seems to be acceptable, too. http://csrc.nist.gov/tools/

Logging Utilities

- *Chklastlog:* chklastlog checks the file/var/adm/lastlog and the file/var/adm/wtmp for inconsistencies. The "zap" utility deletes the last entry for a given username from the/var/adm/wtmp file and the entry in the lastlog file. If there are other entries in the wtmp file, this tool will find the missing entry in the lastlog file. http://csrc.nist.gov/tools/
- *Chkwtmp:* chkwtmp checks the file/var/adm/wtmp for entries that were overwritten with zeros. If such an entry is found, the entries above and following the entry are printed to indicate the time range wherein the deletion has been made. http://csrc.nist.gov/tools/
- *Trimlog:* Trimlog is used to trim system log files to keep them from growing without bound. When invoked, it reads commands from the file that tell it which files to trim, how to trim them, and by how much they should be trimmed. http://csrc.nist.gov/tools/
- *L5:* L5 simply walks down UNIX or DOS file systems, sort of like "ls-R" or "find" would, generating listings of anything it finds there. It tells you everything it can about a file's status, and adds on an MD5 hash of it. Its output is rather "numeric," but it is a very simple format and is designed to be post-treated by scripts that call L5. http://csrc.nist.gov/tools/
- *Traceroute:* Traces the route IP packets take from the current system to some destination system.

Intrusion Detection Tools/Network Monitoring Tools

- *Argus:* A generic IP network transaction auditing tool that has allowed Carnegie Mellon University's Software Engineering Institute to perform a number of powerful network management tasks that are currently not possible using commercial network management tools. Requires the libpcap and tcp_wrappers packages. http://csrc.nist.gov/tools/

- *ARP Monitor:* Arpmon does a popen() to tcpdump and collects data. It writes its pid by default to/home/arpmon/arpmon.pid and dumps its data to/home/arpmon/addrs. Doing a kill -HUP 'cat arpmon.pid' creates or updates the addrs file. A kill -QUIT 'cat arpmon.pid' updates the addrs file and instructs the arpmon process to die. You can change these path names by editing paths.pl; ipreport will write a formatted report of the addrs files to stdout; do an ipreport -h for the other options. http://csrc.nist.gov/tools/

- *ARPWATCH 1.3:* This directory contains source code for ARPWATCH, a tool that monitors Ethernet activity and keeps a database of ethernet/ ip address pairings. It also reports certain changes via e-mail. ARP-WATCH uses libcap, a system-independent interface for user-level packet capture. Before tcpdump is built, retrieve and build libpcap, also from LBL, in ftp://ftp.ee.lbl.gov/libpcap-*.tar.Z. http://csrc.nist.gov/ tools/

- *ASAX (Advanced Security Audit Trail Analysis on UNIX):* A package that allows you to analyze any form of audit trail by customizing the format description of your trail. Analyzing substantial amounts of data and extracting relevant information out of huge sequential files has always been a nightmare, unless you use ASAX, fundp. Using highly sophisticated and powerful algorithms, ASAX tremendously simplifies the intelligent analysis of sequential files. Of course, the data should fit the analyzer. Therefore, ASAX has defined a normalized audit file format (NADF) with built-in flexibility to guarantee a simple and straightforward translation of any stream of native data into the normalized sequential files ASAX understands. But ASAX's real power is unleashed by deploying its embedded, easy-to-use, rule-based language RUSSEL. This tailor-made analysis tool solves very intricate queries on any sequential data. http://csrc.nist.gov/tools/

- *Courtney:* Courtney is the work of CIAC. It monitors the network and identifies the source machines of SATAN probes or attacks. Courtney receives input from tcpdump counting the number of new services a machine originates within a certain time window. If one machine connects to numerous services within that time window, Courtney identifies that machine as a potential SATAN host. http://csrc.nist.gov/ tools/

- *Gabriel:* A SATAN detector similar to Courtney. While it is only available for Sun platforms, it is written entirely in C, and comes pre-built. http:// csrc.nist.gov/tools/

- *Hobgoblin:* Hobgoblin checks file system consistency against a description. Hobgoblin is a language and an interpreter. The language describes properties of a set of hierarchically organized files. The interpreter checks the description for conformity between the described and actual file properties. The description constitutes a model for this set of files. Consistency Ondishko checking verifies that the real state of these files corresponds to the model, flagging any exceptions. Hobgoblin can verify conformity of system files on a large number of systems to a uniform model. Relying on this verification, system managers can deal with a small number of conceptual models of systems, instead of a large number of unique systems. Also, checking for conformity to an appropriate model can enhance system reliability and security by detecting incorrect access permissions or nonconforming program and configuration files. http://csrc.nist.gov/tools/

■ *KarlBridge (package by Doug Karl):* A program that runs on a PC with two Ethernet boards, turning the PC into a sophisticated, high-level, packet-filtering bridge. It can filter packets based on any specified protocol, including IP, XNS, DECNET, LAT, IPX, AppleTalk, etc.

■ *MD5check:* Checks to see if existing binary files match their appropriate cryptographic signatures. http://csrc.nist.gov/tools/

■ *NETMAN:* Network monitoring and visualization tools from Curtin University. The etherman program is an X window system tool that displays a representation of real-time Ethernet communications. The interman program focuses on IP connectivity within a single segment. The packetman tool is a retrospective Ethernet packet analyzer. http://csrc.nist.gov/tools/

■ *NFSwatch (program by Dave Curry and Jeff Mogul):* Monitors the local network for NFS packets and decodes them by client/server name, procedure name, and so forth. Can be used to determine how much traffic each client is sending to a server and determine what users are accessing the server, etc. http://csrc.nist.gov/tools/

■ *NID (Network Intrusion Detector):* Provides a suite of security tools that detects and analyzes network intrusion. NID provides detection and analysis of intrusion from individuals not authorized to use a particular computer and from individuals allowed to use a particular computer, but who perform either unauthorized activities or activities of a suspicious nature on it. http://csrc.nist.gov/tools/

■ *NOCOL (Network Operations Center Online):* Monitors various network variables such as ICMP or RPC reachability, host performance, SNMP traps, modem line usage, AppleTalk and Novell routes and services, BGP peers, etc. The software is extensible and new monitors can be added easily. http://csrc.nist.gov/tools/

■ *Noshell:* This program is designed to provide the system administrator with additional information about who is logging into disabled accounts. Traditionally, accounts have been disabled by changing the shell field of the password entry to "/bin/sync" or some other benign program. Noshell provides an informative alternative to this method by specifying the Noshell program as the login shell in the password entry for any account that has been disabled. http://csrc.nist.gov/tools/

■ *Raudit:* Raudit is a Perl script that audits each user's rhosts file and reports on various findings. Without arguments, Raudit will report on the total number of rhosts entries, the total number of nonoperations entries, for which the host is listed in the/etc/hosts.equiv file, the total number of remote entries, for which the host is a non-NAS host. Raudit will also report on any entries that may be illegal. An entry is considered illegal if the username does not mach the username from the password file or if the entry contains a "+" or a "−." Raudit is normally run on a weekly basis via a cron job that runs rhosts.audit. The output is mailed to the NAS security analyst. http://csrc.nist.gov/tools/

- *RIACS Intelligent Auditing and Categorizing System:* A file system auditing program that compares current contents against previously generated listings and reports differences. http://csrc.nist.gov/tools/
- *SARA (Security Auditor's Research Assistant):* A third-generation, UNIX-based security analysis tool that is based on the SATAN model.
- *Swatch (package by Stephen Hansen and Todd Atkins):* A system for monitoring events on a large number of systems. Modifies certain programs to enhance their logging capabilities and software to then monitor the system logs for "important" messages. http://csrc.nist.gov/tools/
- *swIPe:* swIPe is a network-layer security protocol for the IP protocol suite. swIPe provides confidentiality, integrity, and authentication of network traffic, and can be used to provide both end-to-end and intermediate-hop security. swIPe is concerned only with security mechanisms; policy and key management are handled outside the protocol. http://csrc.nist.gov/tools/
- *TAMU Check Integrity Script:* Invoke it without arguments in the same directory that has the TAMU Security distribution. It will automatically validate the files in the distribution to make sure that they have not been tampered with. http://csrc.nist.gov/tools/
- *Tripwire:* Scans file systems and computes digital signatures for the files therein, then can be used later to check those files for any changes. Tripwire also checks all inode information on a user-selectable basis, and monitors for missing or added files. http://csrc.nist.gov/tools/
- *Watcher:* A configurable and extensible system-monitoring tool that issues a number of user-specified commands, parses the output, checks for items of significance, and reports them to the system administrator. http://csrc.nist.gov/tools/
- *WinDump:* TCPdump is a network capture program developed by Network Research Group (NRG) of the Information and Computing Sciences Division (ICSD) at Lawrence Berkeley National Laboratory (LBNL) in Berkeley, California. Originally available only on UNIX platform, this is the porting on Windows (95/98, NT 4.0). It consists in an executable (the windump main program) with a network capture driver; both are specific for each platform. Source code is available at, http://netgroup-serv.polito.it/windump/install/Default.htm
- *X Connection Monitor:* This program monitors X connections. It uses RFC 931 to display usernames, when the client host supports RFC 931. It allows the user to freeze and unfreeze connections, or kill them, independent of the client, and very importantly independent of the server. The KillClient request can be used to forcibly disconnect a client from the server, but only if the client has created a resource, which, for example, neither xkey nor crowbar does. It monitors the connection,

and if it sees certain dubious requests, currently configurable only by hacking on the source, it pops up a little menu with which the user can allow the request, have it replaced with a NoOperation request, or kill the connection. The dubious requests are, at present, requests to change the host access list, requests to enable or disable access control, and Change Window Attributes requests operating on nonroot windows not created by the same client.

System Status Reporting Tools

- *CPM (Check Promiscuous Mode):* The CPM program from Carnegie Mellon University. A root-compromised system that supports a promiscuous network interface is being used by intruders to collect host and user authentication information visible on the network. There are network monitoring tools that use the promiscuous mode of a specific network interface to capture host and user authentication information on all newly opened FTP, TFTP, TELNET, and RLOGIN sessions. CPM checks a system for any network interfaces in promiscuous mode; this may indicate that an attacker has broken in and started a packet-snooping program. http://csrc.nist.gov/tools/
- *DIG:* This is a command-line tool for querying DNS servers. It is easier to use than nslookup and is well-suited for use within shell scripts. http://csrc.nist.gov/tools/
- *Fremont:* A research prototype for discovering key network characteristics, such as hosts, gateways, and topology. Fremont stores this information in a database and can then notify the administrator of anomalies detected. http://csrc.nist.gov/tools/
- *host:* Program for obtaining information from the DNS. More flexible than nslookup. http://csrc.nist.gov/tools/
- *ICMPINFO:* A tool for looking at the icmp messages received on the running host. The source code is written by Laurent De Mailly and comes from a heavily modified BSD ping source. ICMPINFO comes without warranty. http://csrc.nist.gov/tools/
- *IDENT:* The IDENT package contains the following:
    - *Identify,* a small program that can be used to log "ident" info in conjunction with the "inetd" daemon.
    - *Idlookup,* a small tool that can be used to look up the identifier associated with a particular TCP/IP connection if the remote site is running an ident server.tcplist. Idlookup makes a list of TCP connections to and from the local machine, displaying the user name associated with the local end, and makes use of RFC 931 services if available to determine the "user" at the other end.
    - *TCPlocate,* identifies process(es) that have sockets that are either connected to a remote TCP port or are bound to a given local TCP port. http://csrc.nist.gov/tools/

- *Ifstatus:* Checks a system for any network interfaces in promiscuous mode. This may indicate that an attacker as broken in and started a packet-snooping program.
- *IRTS (Incident Response Ticket System):* The IRTS is a tool for tracking incidents, requests for help, and contact information. It was designed and implemented by CIAC for managing the day-to-day responsibilities of its team members.
- *LSOF:* The LSOF program by Vic Abell is a descendant of Ofiles and FSTAT. LSOF is used to list all open files (and network connections, pipes, streams, etc.) on a system. Can find out which processes have a given file open, which files a specific process has open, and so forth. Useful for tracing network connections to the processes using them as well. http://csrc.nist.gov/tools/
- *STROBE:* Strobe is a network tool that locates and describes all listening TCP ports on a remote host or on many hosts in a network. http://csrc.nist.gov/tools/
- *TCP Port Probing Program:* A TCP port-probing program is fairly self-explanatory. It is known to work on UNIX workstations, but the C code is fairly portable. http://csrc.nist.gov/tools/
- *Tcpwho:* Displays a list of all TCP connections and the corresponding user name along with the process identifier associated with each connection.

Mail Security Tools

- *Alphanumeric Pager via e-mail:* "tpage" or "Tom's Pager System" is a set of programs that let you send messages to alphanumeric pagers using the IXO Protocol. It supports a dialing directory, a "who's on duty now" schedule, and can do special tricks with RFC 822-format e-mail. The system has several features. Tpage sends pages to any pager system that supports the IXO Protocol and additional protocols can be added. Tpage can parse e-mail messages and extract the interesting info from them resulting in shorter messages. Tpage can also copy its input to stdout and therefore can be used as a "tee." It also maintains a directory of people's phone numbers/PINs and can page "the person on duty" by searching a schedule. Schedule can have slots that are empty, but find someone anyway if the message is marked "urgent." With programs like Procmail, tpage permits you to send certain e-mail messages to your pager. A list of modems can be given to the daemon. http://csrc.nist.gov/tools/
- *PGP:* Pretty Good Privacy is a program that gives electronic mail something that it otherwise does not have: privacy. It does this by encrypting your mail so that nobody but the intended person can read it. When encrypted, the message looks like a meaningless jumble of random characters. http://csrc.nist.gov/tools/

- *RPEM (Rabin Privacy Enhanced Mail):* This distribution makes available a nearly public-domain public key encryption system. Included are functions implementing the algorithm, functions implementing related capabilities including a DES implementation for recipients in the USA, and a program, RPEM, that implements a simple privacy-enhanced mail system. The principal applications provided are (1) RPEM, a program (somewhat compatible with RFC 1113) to encrypt a file into an encapsulated postscript file suitable for inclusion into a mail message and (2) Makerkey, a program to create public keys, both public and private components, for use with RPEM. There are also some miscellaneous applications included with RPEM.

Packet Filtering Tools

- *IP Packet Filter for SunOs:* If you have a multihomed Sun server/ workstation (two or more Ethernet interfaces) that performs routing and have a problem with IP headers being forged with no router on the system for assistance, then this package will allow you to set up packet filters for each interface, much like those that can be set up in Ciscos and others. Packets going in or out can be filtered. They can be logged, blocked, or passed. You can filter on any combination of TCP flags, the various ICMP types, as well as the standard variations on IP# source-destination pairs (with variable netmasks) and source-destination ports for TCP and UDP. Packets with nonstandard IP header lengths, such as those with source routing information inside, can be selected apart from standard packets. There is no need to worry about fragments as only complete IP packets are examined. http:// csrc.nist.gov/tools/
- *Ipacl:* The Ipacl package from Siemens forces all TCP and UDP packets to pass through an access control list facility. The configuration file allows packets to be accepted, rejected, conditionally accepted, and conditionally rejected based on characteristics such as source address, destination address, source port number, and destination port number. Should be portable to any system that uses System V STREAMS for its network code. http://csrc.nist.gov/tools/
- *Screend:* The Screend package by Jeff Mogul provides daemon and kernel modifications to allow all packets to be filtered based on source address, destination address, or any other byte or set of bytes in the packet. This package should work on most systems that use Berkeley-style networking in the kernel, but requires kernel modifications (i.e., kernel source code). http://csrc.nist.gov/tools/
- *TCP/Wrappers:* The TCP/Wrappers program monitors and filters incoming requests for network services such as TFTP, EXEC, FTP, RSH, TELNET, RLOGIN, FINGER, and SYSTAT. This package provides tiny daemon wrapper programs that can be installed without any changes

to existing software or existing configuration files. The wrappers report the name of the remote host and of the requested service; the wrappers do not exchange information with the remote process and impose no overhead on the actual communication between the client and server. Optional features are access control to restrict what systems can connect to network daemons, remote user name lookups with the RFC 931 protocol, and additional protection against hosts that pretend to have someone else's host name or address. http://csrc.nist.gov/tools/

■ *Tcpdump:* The Tcpdump program by Van Jacobson is similar to Sun's Etherfind, but somewhat more powerful and slightly easier to use. It captures packets from an Ethernet in promiscuous mode, and displays their contents. Numerous options exist to filter the output down to only those packets of interest. This version runs on a number of different UNIX platforms.

Firewall Tools

■ *Access_list_examples:* A series of Perl scripts that allow one to quickly and easily configure ACL entries for firewall routers. http://csrc.nist.gov/tools/

■ *Fwtk (TIS firewall tool kit):* A software kit for building and maintaining internetwork firewalls. It is distributed in source code form with all modules written in the C programming language. Fwtk runs on many BSD UNIX-derived platforms. http://csrc.nist.gov/tools/

■ *GAU (Gateway Access Utilities):* GAU currently supports access to the Internet through the use of a firewall system. All internal systems are hidden behind a firewall or gateway from the Internet. These utilities allow users from inside the network to get to archives and services on the Internet without requiring that they have an account on the gateway system. http://csrc.nist.gov/tools/

■ *Socks:* Socks is a package by David and Michelle Koblas that allows hosts behind a firewall to gain full access to the Internet without requiring direct IP reachability. The Internet "socket server" consists of a set of client library routines and a daemon that interacts through a simple protocol to provide convenient and secure network connectivity through a firewall host. It works by redirecting requests to talk to Internet sites to a server that authorizes the connection. http://csrc.nist.gov/tools/

■ *Tcpr:* A set of Perl scripts that enable FTP and telnet commands to run across a firewall. Forwarding takes place at the application level for easy control. http://csrc.nist.gov/tools/

■ *TIS Firewall Toolkit:* Trusted Information Systems, Inc. Firewall Toolkit, a software kit for building and maintaining internetwork firewalls. It is distributed in source code form, with all modules written in the C programming language, and runs on many BSD UNIX-derived platforms.

- *UDP Packet Relayer:* This package consists of two components: (1) udprelay is a daemon process by Tom Fitzgerald that runs on a firewall host and forwards UDP packets in and out of a firewalled network as directed by a configuration file, and (2) Rsendto.c provides the routines Rsendto and Rrecvfrom, which allow tunneling through the bastion to arbitrary outside hosts. Rsendto and Rrecvfrom communicate with udprelay using UDP packets encapsulated in a wrapper that includes the address of the remote host/port to transfer traffic to.
- *Xforward6:* The Xforward package by Win Treese is used for relaying X Window System connections across network firewalls. http://csrc.nist.gov/tools/

Real-Time Attack Response Tools

- *Disable modload, modunload modstat:* When you want to lock the door after all kosher modloads and kmem writes have happened, attempt to open the device (for example, add "sh -c").
- *Dummy "SU" program.* This program is intended to help an intruder who does not know the system to trip alarms so the rightful system administration will notice and respond. http://csrc.nist.gov/tools/
- *Fake-Rshd:* fake_rshd echoes the specified arguments to the remote system after satisfying a minimal subset of the Rshd Protocol. It works with the TCP Wrapper to send an arbitrary message back to someone trying to make an rsh/rlogin connection. http://csrc.nist.gov/tools/
- *Rsucker:* Rsucker is a Perl script that acts as a fake r* daemon and log the attempt is syslog. Byte sucker for r* commands.

Encryption Tools

- *DES Package:* This program uses the DES algorithm to read and write the encrypted data. If file name is not given in command line, Des uses standard input or output. The data is transformed by a one-way function into an eight-byte key, which is then used by the algorithm. If no key is given on command line, DES asks one with getpass(3). DES encrypts when given a flag and decrypts with a given flag. With the flag, DES encrypts normally, but it does not produce encrypted output, instead it prints eight-byte cryptographic checksum of input data. http://csrc.nist.gov/tools/
- *Descore:* Descore is a package containing only the core DES functionality: specifying keys, encryption, and decryption. It is for those who want to implement such things as DES filters rather than UNIX password crackers. http://csrc.nist.gov/tools/

- *Libdes:* This kit builds a DES encryption library and a DES encryption program. It supports ECB, CBC, OFB, CFB, triple ECB, triple CBC and MIt in PCBC encryption modes and also has a fast implementation of crypt(3). It contains support routines to read keys from a terminal, generate a random key, generate a key from an arbitrary length string, and read and write encrypted data from or to a file descriptor. The implementation was written to conform with the manual entry for the des_crypt(3) library routines from MIt in project Athena. http://csrc.nist.gov/tools/
- *Snuffle:* Snuffle is a set of generic hash-based encryption and decryption programs. Snuffle and unsnuffle turn any good one-way hash function, such as Merkle's Snefru, into a reasonably fast private-key encryption method. You must have Snefru or something providing the same Hash512() interface for snuffle and unsnuffle to work. Snuffle is rather portable provided the Hash512() interface is present. http://csrc.nist.gov/tools/

Host Configuration Tools

- *ACMAINT:* An account creation and maintenance system for distributed UNIX systems; a network-based, centralized database system used to manage account creation and maintenance similar to NIS/YP. http://csrc.nist.gov/tools/
- *Chrootuid:* Chrootuid makes it easy to run a network service at low-privilege level and with restricted file system access. At Eindhoven University, they use this program to run the gopher and WWW network daemons in a minimal environment. The daemons have access only to their own directory tree and run under a low-privileged userid. The arrangement greatly reduces the impact of possible loopholes in daemon software. http://csrc.nist.gov/tools/
- *OP:* OP is a tool designed to allow customizable superuser access. A user can do everything from emulating giving a superuser shell for nothing to only allowing one or two users access via log-in names or special passwords that are neither root, nor their own. Plus, as an added bonus, for those commands that you would like users to be able to use, but need to place restrictions on the arguments, you can configure that as well. (i.e., if you want your users to be able to mount NFS file systems). http://csrc.nist.gov/tools/
- *Rdist (program from the University of Southern California):* Replacement for the Rdist software distribution utility that originated in Berkeley UNIX and is now shipped with most vendor's releases. In addition to a number of new features and improvements, this version has had all known Rdist security holes fixed. This version does not need to run set-user-id "root," unlike the standard version. http://csrc.nist.gov/tools/ — TOC

- *Sudo:* Sudo is a program designed to allow a system administrator to give limited root privileges to users and log root activity. The basic philosophy is to give as few privileges as possible, but still allow people to get their work done. The purpose of Sudo is to make superuser access easier, self-documenting, and controlled. The Sudo control file is called usr/local/adm/sudoers. You are given "all" permissions, which means you have unlimited superuser access. You may have already been given a lecture at some point as to the moral and social etiquette that you should observe as a superuser. With superuser permissions, it is possible to do great damage by accident. With superuser permissions you may look at any file you wish. Resist all temptation to look in other people's personal files. http://csrc.nist.gov/tools/
- *YPX:* A utility to transfer NIS maps beyond a local (broadcast) network. YPX is a utility to transfer a NIS map from any host running a ypserv daemon. YPX is similar to ypcat, with some additions. To be able to transfer a map, a domain name must be specified. There unfortunately is no way to ask the remote host about its domain name, so it must be known already or guessed to transfer a map successfully. If none is specified, the host name of the remote host is used as the domain name. YPX is able to guess at the remote domain name, by trying parts of the host name only if guessing is enabled with the -g option. If the -s option is used, YPX will connect to the Sendmail daemon, read the host name, and parse that too, to be used as additional guesses. Finally, any additional strings on the command line will be added to the list of domain name guesses.

Antivirus Tools

- *A-VIRUS1:* The A-Virus1 file contains information on the AIDs Trojan Horse program.
- *AAVIRUS:* The AAVIRUS program checks the integrity of the DOS bootstrap system on a bootable disk against a checksum file created by the program at installation. The program is able to restore these bootstrap records if the disk becomes infected.
- *Adinf Advanced Diskinfoscope:* File integrity checker. Dialogue Science, http://www.dials.ru
- *AEDOS:* Anyware Antivirus v3.01.480 antivirus scanner for DOS.
- *ALERT!:* Maintains a table of checksum and file information for sensitive files on the system and will alert the user whenever these files are modified.
- *ANSICHEK:* The ANSICHEK package is a set of programs designed to find hidden ANSI codes that could redefine the keyboard.
- *Antigen 5 for Lotus Notes:* Sybari, http://www.sybari.com.
- *Antigen 5 for Microsoft Exchange:* Sybari, http://www.sybari.com.
- *Antiviral Toolkit Pro:* Kaspersky Labs, http://www.avp.ru.

- *ASTEALTH2:* Astealth2 is a program for finding stealth viruses.
- *AUTOSCAN:* AUTOSCAN will automatically search for viruses in archived files (ZIP, ARC, ICE, LZH, PAK, or ARJ) using McAfee's SCAN program.
- *Antiviral Toolkit Pro:* The Antiviral Toolkit Pro (AVP) evaluation version is an integrated antiviral package combining a scanner, a heuristic code analyzer, file extraction engines, and an antiviral TSR monitor.
- *AVAST:* Securenet, http://www.securenet.org.
- *AVG Anti-Virus System:* Grisoft, http://www.grisoft.com.
- *AVP Virus Encyclopedia:* AVP Virus Encyclopedia, including numerous virus simulations.
- *Bomb Squad:* Attempts to detect Trojan horses in executable code by scanning for suspicious strings and intercepting calls to BIOS code.
- *BootChek:* Detects changes to the boot sector of a disk.
- *BOOTCOMP:* Compares the boot sector and partition table information on a disk with previously saved copies and will alert the user to any changes. When installed, the original BIOS interrupts are used to read the boot sector and partition table, defeating any virus that may be present.
- *BtPrT Version 102:* A program to detect and clean any boot sector virus.
- *CatchMtE:* Designed to recognize viral code based on the Mutation Engine distributed by Dark Avenger from Bulgaria.
- *CheckMate:* A detection tool for new and known file, boot, and partition table viruses. It is designed to augment the use of a good-quality virus scanner.
- *CheckOut:* A virus protection program that is intended for use in environments in which many programs reside in archives such as ZIP or LZH. It breaks open each archive and calls ViruScan by McAfee Associates to check the components for infection. If desired, it can then repackage the archive in a different format.
- *CHECKUP:* Detects viral infections by comparing target file sizes and incremental and cumulative cyclic redundancy checks (CRCs) to previously recorded baseline values, optionally stored on removable media. CHECKUP examines files first by separating them into randomly sized blocks of data, using dynamic block size allocation techniques that allow files as small as one byte to be accurately checked. CHECKUP then scans and compares every byte of the target files on a block-by-block basis. If the recorded file sizes or any of the incremental or cumulative CRC comparisons do not match, CHECKUP alerts users that the target files have been modified.
- *CHEKMATE:* Generic virus detection w/word.
- *Command Antivirus:* Command Software Systems, Inc., http://www.commandcom.com.
- *CRC Check:* Generates and validates 32-bit checksums.
- *CRCSET:* A package of Pascal and C routines that allow programs to verify their own integrity before execution and stop if a virus is detected.

- *CVIRPROT:* Consists of several programs designed to make C programs virus resistant. The programs do not actually prevent virus infection, but will alert the user that such an event has occurred. The technique works by embedding checksum values into the executable file. When the program is started, it checks itself against the values embedded when the file was first compiled.
- *Deform:* A free tool to remove the Form virus from infected systems.
- *Disinfectant (by John Norstad):* A program designed to detect and remove all known Macintosh viruses. Included in the program is a small extension that, once installed, will provide run-time detection of known viruses.
- *DiskNet:* Reflex Magnetics, http://www.reflex-magnetics.co.uk.
- *DISKSECURE II:* Replaces the master boot record on a hard disk with its own code. The necessary elements of the original partition table are stored on an unused part of the disk and presented to the authenticated operating system as required. Unauthorized boot programs (such as the Brain, Stoned, or Azusa viruses) will not be able to access the partition table as expected.
- *DisQuick Diskettes:* OverByte Corporation, http://www.disquick.com.
- *DLCHECK.BAT:* A batch file intended to automate the process of checking downloaded files for computer viruses.
- *Dr. Solomon's Anti-Virus Toolkit:* Network Associates, Inc., http://www.nai.com.
- *Dr. Web:* Dialogue Science, http://www.dials.ru.
- *DSII:* BIOS-level antivirus with access control.
- *EARLY Bird:* Scans program files for OUT instructions or occurrences of the BIOS or DOS disk interrupts in an attempt to detect Trojan code.
- *EMD Armor:* EMD Enterprises, http://www.emdent.com.
- *ESafe Protect Enterprise:* Esafe Technologies, http://www.esafe.com.
- *ESafe Protect Gateway:* Esafe Technologies, http://www.esafe.com.
- *ESDScan:* Searches files for appearances of user specified ASCII and HEX signatures.
- *F-Secure Anti-Virus:* Data Fellows, http://www.datafellows.com.
- *FIBER:* Fiber Anti Virus 1.20d. Antivirus scanner.
- *File Defender Plus:* File protection driver.
- *Fix B SI:* BIOS detection and recovery from BSI viruses.
- *FileSafe:* Computer virus detection system.
- *F-PROT:* Consists of programs designed to detect virus signatures and stop viruses from infecting the system.
- *FixUtils:* A set of utility programs to repair the master boot record, fix boot sectors, prevent floppy boots, and check for suspicious memory usage.
- *FLU_SHOT+:* Memory resident virus monitor and virus prevention program.
- *Gatekeeper (by Chris Johnson) Version 1.3:* A set of Macintosh system extensions and related control panels that offer protection against attacks by all currently known viruses. It also monitors computer activities for what are considered to be suspicious "events" or "operations,"

in an attempt to intercept what could be variants of known viruses or completely new viruses (discontinued software).

- *HARE:* F-Hare. A scanner and disinfector for the Hare viruses.
- *Hcopy Version 15:* Hilgraeve's copy program with virus protection. Scans files as they are copied.
- *HTSCAN:* A user-programmable virus scanner. It is designed to detect and identify known viruses within files, boot-sectors, master boot records, and memory. HTSCAN can scan floppy disks, hard disks, and network drives.
- *InDefense:* Tegam International, http://www.indefense.com.
- *InoculateIT:* Computer Associates, http://www.cai.com/cheyenne.
- *Integrity Master:* A high-performance program offering virus protection, data integrity, security, CMOS protection, and change management all in one easy-to-use package. It detects hardware glitches, software bugs, and deliberate sabotage to data. If a virus strikes, Integrity Master identifies it by name and also identifies any damage caused by the virus. It will even detect new and unknown viruses. Stiller Research, http://www.stiller.com.
- *InVircible:* A virus detection and eradication system based on a rule-based expert system, integrity checker, and real-time memory monitor. NetZ Computing, http://www.invircible.com.
- *iRiS AntiVirus Plus:* iRiS Antivirus, http://www.irisav.com.
- *KillMonk:* Finds and removes the Monkey and Int_10 viruses from hard disks and diskettes.
- *M-Disk:* A program to remove viruses from the boot sector or master boot record (MBR partition table).
- *MacLis Version 1.10:* Padgett's Word macro virus detector.
- *MacroKiller Version 1.2:* A scanner to detect and delete Word macro virus infections.
- *McAfee VirusScan:* Network Associates, Inc., http://www.nai.com
- *Microsoft Macro Virus Detector:* The macro virus detector is a macro detector for Microsoft Word Version 6 or later. The detector scans for the Concept virus and installs a macro that scans every document you open with the File-Open command and displays a dialog box if the document contains a macro.
- *MIMEsweeper:* Content Technologies, Inc., http://www.mimesweeper.com.
- *NETShield (NetWare):* McAfee's NETShield antivirus NLM for Novell NetWare. Network Associates, Inc., http://www.nai.com.
- *NetZ Utilities:* NetZ's antivirus utilities.
- *NOD-iCE:* ESET, http://www.eset.sk.
- *Norman Virus Control:* Norman Data Defense Systems, http://www.norman.com.
- *Norton Anti-Virus:* Symantec Corporation, http://www.symantec.com
- *Nuke MANZON:* Nuke MANZON.1404 and MANZON.1416. v1.2 + source.
- *Nuke REPLICATOR:* Nuke REPLICATOR.649 and .651 v1.1 + source.
- *Nuke TAIPAN:* Nuke TAIPAN.438 virus v2.2 + source.
- NetShieldNT.

- *OfficeScan:* Trend Micro, http://www.antivirus.com
- *Overseer:* Resident virus guardian system.
- *Panda Antivirus:* Panda Software, http://www.pandasoftware.com.
- *PC ScanMaster for VINES:* Netpro, http://www.netpro.com.
- *PC-Virus 4.0 Database:* PC-Virus 4.0 database and program.
- *PC-Virus 4.0 Reports:* PC-Virus 4.0 virus reports in text form.
- *Protector Plus:* For Windows 95/98, Netware, and NT, http://www.pspl.com
- *Quick Heal:* Cat Computer Services, http://www.quickheal.com
- *QWXYC:* QWXYC cleaner for the WXYC virus. Cleans virus from hard disks and diskettes.
- *Res-av:* Programs to detect unknown viruses.
- *ResQProf:* NetZ Computing, http://www.invircible.com.
- *ScanDay:* The ScanDay utility will automatically run the McAfee Associates' VIRUSCAN software on the first boot on selected days of the week.
- *SENTRY:* SENTRY detects virus infections by maintaining a set of checksums of executable files. SENTRY only checksums the beginnings of such files, allowing for significantly smaller scan times when run.server ScanMaster for VINES and NT: Netpro, http://www.netpro.com.
- *ServerProtect:* Trend Micro, http://www.antivirus.com.
- *Sophos Sweep:* Sophos Software, http://www.sophos.com
- *StScan Version 1.7:* Windows-specific virus scanner/cleaner.
- *Symantec Antivirus for Mac Updates:* SAM is a commercial antivirus product for the Macintosh from Symantec. Updates are available from their web site or from the Symantec BBS at (503) 484–6669 and from the Symantec FTP site ftp://ftp.symantec.com. Copies of some of the updates are available on the CIAC archive. The 4.0.8 update finds and removes most Word macro viruses.
- *System Boot Areas Anti-Virus and Crash Recovery:* SBABR, http://www.sbabr.com.
- *The Bridge Terminus:* A shell utility for ARC, LHARC, PAK, and PKZIP archivers. It will automatically perform virus detection during compression and extraction using McAfee's VIRUSCAN tool.
- *The Detective:* A program for verifying the integrity of files on a system.
- *The Virus Terminus:* A shell menu utility program for McAfee Associates antivirus programs VIRUSCAN, CLEAN, and VALIDATE. Virus Terminus is menu driven and may be used with a mouse or keyboard. Program options may be toggled, reports may be viewed, printed, and merged, and virus fact sheets may be examined to obtain information on specific viruses.
- *ThunderBYTE Anti-Virus:* A toolkit designed to protect against and recover from computer viruses. It focuses on several methods to prevent a virus infection, but also includes programs to remove viruses that have managed to infect the system.
- *Trojan Trap:* Trojan activity detector and protector. Norman Data Defense System, http://www.norman.com.

- *V-find Security Toolkit:* Cybersoft, http://www.cyber.com
- *Vcheck Version 285:* Detects changes in files made by known and unknown viruses. VET Anti-Virus. VET Anti-Virus Software Pty LTD, http://www.vet.com.au.
- *VIRBAIT:* This program notifies the user if it has been modified, presumably by a virus infection. Run periodically, it may alert the user to an infection before damage is done.
- *Virex (by Datawatch Corporation):* Package consists of the VPCScan and Virex programs. VPCScan will identify known viruses in memory and on disk and will repair infected files. VPCScan can also maintain a database of file checksums and detect changes to files. Virex is a TSR program that provides continuous virus protection against running infected or untested software.
- *Virus ALERT:* Look Software, http://www.look.com.
- *Virus Detection System (VDS):* VDS is an antivirus package for IBM PC-compatible computer running MSDOS 3.0 and higher. It contains a set of tools that offer detection and removal of PC viruses. Features include "decoy launching," active stealth boot sector virus detection, self-recovery, and real-time antivirus monitoring to deal with both old and new viruses in an effective manner.
- *VirusBuster:* Leprechaun Software, http://www.leprechaun.com.au.
- *VirusNet LAN:* Safetynet, http://www.safetynet.com.
- *VirusNet PC:* Safteynet, http://www.safetynet.com.
- *VRU AV Testing:* Virus Research Unit is antivirus scanner analysis.
- *VSTE Scanner:* FreeWare Novell virus scanning and reporting.
- *Virus Information Summary List (VSUM):* Patricia Hoffman's Virus Information Summary. VSUM is a hypertext database of virus information.
- *VIRUSCAN:* VIRUSCAN, from McAfee Associates, scans and removes viruses in the master boot record, the DOS boot sector, and executable files on the system.
- *Viruschk:* Viruschk is a "shell" or "watchdog" for McAfee's scan.exe. If a virus condition is found, it will lock up the system and alert the user with loud tone and unmistakable screen.
- *Virus Simulation Suite:* The Virus Simulation Suite are 15 programs that simulate the visual and aural effects of several well-known, older viruses such as Cascade and Devil's Dance. The virus infection routines have been removed, leaving only the nondestructive payloads that can be used for demonstration purposes. The Suite was created by Joe Hirst of the British Computer Virus Research Center.
- *VirusNet LAN Version 3.0 and VirusNet PC Version 3.0:* Provides fully automatic virus protection for several or hundreds of workstations. This is an evaluation version.
- *Wave Anti-Virus:* Cybersoft, http://www.cyber.com.
- *WebScan:* McAfee's Virus protection for Web browser downloads and e-mail attached files. This is an evaluation version.

Cryptographic Checksum Tools

- *MD2:* The source code and specification for the MD-2 message DIGest function.
- *MD4:* The source code and specification for the MD-4 message DIGest function.
- *MD5:* The source code and specification for the MD-5 message DIGest function.
- *Snefru:* The source code and documentation for the Snefru message DIGest function (Xerox's Secure Hash Function).

Miscellaneous Tools

- *BCWipe:* The BCWipe utility for Windows 95/NT is designed to securely delete files from the disk. Standard file deletion leaves the contents of the "deleted" file on your disk. Unless files subsequently saved have overwritten it, it can be recovered using standard disk utilities. Working quickly and integrated with Windows Shell, BCWipe shreds data in files so that they cannot be recovered by any means. BCWipe software is a freeware for noncommercial and nongovernmental use. Testing indicates that Versions 1 and 2 of this product only destroy the primary data stream and do not destroy any alternate data streams. Alternate data streams in NTFS are occasionally used to store other data such as thumbnail images. To ensure that you get the alternate data streams, after clearing and deleting the problem file you should securely erase all free space on the drive.
- *DNSwalk:* A DNS debugger. It performs zone transfers of specified domains and checks the database in numerous ways for internal consistency as well as accuracy. DNSwalk requires Perl and DIG. http://csrc.nist.gov/tools/
- *Generate (pseudo) random TCP sequence numbers:* This was developed for Sun4C machines under SunOS 4.1.2. The author believes it should work for any 4.1.x system, possibly with minor tweaks. It treats tcp_iss as a CRC accumulator into which it hashes every IP output packet. This is perhaps not as strong as it might be, but it is better than what was used and if the machine is at all busy on the network, the attacker faces essentially random sequences of numbers. It does cost some CPU cycles for each output packet. http://csrc.nist.gov/tools/
- *The Internet Worm Source Code:* This is a decompiled C version of the infamous Internet Worm released in November 1988. It is not very readable! http://csrc.nist.gov/tools/
- *Merlin:* Merlin is a Hypertext Transfer Protocol front-end system that allows point-and-click internal vulnerability scanning. Merlin runs in conjunction with the Netscape browser and any security package, such as COPS, Crack, TAMU-Tiger, etc. Simply download desired security

packages and then run Merlin. Merlin makes system scanning easy with its innovative http interface. Merlin is a useful tool for system administrators who have little time to perform the necessary security scans. http://csrc.nist.gov/tools/

- *PC-Sentry:* PC-Sentry is a collection of programs and utilities to provide security and accountability on PCs and PC networks. The heart of the system is pcs.exe, a TSR (memory resident) program that maintains daily log files of file based computer activity. It will log all files opened, deleted, created, copied, directories created and deleted, time changes, commands issued from the DOS prompt, and much more. In addition, it will keep a record of average keystrokes per minute and periods of keyboard inactivity. Most logging functions can be toggled on or off at load time to allow the user to customize the logging capabilities of the program. pcs.exe can also be loaded in a "quiet" mode so the user will never be aware it is running. PC-Sentry is also available in a network version. It operates much the same as the single user version except that it will maintain its log files on a specified network drive. It will also automatically detect whether or not the user is logged into the network, and maintain its log files on the local drive when the network connection is broken, and automatically switch back to the network drive when the connection is reestablished.

- *SATAN (System Administrator Tool for Analyzing Networks):* A network security analyzer that scans systems connected to the network noting the existence of well-known, often exploited vulnerabilities. http://csrc.nist.gov/tools/

- *SCRUB Version 1.3:* A UNIX disk sanitization tool that was developed at the Lawrence Livermore National Laboratory. It has been tested on Linux, Solaris, and AIX. The utility can overwrite a single file, all unused space on a disk, or a whole disk drive with six different patterns to make it highly unlikely that anyone could retrieve the original data from the disk.

- *STREAMS:* A pushable-module/driver tap. Its driver is a kernel-loadable-module, meaning no reboot required. STREAMS is a combination of a STREAMS-module and a STREAMS-driver. The pushed-tap-module pass all downstream M_DATA messages coming from above to the tapc0-driver upstream on the read-side. All upstream M_DATA message coming from below to the tapc1-driver upstream on the read_side. All messages coming downstream from the tapc?-driver are discarded. http://csrc.nist.gov/tools/

- *TbFence:* The TbFence causes systems to use a modified floppy disk data format. This prevents accidental use of diskettes from the outside world that might be infected with viruses. It also prevents accidental distribution of internal data to the outside world.

- *The Gate:* An accounting package for PC systems. It creates a log of users, their passwords, dates, and start and stop times of specified activities.

- *Zap:* This program will fill the wtmp and utmp entries corresponding to the entered username. It also zeros out the last log-in data for the specific user, fingering that user will show "never logged in."

Visualization Tools

In addition to everything else that we have discussed, there are a number of data visualization tools that can be very useful. One such tool, Data Analysis and Visualization Environment (DAVE) from Syneca Research Group (SRG), was developed specifically to store and analyze the types of information relevant to information systems, interoperability, and information architecture. Although the user interface is not up to current standards (Exhibits 1–3), this tool still possesses significant capabilities for the analysis of system require-ments. One adaptation of this tool, Architect, was mentioned previously.

I'm Going to Break in and Compromise your Information

In a nutshell, you can spend an impressive amount of money on your system security and a serious attacker could still find holes. Few, if any, systems can be 100 percent secure unless you unplug the system from the Internet and place it in a lead-lined room with no access. Even then it still needs electricity (which can be accidentally or maliciously turned off). So it is possible that the best you can do from a risk management perspective is to prevent 99.999 percent of the hackers from breaking in and compromising or disrupting your information. But that still gives at least these authors the ability to exploit your information using network attack tools and some elementary program-ming. Here is what we consider the most common methods for gaining access to your information. You may notice that the attacks are not very "high-tech" and that is because, unfortunately, they do not have to be. They just need to work. Neither are they physical attacks or malicious attacks that could be caused by disgruntled employees working on the inside. This list is exhaustive, but not complete. These attacks are what you will most likely see the largest percentage of hackers using.

We will not give any details on how to execute the attacks listed below. But anyone who wants to learn how to break in to your system and com-promise your information can find out how with just a little research and the right automated tools.

We would first launch an attack using any of several generic reconnaissance mechanisms available to us, such as finger, systat, netstat, or rusersd. These can all be used to gather user names, network statistics, process accounting, and other information. All of these help us to learn about your host and network. With systat and netstat running, we can view running processes on your host, as well as network configuration information. Various RPC services such as rusersd and rstatd allow us to see who is logged in and to monitor system statistics for planning attacks.

The finger service would be our first choice of general reconnaissance. Finger can be used to grab valid account names from your host. Some versions allow us to issue commands that let us "walk" the user list, thereby allowing us to list out every account on your host. Some versions will also let us "walk" the local utmp file, allowing us to view where users are logging in from and

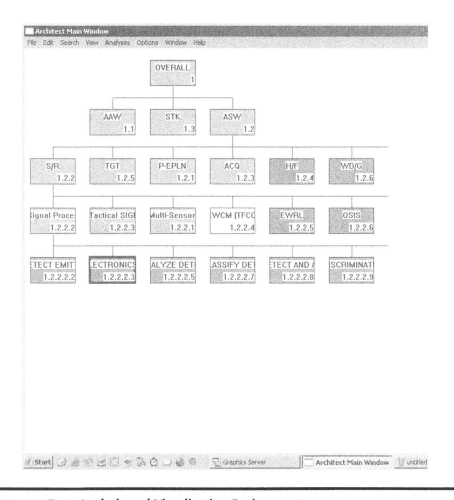

Exhibit 1   Data Analysis and Visualization Environment

when. There are also other versions that allow us to execute commands remotely or to setup.plan files that mail out privileged system information. Do yourself a favor and shut this service off on all your hosts.

We would first try to log into your system by using common accounts that are shipped with many UNIX hosts, such as TEST. Although many modern systems do not succumb to this, many older ones do. Sometimes administrators will reenable the default accounts, even on new hosts as well. Sometimes they have to boot off the original after a system crash or file corruption, and the original default accounts and null passwords sneak back into the system without a warning.

Next, we would try logging in by trying a known username and using the username as the password as well. This works especially well after grabbing names from finger and other sources. Having the username and password the same is not a rare event.

How were we able to get this far? The simple answer is the "r" word — remote. Every administrator should loathe the "r" word. Remote hosts, remote shells, remote log-in, remote executes, etc. Take, for example, rsh, which

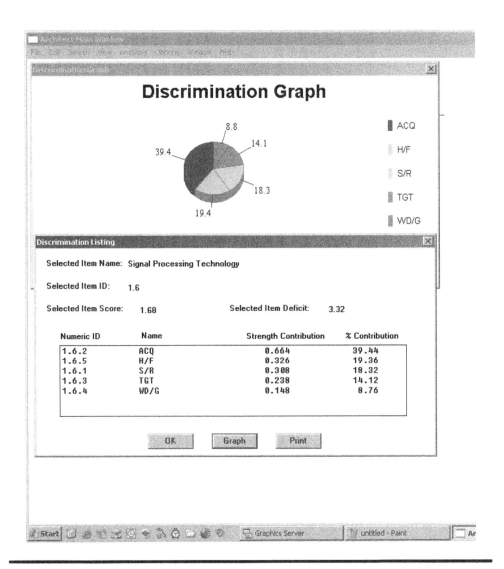

Exhibit 2   Discrimination Analysis

comes shipped with your UNIX operating system and many administrators leave them on their UNIX source trees. They use a poor authentication mechanism that is easily abused and we found that the majority of people who use them are just too lazy to type in a password between hosts. A very large number of sites use transitive trusts between hosts (.rhosts files) and this leads to rapid system compromise if even a single host is hacked. Some vendors ship with a/etc/hosts.equiv file including a "+" that allows any host full access to your system remotely. In addition to this, many of the rsh daemons perform no auditing of any commands. You should shut off the rsh service and remove it from your binary directory to ensure it is never turned on. If you need the remote execution feature and transitive trust feature for automated tasks, you should try SSH instead. Otherwise, consider us arriving at your back door with some simple breaking-and-entering tools like rexecd and rexd.

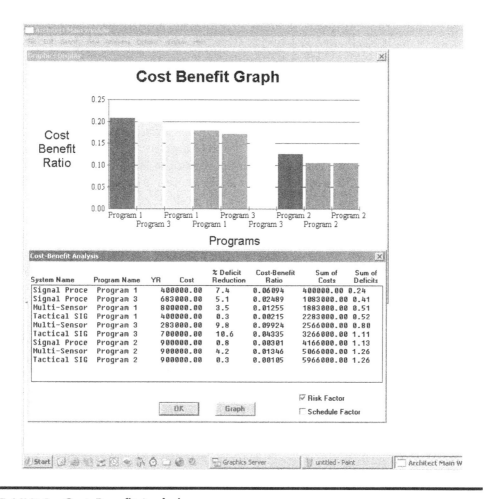

Exhibit 3   Cost–Benefit Analysis

Your rexecd service uses username/password-style authentication, but does not audit failed login attempts. This allows us to beat up on a host with a large password list unknown to the administrator. Not to be confused with rexecd, rexd is a service that allows any remote host to run commands on your system identified as any user we want (sometimes we may not be able to run as root, though). This service is actually shipped with some UNIX versions turned on. It is important to note that all of the rexd security is at the client and not the server. Because we can impersonate any user we wish, you can plainly see what is going to happen next.

Many remote services have problems that can be exploited to one degree or another. If you do not use the service, you should shut it off (rusers, sprayd, walld, rexd, etc.). One particular service, statd (sometimes listed as "status" in portmapper dumps), is used extensively to gain access to systems. This service should be patched or shut down on all hosts that do not require it (it is used by NFS to enable more-reliable file locking, so you may not be able to shut it off if you use NFS). Contact your vendor for an update. Another service making the rounds is "ttdbserverd," which has a remotely exploitable overflow as well. Shut off your RPC services or get them patched.

The best thing we can do now is to go password sniffing. This has got to be one of the most powerful attacks we can use against your system. Not because it is sophisticated, but rather because it allows us to gain access quickly to hundreds of hosts if they have a sniffer setup in a high-traffic location. Once the passwords are obtained, it is difficult to spot us because we appear as a normal user. The only defense against this is to not allow us to obtain access to a host. You may want to consider using encrypted sessions between all hosts with a tool such as SSH. Fortunately for us, most other protocols are open to our attack also (e.g., POP, FTP, HTTP). You can do yourself a favor and force users to use SSH through its tunneling mechanism to access some of these services, but many users will balk at this unless major arm-twisting is employed.

Another way to remotely grab password files (and in some cases remotely execute commands) is through your Network Information Service (NIS, formerly YP). If you need this service, please upgrade to NIS+ and ensure it is properly patched.

Do not run an anonymous FTP server unless you need the service. FTP sites are easily configured in error. Many FTP daemons also have a variety of problems that can lead to system compromise even if anonymous FTP is not enabled. If you do run an anonymous FTP site you need to watch it very closely and follow the guidelines for setting it up correctly. We can use a wrongly configured site to exchange pirate software, corrupt downloadable files, gain remote access, bypass firewall and packet-filter security, and a variety of other misuses.

Once in, we will see if you are running RPC Portmapper. Some older versions allow us to perform "proxy" attacks in that we can bypass local security restrictions by making the RPC call appear to come from the local host. This service can also be used to dump all available RPC services that would help us discover vulnerable services. You should shutdown all RPC services if you do not use them, or use a replacement that fixes a number of these problems. For the typical hacker, this only blocks them from looking at the portmapper for information. However, some of us can bypass portmapper (and hence your wrapper) and probe for services directly. It is important that you shut off all RPC services you are not using. Next, we will go looking for your World Wide Web (WWW) server.

If you do not need to run a WWW server, you should shut it off. We can abuse the default cgi-bin files shipped with these servers to remotely exploit hosts. If you are running a WWW server, you should go into the cgi-bin directory and "rm *" the entire thing and then fill it in with your CGI scripts. Nearly all CGI scripts shipped with WWW servers have had security holes in them, or currently have a hole of some type and should be deleted.

One daemon that we love to find is your Network File Sharing (NFS) daemon. We use this to read and write to files and to gain access through any number of methods. First, you need to be sure you are running the latest version of the daemon for your operating system, as this will fix many common problems. Just make sure you are not exporting directories to the world. Be sure you are only exporting directories to hosts that need them and that you are not exporting more than necessary. In other words, why are you exporting "/" when your users really only need "/usr/local/tools"? Be sure you run fsir and another similar utility after you have applied patches to ensure your file handles are random. Export read-only when you can and if you export read-write, be sure you do not allow root privs to cross the export mount. The mountd service under Linux is especially vulnerable to a nasty remote access hole. Make sure your systems are patched, and if you are not running NFS, shut off all of its associated daemons.

One of the authors was part of the group that designed and wrote the documentation for Transmission Control Protocol/Internet Protocol (TCP/IP), Simple Mail Transport Protocol (SMTP), and other protocols still in use. So trust us when we tell you to make sure your SMTP server is running the latest version of the daemon. Sendmail, smail, and others have all had problems in the past, ranging from denial-of-service to full remote-access exploits. If your host does not process mail, you should shut off local SMTP services. If you are running mail, consider dumping Sendmail and getting either qmail or vmailer, which are far more secure.

Likewise, many SNMP daemons and services are set up with easily guess-able public and private community strings. This allows us to reconfigure key network devices, gain reconnaissance information, and cause general mayhem. You need to disable SNMP on your network or if you need to use it, make sure you are using at least Version 2 and have unguessable community names. Even still, beware that this is still very susceptible to attack.

If you are running Trivial File Transfer Protocol (TFTP), you have basically extended the welcome mat to us. The name says it all. This service allows us to grab key system files, such as/etc/passwd. Because it requires no authentication, any person can connect and read whatever they want.

Another welcome mat is X Windows. We can use open X Windows clients to read keyboard input, dump screen shots, execute commands as the logged-in user, and generally cause mischief. You need to make sure all your X-related devices are secured with either xhost or xauth security mechanisms. If you are running Microsoft Windows X clients, you need to do the same to them as well. We can capture keystrokes just as easily from Reflections X on Windows as we can on UNIX.

One of the easiest ways of breaking into your system is by performing buffer overrun attacks. Once we can get a buffer overrun to crash the system, security holes pop up all over the place. By the time you reboot the system, you are also rebooting one of our own backdoors. Make sure you are using the latest version of DNS on your name servers to prevent cache poisoning and buffer overrun attacks. Make sure you prohibit zone transfers to sites that are not a secondary to you, as this allows us to view your entire namespace to find targets (not foolproof, but good enough to stop most attacks). Be careful how you name your machines as they appear in external DNS. The names should be nondescript to the casual observer. Naming a machine "gauntlet-fw.somedo-main.com" tells us instantly you are probably running a TIS Gauntlet firewall.

Likewise, a machine with a name of "temp123.somedomain.com" lets us know that the machine would be a good target because it is probably not well monitored. You should also consider running BIND in a chroot() environment.

A very common buffer-overrun method known to many attackers is IMAP/POP. Some versions contain a serious and easily exploited buffer overrun that allows remote execution commands as root. Update your daemon or shut this service off if you do not use it. Some POP servers also do not report failed log-ins, so we can brute-force passwords all day long and you will never know.

If you are running the Linux operating system, you are not out of the woods by a long shot. Samba is a popular exploit for Linux systems, as many distributions ship this service enabled by default. Aside from administrators exporting shares with global permission, exporting too much, etc., it also has a serious buffer overrun that allows attackers to execute commands as root. Shut off this service or obtain an update.

Some of our favorite exploits are those "temporary" configurations that get embedded deep in the system somewhere and then are forgotten about. And then we find them. "Temporary changes" are changes that you set up "temporarily" to let someone onto your system, but you later forget to disable. It always seems that we find these at one point or another, no matter how well hidden you think they are. Please do not set up "temporary" configurations for any host that is on the Internet for any length of time.

If all this is overwhelming, we recommend a good basic book for system administrators on what attackers look for when they try to break into your system: *Improving the Security of Your Site by Breaking Into It,* written by Dan Farmer and Wietse Venema.

A Sampling of Software Tools that Attackers Use

L0pht Crack

A Windows NT password cracker, auditing tool, by L0pht Heavy Industries.

NTRecover/Locksmith

Allows you to gain access to a WinNT computer over a serial connection. NTRecover is an advanced Windows NT dead-system recovery utility for x86 NT installations. Using NTRecover, NT machines that fail to boot because of data corruption, improperly installed software or hardware, or faulty configuration, can be accessed and recovered using standard administrative tools, as if the machine were up and running. Using an adjacent NT-based computer connected by a serial cable, NTRecover allows an administrator to:

- Copy files between the nonbooting system and the working NT system
- Edit or delete files that may be preventing the system from booting
- Run virus detection and removal programs
- Repair damaged filesystem structures using chkdsk

NTRecover consists of host and client software, where the host software runs on a "good" NT 3.51 or 4.0 system, and the client software executes on a "dead" system in need of repair. The "dead" system is booted off a floppy disk directly to the NTRecover program, so repair is possible even when basic startup code in NT, such as NTLDR, fails. The host and client machines are connected with a standard null-modem serial cable. The NTRecover host software creates virtual disk drives on the host machine that represent the drives present on the client computer. When native NT file systems, such as NTFS and FAT, access the drives, NTRecover manages communications over the serial cable to the client software to transfer disk data back and forth between the two machines. As far as Windows NT on the host machine is concerned, the drives created by NTRecover are indistinguishable from the local drives present on the host, and so they can be manipulated with Windows NT disk utilities, including high-level tools such as the Windows NT Explorer, and low-level tools such as chkdsk. Be sure to check out Remote Recover, which provides you all the capabilities of NTRecover except that it works over TCP/IP LAN/WANs instead of a serial cable. Remote Recover is ideal for high-speed backup/restore/repair, especially when large amounts of data are involved.

Password Hacker

A utility similar to Snadboy in that it reveals the passwords normally hidden by asterisks in Win95/98.

Snadboy's Revelation

Revelation will uncover those passwords that Windows 95/98 has hidden behind asterisks.

Legion

A sophisticated scanner that specifically looks for "Windows shares" on an IP range.

Port Scanner

Portscan is a utility that allows one to scan specified hosts for open ports in specified port ranges. Port Scanner allows you to scan a group of IP addresses looking for the presence of specific incoming TCP/IP ports. This is a terrific tool for anyone managing a TCP/IP network. Finally, there is an easy way to see who on your network is running a specific TCP/IP daemon. In just a few seconds, Port Scanner can locate and log all the active TCP/IP ports on all machines that you specify. Using an intuitive interface that allows you to specify the start and end addresses of a scan, you can quickly check a specific machine, a subnet, or an entire domain. Port Scanner comes predefined to scan for the most common TCP/IP services, and provides a quick way to add any of your own ports. In addition, Port Scanner lets you scan a subset of the existing ports, and to save subsets into named groups for easy recall. Scan results can be easily printed or saved to a file. Version 1.2b1 introduces the ability to automate Port Scanner. Through the use of simple text-based scripts, you can automate a long series of scans, and have the results of each scan saved into a text file for later analysis. The current version of Port Scanner is 1.2b1. Port Scanner requires a WinSock-compatible TCP/IP stack, and is fully Windows 95- and NT 4.0-compatible.

SATAN

The controversial network analysis tool, SATAN was written because it was realized that computer systems are becoming more and more dependent on the network, and at the same becoming more and more vulnerable to attack via that same network. The rationale for SATAN is given in a paper posted in a December 1993 admin guide to cracking, a flat text compressed with the UNIX compress command. SATAN is a tool to help systems administrators. It recognizes several common networking-related security problems, and reports the problems without actually exploiting them. For each type or problem found, SATAN offers a tutorial that explains the problem and what its impact could be. The tutorial also explains what can be done about the problem: correct an error in a configuration file, install a bugfix from the vendor, and use other means to restrict access, or simply disable service. SATAN collects information that is available to everyone with access to the network. With a properly configured firewall in place, that should be near-zero information for outsiders. We have done some limited research with SATAN. Our finding is that on networks with more than a few dozen systems, SATAN will inevitably find problems. Here is the current problem list:

- NFS file systems exported to arbitrary hosts
- NFS file systems exported to unprivileged programs
- NFS file systems exported via the portmapper
- NIS password file access from arbitrary hosts
- Old (i.e., before 8.6.10) Sendmail versions
- REXD access from arbitrary hosts
- X server access control disabled
- Arbitrary files accessible via TFTP
- Remote shell access from arbitrary hosts
- Writable anonymous FTP home directory

These are well-known problems. They have been the subject of CERT, CIAC, or other advisories, or are described extensively in practical security handbooks. The intruder community has exploited the problems for a long time. We realize that SATAN is a two-edged sword — like many tools, it can be used for good and for evil purposes. We also realize that attackers have much-more-capable tools than offered with SATAN. We have those tools, too, but giving them away to the world at large is not the goal of the SATAN project.

YAPS

YAPS stands for "yet another port scanner." YAPS is a Windows95/NT intelligent IP port scanner. It can quickly analyze a single computer or identify all computers on a specified network. Features include:

- Scans a single host by name
- Scans a range of hosts by IP address
- Scans multiple hosts simultaneously
- Generates reports in HTML format
- Scans TCP ports over a user-defined range of ports
- Identifies Web server version and home page title
- FTP reports with anonymous log-on test
- Reports on telnet response
- Reports on NNTP, SMTP, and POP servers
- Reports on finger response
- User-defined (not system default) time-out
- Scans Windows (SMB) networks, even across the Internet
- Scans up to 65535 unprivileged ports
- Uses multiple asynchronous sockets to scan hundreds of times faster
- Complete control over which services are scanned
- ICMP echo (ping) test
- Option to continue if ping fails
- Scans up to 4096 hosts at one time
- Defines multiple ports and ranges of ports to scan

Sniffit

This is a pretty good packet sniffer that runs on UNIX, Linux, FreeBSD, and Irix. My packet sniffer, developed on LINUX, ported to SunOS/SOLARIS, Irix, and FreeBSD. It has various functions that are not offered in any other noncommercial sniffer.

Web Packet Sniffer

This is actually two CGI scripts that can listen to all TCP/IP traffic on a subnet and more. These are a pair of Perl scripts that together will:

- Listen to all TCP/IP traffic on a subnet
- Intercept all outgoing requests for Web documents and display them
- Intercept all incoming requests for Web documents and display them
- Decode the basic authentication passwords, if any

These scripts (total of 39 lines of code) were demonstrated at the WWW6 conference in Santa Clara, California in April 1997. The demonstration was not to show how to write a great packet sniffer, but to show how vulnerable the Web is to sniffing.

IP Spoofing

Hides your true IP address and appear to have an entirely different IP.

Back Orifice

Back Orifice is a remote administration system that allows a user to control a computer across a TCP/IP connection using a simple console or GUI application. On a local LAN or across the Internet, BO gives its user more control of the remote Windows machine than the person at the keyboard of the remote machine has. BO is small, and entirely self-installing. Simply executing the server on any Windows machine installs the server, moving the executable into the system where it will not interfere with other running applications. To ease distribution, BO can also be attached to any other Windows executable that will run normally after installing the server. Once running, BO does not show up in the task list or close-program list, and is rerun every time the computer is started. The filename that it runs as is configurable before it is installed, and it is as easy to upgrade as uploading the new version and running it.

NetBus

Better than Back Orifice, and runs on NT, too.

Stealth Keyboard Interceptor

A very good and full-featured keyboard logger that runs completely in the background.

Summary

In this chapter you have come to recognize the automated tools that can be used to protect your information, as well as those tools that attackers use to attempt to access your information. In some instances, it is the same tool, just used for different purposes. To recognize the value and limitations of these tools is important, but it is even more important to realize that the use of these tools will not solve all your problems. They are simply an important segment of the overall systemic solution.

Chapter 12

Summary

A good plan executed violently today is better than a perfect plan executed tomorrow.

General George S. Patton, Jr.

We have covered a lot of ground in this volume and it may not always have been clear how the various pieces fit together. So, in the interest of clarity, we will try to summarize here and make explicit connections that may not have been apparent up to this point.

In Chapter 1, we started with the goal, information assurance (IA). By definition, IA is the business of getting:

- The right information
- To the right individual
- At the right time
- With some "reasonable assurance" (confidence) that the information is timely, accurate, and reliable

Information assurance is the single biggest concern of Chief Information Officers (CIOs) and other information managers in both government and industry. Indeed, it is a concern for many citizens as well. IA is more than just user IDs and passwords, but it is not rocket science. Though there are several significant technical issues involved, most organizations could make major improvements in their IA posture with the simple application of policies, procedures, and processes. There is no pie-in-the-sky, technical, whiz-bang widget that will totally fix or eliminate the problem. Instead, as suggested by tried-and-true methodologies such as systems engineering and the Trusted Computer Security Evaluation Criteria (TCSEC), the best approach is a layered approach — building security and, hence, information assurance through layers of safeguards beginning with perimeter fencing, guards, and other physical access controls, to policies and procedures for the use of information systems and the control of access to those systems both physically and virtually through user IDs, passwords, firewalls, PKIs, VPNs, and a large variety of other methods and technologies. The good news is that, because there are so many different combinations, it is fairly easy to devise the one best suited to any particular situation. On the flip side, however, so many different options require a good deal of investigation, preparation, enforcement, monitoring, and routine maintenance.

In order to understand all of the things that make up this problem of information assurance, we proceeded in Chapter 2 with a description of some of the basic, underlying issues and concerns. First, there was the concept of information and system attributes. In the first chapter and again in the introduction in this chapter, we mentioned confidence or "reasonable assurance" that our information is timely, accurate, and reliable; but what does that really mean? The more we think about all of the characteristics or "'ilities" that our information should ideally possess, the longer the list becomes. This issue has been the subject of much writing by many authors and, as stated, we did not try to reinvent the wheel. We did, however, present a short summary of previous work, and tried to show how all of these information properties (and, no doubt, a good deal more) are important to our interpretation of the knowledge they impart.

Speaking of knowledge, just exactly what is it and how do we get there? The cognitive, information, and decision hierarchies are an attempt to understand how we process the large quantity of facts that assault our consciousness daily. The jumble of incoming data first must be categorized or organized in some fashion that is intelligible to humans, then fused with other information and real-world sense; thus working our way up the pyramid from data to organized information, to recognized, useful knowledge. Again, the accuracy or "goodness" of that knowledge is heavily dependent on how many of the attributes have been satisfied and how well. From there, human cognition takes over, and we begin to understand the situation and become aware of our environment until we get to the point where we feel comfortable enough to make a decision. Somewhere along the line, probably after years of struggling with loads of information, knowledge, and decisions, some of us develop a "sixth sense" or wisdom associated with the domain or perhaps the world in general.

Combined with all of this is the issue of the quickness with which we navigate the information maze — what Colonel John Boyd called "the OODA Loop." Col. Boyd argued that it is not enough to collect "good" information and build it into understanding and awareness; we must do it faster and better than the other guy. Whether we are referring to air-to-air combat or day-to-day business applications, there is always an opponent or competitor that we are trying to outperform. The OODA Loop shows us that it is the relative speed of decision making that counts, not necessarily the absolute speed with which it is accomplished. These concepts all come together in the Information Pinwheel (Exhibit 1).

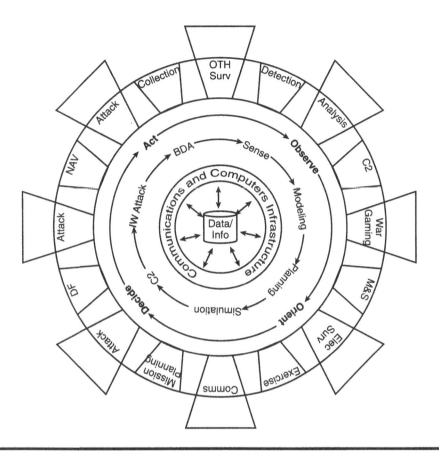

Exhibit 1   The Information Pinwheel

Exhibit 2   Risk Assessment

In Chapter 3, we discussed three more important concepts: risk, threat, and vulnerability. Although these terms are often used interchangeably, we show how they are significantly different concepts. Risk is some combination of threat, vulnerability, and value (Exhibit 2). In the absence of any one of these, risk is virtually nonexistent. But more often it is some multiattribute utility (MAU) measure that takes all of these things into account.

A threat can be defined as any circumstance or event with the potential to harm an information system. Threats can be naturally occurring phenomena such as hurricanes and lightning strikes, or unintentional man-made events, or a hostile attack. There are ways to guard against all of these, but the hostile attack generally causes us the most concern. Many factors influence such an attack, as we discussed, but in general they are some combination of hostile intent, commitment on the part of the perpetrator, and the capability to carry out the intent. If there were no threats (naturally occurring, accidental, or otherwise), there would be little reason to "harden" information systems. Unfortunately, real threats do exist, which brings us to the vulnerability of our information systems to these potential threats.

Vulnerability is a measure of how open a particular system may be to potential attack. If a system has no vulnerabilities, the threat, however intense or imminent, is unimportant. With a house of brick, the big bad wolf can huff and puff all he likes, but he will not get in. Unfortunately, we have also shown how it is virtually impossible to make any information system impregnable. There simply is not enough time nor money to do so, and even if there were, we must consider the concept of value.

It does not make a good deal of sense to spend large sums of time and money to protect information that is relatively unimportant or of little value (Exhibit 3). Although monetary value is something that we all deal with every day, this is a difficult concept for some information managers to grasp. All information has some value. The extent of that worth depends on its sensitivity, importance, criticality, and other domain-specific measures. Information categorized as intellectual property (IP), company proprietary or competition sensitive, for example, tends to be difficult for information managers to quantify from the perspective of worth. Yet, investment bankers, loan officers, financial analysts, and lawyers attach monetary values to such things every day. In fact, individual investors do so when they evaluate the comparative advantages of

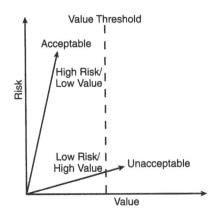

Exhibit 3   Value

one corporate stock over another, although they may not do so consciously. If we do not know the worth of our information or information system, how are we to make informed business decisions concerning the time, effort, and cost associated with the security of it? In Chapter 3, we hope to have shown that risk, threat, and vulnerability are complex and interrelated though separate issues that must be addressed if we are to achieve information assurance.

One more topic remains before we can address the actual process of building, operating, and maintaining any system — systems engineering, the subject of Chapter 4. Here again our intent was to lay the foundation for what is to come, not to reinvent structured engineering approaches. We present a number of views of systems engineering and engineering management as described by several well-respected pioneers in the field without attempting to choose among them. It is our belief that nearly any good, organized, structured approach will work if it is followed thoroughly and consistently. Whether you choose the Spiral Model (Exhibit 4) or the more traditional Waterfall (Exhibit 5), the key is the rigor with which the methodology is applied. The choice of methods depends on many factors and, of course, all of these methods must be customized to each individual project to account for complexity, the availability of resources, the acceptable level of risk, the level of experience the team possesses in the method, and many more factors. Here, we simply discuss some alternatives and advocate the use of some structured approach.

In order to actualize a system design, we must first collect a core team of experts to manage the project; which is the subject of Chapter 5. Far too many

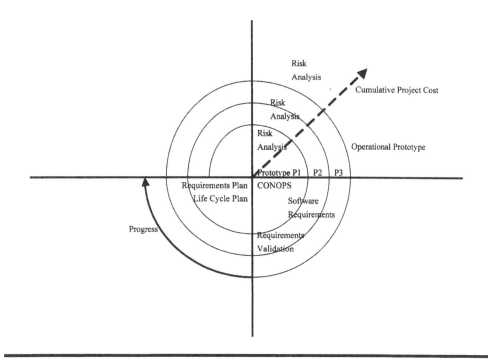

Exhibit 4   The Spiral Model [Krutz, 2001]

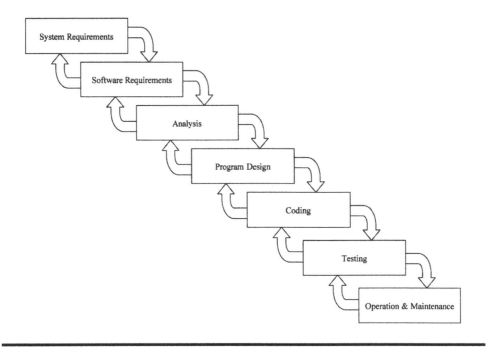

Exhibit 5   The Waterfall Model [Krutz, 2001]

organizations engage in defining requirements and procuring funding or a variety of other activities before selecting a team or even a team leader to manage the process. It is important to achieve some level of continuity in any project. In addition, many of the decisions that will be made along the way will depend on the individuals involved. Project timelines, work breakdown structures, choice of tools, and many other factors depend on the expertise and experience of the core team. Making some of these selections before the team is established can force the individuals and the organization into less-than-optimal situations. In Chapter 5, we discuss some of the key considerations in choosing and organizing a team, along with a few of the basic functions of the team once it is established.

Having addressed these background, underlying issues, we then outline a structured, systems engineering approach to defining, building, and maintaining an information system, beginning in Chapter 6. The beginning of any systems development is the definition of requirements — just exactly what is the system intended to do, in what environment, under what circumstances? Systems engineering, information management, knowledge management, and other disciplines have addressed the issue of functional requirements collection, analysis, and allocation adequately. Many authors have presented various methodologies and discuss different aspects of the problem. Alhough we presented a brief summary of these concepts in Chapter 4, our primary focus is on how to capture these requirements and what to do with them once they have been adequately defined. As we have shown, simply collecting requirements is not enough. If they are not readily accessible to analysts, developers, users, and acquisition agents to study, compare, cost-out and trade-off, the job becomes (or perhaps remains) more difficult than required. In our opinion, automated tools can provide a good deal of capability in this area, yet are largely unused (Exhibits 6 and 7). This goes back to the cognitive hierarchy. While simply recording requirements in some list or textual document may at least collect the required data in one place, it does very little with respect to helping us understand the requirements and being aware of system concepts at the micro and macro levels and everywhere in between.

Several commercial off-the-shelf (COTS) automated tools are available to help organize and visualize data, beginning with something as simple as a database (Exhibit 6). Several organizations have successfully implemented databases to capture requirements of one sort or another, but most are limited to producing interesting sorts, queries, and reports rather than interfacing with other automated tools for visualization and analysis. Other government off-the-shelf (GOTS) tools and corporate proprietary tools have been developed to interface with data captured in a database and allow various analyses and interesting views of the data (Exhibit 7). This began the discussion of tools that we elaborate on later.

The most important concept in this chapter is the notion of a single, unified architecture, or what we refer to as the *Rubik's Cube architecture* (Exhibit 8). Many different individuals and groups are interested in varying aspects of the architecture. Hence, a variety of architectural views or specialized blueprints, if you prefer, are required. But just like the blueprints for a building, these are all just context-specific pictures of the same architecture — the plumbers' view versus the electricians' view versus the structural details. As a Rubik's Cube, the faces can change in innumerable ways, but they always come back to the same thing.

In Chapter 7, we move on to actually designing the system. From conceptual to final design, many things must be considered. All too often, some critically important items, such as security, documentation, and training, get pushed aside until much later. Band-aid fixes are then applied to solve problems that should never have developed in the first place. In some circles, this design has been termed *system architecture*. Unfortunately, while descriptive, the term has been overused and has picked up some less-than-desirable connotations along the way. Nonetheless, architectures or blueprints are essential to clean, accurate system design, especially when we consider interoperability issues.

By the end of this chapter, it should be clear how all the concepts that we have discussed (IA, interoperability, attributes, the cognitive hierarchy, the OODA Loop, etc.) come together to produce a well-designed, interoperable system (Exhibit 9).

Implementation and testing (Chapter 8) is the next step. While all of the traditional systems engineering concepts related to these areas definitely apply, information systems are generally subjected to a unique certification and accreditation process. Building on early work with the TCSEC [DoD5200, 1985], the Department of Defense (DoD) first codified the process in the DoD Information Technology System Certification and Accreditation Program (DITSCAP) [DoD8510, 2000]. Later DITSCAP, with minor modifications, was

Exhibit 6   Requirements Data

Bx	Rx	Bname	O/D	Tier3	Rof_title	WMA	System	Imp	Cap	Plat	Arch	IOC	MSC	POM	D/I	C/N	Assumption
1	1	P-EPLN	D	EWC2	Conduct tactical mission planning	STK	TAMPS	3	4	A	W	1990	NPLR	C			TF organic systems; System needs update; Not a primary EW tool
1	1	P-EPLN	D	EWC2	Conduct tactical mission planning	STK	TEAMS	5	4	A	W	1990	NPLR	C	D	C	TF organic systems; Requires update for EA-6B
1	2	P-EPLN	D	ELINT	Develop electronic OOBs	AAW	EWRL	2	3	Z	W	1990	NPLR	C			Does not cover all spectrums/freqs needed for planning; Availability of input data
1	2	P-EPLN	D	ELINT	Develop electronic OOBs	AAW	BGPHES	5	4	M	+	2000	NPLR	C	D	C	Does not cover all spectrums/freqs needed for planning
1	2	P-EPLN	D	ELINT	Develop electronic OOBs	AAW	CDF	5	3	S	W	1990	NPLR	C	D	C	Databases and TACINTEL; Good now, but will not handle the threat ca. 2010 without significant upgrades; Comms only
1	2	P-EPLN	D	ELINT	Develop electronic OOBs	AAW	OSIS	4	3	Z	W	1990	NPLR	C	D	N	Databases and TACINTEL
1	2	P-EPLN	D	ELINT	Develop electronic OOBs	AAW	ES-3A	5	4	A	W	1990	NPLR	C	D	C	Does not cover all spectrums and freqs needed for planning
1	2	P-EPLN	D	ELINT	Develop electronic OOBs	AAW	TENCAP	5	3	Z	W	1990	NPLR	C	D	C	Databases and TACINTEL; Excellent capability, but limited availability
5	54	WD/G	D	EWC2	Confirm target identification in real-time	STK	CDF	5	4	S	W	1990	NPL	C	D	C	Requires radiating target
5	54	WD/G	D	EWC2	Confirm target identification in real-time	STK	CILOP	5	5	A	+	2000	NPL	C	D	C	Confirmation of a detected emitter or platform (or both) as a target is good
6	66	H/F	D	Noise jam	Counter enemy terminal defense systems	AAW	Tacit Rainbow	5	3	A	+	2000	NP	B	D	C	Limited accuracy
6	66	H/F	D	Noise jam	Counter enemy terminal defense systems	STK	ASPJ & P3	5	3	A	+	2000	NP	B	D	C	Designed for terminal defense
6	71	H/F	O		Employ directed energy weapons	AAW	EA-6B	3	5	A	W	1990	NPL	BDE			HARM only

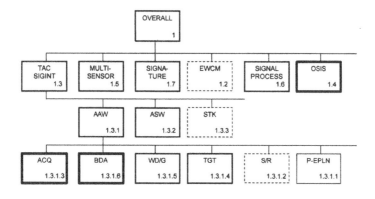

Exhibit 7   Visualizing Requirements

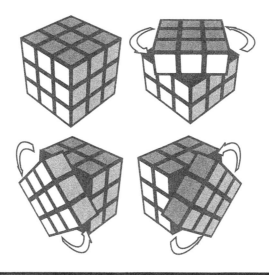

Exhibit 8   Rubik's Cube Architecture

adopted as a national standard under the title National Information Assurance Certification and Accreditation Program (NIACAP) [NIST, 2000]. The certification and accreditation (C&A) program specifies three basic steps:

1. *Evaluation:* The technical analysis of the security of a component, product, subsystem, or system that establishes whether or not it meets a specific set of requirements.
2. *Certification:* The inspection and testing of a specific hardware and software site implementation against accepted information assurance/ information security standards.
3. *Accreditation:* Formal declaration by a designated approving authority (DAA) that an AIS is approved to operate in a particular security mode using a prescribed set of safeguards.

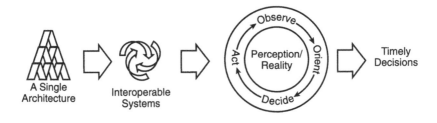

Exhibit 9   The Big Picture

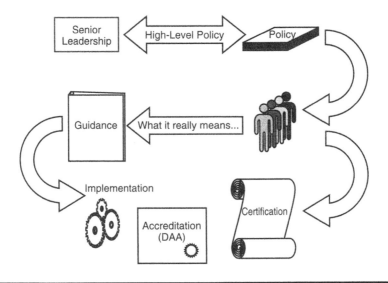

Exhibit 10   The C&A Process

Beginning with *evaluation,* this ensures that each hardware and software component is inspected and tested for applicable security compliance; the assembled system is then *certified* in its intended operational environment, and finally, some designated approving authority (DAA) *accredits* the system installation and accepts responsibility for the operation of the system within the limitations of the system and the environment (Exhibit 10). Certifications and accreditations are typically accomplished by the owner of the system, while evaluations are usually conducted by an independent third party or government agency.

Recently, the Common Criteria [ISO15408, 1999] has been developed to take the place of earlier, individual, country-specific security requirements. In the United States, Common Criteria replaces the old TCSEC and is sponsored by the National Information Assurance Partnership (NIAP), a joint venture between the National Security Agency (NSA) and the National Institute of Standards and Technology (NIST). The Common Evaluation Methodology (CEM) [NIST, 1999], an alternative to the C&A process, is a related standard.

Moving on to Chapter 9, we discussed some of the issues involved with life-cycle support and day-to-day operations. In order for any system to deliver the functionality for which it was designed:

- It must operate reliably
- The operators, maintainers, and users must be properly trained
- Processes and procedures must be in place, in use, and enforced
- Routine ·maintenance must, of course, be performed
- Data must be updated continually
- A whole host of other routine functions must be performed

Most of these things are common practice, but often designers, developers, implementers, and operators forget just what is involved. If consideration is given to all of these issues early in the development, considerable time, money, and other resources can be saved later, while significantly increasing the performance of both the system and the people who use it.

In Chapter 10, we addressed the issue of information assurance organizations and described a solution that we call the Information Assurance Center (IAC). This is a simple, scalable, executable formula for an establishment to deal with IA issues. In large organizations with diverse systems and responsibilities, the IAC could be very large and may even be a completely separate agency, department, or some other corporate entity. In smaller applications, it may simply be a division or group within the parent. In either case, the IAC is intended to be the one-stop authority on IA issues, a place to find up-to-date information, and get assistance when needed (Exhibit 11). The IAC concept was modeled after very successful organizations with similar responsibilities in the aviation-safety domain within the DoD [Campbell, 1997; Curts, 2000]. This chapter offers some insight into the functions that might be performed by such an organization, and some suggested organizational constructs.

Automated tools are a very important part of the IT domain and were discussed briefly in Chapter 11. We believe that tools are grossly underutilized

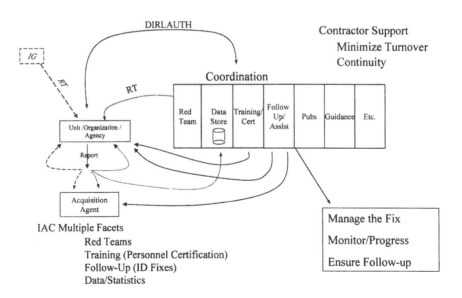

Exhibit 11

in the world of systems engineering, information technology, architecture development, and information assurance, particularly in the area of data visualization (Exhibit 7). Tools come in all shapes and sizes, and there is a huge, off-the-shelf variety available. The trick is to match the tools to the environment. All too often those who do realize the value of tools choose an application and then become a slave to the huge data requirements that drive it. Project management and scheduling tools are a good example. Almost all projects, big or small, require some sort of timeline to show schedules and management, if nothing else. Many good tools exist to perform this function and much more; much more is often the problem. Some users feel compelled to input all the data the tool will accept instead of tailoring the data input to the required functionality and output. This can be a large drain on resources for little or no return.

At the other end of the spectrum, we find seemingly simple applications that are either not developed or underutilized. As we discussed in earlier chapters, requirements, architectural details, and other data elements lend themselves nicely to simple database applications, yet they are much more often captured as text. Admittedly, a little more time is required on the front end to design database schemas and set up the appropriate tables, relationships, constraints, and other such constructs. A different skill set is generally required to do so successfully. However, the process of instantiating the database is often less resource intensive than publishing a document and the long-term payoff in terms of functionality is enormous — well worth the up-front costs. Opponents of this approach will point to the increased costs of data maintenance as a detractor. But consider the typical textual documents where maintenance does not take place at all until the next scheduled revision, two, three, or five years later, at which time the entire premise on which the earlier version was based may be totally out of date, requiring a good deal of study and update. We could argue that with a database approach, the costs are actually less, are spread out over a longer period (thus they are more affordable), and the data remains up-to-date and useful at all times.

The tools listed in Chapter 11 are intended to be a representative sample of the types of applications that are currently available. It is not an all-inclusive set. They are not necessarily the best tools available for every situation, and they are not necessarily recommended by us. Tools should be utilized, but they must be matched to each individual situation or project and implemented to the extent required.

Conclusions and Recommendations

That brings us to this summary. In closing, we would like to offer five specific recommendations. If true interoperability is ever to be achieved, the concept of a single unifying construct, however imperfect or incomplete, must receive support at the highest levels of the organization. Although the following plan (which we've mentioned previously) is, no doubt, imperfect, it is at least a start, and is offered as a first step toward a widespread, interoperable IT architecture.

Recommendation #1: Compile a Common Lexicon

First, we must compile and use a common lexicon. If IT architectures are ever to be interoperable, the developers of those documents must be able to communicate efficiently and effectively. Terms such as architecture, master plan, functional requirement, etc., must be defined and used consistently by all players.

This does not sound like a particularly difficult task, but.... All organizations have a default lexicon (official or unofficial) and they all use slightly different terminologies with varying connotations. The interoperability problem is tough enough *if we can* communicate. It is nearly impossible if everyone is speaking a different language. Although there have been great strides in this area, we still have significant diversity in terminology and taxonomy. Why not use existing materials as a starting point and merge them into a common standard? Speaking of standards....

"Compile and use a common lexicon / taxonomy."

Exhibit 12

Recommendation #2: Define and Enforce Common Interface Standards

Next, we must define architecture development, definition, maintenance, and interface standards as necessary to:

- *Ensure* interoperability and connectivity of architectures, consistency, compliance with applicable directives, and architectural information dissemination
- *Facilitate* implementation of policies and procedures, acquisition strategies, systems engineering, configuration management, and technical standards
- *Standardize* terms of reference, modeling tools, architecture data elements, architecture data structures, hardware and software interfaces, architectural representations and architectural scope, and level of detail and abstraction (Exhibit 13).

The goal should not be forced procurement of a single, standard system that performs some specific set of functions. The real issue, at least in the near term, is not "Who is using what system?," but rather "Are these various systems compatible/interoperable?" In other words, all that we really need, at least to start, are interface/interoperability *standards*. It is time to stop investigating architectural concepts and start defining and building joint, interoperable, standardized architectures.

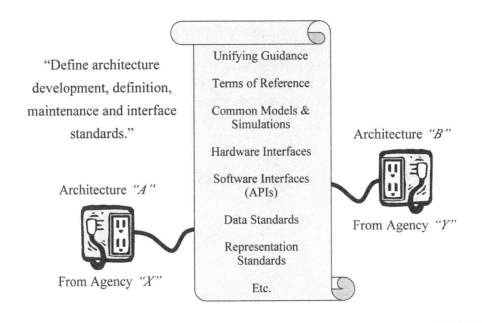

Exhibit 13

Recommendation #3: Develop a Well-Defined Architecture Development Process

A standardized, well-defined architectural process would significantly simplify the evolution of architectures, while adding a certain amount of rigor, reproducibility, and confidence to the procedure. Earlier works [Curts, 1989a,b, 1990a, 1995] have discussed these concepts in greater detail. The process must, as a minimum, contain well-defined authority, designated cognizant activities, processes, milestones, architectural outlines and formats, deliverables, documentation, and maintenance and update schedules.

For all of its shortcomings, SPAWAR's WSA&E effort described in Chapter 2 was a step in the right direction. Unfortunately, the process took too long, was very costly, and eventually ran out of steam. Other examples exist within government and industry. Additionally, as discussed in Chapter 11, an effort must be supported by a good set of tools. Without the help of automation, we can never hope to keep track of all the pieces (Exhibit 14).

"Standardize a well defined, automated architecture
process to simplify the evolution of architectures
while adding a certain amount of rigor,
reproducibility and confidence to the process."

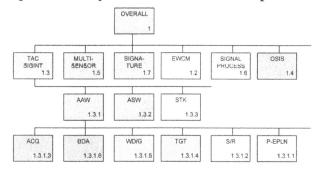

Exhibit 14

Recommendation #4: Commit to IT System Interoperability

Acquisition Managers, Acquisition Authorities, and Operational Managers must
be evaluated on meeting all of their requirements including interoperability
and information assurance. It appears that these measures are beginning to
be graded at the operational level, especially within IRM, CIO, and other IT
organizations. They are receiving more attention than ever before, but it is an
important issue that bears emphasis (Exhibit 15).

"A commitment to
interoperability on the part of
both agencies and individuals,
backed up by accountability
through a strong report card for
compliance, is needed as part of
the existing performance
evaluation system."

Exhibit 15

Recommendation #5: Assign an IT Architect

Finally, an IT architect must be assigned at the very highest levels of the organization, embodied with the responsibility and authority to enforce compliance with IT architectural concepts. Although this has been a key recommendation of many studies, committees, and reports, and although most major organizations have established an office of Chief Information Officer (CIO), it seems that it is very difficult to exercise sufficient control in all of the necessary areas. Clearly, we need a different paradigm.

It may appear that these recommendations are very basic — they are. Yet, a surprising number of institutions have yet to embrace these concepts. While there are, no doubt, sufficient technical issues to keep us busy for some time to come, we believe that a truly successful, interoperable, IT infrastructure must first be founded on these basic principles (Exhibit 16).

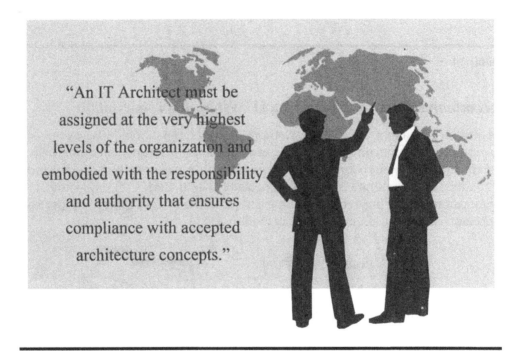

"An IT Architect must be assigned at the very highest levels of the organization and embodied with the responsibility and authority that ensures compliance with accepted architecture concepts."

Exhibit 16

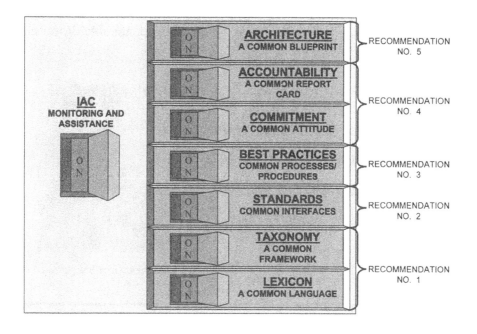

Exhibit 17

Future Work

We have been involved with a number of projects where a variety of the items discussed here have been implement at some level. The one piece that remains to be attempted on a large-scale, real-world system, is the object-oriented database concepts in Chapter 4. There will, no doubt, be challenges, but we look forward to the opportunity.

A major technical goal of the next ten years will be the utilization of an architecture that allows interoperability between IT systems and modeling and simulation (M&S). Current technologies do not support such interoperability, without unique hardware (human-in-the-loop in many cases) and software. The goal within the next decade should be to allow the majority of IT systems to "plug-and-play" to the majority of military M&S applications and exchange information without having to build unique interfaces. In other words, to give end users the needed interoperability and reusability of M&S programs running in a common browser. This will provide an increased ease-of-use for the user community, and this will promote the ability to train users on the same IT systems that they will use in daily practice, at reduced training and development costs for specialized interfaces to models. As expressed by the Defense Science Board (DSB) Task Force on Readiness [DSB, 1994]:

> Modeling and simulation technology should be exploited to enhance joint and combined training and doctrine. It offers a tremendous

opportunity to leverage our existing training at all levels through enhancement or even replacement where appropriate after thorough review (Exhibit 18).

"A good plan executed violently today is better than a perfect plan executed tomorrow. "

General George S. Patton, Jr.

Exhibit 18

Appendix A

Acronyms

I will be so brief I have already finished.

Salvador Dali

A1: Verified Design, the highest level of security, Verified Protection, as specified by the TCSEC

AAW: anti-air warfare

ABCP: Associate Business Continuity Planner

ACM: Association for Computing Machinery

ACR: acoustic conference room

ACT: aircrew coordination training

AD: *Action Directe* (Direct Action), a terrorist organization

ADP: automated data processing

ADPE: automated data processing equipment

AF: Air Force

AFCEA: Armed Forces Communications and Electronics Association

AHU: air handling unit

AIMD: Aircraft Intermediate Maintenance Department

AIS: automated information system

AISS: automated information systems security

Al Fatah: A terrorist organization

ALMEN: air-land-maritime engagement model

AM: Accreditation Manager

AMHH: a miracle happens here

ANSI: American National Standards Institute

API: application program interface

ARPANET: Advanced Research Projects Agency Network

ASAP: Architecture Simulation and Analysis Platform

ASAS: all-source analysis system

ASCII: American Standard Code for Information Interchange

ASD: Assistant Secretary of Defense

ASD(C3I): Assistant Secretary of Defense for Command, Control, Communications, and Intelligence

ASE: acoustical shielded enclosure

ASIS: American Society for Industrial Security

ASO: Aviation Safety Office (Officer)

ASSIST: Automated Systems Security Incident Support Team

ASUW: anti-surface warfare

ASW: anti-submarine warfare

AT&T: American Telephone & Telegraph

ATM: Asynchronous Transfer Mode; automatic teller machine

AWG: Architecture Working Group

B1: Labeled Security Protection, the lowest of three mandatory protection levels, as specified in the TCSEC

B2: Structured Protection, a mandatory protection level, as specified in the TCSEC

B3: Security Domains, the highest of three mandatory protection levels, as specified in the TCSEC

BAP: battlespace awareness picture

BDA: battle damage assessment

BF: battle force

BKA: German Federal Criminal Investigation Department

BOGSAT: bunch of guys sitting around a table

C&A: Certification and Accreditation

C1: Discretionary Security Protection, the lowest of two discretionary protection levels, as specified in the TCSEC

C2: Command and Control; Controlled Access Protection, the highest of two discretionary protection levels, as specified in the TCSEC

C2W: Command And Control Warfare

C3: Command, Control, and Communications

C3I: Command, Control, Communications, and Intelligence

C4: Command, Control, Communications, and Computers

C4I: Command, Control, Communications, Computers, and Intelligence

C4ISP: C4I Support Plan

C4ISR: Command, Control, Communications, Computers, Intelligence, Surveillance, and Reconnaissance

CA: certification authority; command authority; COMSEC account; controlling authority

CAAP: critical asset assurance program

CADM: C4ISR Core Architecture Data Model

CADP: conceptual architecture design principles

CAF: C4ISR Architecture Framework

CAPE: C4ISR Analytic Performance Evaluation

CASE: Computer Aided System Engineering

CBA: cost–benefit analysis

CBCP: Certified Business Continuity Professional

CBK: common body of knowledge
CC: common criteria
CCA: Clinger-Cohen Act
CCC: Combatant Communist Cells (*Cellules Communistes Combattantes*)
C-CDR: component complete design review
CCRP: C4ISR Cooperative Research Program
CCRTS: Command and Control Research and Technology Symposium
CCS: common cryptographic service
CDC: Control Data Corporation
CDR: complete design review
CDR: critical design review
CEM: common evaluation methodology
CERIAS: Center for Education and Research in IA and Security at Purdue University
CERT: Computer Emergency Response Team
CSERT: Computer Security Emergency Response Team
CIA: Central Intelligence Agency
CIAO: Critical Infrastructure Assurance Officer
CIAP: C4ISR Integrated Architecture Program
CINC: Commander-in-Chief
CIO: Chief Information Officer
CIP: critical infrastructure protection
CIRT: Computer Incident Response Team
CISA: C4ISR Integration Support Activity
CISA: Certified Information Systems Auditor
CISSP: Certified Information Systems Security Professional
CJCS: Chairman, Joint Chiefs of Staff
CJCSI: Chairman, Joint Chiefs of Staff Instruction
CLODO: *Comite Liquidant ou Detoumant les Ordinateurs* (Committee on the Liquidation or Deterrence of Computers)
CM: configuration management
CMM: capability maturity model
CMMI: capability maturity model integrated
CMU: Carnegie Mellon University
CNA: Center for Naval Analysis
CNO: Chief of Naval Operations
CO: Commanding (or Contracting) Officer
COE: common operating environment
COI: communications operating instruction
COI: community of interest
COMMS: Communications
Comp-Terror: computer terrorism
COMPUSEC: computer security
COMSEC: communications security
CONOPS: concept of operation
COOP: continuity of operations plan
COP: Common Operational Picture (Plan)
COTS: commercial off-the-shelf

CPA: certified public accountant
CPE: Continuing Professional Education
CPI: critical program information
CPP: Certified Protection Professional
CPU: central processing unit
CRD: Capstone Requirements Document
CRR: Certification Requirements Review
CSA: Computer Security Act (of 1987)
CSD: Computer Security Division (NIST)
CSIRT: Computer Security Incident Response Team
CSIS: Georgetown University's Center for Strategic and International Studies, Washington, D.C.
CSRC: Computer Security Resource Center (NIST CSD)
CSSO: Computer Systems Security Officer
CSTVRP: Computer Security Technical Vulnerability Reporting Program
CT&E: certification test and evaluation
CTAPS: Contingency Tactical Air Planning System
C-TEP: Compu-Terror Evaluation Plan
CTO: Chief Technology Officer
D: Minimal Protection as specified in the TCSEC
DAA: designated approving authority
DAC: discretionary access control
DACS: Data and Analysis Center for Software at DTIC
DAI: Donnell Associates, Inc.
DARPA: Defense Advanced Research Projects Agency
DAU: Defense Acquisition University
DBMS: database management system
DCI: Director of Central Intelligence
DCID: Director of Central Intelligence Directive
DDD: Defense data dictionary
DDM: data distribution management
DDN: Defense data network
DFD: data flow diagram
DGMS: Dialogue Generation and Management System
DIA: Defense Intelligence Agency
DII: Defense information infrastructure
DINCOTE: Peruvian National Anti-Terrorist Directorate
DISA: Defense Information Systems Agency
DISN: Defense Information Systems Network
DITSCAP: Defense Information Technology Security Certification and Accreditation Program
DNA: deoxyribonucleic acid
DoD: Department of Defense
DoD TCSEC: Department of Defense Trusted Computer System Evaluation Criteria
DoDD: Department of Defense Directive
DoDI: Department of Defense Instruction
DoE: Department of Energy

DON: Department of the Navy
DOP: Development Options Paper
DOS: disk operating system
DOSTN: Department of State Telecommunications Network
DOT&E: Director of Operational Test and Evaluation
DOTE: Director (or Directorate) of Operational Test and Evaluation
DP: data processing
DRDA: distributed relational database architecture
DRII: Disaster Recovery Institute International
DSB: Defense Science Board
DSC: decision support center
DSMC: Defense Systems Management College
DSS: decision support system
DT&E: developmental test and evaluation
DTIC: Defense Technical Information Center (Alexandria, VA)
E3S: Electronic Safeguards and Security System
EA: electronic attack
EA: executive agent/agency
ECCM: electronic counter-countermeasures
ECM: electronic countermeasures
EDP: electronic data processing
EFFBD: enhanced functional flow block diagram
EFTS: Electronic Funds Transfer System
EIC: equipment identification code
ELINT: electronic intelligence
ELSEC: electronic security
e-mail: electronic mail
EMP: electromagnetic pulse
EMP-T: electromagnetic pulse transformer (bomb)
EMSEC: emission security
EO: Executive Order
EP: electronic protection
EPL: evaluated products list
EPO: emergency power off
ERD: entity relationship diagram
ES: electronic warfare support
EW: electronic warfare
FA: functional analysis
FALN: *Fuerzas Armadas de Liberación Nácional*, a terrorist organization
FAR: Federal Acquisition Regulation
FAX: facsimile transmission
FBI: Federal Bureau of Investigation
FBIS: Foreign Broadcast Information Service
FCA: functional configuration audit
FFBD: functional flow block diagram
FIPS: Federal Information Processing Standard
FIPS PUB: Federal Information Processing Standard Publication

FIWC: Fleet Information Warfare Center (U.S. Navy)

FM: field manual (U.S. Army)

FOIA: Freedom of Information Act (of 1974)

FOT&E: follow-on test and evaluation

FOUO: For Official Use Only

FPM: force performance metrics

FTP: file transfer protocol

FYDP: Five-Year Defense Plan

GAO: General Accounting Office

GCCS: Global Command and Control System

GCSS: Global Command Support System

GIG: global information grid

GIS: Geographic Information System

GMT: Greenwich Mean Time, also known as Zulu Time, now called UTC Coordinated Universal Time

GMU: George Mason University

GOTS: government off-the-shelf

GPRA: Government Performance Results Act

GPS: Global Positioning System

GSA: General Services Administration

GUI: graphical user interface

GWU: George Washington University

HAZREP: Hazard Report

HDD: hierarchical data dictionary

HERF: high energy radio frequency (Gun)

HLA: high-level architecture

HR: House of Representatives

HTML: Hypertext Markup Language

HTTP: Hypertext Transfer Protocol

I&A: Identification and Authentication

I/O: input/output

IA: information assurance

IAC: Information (or Intelligence) Analysis Center; Information Assurance Center

IAP: Information Assurance Program/Panel

IASE: Information Assurance Support Environment

IASEPMT: Information Assurance Systems Engineering Program Management Team

IATAC: Information Assurance Technology Analysis Center (DoD)

IATF: information assurance technical framework

IATFF: information assurance technical framework forum

IATO: interim approval to operate; interim authority to operate

IATP: Information Assurance Test Plan

IBM: International Business Machines Corporation

IC: Intelligence Community

ICEP: Interoperability Certification Evaluation Plan

ID: identification/identity/identify

IDA: Institute for Defense Analysis
IDS: Intrusion Detection System
IEC: International Electrotechnical Commission
IEEE: Institute of Electrical & Electronic Engineers (or Engineering)
IER: information exchange requirements
IFIP: International Federation for Information Processing
ILS: integrated logistics support
ILSMT: Integrated Logistics Support Management Team
INCOSE: International Council on Systems Engineering
InfoSec: information security
INTEL: Intelligence
Interpact: International Partnership Against Computer Terrorism
IO: information operations
IOC: initial operational (or operating) capability
IOT: initial operational test
IOT&E: initial operational test and evaluation
IP: Internet Protocol; Interoperability Policy
IPSO: Internet Protocol Security Option
IPT: Integrated Product Team
IPT: Interoperability Policy Test
IPTP: Interoperability Policy Test Panel
IRA: Irish Republican Army
IRM: information resource management
IS: information system
ISACA: Information Systems Audit and Control Association
ISDN: Integrated Services Digital Network
ISEA: in-service engineering activity
ISO: International Standards Organization
ISS: information systems security
ISSEP: information system security engineering principles
ISSM: Information Systems Security Manager
ISSO: Information Systems Security Officer
ISSPP: Information Systems Security Program Plan
IT: information technology
ITA: information technology architecture
ITAA: Information Technology Association of America
ITAC: Intelligence and Threat Analysis Center
ITI: information technology infrastructure
ITL: Information Technology Laboratory (NIST CSD)
ITMRA: Information Technology Management Reform Act (of 1996) (aka Clinger-Cohen Act)
ITT: International Telephone and Telegraph
IV&V: independent verification and validation
IW: information warfare
JCAPS: Joint C4ISR Architecture Planning/Analysis System
JCS: Joint Chiefs of Staff

JIC: Joint Intelligence Center

JIER: Joint Information Exchange Requirement

JIERAD: Joint Interoperability Exchange Requirements Analysis Database

JITC: Joint Interoperability Test Command (formerly Joint Interoperability Test Center)

JP: Joint (Chiefs of Staff) Publication

JTA: Joint Task Analysis

JTF: Joint Task Force

JTTP: Joint Tactics, Techniques, and Procedures

JV: Joint Vision

JWARS: Joint Warfare Simulation

JWCA: Joint War-fighting Capability Assessment

KGB: *Komitet Gosudarstvennoye Bezopastnosti,* the State Security Committee of the former Soviet Union

KISS: keep it simple, stupid

LABLN: Union of Basque Patriotic Workers, the labor arm of the radical Basque Party

LAN: local area network

LCC: life-cycle cost (or costing)

LCCA: life-cycle cost analysis

LCD: liquid crystal display

LCM: life-cycle management; Life-Cycle Manager

LDAP: Lightweight Directory Access Protocol

LISI: levels of information system interoperability

LOE: level of effort

M&S: Modeling and Simulation

MAA: Anti-Imperialistic Military Movement

MAN: metropolitan area network; *Maschinenfabrick Ausburg-Nuernberg,* a West German company

MAU: multiattribute utility

MAUT: multiattribute utility theory

MBCP: Master Business Continuity Professional

MBMS: model base management system

MCA: micro channel architecture

MCCB: Modification/Configuration Control Board

MD2: Message Digest #2. A hash algorithm developed by Ron Rivest for 8-bit applications

MD4: Message Digest #4. A hash algorithm developed by Ron Rivest for 32-bit applications

MD5: Message Digest #5. A hash algorithm developed by Ron Rivest for 32-bit applications

MDA: Milestone Decision Authority

MEI: mission essential infrastructure

MER: minimum essential requirements

MIL: military

MIL-SPEC: Military Specification

MIL-STD: Military Standard

MIME: Multipurpose Internet Main Extension
MIT: Massachusetts Institute of Technology
MLS: multilevel security
MML: magnetic media library
MNS: Mission Need Statement
MOA: Memorandum of Agreement
MOE: measure of effectiveness
MOP: measure of performance
MRTA: *Movimento Revolucionario Tupac Amaru,* also known as the Tupac Amaru Revolutionary Movement
MSG: message
MTBF: mean time between failures
NAC: National Agency Check
NACSEM: National Communications Security Engineering Memorandum
NACSIM: National Communications Security Information Memorandum
NAMP: Naval Aircraft Maintenance Program
NASC: Naval Aviation Safety Center
NATO: North Atlantic Treaty Organization
NATOPS: Naval Air Training & Operating Procedure and Standard
NAVAIR: Naval Air Systems Command
NAVCIRT: Naval Computer Incident Response Team
NAVICP: Navy Inventory Control Point
NAVOAT: Naval Operational Assessment Tool
NAVOSH: Navy Occupational Safety and Health
NBS: National Bureau of Standards (now NIST)
NCAVC: National Center for the Analysis of Violent Crime (FBI)
NCR: National Cash Register Company
NCSA: National Computer Security Association
NCSC: National Computer Security Center
NDI: nondevelopmental item
NDIA: National Defense Industrial Association
NDT&A: nondestructive test and analysis
NDU: National Defense University
NETVIZ: network visualization tool
NETWARS: Networks and Warfare Simulation Model
NIAC: Naval Information Assurance Center
NIACAP: National Information Assurance Certification and Accreditation Process
NIAP: National Information Assurance Partnership (between NSA & NIST)
NIDS: network intrusion detection system
NII: National Information Infrastructure
NIPC: National Infrastructure Protection Center
NIPRNET: Nonclassified Internet Protocol Router Network (part of the Defense Information System Network)
NIS: network information system
NIST: National Institute of Standards and Technology (formerly NBS)
NITF: Natural Image Transfer Format
NORAD: North American Air Defense Command

NPA: New People's Army, the armed wing of the outlawed Communist Party of the Philippines

NPS: Naval Postgraduate School

NRC: National Research Council

NSA: National Security Agency (Ft. Meade)

NSC: Naval Safety Center

NSS: national security strategy

NSS: National Security System

NSS: network systems security

NSTISS: National Security Telecommunications and Information Systems

NSTISSAM: National Security Telecommunications and Information Systems Security Advisory/Information Memorandum

NSTISSC: National Security Telecommunications and Information Systems Security Committee

NSTISSD: National Security Telecommunications and Information Systems Security Directive

NSTISSI: National Security Telecommunications and Information Systems Security Instruction

NSTISSP: National Security Telecommunications and Information Systems Security Policy

NTCB: network trusted computing base

NTDS: Navy Tactical Data System

NTIA: National Telecommunications and Information Administration

NTIC: Naval Technical Intelligence Center

NTISS: National Telecommunications and Information Systems Security

NTISSAM: National Telecommunications and Information Systems Security Advisory Memorandum

NTISSD: National Telecommunications and Information Systems Security Directive

NTISSI: National Telecommunications and Information Systems Security Instruction

NTISSP: National Telecommunications and Information Systems Security Policy

NWTDB: Naval (Navy) warfare tactical database

O/S: operating system

OAN: operational area network

OASD: Office of the Assistant Secretary of Defense

OLAP: online analytical processing

OLTP: online transaction processing

OMB: Office of Management and Budget

ONR: Office of Naval Research

ONT: Office of Naval Technology

OO: object-oriented

OOA: object-oriented analysis

OOAD: object-oriented analysis and design

OOD: object-oriented design

OODA (OODA Loop): Observe, Orient, Decide, and Act

OODBMS: object-oriented data base management system

OOP: object-oriented programming

OPNAV: Office of the Chief of Naval Operations

OPPLAN: operational plan
OPS: Operations
OPSEC: operational security; operations security
OR: operational requirement
ORD: Operational Requirements Document
OS: operating system
OSD: Office of the Secretary of Defense
OSE: open security environment
OSI: open systems interconnection
OSPB: Overseas Security Policy Board (formerly OSPG)
OSPG: Overseas Security Policy Group (currently OSPB)
OT&E: operational test and evaluation
OTA: Operational Test Agency/Activity
OTC: Officer in Tactical Command
OTRR: Operational Test Readiness Review
PAA: policy approving authority
PAID: Procedures, Applications, Infrastructure, Data
PAT: Process Action Team
PC: personal computer
PCA: physical configuration audit; policy creation authority
PCI: peripheral component interconnect
PCS: physical control space
PDD: Presidential Decision Directive
PDI: project development and implementation
PDR: Preliminary Design Review
PDS: protected distribution system
PEO: Program Executive Office/Officer
PFLP: Popular Front for the Liberation of Palestine
PIOS: *Personen, Institutionen, Objekte, Sachen* (Persons, Institutions, Movable and Immovable Objects)
PKI: public key infrastructure (Classes 1–5)
PL: Public Law
PM: Program (Or Project) Manager
PMA: primary mission area; Program (Or Project) Manager, Air (NAVAIR)
PMO: Program/Project Management Office
POA&M: plan of action and milestones
POM: Program Objective Memorandum
PPL: Preferred Products List (a section in the InfoSec Products and Services Catalogue)
PRD: Presidential Review Directive
PSL: Protected Services List
PSYOP: psychological operations
PWMA: primary warfare mission area
QA: quality assurance
QC: quality control
QM: quality management
R&D: research and development

R&M: reliability and maintainability
RAF: Red Army Faction, a terrorist organization
RAG: Replacement Air Group
RAM: random access memory
RAS: requirements allocation sheet
RDA: research, development, and acquisition
RDT&E: research, development, test, and evaluation
REQS: requirements
RFP: request for proposal
RISOS: Research in Secure Operating Systems
RMA: reliability, maintainability, and availability
ROF: required operational function
RSA: Rivest, Shamir and Adleman (an encryption algorithm invented in 1978 by Ron Rivest, Adi Shamir, and Leonard Adleman)
RTM: requirements traceability matrix
S: U.S. Senate
S/MIME: Secure Multipurpose Internet Mail Extension
SA: situational awareness
SA: System Administrator
SABI: secret and below interoperability
SAFCEN: Safety Center (U.S. Navy)
SAT: security awareness training
SATAN: Security Administrator Tool for Analyzing Networks
SBU: sensitive but unclassified
SCI: sensitive compartmented information
SDE: security development and engineering
SDI: Strategic Defense Initiative
SDLC: software development life cycle
SDNS: secure data network system
SDR: system design review
SDS: Students for a Democratic Society
SE: systems engineering
SE-CMM: Systems Engineering Capability Maturity Model
SECNAV: Secretary of the Navy
SECNAVINST: Secretary of the Navy Instruction
SEI: Software Engineering Institute at Carnegie Mellon University
SIGINT: Signals Intelligence
SIOP: single integrated operational plan
SIPRNET: Secret Internet Protocol Router Network (part of the Defense Information System Network)
SIWG: Security Infrastructure Working Group
SMA: support mission area
SMART: specific, measurable, accurate, reliable, timely
SNMP: Simple Network Management Protocol
SoS: system of systems
SPAWAR: Space and Naval Warfare
SPAWARSYSCOM: Space and Naval Warfare Systems Command

SQL: structured query language
SSA: System Security Administrator
SSAA: System Security Authorization Agreement
SSE: software support environment; software systems engineering
SSE-CMM: Software Systems Engineering Capability Maturity Model
SSL: Secure Sockets Layer
ST: security technology
ST&E: security test and evaluation
STRIKE: strike warfare
T&E: test and evaluation
TADIL: tactical digital (or data) information link
TADIL-J: tactical digital interface link-joint
TCB: trusted computing base
TCO: total cost of ownership
TCP: Transmission Control Protocol
TCSEC: Trusted Computer System Evaluation Criteria (DoD), the "Orange Book"
TE: task element
TELNET: telecommunications network
TEMP: Test and Evaluation Master Plan
TF: task force
TG: task group
TIBS: Tactical Information Broadcast System
TLS: top-level specification
TLWR: top-level warfare requirement
TNI: Trusted Network Interpretation (known as the "Red Book," network interpretation of the TCSEC ("Orange Book"; originally the "White Book"))
TOE: target of evaluation
TOPSIGHT: NRO-sponsored tool for C4ISR System of Systems Analysis
TOR: tentative (or tactical) operational requirement
TPEP: Trusted Products Evaluation Program
TRANSEC: transmission security
TSCM: technical surveillance countermeasures
TSEC: telecommunications security
TSS: technical security safeguards
TTP: tactics, techniques, and procedures
TU: task unit
UIS: user interface system
UIUC: University of Illinois, Urbana-Champaign Campus
UJTL: Unified Joint Task List
UML: Unified Modeling Language
UPS: uninterruptible power supply/system
USA: U.S. Army
USAF: U.S. Air Force
USC: U.S. Code
USD: Under Secretary of Defense
USMC: U.S. Marine Corps
USMTF: U.S. Message Text Format

USN: U.S. Navy

UTC: Coordinated Universal Time, also known as Greenwich Mean Time (GMT) and Zulu Time.

VHF: very high frequency

VMF: voice message format

VMM: virtual machine monitor

VOR: VHF omnidirectional range

VPN: virtual private network

WAIS: wide area information service

WAN: wide area network

WMA: warfare mission area

WRB: Warfare Requirements Board

WSA&E: Warfare Systems Architecture and Engineering

WSCID: warfare system control interface drawing

WSPS: warfare systems performance specification

WSTS: warfare systems test specification

WWW: World Wide Web

XA: Executive Agent

Y2K: Year 2000

Appendix B

Glossary

The beginning of vision is the definition of terms.

Socrates

As explained in the text, terminology is far from standardized in the areas discussed. Many organizations assign different meanings to commonly used terms; some are only minor deviations while others are significant. Where multiple definitions exist in every day use, we have included several of the more common ones here. The reader is left to decide for himself which, if any, might best suit his purpose.

Abduction [AAAI, 1999]: A form of inference that generates plausible conclusions (which may not necessarily be true). As an example, knowing that if it is night, then a movie is on television and that a movie is on television, then abductive reasoning allows the inference that it is night.

Ability [JITC, 1999]: Capacity, fitness, or tendency to act in specified or desired manner. Skill, especially the physical, mental, or legal power to perform a task.

Acceptance Inspection [NCSC004, 1988]: The final inspection to determine whether or not a facility or system meets the specified technical and performance standards. *Note:* This inspection is held immediately after facility and software testing and is the basis for commissioning or accepting the information system.

Access [NCSC004, 1988]: A specific type of interaction between a subject and an object that results in the flow of information from one to the other.

Access Control [NCSC004, 1988]: The process of limiting access to the resources of a system only to authorized programs, processes, or other systems (in a network). Synonymous with controlled access and limited access.

Accountability [DoD8510, 2000]: Property that allows auditing of IS activities to be traced to persons or processes that may then be held responsible for their actions. Accountability includes authenticity and nonrepudiation. [ISSEP, 2000]:

Accountability (to the individual level) is the security goal generating the requirement that actions of an entity may be traced uniquely to that entity. This supports nonrepudiation, deterrence, fault isolation, intrusion detection and prevention, and after-action recovery and legal action.

Accreditation [Authors]: A management or administrative process of accepting a specific site installation/implementation for operational use based upon evaluations and certifications. [NCSC004, 1988]: A formal declaration by the DAA that the AIS is approved to operate in a particular security mode using a prescribed set of safeguards. Accreditation is the official management authorization for operation of an AIS and is based on the certification process as well as other management considerations. The accreditation statement affixes security responsibility with the DAA and shows that due care has been taken for security. [NSTISSI 4009]: Formal declaration by a Designated Approving Authority (DAA) that an information system is approved to operate in a particular security mode using a prescribed set of safeguards at an acceptable level of risk.

Accreditation Authority [NCSC004, 1988]: Synonymous with Designated Approving Authority (DAA).

Accreditation Package [NCSC029, 1994]: A product of the certification effort and the main basis for the accreditation decision. *Note:* The accreditation package, at a minimum, will include a recommendation for the accreditation decision and a statement of residual risk in operating the system in its environment. Other information included may vary depending on the system and the DAA.

Accredited [NIAP, 1999]: Formally confirmed by an accreditation body as meeting a predetermined standard of impartiality and general technical, methodological, and procedural competence.

Accrediting Authority [NSTISSI 4009]: Synonymous with Designated Approving Authority (DAA).

Accuracy [Authors]: The ability to ensure freedom from error, and convey in a useable format the true situation at the required level of detail or granularity as related to programs, operations, and machine capabilities.

Acquisition Organization [DoD8510, 2000]: The government organization that is responsible for developing a system.

ACR [12 FAM 090]: Abbreviation for Acoustic Conference Room, an enclosure which provides acoustic but not electromagnetic emanations shielding; ACRs are no longer procured; TCRs are systematically replacing them.

Active System [DoD8510, 2000]: A system connected directly to one or more other systems. Active systems are physically connected and have a logical relationship to other systems.

Adversary [BAH, 1998]: Any individual, group, organization, or government that conducts activities, or has the intention and capability to conduct activities, detrimental to critical assets.

Advisory Sensitivity Attributes [12 FAM 090]: User-supplied indicators of file sensitivity that alert other users to the sensitivity of a file so that they may handle it appropriate to its defined sensitivity. Advisory sensitivity attributes are not used by the AIS to enforce file access controls in an automated manner.

Affordability [Authors]: Extent to which C4I features are cost effective on both a recurring and nonrecurring basis.

Agency [12 FAM 090]: A federal agency including department, agency, commission, etc., as defined in 5 U.S.C. 552(e).

Anti-Air Warfare (AAW) [JP 1–02]: A primary warfare mission area dealing with air superiority.

Anti-Submarine Warfare (ASW) [JP 1–02]: A primary warfare mission area aimed against the subsurface threat.

Anti-Surface Warfare (ASUW) [JP 1–02]: A primary warfare mission area dealing with sea-going, surface platforms.

Architecture [CIMPIM, 1993]: An organized framework consisting of principles, rules, conventions, and standards that serve to guide development and construction activities such that all components of the intended structure will work together to satisfy the ultimate objective of the structure. [DAD, 2002]: The structure of components, their interrelationships, and the principle guidelines governing their design and evolution over time.

Assessment [JITC, 1999]: An effort to gain insight into system capabilities and limitations. May be conducted in many ways including a paper analysis, laboratory type testing, or even through limited testing with operationally representative users and equipment in an operational environment. Not sufficiently rigorous in and of itself to allow a determination of effectiveness and suitability to be made for purposes of operational testing. [NSA, 2002]: Surveys and Inspections; an analysis of the vulnerabilities of an AIS. Information acquisition and review process designed to assist a customer to determine how best to use resources to protect information in systems.

Asset [BAH, 1998]: Any person, facility, material, information, or activity which has a positive value to an owner.

Assumptions [Authors]: Accepted state of affairs or supposition.

Assurance [ISSEP, 2000]: grounds for confidence that the other four security goals (integrity, availability, confidentiality, and accountability) have been adequately met by a specific implementation. "Adequately met" includes the following: functionality that performs correctly, sufficient protection against unintentional errors (by users or software), and sufficient resistance to malicious penetration or by-pass. [NCSC004, 1988]: A measure of confidence that the security features and architecture of an AIS accurately mediate and enforce the security policy. [NCSC029, 1994]: A measure of confidence that the security features and architecture of an AIS accurately mediate and enforce the security policy. *Note:* Assurance refers to a basis for believing that the objective and approach of a security mechanism or service will be achieved. Assurance is generally based on factors such as analysis involving theory, testing, software engineering, validation, and verification. Life-cycle assurance requirements provide a framework for secure system design, implementation, and maintenance. The level of assurance that a development team, certifier, or accreditor has about a system reflects the confidence that they have that the system will be able to enforce its security policy correctly during use and in the face of attacks. Assurance may be provided through four means: (1) the way the system is designed and built, (2) analysis of the system description for conformance to requirement and for vulnerabilities, (3) testing the system itself to determine its operating characteristics, and (4) operational experience. Assurance is also provided through complete documentation of the design, analysis, and testing.

Attribute [Authors]: An abstraction of a single characteristic possessed by all the entities that were, themselves, abstracted as objects.

Audit [NSA, 2002]: The independent examination of records and activities to ensure compliance with established controls, policy, and operational procedures, and to recommend any indicated changes in controls, policy, or procedures.

Audit Review [AISSIM, 1996]: The independent review and examination of records and activities to assess the adequacy of system controls, to ensure compliance with established policies and operational procedures, and to recommend necessary changes in controls, policies or procedures.

Audit Trail [NSA, 2002]: In computer security systems, a chronological record of system resource usage. This includes user login, file access, other various activities, and whether any actual or attempted security violations occurred, legitimate and unauthorized.

Audit Trail (Management Trail) [Peltier, 1998]: The chronological set of records that provides evidence of activity. These records can be used to reconstruct, review, and examine transactions from inception to final results.

Audit Trail/Log [12 FAM 090]: Application or system programs when activated automatically monitor system activity in terms of on-line users, accessed programs, periods of operation, file accesses, etc.

Authenticate [AISSIM, 1996]: To verify the identity of a user, user device, or other entity, or the integrity of data stored, transmitted, or otherwise exposed to possible unauthorized modification in an automated information system, or establish the validity of a transmitted message.

Authentication [NSTISSI 4009]: Security measure designed to establish the validity of a transmission, message, or originator, or a means of verifying an individual's authorization to receive specific categories of information.

Authenticity [Authors]: The ability to ensure that the information originates or is endorsed from the source which is attributed to that information. [NCSC029, 1994]: The service that ensures that system events are initiated by and traceable to authorized entities. It is composed of authentication and nonrepudiation.

Authorization [Stoneburner, 2001]: The granting or denying of access rights to a user, program, or process.

Authorized Access List [12 FAM 090]: A list developed and maintained by the information systems security officer of personnel who are authorized unescorted access to the computer room.

Automated Information System (AIS) [12 FAM 090]: (1) An assembly of computer hardware, software, firmware, and related peripherals configured to collect, create, compute, disseminate, process, store, and control data or information; and (2) Information systems that manipulate, store, transmit, or receive information, and associated peripherals such as input/output and data storage and retrieval devices and media.

Autonomy [Authors]: The ability of a system to function independently.

Availability [Authors]: The ability to ensure that the information is available when needed by the decision process. [ISSEP, 2000]: The security goal that generates the requirement for protection against intentional or accidental attempts to (1) perform unauthorized deletion of data, or (2) otherwise cause a denial-of-service or data.

Awareness [Authors]: An individual's perception of reality ? ground truth, the "Big Picture."

Baseline [NCSC029, 1994]: A set of critical observations or data used for a comparison or control. *Note:* Examples include a baseline security policy, a baseline set of security requirements, and a baseline system.

Baseline Architecture [SPAWAR, 1987b]: A complete list and description of equipment that can be found in operation today.

Behaviorally Object-Oriented [Manola, 1990]: The data model incorporates features to define arbitrarily complex object types together with a set of specific operators (abstract data types).

Benign Environment [NCSC004, 1988]: A nonhostile environment that may be protected from external hostile elements by physical, personnel, and procedural security countermeasures.

Benign System [DoD8510, 2000]: A system that is not related to any other system. Benign systems are closed communities without physical connection or logical relationship to any other system. Benign systems are operated exclusive of one another and do not share users, information, or end processing with other systems.

Black [12 FAM 090]: In the information processing context, black denotes data, text, equipment, processes, systems or installations associated with unencrypted information that requires no emanations security related protection. For example, electronic signals are "black" if bearing unclassified information. Antonym: Red. [NSTISSI 4009]: Designation applied to information systems, and to associated areas, circuits, components, and equipment, in which national security information is not processed.

Boyd Cycle [JITC, 1999]: See OODA Loop and J. Boyd, Patterns of Conflict, December 1986. Unpublished study, 196 pages [Boyd, 1986].

C2 [12 FAM 090]: A formal product rating awarded to a product by the National Computer Security Center (NCSC). A C2 rated system incorporates controls capable of enforcing access limitations on an individual basis, making users individually accountable for their actions through logon procedures, auditing of security relevant events, and resource isolation.

C2 [NSA, 2002]: Command and Control.

Central Office of Record [NSTISSI 4009]: Office of a federal department or agency that keeps (COR) records of accountable COMSEC material held by elements subject to its oversight.

Certification [Authors]: The inspection and testing of a specific hardware and software site implementation against accepted Information Assurance/Information Security standards.

Certification Agent [NCSC029, 1994]: The individual(s) responsible for making a technical judgment of the system's compliance with stated requirements, identifying and assessing the risks associated with operating the system, coordinating the certification activities, and consolidating the final certification and accreditation packages.

Certification and Accreditation Plan [NCSC029, 1994]: A plan delineating objectives, responsibilities, schedule, technical monitoring, and other activities in support of the C&A process.

Certification and Repair Center (CRC) [12 FAM 090]: A U.S. Department of State (DoS) facility utilized by IM/SO/TO/OTSS departments for program activities.

Certification Authority (CA) [DoD8510, 2000]: Individual responsible for making a technical judgment of the system's compliance with stated requirements, identifying and assessing the risk associated with operating the system, coordinating the certification activities, and consolidating the final certification and accreditation package. [IATF, 1999]: A trusted agent that issues digital certificates to principals. Certification authorities may themselves have a certificate that is issued to them by other certification authorities. The highest certification authority is called the root CA. [NSTISSI 4009]: Third level of the Public Key Infrastructure (PKI) Certification Management Authority responsible for issuing and revoking user certificates, and exacting compliance to the PKI policy as defined by the parent Policy Creation Authority (PCA).

Certification Package [NCSC029, 1994]: A product of the certification effort documenting the detailed results of the certification activities. *Note:* The contents of this package will vary depending on the system.

Certification Requirements Review (CRR) [DoD8510, 2000]: The review conducted by the DAA, Certifier, program manager, and user representative to review and approve all information contained in the System Security Authorization Agreement (SSAA). The CRR is conducted before the end of Phase 1.

Certification Test and Evaluation (CT&E) [NSTISSI 4009]: Software and hardware security tests conducted during development of an IS.

Certifier [DoD8510, 2000]: See Certification Authority.

Classification [12 FAM 090]: The determination that certain information requires protection against unauthorized disclosure in the interest of national security, coupled with the designation of the level of classification Top Secret, Secret, or Confidential.

Classification Authority [12 FAM 090]: The authority vested in an official of an agency to originally classify information or material which is determined by that official to require protection against unauthorized disclosure in the interest of national security.

Classification Guides [12 FAM 090]: Documents issued in an exercise of authority for original classification that include determinations with respect to the proper level and duration of classification of categories of classified information.

Classified Information [NSTISSI 4009]: Information that has been determined pursuant to Executive Order 12958 or any predecessor order, or by the Atomic Energy Act of 1954, as amended, to require protection against unauthorized disclosure and is marked to indicate its classified status.

Classifier [12 FAM 090]: An individual who makes a classification determination and applies a security classification to information or material. A classifier may either be a classification authority or may assign a security classification based on a properly classified source or a classification guide.

Clear mode [12 FAM 090]: Unencrypted plain text mode.

Cleared U.S. citizen [12 FAM 090]: A citizen of the United States who has undergone a favorable background investigation resulting in the issuance of a security clearance by the Bureau of Diplomatic Security permitting access to classified information at a specified level.

Code Room [12 FAM 090]: The designated and restricted area in which cryptographic operations are conducted.

Collaboration [Alberts, 2000]: Enabling collaboration which transforms shared awareness into actions which can achieve a competitive advantage.

Collateral Information [12 FAM 090]: National security information classified in accordance with E.O. 12356, dated April 2, 1982.

Command and Control [JP 1–02]: The exercise of authority and direction by a properly designated commander over assigned and attached forces in the accomplishment of the mission.

Command and Control Warfare (C2W) [MOP 30]: The integrated use of operations security (OPSEC), military deception, psychological operations (PSYOP), electronic warfare (EW) and physical destruction, mutually supported by intelligence, to deny information to, influence, degrade or destroy adversary C2 capabilities, while protecting friendly C2 capabilities against such actions.

Common Criteria Testing Laboratory (CCTL) [NIAP, 1999]: Within the context of the NIAP Common Criteria Evaluation and Validation Scheme, an IT security evaluation facility, accredited by the National Voluntary Laboratory Accreditation Program (NVLAP) and approved by the NIAP Oversight Body to conduct CC-based evaluations.

Common Operating Environment [DSD IA, 2000]: The collection of standards, specifications, and guidelines, architecture definitions, software infrastructures, reusable components, application programming interfaces (APIs), methodology, runtime environment definitions, reference implementations, and methodology, that establishes an environment on which a system can be built. The COE is the vehicle that assures interoperability through a reference implementation that provides identical implementation of common functions. It is important to realize that the COE is both a standard and an actual product.

Communication Protocols [12 FAM 090]: A set of rules that govern the operation of hardware or software entities to achieve communication.

Communications Security (COMSEC) [NCSC004, 1988]: Measures taken to deny unauthorized persons information derived from telecommunications of the U.S. government concerning national security, and to ensure the authenticity of such telecommunications. Communications security includes crypto-security, transmission security, emission security, and physical security of communications security material and information.

Communications System [12 FAM 090]: A mix of telecommunications and automated information systems used to originate, control, process, encrypt, and transmit or receive information. Such a system generally consists of the following connected or connectable devices (1) Automated information equipment (AIS) on which information is originated; (2) A central controller (i.e., CIHS, C-LAN) of, principally, access rights and information distribution; (3) A telecommunications processor (i.e., TERP, IMH) which prepares information for transmission; and (4) National-level devices which encrypt information (COMSEC/CRYPTO/CCI) prior to its transmission via Diplomatic Telecommunications Service (DTS) or commercial carrier.

Compartmented Mode [DoD8510, 2000]: INFOSEC mode of operation wherein each user with direct or indirect access to a system, its peripherals, remote terminals, or remote hosts has all of the following: (1) valid security clearance for the most restricted information processed in the system; (2) formal access approval and signed nondisclosure agreements for that information which a user is to have access; and (3) valid need-to-know for information which a user is to have access.

Completeness [FM 100–6]: The ability to assemble necessary and sufficient information upon which to base a rapid, active information presentation and mission decision. Information encompasses all that is necessary and sufficient about the mission, task, or situation at hand to form a rapid, active presentation and decision.

Component [Authors]: Basic unit designed to satisfy one or more functional requirements.

Composite Threat List [12 FAM 090]: A Department of State threat list intended to cover all localities operating under the authority of a chief of mission and staffed by direct-hire U.S. personnel. This list is developed in coordination with the intelligence community and issued semiannually by the Bureau of Diplomatic Security.

Comprehension [Webster, 1984]: The capacity to include. Knowledge acquired by grasping mentally.

Compromise [NSTISSI 4009]: Disclosure of information to unauthorized persons or a violation of the security policy of a system in which unauthorized intentional or unintentional disclosure, modification, destruction, or loss of an object may have occurred.

Compromising Emanations [NSTISSI 4009]: Unintentional signals that, if intercepted and analyzed, would disclose the information transmitted, received, handled, or otherwise processed by information systems equipment. See TEMPEST.

Computer [NCSC029, 1994]: The hardware, software, and firmware components of a system that are capable of performing calculations, manipulations, or storage of data. It usually consists of arithmetic, logical, and control units, and may have input, output, and storage devices.

Computer Security [IATF, 1999]: Measures and controls that ensure confidentiality, integrity and availability of information system assets including hardware, software, firmware and information being processed, stored, or communicated.

Computer Security (COMPUSEC) [NCSC029, 1994]: Measures and controls that ensure confidentiality, integrity, and availability of the information processed and stored by a computer.

Computing Environment [DoD8510, 2000]: The total environment in which an automated information system, network, or component operates. The environment includes physical, administrative, and personnel procedures as well as communication and networking relationships with other information systems.

COMSEC Account [NSTISSI 4009]: Administrative entity, identified by an account number, used to maintain accountability, custody, and control of COMSEC material.

COMSEC Custodian [NSTISSI 4009]: Person designated by proper authority to be responsible for the receipt, transfer, accounting, safeguarding, and destruction of COMSEC material assigned to a COMSEC account.

COMSEC Facility [NSTISSI 4009]: Space used for generating, storing, repairing, or using COMSEC material.

COMSEC Manager [NSTISSI 4009]: Person who manages the COMSEC resources of an organization.

COMSEC Material [NSTISSI 4009]: Item designed to secure or authenticate telecommunications. COMSEC material includes, but is not limited to key, equipment, devices, documents, firmware, or software that embodies or describes cryptographic logic and other items that perform COMSEC function.

COMSEC Material Control System (CMCS) [NSTISSI 4009]: Logistics and accounting system through which COMSEC material marked "CRYPTO" is distributed, controlled, and safeguarded. Included are the COMSEC central offices of record, crypto-logistic depots, and COMSEC accounts. COMSEC material other than key may be

COMSEC Officer [12 FAM 090]: The properly appointed individual responsible to ensure that COMSEC regulations and procedures are understood and adhered to, that the COMSEC facility is operated securely, that personnel are trained in proper COMSEC practices, and who advises on communications security matters. Only Department of State personnel will be appointed.

Confidence [Entrust, 2000]: Confidence in electronic interactions can be significantly increased by solutions that address the basic requirements of integrity, confidentiality, authentication, authorization and access management or access control.

Confidentiality [NCSC029, 1994]: Assurance that information is not disclosed to unauthorized entities or processes. [NIAP, 1999]: The prevention of unauthorized disclosure of information. [NSA, 2002]: Assuring information will be kept secret, with access limited to appropriate persons. [NSTISSI 4009]: Assurance that information is not disclosed to unauthorized persons, processes, or devices. [Stoneburner, 2001]: The security goal that generates the requirement for protection from intentional or accidental attempts to perform unauthorized data reads. Like integrity, confidentiality covers data in storage, during processing, and while in transit.

Confidentiality Loss [JITC, 1999]: The compromise of sensitive, restricted, or classified data or software.

Configuration Control [NCSC004, 1988]: The process of controlling modifications to the system's hardware, firmware, software, and documentation that provides sufficient assurance that the system is protected against the introduction of improper modifications prior to, during, and after system implementation. Compare configuration management.

Configuration Management [NSTISSI 4009]: Management of security features and assurances through control of changes made to hardware, software, firmware, documentation, test, test fixtures, and test documentation throughout the life cycle of an IS.

Configuration Manager [DoD8510, 2000]: The individual or organization responsible for configuration control or configuration management.

Connectivity [FM 100–6]: The uninterrupted availability of information paths for the effective performance of C2 functions.

Consistency [Alberts, 2000]: Degree of shared understanding/common outlook regarding intent.

Consumer Electronics [12 FAM 090]: Any electronic/electrical devices, either AC- or battery-powered, which are not part of the facility infrastructure. Some examples are radios, televisions, electronic recording or playback equipment, PA systems, paging devices, and dictaphones (see also electronic equipment).

Content [Authors]: See Completeness.

Continuity [FM 100–6]: The uninterrupted availability of information paths for the effective performance of organizational function.

Controlled Access Area [12 FAM 090]: Controlled access areas are specifically designated areas within a building where classified information may be handled, stored, discussed, or processed.

Controlled Cryptographic Item (CCI) [12 FAM 090]: Secure telecommunications or information handling equipment, or associated cryptographic components, which are unclassified but governed by a special set of control requirements.

Controlled Shipment [12 FAM 090]: The transport of material from the point at which the destination of the material is first identified for a site, through installation and use, under the continuous 24-hour control of Secret cleared U.S. citizens or by DS-approved technical means and seal.

Corruption [JITC, 1999]: Departure from an original, correct data file or correctly functioning system to an improper state.

Criticality [JITC, 1999]: The severity of the loss of either data or system functionality. Involves judicious evaluation of system components and data when a property or phenomenon undergoes unwanted change.

CRYPTO [NSTISSI 4009]: Marking or designator identifying COMSEC keying material used to secure or authenticate telecommunications carrying classified or sensitive U.S. government or U.S. government-derived information.

Crypto ignition key (CIK) [12 FAM 090]: The device or electronic key used to unlock the secure mode of crypto equipment.

Cryptographic Access [12 FAM 090]: The prerequisite to, and authorization for, access to crypto information, but does not constitute authorization for use of crypto equipment and keying material issued by the Department.

Cryptographic Material [12 FAM 090]: All COMSEC material bearing the marking "CRYPTO" or otherwise designated as incorporating cryptographic information.

Cryptography [NCSC004, 1988]: The principles, means and methods for rendering information unintelligible, and for restoring encrypted information to intelligible form.

Cryptology [NSA, 2002]: The science which deals with hidden, disguised, or encrypted communications.

Current Architecture [SPAWAR, 1987b]: Baseline architecture plus upgrades planned through the Five Year Defense Plan (FYDP).

Custodian [12 FAM 090]: An individual who has possession of or is otherwise charged with the responsibility for safeguarding and accounting for classified information.

D2 [12 FAM 090]: A rating provided by the NCSC for PC security subsystems which corresponds to the features of the C2 level. A computer security subsystem is any hardware, firmware and software which are added to a computer system to enhance the security of the overall system.

Data [Authors]: a loose collection of facts collected from one or more sources. [Webster, 1984]: Information organized for analysis or used as the basis for decision making.

Data Integrity [DoD8510, 2000]: Condition existing when data is unchanged from its source and has not been accidentally or maliciously modified, altered, or destroyed. [NCSC004, 1988]: The property that data meet an a priori expectation of quality. [Stoneburner, 2001]: The property that data has not been altered in an unauthorized manner. Data integrity covers data in storage, during processing, and while in transit.

Data Origin Authentication [ISSEP, 2000]: The corroboration that the source of data received is as claimed.

Decision Superiority [JV 2020]: Better decisions arrived at and implemented faster than an opponent can react, or in a noncombat situation, at a tempo that allows the force to shape the situation or react to changes and accomplish its mission.

Declassification [12 FAM 090]: The determination that particular classified information no longer requires protection against unauthorized disclosure in the interest of national security. Such determination shall be by specific action or automatically after the lapse of a requisite period of time or the occurrence of a specified event. If such determination is by specific action, the material shall be so marked with the new designation.

Declassification Event [12 FAM 090]: An event which would eliminate the need for continued classification.

Decontrol [12 FAM 090]: The authorized removal of an assigned administrative control designation.

Dedicated Mode [NCSC029, 1994]: Security mode of operation wherein each user, with direct or indirect access to the system, its peripherals, remote terminals, or remote hosts, has all of the following: a. Valid security clearance for all information within the system, b. Formal access approval and signed nondisclosure agreements for all the information stored and processed (including all compartments, subcompartments, and special access programs), c. Valid need-to-know for all information contained within the system. *Note:* When in the dedicated security mode, a system is specifically and exclusively dedicated to and controlled for the processing of one particular type or classification of information, either for full-time operation or for a specified period of time.

Deduction [AAAI, 1999]: A method of logical reasoning which results in necessarily true statements. As an example, if it is known that every man is mortal and that George is a man, then it can be deduced that George is mortal. Deduction is equivalent to the logical rule of *modus ponens*.

Defense in Depth [IATF, 1999]: The security approach whereby layers of protection are needed to establish an adequate security posture for a system; strategy is based on concept that attacks must penetrate multiple protections that have been placed throughout the system to be successful.

Defense Information Infrastructure (DII) [JROCM 134–01]: The complete set of DoD information transfer and processing resources, including information and data storage, manipulation, retrieval, and display. More specifically, the DII is the shared or interconnected system of computers, communications, data, applications, security, people, training, and other support structure, serving the DoD's local and worldwide information needs. It connects DoD mission support, command and control, and intelligence computers and users through voice, data, imagery, video, and multimedia services; and it provides information processing and value-added services to subscribers over the DISN and interconnected Service and Agency networks. Data, information, and user applications software unique to a specific user are not considered part of the DII.

Defense Information Systems Network (DISN) [DSD IA, 2000]: A subelement of the Defense Information Infrastructure (DII), the DISN is the DoD's consolidated worldwide enterprise level telecommunications infrastructure that provides the end-to-end information transfer network for supporting military operations. It is transparent to its users, facilitates the management of information resources, and is responsive to national security and defense needs under all conditions in the most efficient manner.

Degree [JITC, 1999]: A measure of damage achieved in an Information Operations attack. [Webster, 1984]: Relative amount or intensity, as of a quality or attribute. The measure or extent of a state of being, action, or relation.

Delegated Accrediting Authority (DAA) [DoD8510, 2000]: Official with the authority to formally assume responsibility for operating a system at an acceptable level of risk. This term is synonymous with designated accrediting authority and designated approval authority.

Denial-of-service [Stoneburner, 2001]: The prevention of authorized access to resources or the delaying of time-critical operations. Time-critical may be milliseconds or it may be hours, depending upon the service provided.

Depth [JITC, 1999]: Penetration layer achieved during or the degree of intensity of an IO attack. [Webster, 1984]: The most profound or intense part or stage. The severest or worst part. The degree of richness or intensity.

Derivative Classification [12 FAM 090]: A determination that information is in substance the same as information currently classified, coupled with the designation of the level of classification.

Descriptive Attributes [Authors]: The intrinsic characteristics of an object.

Designated Accrediting Authority (DAA) [DoD8510, 2000]: Official with the authority to formally assume responsibility for operating a system at an acceptable level of risk. This term is synonymous with designated approval authority and delegated accrediting authority.

Designated Approving Authority (DAA) [NCSC004, 1988]: The official who has the authority to decide on accepting the security safeguards prescribed for an AIS or that official who may be responsible for issuing an accreditation statement that records the decision to accept those safeguards.

Destruction [JITC, 1999]: Irretrievable loss of data file, or damage to hardware or software.

Detect [JITC, 1999]: To discover threat activity within information systems, such as initial intrusions, during the threat activity or post-activity. Providing prompt awareness and standardized reporting of attacks and other anomalous external or internal system and network activity.

Developer [DoD8510, 2000]: The organization that develops the IS.

Distributed System [12 FAM 090]: A multi-work station, or terminal system where more than one workstation shares common system resources. The work stations are connected to the control unit/data storage element through communication lines.

Document [12 FAM 090]: Any recorded information regardless of its physical form or characteristics, including, without limitation, written or printed material; data processing cards and tapes; maps; charts; paintings; drawings; engravings; sketches; working notes and papers; reproductions of such things by any means or process; and sound, voice, or electronic recordings in any form.

DoD Information Technology Security Certification and Accreditation Process (DITSCAP) [DoD8510, 2000]: The standard DoD process for identifying information security requirements, providing security solutions, and managing IS security activities.

DoD Trusted Computer System Evaluation Criteria (TCSEC) [NSTISSI 4009]: Document containing basic requirements and evaluation classes for assessing degrees of effectiveness of hardware and software security controls built into an IS. This document, DoD 5200.28 STD, is frequently referred to as the Orange Book.

Domain [ISSEP, 2000]: See Security Domain.

Domain Dimension [Ryberg, 1988]: The dimension dealing with the structural aspects of the system involving broad, static patterns of internal behavior.

Downgrading [12 FAM 090]: The determination that particular classified information requires a lesser degree of protection or no protection against unauthorized disclosure than currently provided. Such determination shall be by specific action or automatically after lapse of the requisite period of time or the occurrence of a specified event. If such determination is by specific action, the material shall be so marked with the new designation.

Dynamic Binding [Meyer, 1988]: The responsibility for executing an action on an object resides within the object itself. The same message can elicit a different response depending upon the receiver.

Dynamic Dimension [Ryberg, 1988]: The dimension concerned with the non-static, process related properties of the system.

Ease [JITC, 1999]: Amount of time and skill level required to either penetrate or restore function. Measures the degree of difficulty.

Ecological Dimension [Ryberg, 1988]: The dimension dealing with the interface properties of a system; inflow and outflow of forces in a system.

Economy [FM 100–6]: Scaleable system packages ease the application of economy. Space, weight, or time constraints limit the quantity or capability of systems that can be deployed. Information requirements must be satisfied by consolidating similar functional facilities, integrating commercial systems into tactical information works, or accessing to a different information system.

Effectiveness [JITC, 1999]: Efficiency, potency, or capability of an act in producing a desired (or undesired) result. The power of the protection or the attack.

Efficiency [JITC, 1999]: Capability, competency, or productivity. The efficiency of an act is a measure of the work required to achieve a desired result.

Electronic Attack (EA) [MOP 30]: Use of EM or Directed Energy to attack personnel, facilities or equipment to destroy/degrade combat capability.

Electronic Protect (EP) [MOP 30]: Actions to protect personnel, facilities and equipment from enemy/friendly EW that degrade or destroy own-force combat capability.

Electronic Warfare (EW) [MOP 30]: Action involving the use of electromagnetic (EM) and directed energy to control the EM spectrum or to attack the enemy.

Electronic Warfare Support (ES) [NSA, 2002]: That division of EW involving actions tasked by, or under direct control of, an operational commander to search for, intercept, identify, and locate sources of intentional and unintentional radiated electromagnetic energy for the purpose of immediate threat recognition. Thus, electronic warfare support provides information required for immediate decisions involving EW operations and other tactical actions such as threat avoidance, targeting and homing. ES data can be used to produce signals intelligence (JP 1–02).

Emission Security (EMSEC) [NCSC004, 1988]: The protection resulting from all measures taken to deny unauthorized persons information of value that might be derived from intercept and from an analysis of compromising emanations from systems.

Encapsulation [Cox, 1986]: A technique for minimizing interdependencies among separately written modules by defining strict external interfaces.

Enclave [DSD IA, 2000]: An environment that is under the control of a single authority and has a homogeneous security policy, including personnel and physical security. Local and remote elements that access resources within an enclave must satisfy the policy of the enclave. Enclaves can be specific to an organization or a mission and may also contain multiple networks. They may be logical, such as an operational area network (OAN) or be based on physical location and proximity.

Encrypted Text [12 FAM 090]: Data which is encoded into an unclassified form using a nationally accepted form of encoding.

Encryption [Peltier, 1998]: The act of making information unreadable by scrambling the characters in a predefined manner determined by a private key; decryption returns the information to readable form.

Endorsed Cryptographic Products List [NCSC029, 1994]: A list of products that provide electronic cryptographic coding (encrypting) and decoding (decrypting), and which have been endorsed for use for classified or sensitive unclassified U.S. government or government-derived information during its transmission.

Endorsed TEMPEST Products List [12 FAM 090]: A list of commercially developed and commercially produced TEMPEST telecommunications equipment that NSA has endorsed, under the auspices of the NSA Endorsed TEMPEST Products Program, for use by government entities and their contractors to process classified U.S. government information.

Entity [Stoneburner, 2001]: Either a subject (an active element that operates on information or the system state) or an object (a passive element that contains or receives information).

Environment (System) [NCSC029, 1994]: The aggregate of procedures, conditions, and objects that affects the development, operation, and maintenance of a system. *Note:* Environment is often used with qualifiers such as computing environment, application environment, or threat environment, which limit the scope being considered.

Evaluated Products List (EPL) [NCSC004, 1988]: A list of equipments, hardware, software, and firmware that have been evaluated against, and found to be technically compliant, at a particular level of trust, with the DoD TCSEC by the NCSC. The EPL is included in the National Security Agency Information Systems Security Products and Services Catalogue, which is available through the Government Printing Office.

Evaluation [Authors]: The inspection and testing of specific hardware and software products against accepted Information Assurance/Information Security standards.

Evaluation Criteria [NIAP, 1999]: See IT Security Evaluation Criteria.

Evaluation Methodology [NIAP, 1999]: See IT Security Evaluation Methodology.

Event [Authors]: A trigger for an activity.

Evolutionary Program Strategies [DoD8510, 2000]: Generally characterized by design, development, and deployment of a preliminary capability that includes provisions for the evolutionary addition of future functionality and changes, as requirements are further defined.

External Certificate Authority [DSD IA, 2000]: An agent that is trusted and authorized to issue certificates to approved vendors and contractors for the purpose of enabling secure interoperability with DoD entities. Operating requirements for ECAs must be approved by the DoD CIO, in coordination with the DoD Comptroller and the DoD General Counsel.

Fidelity [Webster, 1984]: Accuracy, exact correspondence to truth or fact, the degree to which a system or information is distortion-free.

Flexibility [JP 6–0]: Responsiveness to change, specifically as it relates to user information needs and operational environment.

Force [Authors]: A group of platforms and sites organized for a particular purpose.

Foreign Government Information [12 FAM 090]: (1) Information provided to the United States by a foreign government or international organization of governments in the expectation, express or implied, that the information is to be kept in confidence; or (2) Information, requiring confidentiality, produced by the United States pursuant to a written joint arrangement with a foreign government or international organization of governments. A written joint arrangement may be evidenced by an exchange of letters, a memorandum of understanding, or other written record of the joint arrangement.

Forgery [JITC, 1999]: A false, fake, or counterfeit datum, document, image, or act.

Formerly Restricted Data [12 FAM 090]: Information removed from the restricted data category upon determination jointly by the Department of Energy and Department of Defense that such information relates primarily to the military utilization of atomic weapons and that such information can be adequately safeguarded as classified defense information subject to the restrictions on transmission to other countries and regional defense organizations that apply to restricted data.

Full Operational Capability (FOC) [Authors]: The time at which a new system has been installed at all planned locations and has been fully integrated into the operational structure.

Function [SPAWAR, 1987b]: A discrete action required to achieve a given objective.

Functional Analysis [Pollard, 1988]: Translating requirements into operational and systems functions and identifying the major elements of the system and their configurations and initial functional design requirements.

Functional Domain [DSD IA, 2000]: An identifiable DoD functional mission area. For purposes of the DoD policy memorandum, the functional domains are: command and control, space, logistics, transportation, health affairs, personnel, financial services, public works, research and development, and Intelligence, Surveillance, and Reconnaissance (ISR).

Functional Requirements [Authors]: Architectural atoms; the elementary building blocks of architectural concepts; made up of activities/functions, attributes associated with activities/processes and processes/methods sequencing activities.

Functional Testing [NCSC004, 1988]: The segment of security testing in which the advertised security mechanisms of the system are tested, under operational conditions, for correct operation.

Functionality [JITC, 1999]: Degree of acceptable performance of an act.

General Support System [Stoneburner, 2001]: An interconnected information resource under the same direct management control that shares common functionality. It normally includes hardware, software, information, data, applications, communications, facilities, and people and provides support for a variety of users and applications. Individual applications support different mission-related functions. Users may be from the same or different organizations.

Global Information Grid [DSD EB, 2000]: The globally interconnected, end-to-end set of information capabilities, associated processes and personnel for collecting, processing, storing, disseminating and managing information on demand to warfighters, policy makers, and support personnel. The GiG includes all owned and leased communications and computing systems, services, software (including applications), data, security services and other associated services necessary to achieve Information Superiority.

Global Information Grid Architecture [DSD GiG, 2000]: The architecture, composed of interrelated operational, systems and technical views, which defines the characteristics of and relationships among current and planned Global Information Grid assets in support to National Security missions.

Governing Security Requisites [DoD8510, 2000]: Those security requirements that must be addressed in all systems. These requirements are set by policy, directive, or common practice; e.g., by Executive Order, Office of Management and Budget (OMB), Office of the Secretary of Defense, a Military Service or DoD Agency. Governing security requisites are typically high-level requirements. While implementations will vary from case to case, these requisites are fundamental and must be addressed.

Grand Design Program Strategies [DoD8510, 2000]: Characterized by acquisition, development, and deployment of the total functional capability in a single increment.

Halon [Gann, 1975]: An abbreviation for halogenated hydrocarbon coined by the U.S. Army Corps of Engineers. Halon nomenclature follows the following rule: if a hydrocarbon compound contains the elements CaFbClcBrdIe, it is designated as Halon abcde (terminal zeros are dropped). Thus, Halon 1211 is chlorobromodifluoromethane, etc.

Identification Media [12 FAM 090]: A building or visitor pass.

Identifier [Booch, 1986]: A set of one or more attributes that uniquely distinguishes each instance of an object.

Identity [Stoneburner, 2001]: Information that is unique within a security domain and which is recognized as denoting a particular entity within that domain.

Identity-Based Security Policy [ISSEP, 2000]: A security policy based on the identities and attributes of the object (system resource) being accessed and of the subject (user, group of users, process, or device) requesting access.

Impact [BAH, 1998]: The amount of loss or damage that can be expected, or may be expected from a successful attack of an asset.

Importance [JITC, 1999]: A subjective assessment of the significance of a system's capability and the consequences of the loss of that capability.

Inadvertent Disclosure [NSTISSI 4009]: Accidental exposure of information to a person not authorized access.

Inadvertent Loss [JITC, 1999]: The unplanned loss or compromise of data or system.

Incremental Program Strategies [DoD8510, 2000]: Characterized by acquisition, development, and deployment of functionality through a number of clearly defined system "increments" that stand on their own.

Induction [AAAI, 1999]: A process of logically arriving at a conclusion about a member of a class from examining a few other members of the same class. This method of reasoning may not always produce true statements. As an example, suppose it is known that George's car has four tires and that Fred's car has four tires. Inductive reasoning would allow the conclusion that all cars have four tires. Induction is closely related to learning.

Information [Authors]: Data organized into some form that is useful to a human operator. Must be presented in a useful, recognizable form. [Webster, 1984]: Knowledge derived from study, experience or instruction.

Information Assurance (IA) [IATF, 1999]: Information operations (IO) that protect and defend information and information systems by ensuring their availability, integrity, authentication, confidentiality, and nonrepudiation. This includes providing for restoration of information systems by incorporating protection, detection, and reaction capabilities.

Information Assurance Support Environment (IASE) [DoD8510, 2000]: The IASE is an on-line Web-based help environment for DoD INFOSEC and IA professionals.

Information Assurance Vulnerability Alert (IAVA) [DSD IA, 2000]: The comprehensive distribution process for notifying CINC's, Services and agencies (C/S/A) about vulnerability alerts and countermeasures information. The IAVA process requires C/S/A receipt acknowledgment and provides specific time parameters for implementing appropriate countermeasures depending on the criticality of the vulnerability.

Information Attributes [Authors]: The qualities, characteristics, and distinctive features of information.

Information Category [DoD8510, 2000]: The term used to bind information and tie it to an information security policy.

Information Environment [JP 1–02]: The aggregate of individuals, organizations, and systems that collect, process, or disseminate information, including the information itself.

Information Hiding [Cox, 1986]: The state of a software module is contained in private variables, visible only from within the scope of the module.

Information Interoperability [JITC, 1999]: The exchange and use of information in any electronic form.

Information Operations (IO) [NSTISSI 4009]: Actions taken to affect adversary information and information systems while defending one's own information and information systems.

Information Operations Condition (INFOCON) [DSD IA, 2000]: The INFOCON is a comprehensive defense posture and response based on the status of information systems, military operations, and intelligence assessments of adversary capabilities and intent. The INFOCON system presents a structured, coordinated approach to defend against a computer network attack. INFOCON measures focus on computer network-based protective measures. Each level reflects a defensive posture based on the risk of impact to military operations through the intentional disruption of friendly information systems. INFOCON levels are: NORMAL (normal activity); ALPHA (increased risk of attack); BRAVO (specific risk of attack); CHARLIE (limited attack); and DELTA (general attack). Countermeasures at each level include preventive actions, actions taken during an attack, and damage control/mitigating actions.

Information Owner [DSD IA, 2000]: The organization which creates and is responsible for managing specific information. Usually the principal user of the information created.

Information Requirements [JP 1–02]: Those items of information regarding the enemy and his environment which need to be collected and processed in order to meet the intelligence requirements of a commander.

Information Security [12 FAM 090]: Safeguarding information against unauthorized disclosure; or, the result of any system of administrative policies and procedures for identifying, controlling, and protecting from unauthorized disclosure, information the protection of which is authorized by Executive Order or statute.

Information Superiority [DoD5000, 2001]: The capability to collect, process, and disseminate an uninterrupted flow of information while exploiting or denying an adversary's ability to do the same. Forces attain information superiority through the acquisition of systems and families-of-systems that are secure, reliable, interoperable, and able to communicate across a universal Information Technology (IT) infrastructure, to include National Security Systems (NSS). This IT infrastructure includes the data, information, processes, organizational interactions, skills, and analytical expertise, as well as systems, networks, and information exchange capabilities.

Information System [OMB A130, 1996]: A discrete set of information resources organized for the collection, processing, maintenance, transmission, and dissemination of information, in accordance with defined procedures, whether automated or manual.

Information Systems Security (INFOSEC) [NCSC029, 1994]: The protection of information systems against unauthorized access to or modification of information, whether in storage, processing, or transit, and against the denial-of-service to authorized users or the provision of service to unauthorized users, including those measures necessary to detect, document, and counter such threats.

Information Systems Security Officer (ISSO) [NSTISSI 4009]: Person responsible to the designated approving authority for ensuring the security of an information system throughout its life cycle, from design through disposal. Synonymous with system security officer.

Information Technology (IT) [DoD8510, 2000]: The hardware, firmware, and software used as part of the IS to perform DoD information functions. This definition includes computers, telecommunications, automated information systems, and automatic data processing equipment. IT includes any assembly of computer hardware, software, and firmware configured to collect, create, communicate, compute, disseminate, process, store, and control data or information.

Information Technology (IT) [OMB A130, 1996]: The hardware and software operated by a federal agency or by a contractor of a federal agency or other organization that processes information on behalf of the federal government to accomplish a federal function, regardless of the technology involved, whether computers, telecommunications, or others. It includes automatic data processing equipment as that term is defined in Section 111(a)(2) of the Federal Property and Administrative Services Act of 1949. For the purposes of this Circular, automatic data processing and telecommunications activities related to certain critical national security missions, as defined in 44 U.S.C. 3502(2) and 10 U.S.C. 2315, are excluded.

Information Warfare (IW) [JCS3210, 1996]: Actions taken to achieve information superiority by affecting adversary information, information-based processes, information systems and computer-based networks while defending one's own information, information-based processes, information systems and computer-based networks.

Infrastructure [DSD IA, 2000]: The framework of interdependent networks and systems comprising identifiable industries, institutions, and distribution capabilities that provide a continual flow of goods and services essential to the defense and economic security of the United States, the smooth functioning of government at all levels, or society as a whole.

Infrastructure-Centric [DoD8510, 2000]: A security management approach that considers information systems and their computing environment as a single entity.

Inheritance [Cox, 1986]: In the Object-Oriented paradigm, instance variables, class variables and methods are passed down from a superclass to its subclasses. A technique that allows new classes to be built on top of older, less specialized classes instead of being rewritten from scratch.

Initial Operational Capability (IOC) [Authors]: The first time a new system is introduced into operation.

Integrator [DoD8510, 2000]: The organization that integrates the IS components.

Integrity [DoD8510, 2000]: Quality of an IS reflecting the logical correctness and reliability of the operating system; the logical completeness of the hardware and software implementing the protection mechanisms; and the consistency of the data structures and occurrence of the stored data. Note that, in a formal security mode, integrity is interpreted more narrowly to mean protection against unauthorized modification or destruction of information. [Stoneburner, 2001]: The security goal that generates the requirement for protection against either intentional or accidental attempts to violate data integrity (the property that data has not been altered in an unauthorized manner) or system integrity (the quality that a system has when it performs its intended function in an unimpaired manner, free from unauthorized manipulation).

Intelligence Method [12 FAM 090]: The method which is used to provide support to an intelligence source or operation, and which, if disclosed, is vulnerable to counteraction that could nullify or significantly reduce its effectiveness in supporting the foreign intelligence or foreign counterintelligence activities of the United States, or which would, if disclosed, reasonably lead to the disclosure of an intelligence source or operation.

Intelligence Source [12 FAM 090]: A person, organization, or technical means which provides foreign intelligence or foreign counterintelligence and which, if its identity or capability is disclosed, is vulnerable to counteraction that could nullify or significantly reduce its effectiveness in providing foreign intelligence or foreign counterintelligence to the United States. An intelligence source also means a person or organization which provides foreign intelligence or foreign counterintelligence to the United States only on the condition that its identity remains undisclosed.

Interagency Coordination [JP 1–02]: Within the context of Department of Defense involvement, the coordination that occurs between elements of the Department of Defense and engaged U.S. government agencies, nongovernment organizations, private voluntary organizations, and regional and international organizations for the purpose of accomplishing an objective.

Interim Approval to Operate (IATO) [DoD8510, 2000]: Temporary approval granted by a DAA for an IS to process information based on preliminary results of a security evaluation of the system.

International Organization [12 FAM 090]: An organization of governments.

Interoperability [FM 100–6]: The capability of information systems working together as a system-of-systems. Interoperability implies compatibility of combined, joint, and service common information or data elements procedures. Interoperability is the foundation on which information systems capabilities depend.

Intrusion Detection [NSA, 2002]: Pertaining to techniques which attempt to detect intrusion into a computer or network by observation of actions, security logs, or audit data. Detection of break-ins or attempts either manually or via software expert systems that operate on logs or other information available on the network.

IS Security Goal [ISSEP, 2000]: See Security Goal.

IS-Related Risk [ISSEP, 2000]: The probability that a particular threat agent will exploit, or trigger, a particular information system vulnerability and the resulting mission/business impact if this should occur. IS related-risks arise from legal liability or mission/business loss due to (1) Unauthorized (malicious, nonmalicious, or accidental) disclosure, modification, or destruction of information; (2) Nonmalicious errors and omissions; (3) IS disruptions due to natural or man-made disasters; (4) Failure to exercise due care and diligence in the implementation and operation of the IS.

IT Security Architecture [Stoneburner, 2001]: A description of security principles and an overall approach for complying with the principles that drive the system design; i.e., guidelines on the placement and implementation of specific security services within various distributed computing environments.

IT Security Goals [Stoneburner, 2001]: See Security Goals.

IT-Related Risk [Stoneburner, 2001]: The net mission/business impact considering the probability that a particular threat source will exploit, or trigger, a particular information system vulnerability, and the resulting impact if this should occur. IT-related risks arise from legal liability or mission/business loss due to, but not limited to (1) Unauthorized (malicious, nonmalicious, or accidental) disclosure, modification, or destruction of information; (2) Non-malicious errors and omissions; (3) IT disruptions due to normal or man-made disasters; (4) Failure to exercise due care and diligence in the implementation and operation of the IT.

Java [Sun, 2002]: A general purpose, class based, Object-Oriented programming language. Based on a programming language called Oak that was originally intended for embedded consumer electronics applications. It was later retargeted at the internet and renamed.

Judgment [Webster, 1984]: The ability to make a decision or form an opinion by discerning and evaluating.

Knowledge [Authors]: Information from multiple sources integrated with common, environmental, real-world experience.

Layered Defense [DSD IA, 2000]: A combination of security services, software and hardware, infrastructures, and processes which are implemented to achieve a required level of protection. These mechanisms are additive in nature with the minimum protection being provided by the network and infrastructure layers.

Legacy Information System [DoD8510, 2000]: An operational IS that existed prior to the implementation of the DITSCAP.

Logged-on but Unattended [12 FAM 090]: A workstation is considered logged on but unattended when the user is (1) Logged on but is not physically present in the office; and (2) There is no one else present with an appropriate level of clearance safeguarding access to the workstation. Coverage must be equivalent to that which would be required to safeguard hard copy information if the same employee were away from his or her desk. Users of logged on but unattended classified workstations are subject to the issuance of security violations.

Logically Disconnect [12 FAM 090]: Although the physical connection between the control unit and a terminal remains intact, a system enforced disconnection prevents communication between the control unit and the terminal.

Lost Pouch [12 FAM 090]: Any pouch-out-of-control which is not recovered.

Maintainability [Eisner, 1987]:... the general ease of a system to be maintained, at all levels of maintenance.

Maintenance Organization [DoD8510, 2000]: The government organization responsible for the maintenance of an IS. (Although the actual organization performing maintenance on a system may be a contractor, the maintenance organization is the government organization responsible for the maintenance.)

Major Application [Stoneburner, 2001]: An application that requires special attention to security due to the risk and magnitude of the harm resulting from the loss, misuse, or unauthorized access to, or modification of, the information in the application. A breach in a major application might comprise many individual application programs and hardware, software, and telecommunications components. Major applications can be either major software applications or a combination of hardware/software where the only purpose of the system is to support a specific mission-related function.

Maritime Strategy [Authors]: Naval objectives for sea control, maritime power projection, and control and protection of shipping. The Naval objectives in support of the National Strategy.

Master Plan [SPAWAR, 1987b]: A long-range plan, derived from the notional architecture, for development and procurement of capabilities.

Message [Authors]: A form of indirect procedure call. In the Object-Oriented Paradigm, a message must be sent to an object in order to find out anything about it.

Message Digest [Authors]: A term associated with the MD2, 4, 5 series of hash algorithms designed for use with digital signature schemas. A "fingerprint" or Message Digest (MD) of a message of arbitrary length. It is conjectured that the difficulty of coming up with two messages having the same message digest is on the order of 2^{64} operations, and that the difficulty of coming up with any message having a given message digest is on the order of 2^{128} operations.

Message Stream [12 FAM 090]: The sequence of messages or parts of messages to be sent.

Method [Authors]: A function, capability, algorithm, formula, or process that an object is capable of performing.

Mission [NCSC029, 1994]: A specific task with which a person, or group of individuals, or organization is entrusted to perform.

Mission Justification [DoD8510, 2000]: The description of the operational capabilities required to perform an assigned mission. This includes a description of a system's capabilities, functions, interfaces, information processed, operational organizations supported, and the intended operational environment.

Modification [JITC, 1999]: Change to data or software (to include forgery or insertion of viruses or back doors into computer system, server, or router), whose unauthorized disclosure or tampering could damage persons or national security.

Modular Treated Conference Room (MTCR) [12 FAM 090]: A second-generation design of the treated conference room (TCR), offering more flexibility in configuration and ease of assembly than the original TCR, designed to provide acoustic and RF emanations protection.

Modularity [FM 100–6]: Modular packages consist of sets of equipment, people, and software tailorable for a wide range of missions.

Multilevel Mode [DoD8510, 2000]: INFOSEC mode of operation wherein all the following statements are satisfied concerning the users who have direct or indirect access to the system, its peripherals, remote terminals, or remote hosts: (1) Some users do not have a valid security clearance for all the information processed in the IS; (2) all users have the proper security clearance and appropriate formal access approval for that information to which they have access; and (3) all users have a valid need-to-know only for information for which they have access.

Multilevel Security (MLS) [NCSC029, 1994]: Concept of processing information with different classifications and categories that simultaneously permits access by users with different security clearances, but prevents users from obtaining access to information for which they lack authorization.

Multinational Operations [JP 1–02]: A collective term to describe military actions conducted by forces of two or more nations usually undertaken within the structure of a coalition or alliance

Naming Attributes [Booch, 1986]: Names carried by each instance of an object, such as name, or identification number.

National Computer Security Center (NCSC) [NCSC004, 1988]: Originally named the DoD Computer Security Center, the NCSC is responsible for encouraging the widespread availability of trusted computer systems throughout the federal government. With the signing of NSDD-145; the NCSC is responsible for encouraging the widespread availability of trusted computer systems throughout the federal government.

National Information Assurance Partnership (NIAP) [IATF, 1999]: A joint industry/government initiative, lead by NIST and NSA, to establish commercial testing laboratories where industry product providers can have security products tested to verify their performance against vendor claims.

National Security [12 FAM 090]: The national defense or foreign relations of the United States.

National Security Information [NSTISSI 4009]: Information that has been determined, pursuant to (NSI) Executive Order 12958 or any predecessor order, to require protection against unauthorized disclosure

National Security System [DSD IA, 2000]: Any telecommunications or information system operated by the Department of Defense, the function, operation, or use of which (1) involves intelligence activities; (2) involves cryptologic activities related to national security; (3) involves command and control of military forces; (4) involves equipment that is an integral part of a weapon or weapon system; or (5) is critical to the direct fulfillment of military or intelligence missions and does not include a system that is to be used for routine administrative and business applications (including payroll, finance, logistics, and personnel management applications).

National Strategy [Authors]: Objectives of the nation for dealing in the arena of international politics, military confrontation, and national defense.

Network Centric [DSD IA, 2000]: A holistic view of interconnected information systems and resources that encourages a broader approach to security management than a component-based approach.

NIAP Common Criteria Evaluation and Validation Scheme [NIAP, 1999]: The scheme developed by NIST and NSA as part of the National Information Assurance Partnership (NIAP) establishing an organizational and technical framework to evaluate the trustworthiness of IT products.

NIAP Oversight Body [NIAP, 1999]: A governmental organization responsible for carrying out validation and for overseeing the day-to-day operation of the NIAP Common Criteria Evaluation and Validation Scheme.

Node [Authors]: A compound object of functional requirements.

Noncomputing Security Methods [ISSEP, 2000]: Noncomputing methods are security safeguards which do not use the hardware, software, and firmware of the IS. Traditional methods include physical security (controlling physical access to computing resources), personnel security, and procedural security.

Nondevelopmental Item (NDI) [DoD8510, 2000]: Any item that is available in the commercial marketplace; any previously developed item that is in use by a Department or Agency of the United States, a state or local government, or a foreign government with which the United States has a mutual defense cooperation agreement; any item described above that requires only minor modifications in order to meet the requirements of the procuring Agency; or any item that is currently being produced that does not meet the requirements of definitions above, solely because the item is not yet in use or is not yet available in the commercial marketplace.

Nonrecord Material [12 FAM 090]: Extra and duplicate copies that are only of temporary value, including shorthand notes, used carbon paper, preliminary drafts, and other material of similar nature.

Nonrepudiation [Entrust, 2000]: The parties involved in an electronic exchange should not be able to deny or repudiate the exchange.

Notional Architecture [SPAWAR, 1987b]: An alternative architecture composed of current systems, as well as, new procurements proposed for some future date.

Null Option [SPAWAR, 1987b]: The option to take no action.

Object [AAAI, 1999]: An entity that can have many properties (either declarative, procedural, or both) associated with it.

Object Identity [Authors]: In the Object-Oriented paradigm, each object has a unique identifier independent of the values of other properties.

Object Reuse [NSTISSI 4009]: Reassignment and re-use of a storage medium containing one or more objects after ensuring no residual data remains on the storage medium.

Observe, Orient, Decide, Act (OODA) [JITC, 1999]: See OODA Loop.

Official Information [12 FAM 090]: That information or material which is owned by, produced for or by, or under the control of the U.S. government.

OODA Loop [JITC, 1999]: The Observe, Orient, Decide, Act (OODA) cycle (or Boyd Cycle) first introduced by Col. John Boyd, USAF. Refers to steps in the decision-making process. See Boyd Cycle and J. Boyd, Patterns of Conflict, December 1986. Unpublished study, 196 pages [Boyd, 1986].

Operating Environment [DSD IA, 2000]: The total environment in which an information system operates. Includes the physical facility and controls, procedural and administrative controls, personnel controls (e.g., clearance level of the least cleared user).

Operational Security (OPSEC) [DoD8510, 2000]: Process denying information to potential adversaries about capabilities and intentions by identifying, controlling, and protecting unclassified generic activities.

Operationally Object-Oriented [Dittrich, 1986]: The data model includes generic operators to deal with complex objects in their entirety.

Operations Security (OPSEC) [NCSC029, 1994]: A process denying to potential adversaries information about capabilities and intentions by identifying, controlling, and protecting generally unclassified evidence of the planning and execution of sensitive activities.

Operator Overloading [Elmasri, 2000]: See Polymorphism.

Orange Book [DoD5200, 1985]: Common name used to refer to the DoD Trusted Computing System Evaluation Criteria (TCSEC), DoD 5200.28-STD.

Orange Forces [Authors]: Forces of the United States operating in an exercise in emulation of the opposing force.

Original Classification [12 FAM 090]: An initial determination that information requires protection against unauthorized disclosure in the interest of national security, and a designation of the level of classification.

Original Classifier [12 FAM 090]: An authorized individual in the executive branch who initially determines that particular information requires a specific degree of protection against unauthorized disclosure in the interest of national security and applies the classification designation "Top Secret," "Secret," or "Confidential."

Overlaps [SPAWAR, 1987b]: Areas in which too much capability exists. Unnecessary redundancy of coverage in a given area or function.

Overseas Security Policy Board (OSPB) [12 FAM 090]: The Overseas Security Policy Board (OSPB) is an interagency group of security professionals from the foreign affairs and intelligence communities who meet regularly to formulate security policy for U.S. missions abroad. The OSPB is chaired by the Director, Diplomatic Security Service.

Passive System [DoD8510, 2000]: A system related indirectly to other systems. Passive systems may or may not have a physical connection to other systems, and their logical connection is controlled tightly.

Password [Peltier, 1998]: A confidential sequence of characters used to authenticate an individual's identity, usually during a log-on process.

Plain Text [12 FAM 090]: Information, usually classified, in unencrypted form.

Platform [Authors]: A mobile collection of systems (e.g., ship, aircraft, satellite, truck, etc.).

Polymorphism [Elmasri, 2000]: Allows the same message to be handled in different ways depending on the object that receives it. Allows the use of the same name for the same operation everywhere in the program.

Precision Engagement [JP 1–02]: The ability of joint forces to locate, surveil, discern, and track objectives or targets; select, organize, and use the correct systems; generate desired effects; assess results; and reengage with decisive speed and overwhelming operational tempo as required, throughout the full range of military operations.

Preferred Products List (PPL) [NCSC004, 1988]: A list of commercially produced equipments that meet TEMPEST and other requirements prescribed by the National Security Agency. This list is included in the NSA Information Systems Security Products and Services Catalogue, issued quarterly and available through the Government Printing Office.

Primary Mission Area [Authors]: Synonymous with Primary Warfare Mission Area (PWMA). A warfare mission area concerned with a specific, major phase or portion of naval warfare.

Process [Authors]: A sequence of activities.

Product Certification Center [12 FAM 090]: A facility which certifies the technical security integrity of communications equipment. The equipment is handled and used within secure channels.

Professional Courier (or Diplomatic Courier) [12 FAM 090]: A person specifically employed and provided with official documentation (see section 12 FAM 141) by the U.S. Department of State to transport properly prepared, addressed, and documented diplomatic pouches between the Department and its Foreign Service posts and across other international boundaries.

Program Manager [DoD8510, 2000]: The person ultimately responsible for the overall procurement, development, integration, modification, or operation and maintenance of the IS.

Protect [JITC, 1999]: To keep information systems away from intentional, unintentional, and natural threats: (1) preclude an adversary from gaining access to information for the purpose of destroying, corrupting, or manipulating such information; or (2) deny use of information systems to access, manipulate, and transmit mission-essential information.

Protected Distribution System (PDS) [NSTISSI 4009]: Wire line or fiber optic distribution system used to transmit unencrypted classified national security information through an area of lesser classification or control.

Protection Schema [12 FAM 090]: An outline detailing the type of access users may have to a database or application system, given a user's need-to-know, e.g., read, write, modify, delete, create, execute, and append.

Protective Layers [JITC, 1999]: Mechanisms for insuring the integrity of systems or data. See Defense in Depth.

Rainbow Series [Authors]: A multi-volume set of publications on Information Assurance, Information Security and related topics. Published by the National Computer Security Center (NCSC) at the National Security Agency (NSA) in Fort Meade, MD. Each volume is published under a different color cover, hence the term "Rainbow" series.

Reach [Alberts, 2000]: An aggregate measure of the degree to which information is shared.

React [JITC, 1999]: To respond to threat activity within information systems, when detected, and mitigate the consequences by taking appropriate action to incidents that threaten information and information systems.

Reality [Authors]: The real world.

Record Material [12 FAM 090]: All books, papers, maps, photographs, or other documentary materials, regardless of physical form or characteristics, made or received by the U.S. government in connection with the transaction of public business and preserved or appropriated by an agency or its legitimate successor as evidence of the organization, functions, policies, decisions, procedures, or other activities of any agency of the government, or because of the informational data contained therein.

Red [NSTISSI 4009]: Designation applied to information systems, and associated areas, circuits, components, and equipment in which national security information is being processed.

Red Book [DoD5200, 1985]: Common name used to refer to the Network Interpretation of the TCSEC (Orange Book). Originally referred to in some circles as the "White Book."

Red Forces [Authors]: Forces of countries considered unfriendly to the United States and her Allies.

Red Team [JITC, 1999]: A group of people duly authorized to conduct attacks against friendly information systems, under prescribed conditions, for the purpose of revealing the capabilities and limitations of the information assurance posture of a system under test. For purposes of operational testing, the Red team will operate in as operationally realistic an environment as feasible and will conduct its operations in accordance with the approved operational test plan.

Red/Black Concept [NSTISSI 4009]: Separation of electrical and electronic circuits, components, equipment, and systems that handle national security information (RED), in electrical form, from those that handle nonnational security information (BLACK) in the same form.

Red-Black Separation [12 FAM 090]: The requirement for physical spacing between "red" and "black" processing systems and their components, including signal and power lines.

Redundancy [FM 100–6]: From a information systems network perspective, planners provide diverse paths over multiple means to ensure timely, reliable information flow. From an equipment perspective, planners ensure that sufficient backup systems and repair parts are available to maintain the system's or network's capabilities.

Redundant Control Capability [12 FAM 090]: Use of active or passive replacement, for example, throughout the network components (i.e., network nodes, connectivity, and control stations) to enhance reliability, reduce threat of single-point-of-failure, enhance survivability, and provide excess capacity.

Reference Monitor [ISSEP, 2000]: The security engineering term for IS functionality that (1) controls all access, (2) cannot be bypassed, (3) is tamper-resistant, and (4) provides confidence that the other three items are true.

Referential Attributes [Booch, 1987]: The facts that tie an instance of one object to an instance of another object.

Regional Diplomatic Courier Officer (RDCO) [12 FAM 090]: The RDCO oversees the operations of a regional diplomatic courier division.

Relevance [Webster]: Related to the matter at hand; directly bearing upon the current matter.

Reliability [Authors]: A measure of system dependability.

Remote Diagnostic Facility [12 FAM 090]: An off-premise diagnostic, maintenance, and programming facility authorized to perform functions on the Department computerized telephone system via an external network trunk connection.

Residual Risk [NCSC004, 1988]: The portion of risk that remains after security measures have been applied.

Restricted Area [12 FAM 090]: A specifically designated and posted area in which classified information or material is located or in which sensitive functions are performed, access to which is controlled and to which only authorized personnel are admitted.

RF Shielding [12 FAM 090]: The application of materials to surfaces of a building, room, or a room within a room, that makes the surface largely impervious to electromagnetic energy. As a technical security countermeasure, it is used to contain or dissipate emanations from information processing equipment, and to prevent interference by externally generated energy.

Richness [Evans, 1997]: Defined by three aspects of the information itself: bandwidth (the amount of information), the degree to which the information is customized, and interactivity (the extent of two way communication).

Risk [BAH, 1998]: The potential for damage to, or loss of an asset. The level of risk is a combination of Impact on the asset, a specific Vulnerability and a particular Threat (R = I (Impact) x T (Threat) x V (Vulnerability)).

Risk Analysis [Stoneburner, 2001]: The process of identifying the risks to system security and determining the probability of occurrence, the resulting impact, and the additional safeguards that mitigate this impact. Part of risk management and synonymous with risk assessment.

Risk Assessment [NSTISSI 4009]: Process of analyzing threats to and vulnerabilities of an IS and the potential impact the loss of information or capabilities of a system would have on national security. The resulting analysis is used as a basis for identifying appropriate and cost-effective measures.

Risk Index [NCSC004, 1988]: The disparity between the minimum clearance or authorization of system users and the maximum sensitivity (e.g., classification and categories) of data processed by a system.

Risk Management [DSD IA, 2000]: The discipline of identifying and measuring security risks associated with an information system, and controlling and reducing those risks to an acceptable level. The goal of risk management is to invest organizational resources to mitigate security risks in a cost-effective manner, while enabling timely and effective mission accomplishment. Risk management is an important aspect of information assurance and defense-in-depth.

Robustness [FM 100–6]: The system's ability to operate despite service interruption, system errors and other anomalous events.

Rule-Based Security Policy [ISSEP, 2000]: A security policy based on global rules imposed for all subjects. These rules usually rely on a comparison of the sensitivity of the objects being accessed and the possession of corresponding attributes by the subjects requesting access.

Rules [Authors]: Constraints.

Sanitize [12 FAM 090]: The degaussing or overwriting of information on magnetic or other storage media.

Secure Interoperability [JITC, 1999]: The ability to have secure, successful transactions. Today's interoperability expands that previous focus to also include information assurance considerations, and include the requirement to formally assess whether that traditional, successful transaction is also secure (i.e., secure interoperability meaning a secure, successful transaction exists).

Secure Room [12 FAM 090]: Any room with floor-to-ceiling, slab-to-slab construction of some substantial material, i.e., concrete, brick, cinder block, plywood, or plaster board. Any window areas or penetrations of wall areas over 15.25 cm (six inches) must be covered with either grilling or substantial type material. Entrance doors must be constructed of solid wood, metal, etc., and be capable of holding a DS-approved three-way combination lock with interior extension.

Secure Voice [12 FAM 090]: Systems in which transmitted conversations are encrypted to make them unintelligible to anyone except the intended recipient. Within the context of Department security standards, secure voice systems must also have protective features included in the environment of the systems terminals.

Security [DoD8510, 2000]: Measures and controls that ensure confidentiality, integrity, availability, and accountability of the information processed and stored by a computer.

Security Anomaly [12 FAM 090]: An irregularity possibly indicative of a security breach, an attempt to breach security, or of noncompliance with security standards, policy, or procedures.

Security Classification Designations [12 FAM 090]: Refers to "Top Secret," and "Secret," and "Confidential" designations on classified information or material.

Security Domain [Stoneburner, 2001]: A set of subjects, their information objects, and a common security policy.

Security Equipment [12 FAM 090]: Protective devices such as intrusion alarms, safes, locks, and destruction equipment which provide physical or technical surveillance protection as their primary purpose.

Security Evaluation [NCSC004, 1988]: An evaluation done to assess the degree of trust that can be placed in systems for the secure handling of sensitive information. One type, a product evaluation, is an evaluation performed on the hardware and software features and assurances of a computer product from a perspective that excludes the application environment. The other type, a system evaluation, is done for the purpose of assessing a system's security safeguards with respect to a specific operational mission and is a major step in the certification and accreditation process.

Security Goals [Stoneburner, 2001]: The five security goals are integrity, availability, confidentiality, accountability, and assurance.

Security Incident [NSA, 2002]: Any act or circumstance that involves classified information that deviates from the requirements of governing security publications. For example, compromise, possible compromise, inadvertent disclosure, and deviation.

Security Inspection [NSTISSI 4009]: Examination of an IS to determine compliance with security policy, procedures, and practices.

Security Label [NSA, 2002]: Piece of information that represents the sensitivity of a subject or object, such as its hierarchical classification (CONFIDENTIAL, SECRET, TOP SECRET) together with any applicable nonhierarchical security categories (e.g., sensitive compartmented information, critical nuclear weapon design information).

Security Policy [NCSC029, 1994]: The set of laws, rules, and practices that regulate how sensitive or critical information is managed, protected, and distributed. *Note:* A security policy may be written at many different levels of abstraction. For example, a corporate security policy is the set of laws, rules, and practices within a user organization; system security policy defines the rules and practices within a specific system; and technical security policy regulates the use of hardware, software, and firmware of a system or product.

Security Policy Model [NSA, 2002]: A formal presentation of the security policy enforced by the system. It must identify the set of rules and practices that regulate how a system manages, protects, and distributes sensitive information.

Security Process [DoD8510, 2000]: The series of activities that monitor, evaluate, test, certify, accredit, and maintain the system accreditation throughout the system life cycle.

Security Purpose [ISSEP, 2000]: The IS security purpose is to provide value by enabling an organization to meet all mission/business objectives while ensuring that system implementations demonstrate due care consideration of risks to the organization and its customers.

Security Requirements [NCSC004, 1988]: The types and levels of protection necessary for equipment, data, information, applications, and facilities to meet security policy.

Security Requirements Baseline [NCSC004, 1988]: A description of minimum requirements necessary for a system to maintain an acceptable level of security.

Security Service [Stoneburner, 2001]: A capability that supports one, or many, of the security goals. Examples of security services are key management, access control, and authentication.

Security Specification [NCSC004, 1988]: A detailed description of the safeguards required to protect a system.

Security Test and Evaluation (ST&E) [NCSC004, 1988]: An examination and analysis of the security safeguards of a system as they have been applied in an operational environment to determine the security posture of the system.

Security Testing [NCSC004, 1988]: A process used to determine that the security features of a system are implemented as designed. This includes hands-on functional testing, penetration testing, and verification.

Sensitive Information [DoD8510, 2000]: Information, the loss, misuse, or unauthorized access to or modification of which could adversely affect the national interest or the conduct of federal programs, or the privacy to which individuals are entitled under 5 USC Section 552a (the Privacy Act), but that has not been specifically authorized under criteria established by an Executive Order or an Act of Congress to be kept secret in the interest of national defense or foreign policy. (Systems that are not national security systems, but contain sensitive information, are to be protected in accordance with the requirements of the Computer Security Act of 1987.)

Sensitive Information [NCSC029, 1994]: Information designated to require protection because its unauthorized disclosure, alteration, loss, or destruction could cause damage. *Note:* It includes both classified and sensitive unclassified information.

Sensitive Intelligence Information [12 FAM 090]: Such intelligence information, the unauthorized disclosure of which would lead to counteraction (1) jeopardizing the continued productivity of intelligence sources or methods which provide intelligence vital to the national security; or (2) offsetting the value of intelligence vital to the national security.

Sensitive Unclassified Information [NCSC029, 1994]: Any information, the loss, misuse, or unauthorized access to or modification of which could adversely affect the national interest or the conduct of federal programs, or the privacy to which individuals are entitled under 5 U.S.C Section 552a (the Privacy Act) [18], but that has not been specifically authorized under criteria established by an Executive Order or an Act of Congress to be kept secret in the interest of national defense or foreign policy. *Note:* Systems that are not national security systems, but contain sensitive information, are to be protected in accordance with the requirements of the Computer Security Act of 1987 (Public Law 100–235).

Sensitivity Attributes [12 FAM 090]: User-supplied indicators of file sensitivity that the system uses to enforce an access control policy.

Sharing [Alberts, 2000]: Providing access to and facilitating the sharing of information which enhances reach and creates shared awareness.

Shorfalls [SPAWAR, 1987b]: Functional areas in which additional capability or coverage is required.

Simplicity [Authors]: The simplest correct structure is the most desirable.

Site [Authors]: An immobile collection of systems at a specific location.

Special Agent [12 FAM 090]: A special agent in the Diplomatic Security Service (DSS) is a sworn officer of the Department of State or the Foreign Service, whose position is designated as either a GS-1811 or FS-2501, and has been issued special agent credentials by the Director of the Diplomatic Security Service to perform those specific law enforcement duties as defined in 22 U.S.C. 2712.

Special Investigators [12 FAM 090]: Special investigators are contracted by the Department of State. They perform various noncriminal investigative functions in DS headquarters, field, and resident offices. They are not members of the Diplomatic Security Service and are not authorized to conduct criminal investigations.

Spherical Zone of Control [12 FAM 090]: A volume of space in which uncleared personnel must be escorted which extends a specific distance in all directions from TEMPEST equipment processing classified information or from a shielded enclosure.

Standardization [FM 100–6]: The commander's information requirements must not be comprised by the use of nonstandard equipment.

State [Authors]: A static condition of an object or group of objects.

State Space [Authors]: The total collection of possible states for a particular object or group of objects.

Storage Media [12 FAM 090]: Floppy diskettes, tapes, hard disk drives, or any devices that store automated information.

Storage Object [NCSC004, 1988]: An object that supports both read and write accesses.

Strength [JITC, 1999]: The power of the information assurance protection.

Strength of Mechanism (SML) [IATF, 1999]: A scale for measuring the relative strength of a security mechanism hierarchically ordered from SML 1 through SML 3.

Strike Warfare [Authors]: A primary warfare mission area dealing with preemptive or retaliatory offensive strikes against inland or coastal ground targets.

Structurally Object-Oriented [Manola, 1990]: The data model allows definitions of data structures to represent entities of any complexity (complex objects).

Subject [Stoneburner, 2001]: An active entity, generally in the form of a person, process, or device, that causes information to flow among objects or changes the system state.

Suite [Authors]: A named set of resources and interfaces; a collection of resources; not a physical space.

Support Mission Area [Authors]: Synonymous with Support Warfare Mission Area. Areas of Naval warfare that provide support functions that cut across the boundaries of all (or most) other warfare mission areas.

Survivability [FM 100–6]: Information systems must be reliable, robust, resilient, and at least as survivable as the supported force. Distributed systems and alternate means of communication provide a measure of resilience. Systems must be organized and deployed to ensure that performance under stress degrades gradually and not catastrophically. Command procedures must be capable of adaptation to cope with degradation or failure.

System [Authors]: A collection of components designed to satisfy functional requirements in a specific functional area.

System [NCSC029, 1994]: A collection of components that may include computer hardware, firmware, software, data, procedures, environment, and people, so related as to behave as an interacting or interdependent unit. *Note:* A system has a particular purpose and operational environment. A system may contain one or more components, subsystems, or products. The operational environment may encompass the computing facility or the site installation.

System Accreditation [12 FAM 090]: The official authorization granted to an information system to process sensitive information in its operational environment based on a comprehensive security evaluation of the system's hardware, firmware, and software security design, configuration and implementation and of the other system procedural, administrative, physical, TEMPEST, personnel, and communications security controls.

System Attributes [Authors]: The qualities, characteristics, and distinctive features of information systems.

System Certification [12 FAM 090]: The technical evaluation of a system's security features that established the extent to which a particular information system's design and implementation meets a set of specified security requirements.

System Entity [DoD8510, 2000]: A system subject (user or process) or object.

System High Mode [DoD8510, 2000]: IS security mode of operation wherein each user, with direct or indirect access to the IS, its peripherals, remote terminals, or remote hosts, has all of the following: a. Valid security clearance for all information within an IS; b. Formal access approval and signed nondisclosure agreements for all the information stored and processed (including all compartments and special access programs); and c. Valid need-to-know for some of the information contained within the IS.

System Integrity [DoD8510, 2000]: The attribute of an IS when it performs its intended function in an unimpaired manner, free from deliberate or inadvertent unauthorized manipulation of the system.

System Security Authorization Agreement (SSAA) [DoD8510, 2000]: The SSAA is a formal agreement among the DAA(s), the Certifier, user representative, and program manager. It is used throughout the entire DITSCAP to guide actions, document decisions, specify IA requirements, document certification tailoring and level-of-effort, identify potential solutions, and maintain operational systems security.

Systems Architecture [INCOSE, 2002]: The fundamental and unifying system structure defined in terms of system elements, interfaces, processes, constraints, and behaviors.

Systems Engineering [DoD5000, 2000]: An integrated composite of people, products, and processes that provides a capability or satisfies a stated need or objective.

Systems Security [AISSIM, 1996]: There are three parts to Systems Security. a. Computer Security (COMPUSEC) is composed of measures and controls that protect an AIS against denial-of-service, unauthorized disclosure, modification, or destruction of AIS and data (information). b. Communications Security (COMSEC) is measures and controls taken to deny unauthorized persons information derived from telecommunications of the U.S. government. government communications regularly travel by computer networks, telephone systems, and radio calls. c. Information Systems Security (INFOSEC) is controls and measures taken to protect telecommunications systems, automated information systems, and the information they process, transmit, and store.

Technical Certification [12 FAM 090]: A formal assurance by the Undersecretary for Management to Congress that standards are met which apply to an examination, installation, test or other process involved in providing security for equipment, systems, or facilities. Certifications may include exceptions and are issued by the office or person performing the work in which the standards apply.

Technical Penetration [12 FAM 090]: An unauthorized RF, acoustic, or emanations intercept of information. This intercept may occur along a transmission path which is (1) known to the source, (2) fortuitous and unknown to the source, or (3) clandestinely established.

Technical Surveillance [12 FAM 090]: The act of establishing a technical penetration and intercepting information without authorization.

Telecommunications [12 FAM 090]: Any transmission, emission, or reception of signs, signals, writings, images, sounds, or information of any nature by wire, radio, visual, or other electromagnetic, mechanical, or optical means.

TEMPEST [IATF, 1999]: The investigation, study and control of compromising emanations from telecommunications and automated information systems equipment.

TEMPEST Certification [12 FAM 090]: Nationally approved hardware that protects against the transmission of compromising emanations, i.e., unintentional signals from information processing equipment which can disclose information being processed by the system.

TEMPEST Equipment (or TEMPEST-Approved Equipment) [12 FAM 090]: Equipment that has been designed or modified to suppress compromising signals. Such equipment is approved at the national level for U.S. classified applications after undergoing specific tests. National TEMPEST approval does not, of itself, mean a device can be used within the foreign affairs community. Separate DS approval is required.

TEMPEST Hazard [12 FAM 090]: A security anomaly that holds the potential for loss of classified information through compromising emanations.

TEMPEST Test [12 FAM 090]: A field or laboratory examination of the electronic signal characteristics of equipment or systems for the presence of compromising emanations.

TEMPEST-Approved Personal Computer (TPC) [12 FAM 090]: A personal computer that is currently listed on the Preferred Products List (PPL) or Evaluated Products List (EPL).

Tenant Agency [12 FAM 090]: A U.S. government department or agency operating overseas as part of the U.S. foreign affairs community under the authority of a chief of mission. Excluded are military elements not under direct authority of the chief of mission.

Threat [NCSC004, 1988]: Any circumstance or event with the potential to cause harm to a system in the form of destruction, disclosure, modification of data, and denial-of-service.

Threat Agent [AISSIM, 1996]: A means or method used to exploit a vulnerability in a system, operation, or facility.

Threat Analysis [ISSEP, 2000]: The examination of threat agents against system vulnerabilities to determine the threats for a particular system in a particular operational environment.

Threat Assessment [NSA, 2002]: Process of formally evaluating the degree of threat to an information system and describing the nature of the threat.

Threat Source [Stoneburner, 2001]: Either (1) intent and method targeted at the intentional exploitation of a vulnerability or (2) the situation and method that may accidentally trigger a vulnerability.

Timeliness [Stoneburner, 2001]: The ability to ensure the delivery of required information within a defined time frame. Availability of required information in time to make decisions and permit execution within an adversary's decision and execution cycle.

Timely [JITC, 1999]: In-time, reasonable access to data or system capabilities.

Traffic Analysis [ISSEP, 2000]: The inference of information from observation of traffic flows (presence, absence, amount, direction, and frequency).

Traffic Flow Confidentiality [ISSEP, 2000]: A confidentiality service to protect against traffic analysis.

Treated Conference Room (TCR) [12 FAM 090]: A shielded enclosure that provides acoustic and electromagnetic attenuation protection.

Trusted Computing Base (TCB) [12 FAM 090]: The totality of protection mechanisms within an AIS (including hardware, firmware and software), the combination of which is responsible for enforcing a security policy. A trusted computing base consists of one or more components that together enforce a unified security policy over a product or AIS. The ability of a trusted computing base to correctly enforce a security policy depends solely on the mechanisms within the trusted computing base and on the correct input by system administrative personnel of parameters (e.g., a user's clearance) related to the security policy.

Trusted Computing Base (TCB) [IATF, 1999]: The totality of protection mechanisms within a computer system, the combination of which is responsible for enforcing a security policy.

Unauthorized Disclosure [NSTISSI 4009]: Exposure of information to individuals not authorized to receive it.

Understanding [Authors]: Real-world knowledge in context.

Unit Security Officer [12 FAM 090]: A U.S. citizen employee who is a nonprofessional security officer designated with a specific or homogeneous working unit to assist the office of security in carrying out functions prescribed in these regulations.

Upgrading [12 FAM 090]: The determination that particular unclassified or classified information requires a higher degree of protection against unauthorized disclosure than currently provided. Such determination shall be coupled with a marking of the material with the new designation.

User [IATF, 1999]: The party, or his designee, responsible for the security of designated information. The user works closely with an ISSE. Also referred to as the customer. [NCSC004, 1988]: Person or process accessing an AIS either by direct connections (i.e., via terminals), or indirect connections (i.e., prepare input data or receive output that is not reviewed for content or classification by a responsible individual).

User Information [Peltier, 1998]: The individual, or organization, who has been authorized access to the information asset by the owner.

User Representative [DoD8510, 2000]: The individual or organization that represents the user or user community in the definition of IS requirements.

User's Identification [12 FAM 090]: A character string which validates authorized user access.

Valid [JITC, 1999]: Logically correct (with respect to original data, software, or system).

Validation [AAAI, 1999]: A process of ensuring that a software product computes correct results; a "did we build a correct program" check. [NIAP, 1999]: The process carried out by the NIAP Oversight Body leading to the issue of a validation certificate.

Validation Phase [DoD8510, 2000]: The users, acquisition authority, and DAA agree on the correct implementation of the security requirements and approach for the completed IS.

Verification [NCSC004, 1988]: The process of comparing two levels of system specification for proper correspondence (e.g., security policy model with top-level specification, top-level specification with source code, or source code with object code). This process may or may not be automated.

Verification Phase [DoD8510, 2000]: The process of determining compliance of the evolving IS specification, design, or code with the security requirements and approach agreed on by the users, acquisition authority, and DAA.

Versatility [FM 100–6]: Versatility is the ability to adapt readily to unforeseen requirements. The subordinate elements of versatility are flexibility, interoperability, and autonomy.

Vulnerability [NCSC029, 1994]: A weakness in an information system or component (e.g., security procedures, hardware design, internal controls) that could be exploited.

Vulnerability Analysis [NCSC004, 1988]: The systematic examination of systems in order to determine the adequacy of security measures, identify security deficiencies, and provide data from which to predict the effectiveness of proposed security measures.

Vulnerability Assessment [DoD8510, 2000]: Systematic examination of an IS or product to determine the adequacy of security measures identify security deficiencies, provide data from which to predict the effectiveness of proposed security measures, and confirm the adequacy of such measures after implementation.

White Book [DoD5200, 1985]: See Red Book

Wisdom [Webster, 1984]: Understanding of what is true, right or lasting.

Appendix C

Links

This appendix is not intended as an all-inclusive list of IA-related links. It is, however, a sample of the types of information readily available on the World Wide Web and is a good entry point to further research for those who are interested. **All of these links were operational at the time of this publication. However, due to the volatile nature of the Internet, some may become outdated over time.**

Best Practices

Commercial

- *CMU SEI Engineering Best Practices:* http://www.sei.cmu.edu/engineering/engineering.html — Best practices for several areas of software, information systems, and systems engineering.
- *Microsoft's Best Security Practices:* http://www.microsoft.com/technet/security/bestprac.asp — Security Best Practices as compiled by Microsoft Corporation.
- *Software Program Manager's Network (SPMN):* http://www.spmn.com/16CSP.html — 16 Critical Software Practices™.
- *Zachman Institute for Framework Advancement:* http://www.zifa.com — The Zachman Institute for Framework Advancement (ZIFA) is a network of information professionals who understand the critical role of enterprise architecture in the ability of the enterprise to successfully participate in the global economy of the 21st century. To this end, the mission of ZIFA is to promote the exchange of knowledge and experience in the use, implementation, and advancement of the Zachman Framework for Enterprise Architecture.

Government

- *Defense Acquisition Deskbook:* http://web2.deskbook.osd.mil/default.asp — Defense Acquisition-related policy, procedure, and Best Practices.
- *Internet Security Policy: A Technical Guide:* http://csrc.nist.gov/ — A technical guide to developing an Internet security policy.
- *Introduction to the Internet and Internet Security:* http://csrc.nist.gov/publications/nistpubs/800–10/node11.html — NIST Special Publication (SP) 800–10.
- *National Institute for Standards and Technology (NIST) Publications Index:* http://csrc.nist.gov/publications/nistpubs/index.html — Index of NIST Special Publications with several references to generally accepted principles and practices for securing information technology systems.
- *Software Program Manager's Network:* http://www.spmn.com/ — Sponsored by the Deputy Under-Secretary of Defense for Science and Technology, Software Intensive Systems Directorate with a charter to seek out proven industry and government software Best Practices and convey them to managers of large-scale DoD software-intensive acquisition programs.
- *U.S. Government Best Practices:* http://www.bsp.gsa.gov/ — Best Practices compiled by the U.S. Government, General Services Administration (GSA).

C&A

DoD

- *DoD Information Technology Systems Certification and Accreditation Process (DITSCAP):* http://iase.disa.mil/ditscap/index.html — Information Assurance Support Environment (IASE) DITSCAP Web site.

NIACAP

- *National Information Assurance Certification and Accreditation Process (NIACAP):* http://nstissc.gov/html/library/html. The federal government's version of DoD's Defense Information Technology Certification and Accreditation Process (DITSCAP).

NIAP

- *NIAP Validated Products List:* http://www.niap.nist.gov/cc-scheme/validatedproducts.html — National Information Assurance Partnership's (NIAP) Common Criteria Validated Products List; see also NSA Certified Products List.

NSA

- *NSA Certified Products List:* http://www.radium.ncsc.mil/tpep/epl/index.html — National Security Agency's (NSA) Common Criteria Certified Products List; see also NIAP's CC Validated Products List.

CERT/CIRT

DoD

- *CERT Technical Tips:* http://www.cert.mil/techtips/index.htm — Incident handling.
- *DoD Computer Emergency Response Team (CERT):* http://www.cert.mil/ — Virus downloads, critical IA information and service CERTS.

DoE

- *DoE Computer Incident Advisory Capability (CIAC):* http://www.ciac.org/ciac/ — Hacks, viruses, and hoaxes.

Federal

- *Federal Computer Incident Response Center (FedCirc):* http://www.fedcirc.gov/ — U.S. federal government computer incident response.

International

- *Australian Computer Emergency Response Team (AUSCERT):* http://www.auscert.org.au/ — Australian Computer Emergency Response Team.

Decision Making

OODA

- *War, Chaos, and Business:* http://www.belisarius.com/ — Boyd's Observe, Orient, Decide, and Act (OODA) philosophy.

Definitions

DoD

- *DoD Dictionary of Military Terms:* http://www.dtic.mil/doctrine/jel/doddict — Joint Publications (JP) 1–02. A complete list of military terminology including information-, IS-, IA-, and interoperability-related terms.

NIST

- *National Information Systems Security (InfoSec) Glossary:* http://www.nstissc.gov/assets/pdf/4009.pdf — Large glossary of IT-related terminology.

Education/Training

Army

- *Information Assurance Security Officer (IASO) Certification Course:* http://www.gordon.army.mil/fa24/iaso.htm — School of Information Technology, Fort Gordon, Georgia.

DITSCAP

- *DITSCAP Training Table of Contents:* http://147.51.219.9/otd/c2protect/isso/contents.htm — Complete DITSCAP training program.

JMU

- *JMU Information Security Program:* http://www.infosec.jmu.edu/ — Masters Degree in Information Security.

Infrastructure

DoD

- *Department of Defense Global Information Grid Information Assurance:* http://www.c3i.osd.mil/org/cio/doc/gigia061600.pdf — Information assurance as it applies to the U.S. Department of Defense's Global Information Grid (GiG), the underlying infrastructure for DoD IT systems.
- *DoD Chief Information Officer Guidance and Policy Memorandums:* http://cno-n6.hq.navy.mil/gig/GIGInformationAssuranceG&PM.doc — CIO Policy and Guidance Memos pertaining to the GiG, PKI, DMS, and other IT issues.
- *Global Information Grid (GiG):* http://cno-n6.hq.navy.mil/files.htm — GiG Guidance and Policy.

Interoperability

DISA/JITC

- *Interoperability Policy Documents:* http://jitc.fhu.disa.mil/ciidocs.htm — Links to DISA/JITC Interoperability Policy documents.

DoD

- *C4I Interoperability: Testing, Assessment, and Certification:* http://jitc.fhu.disa.mil/testing/interop/interop.htm — Background on interoperability issues.
- *Interoperability Policy Directives Online:* http://jitc.fhu.disa.mil/ciidocs.htm — Electronic copies of many Interoperability Policy Directives.

Law

U.S. Code

- *Title 10, Armed Forces:* http://www.access.gpo.gov/uscode/title10/title10.html — Title 10 of the U.S. Code. Legislation related to the Armed Forces of the United States.
- *Title 18, Crimes and Criminal Procedures:* http://www.access.gpo.gov/uscode/title18/title18.html — Title 18 of the U.S. Code. Legislation related to the handling of crimes and criminal proceedings with specific reference to IT-related crime.

Links

DISA

- *DISA Offices and Programs:* http://www.disa.mil/ — Links to DISA offices, programs, and related sites.

DISA/JITC

- *JITC Testing Projects:* http://jitc.fhu.disa.mil/projects.htm — Links to DISA/JITC projects.

DoD

- *IT Links:* http://www.itsi.disa.mil/links.html — Interoperability-, IT-, and IA-related links.
- *Joint Information for Systems Technology, Test, and Training (JIST3):* http://jcs.mil/jist3/ — Links to testing, training, organizations, and resources.

Organizations

DISA

- *DISA Organization Structure Page:* http://www.disa.mil/main/disaorga.html — Organizational structure of DISA including departments, directors, and field organizations.
- *IA Library:* https://iase.disa.mil/documentlib.html — Must be accessed from a .gov or .mil address or with special permission.
- *IA Support Environment:* https://iase.disa.mil/index2.html — Tremendous IA resource; must be accessed from a .gov or .mil address or with special permission.
- *IA Vulnerability Alert (IAVA):* https://iase.disa.mil/IAalerts/index.html — Vulnerability Compliance Tracking Systems (VCTS); must be accessed from a .gov or .mil address or with special permission.
- *IA Workshop:* https://iase.disa.mil/dio/index.html — Must be accessed from a .gov or .mil address or with special permission.
- *Information Assurance:* http://www.disa.mil/infosec/iaweb/default.html — DISA, D25, IA Program Management Office (PMO) programs and links.
- *Network Connection Approval Process (CAP):* https://iase.disa.mil/CAP/index.html — DISN, NIPRNet, and SIPRNet; must be accessed from a .gov or .mil address or with special permission.
- *Public Key Infrastructure (PKI):* https://iase.disa.mil/PKI/index.html — Must be accessed from a .gov or .mil address or with special permission.

DISA/JITC

- *DISA/JITC Software Testing:* http://jitc.fhu.disa.mil/brochure/software.pdf — Software interoperability and conformance testing. Overview and contact information.
- *DoD PKI Test Facility:* http://jitc.fhu.disa.mil/brochure/pki.pdf — Premier DoD PKI Test Facility. Overview and contact information.
- *JITC IA T&E Team:* http://jitc.fhu.disa.mil/brochure/ia.pdf — Information Assurance Test and Evaluation Team. Overview, contact information, and links.
- *JITC Organization Page:* http://jitc.fhu.disa.mil/org.htm — Organization, departments, programs, and mission of the Joint Interoperability Test Command (JITC).
- *JITC Product Registers:* http://jitc.fhu.disa.mil/register.htm — Certification, interoperability, and conformance commercial product register.
- *Joint Interoperability Test Command:* http://jitc.fhu.disa.mil/ — Information Operations Test and Evaluation.
- *Joint Interoperability Testing Starter Guide:* http://jitc.fhu.disa.mil/jist/cover.htm — Introduction to JITC policy, directives, resources, capabilities, and mission. Links to JITC's Guide to Interoperability Testing.

DoD

- *Acquisition Web:* http://www.acq.osd.mil — USD(AT&L) Acquisition Web site. DoD acquisition information, regulations, news, and links.
- *ASD(C3I) IA Directorate:* http://www.c3i.osd.mil/faq/index.html — U.S. Department of Defense, Assistant Secretary of Defense for Command, Control, Communications, and Intelligence (ASD(C3I)), Information Assurance Directorate.
- *Defense Acquisition University (DAU):* http://www.dau.mil — Defense Acquisition Deskbook, DoD 5000 Series, and other acquisition related materials. DSMC Systems Engineering fundamentals.
- *Defense Technical Information Center (DTIC):* http://www.dtic.mil/ — Access to and facilitation of the exchange of scientific and technical information.
- *Defense Technical Information Center (DTIC) home page:* http://www.dtic.mil/ — Central access to defense-related technical information including most of the information-, IA-, interoperability-, and architecture-related documents within DoD.
- *DoD CIO home page:* http://www.c3i.osd.mil/org/cio/gpmlinks.html — Global Information Grid and IA Implementation Guidance.
- *DoD CIP:* http://www.fas.org/irp/offdocs/pdd/DOD-CIP-Plan.htm — Department of Defense (DoD) Critical Infrastructure Protection (CIP) Plan.
- *DoD IA Policy:* http://iase.disa.mil/policy.html — DISA's Information Assurance Support Environment (IASE) Policy and Guidance.
- *General Accounting Office (GAO):* www.gao.gov — GAO reports, products, and publications.
- *USAF Communications Agency:* https://public.afca.scott.af.mil/ — Supports air and space operations by bringing to the fight expertise in the communications and information arena; must be accessed from a .gov or .mil address or with special permission.

DTIC

- *Data Analysis Center for Software (DACS):* http://www.dacs.dtic.mil/databases/url/key.hts?keycode = 120:134&islowerlevel = 1 — Technical reports, papers, and abstracts. Information assurance and information warfare reports.

Federal

- *Critical Infrastructure Assurance Office (CIAO):* http://www.ciao.gov/ — The Critical Infrastructure Assurance Office (CIAO) was created in response to a Presidential Decision Directive (PDD-63) in May 1998 to coordinate the federal government's initiatives on critical infrastructure assurance.

- *Federal Bureau of Investigation (FBI):* http://www.fbi.gov/ — Home of the National Infrastructure Protection Center (NIPC).
- *InfraGard:* http://www.infragard.net/ — InfraGard is an information-sharing and analysis effort serving the interests and combining the knowledge base of a wide range of members. At its most basic level, InfraGard is a cooperative undertaking between the U.S. government (led by the FBI and the NIPC) and an association of businesses, academic institutions, state and local law enforcement agencies, and other participants dedicated to increasing the security of U.S. critical infrastructures.
- *National Information Protection Center (NIPC):* http://www.nipc.gov/ — The National Infrastructure Protection Center (NIPC) serves as a national critical infrastructure threat assessment, warning, vulnerability, and law enforcement investigation and response entity.

IDA

- *IDA, Director of Operational Test and Evaluation (DOTE):* http://www.ida.org/DIVISIONS/oed/iametricsandpolicy/ — Institute for Defense Analysis (IDA), Directorate of Operational Test and Evaluation. IA policy and metrics.

International

- *International Telecommunication Union (ITU):* http://www.itu.int — International IA, IT, InfoSec, interoperability, and architecture issues.

IWS

- *The Information Warfare Site (IWS):* http://www.iwar.org.uk/ — Information and links to a wide variety of information, information system, information assurance, critical infrastructure protection, interoperability, information warfare, information architecture, and related issues.

Military

- *Andrews Air Force Base Information Assurance home page:* http://www.andrews.af.mil/89cg/89cs/scbsi/info.html
- *National Defense University (NDU)* — http://nduknowledge.net/Information/infoassr_faqs.htm
- *U.S. Department of Defense C3I home page:* http://www.c3i.osd.mil/faq/ — 18: U.S. DoD C3I Frequently Asked Questions.
- *U.S. Secretary of the Navy:* http://fas.org/irp/doddir/navy/secnavinst/ — Links to Secretary of the Navy Instructions, Doctrine, and related documents.

Professional

- *American National Standards Institute (ANSI):* http://www.ansi.org/ — IT standards, databases, services, and committees.
- *Extranet for Security Professionals (ESP):* http://www.xsp.org/ — A collaboration of U.S. government agencies for better security.
- *Federation of American Scientists (FAS) home page:* http://www/fas.org/— Links to a wide variety of military, intelligence, and security-related sites.
- *IA Technical Framework (IATF):* http://www.iatf.net/framework_docs/version-3_0/index.cfm — Information Assurance Technical Framework documents.
- *Information Assurance Technical Framework Forum (IATFF):* http://www.iatf.net/ — IA documents and fora.
- *InfoWar.com:* http://www.infowar.com/ — General information security information, history, and interest groups.
- *Institute of Electrical and Electronics Engineers (IEEE):* http://www.ieee.org/ — Standards, committees, publications, and conferences.
- *International Council on Systems Engineering (INCOSE):* www.incose.org — Systems engineering references and materials.
- *Systems Administrator and Network Security (SANS):* http://www.sans.org/ — IA training and solutions.

Publications

CMU SEI

- *CMU SEI Publications:* http://www.sei.cmu.edu/publications/publications.html — Index of industry standard publications on a variety of software, information systems, and systems engineering concepts.

Commercial

- *FAS News References:* http://www.fas.org/news/reference/ — Federation of American Scientists (FAS) news and reference links.

DoD

- *AIS Security:* http://www.dtic.mil/whs/directives/corres/html/520028.htm — Security Requirements for Automated Information Systems, DoD Directive 5200.28.
- *DoD Acquisition Deskbook:* http://web2.deskbook.osd.mil/default.asp — Regulations, directives, and other guidance related to DoD IT acquisition.
- *DoD Publications:* http://www.dtic.mil/whs/directives — U.S. Department of Defense Directives and Regulations.

- *Information Operations Implementation:* http://www.cert.mil/policy/ 6510_01b.pdf — DoD, Joint Chiefs of Staff, Defensive Information Operations Implementation Directive. JCS Instruction 6510.01 B/CH1.
- *Joint Doctrine Encyclopedia:* http://www.dtic.mil/doctrine/jrm/ ency.htm — Part of DoD JCS Joint Doctrine home page. A plethora of information on information and information systems-related issues.
- *Joint Doctrine home page:* http://www.dtic.mil/doctrine/index.html — Information Age Doctrine — Information Operations, Assurance, and Warfare.
- *Joint Electronic Library:* http://www.dtic.mil/doctrine/doctrine.htm — Universal Joint Task List (UJTL), Joint Tactics, Techniques, and Procedures and other Joint publications and reference materials.
- *Joint Vision 2020:* http://www.dtic.mil/jv2020/index.html — Future warfare and the implications of IT.

Executive

- *Federal IT Management:* http://www.whitehouse.g.,ov/omb/circulars/ a130/a130.html — Management of federal information resources.
- *PDD-63: Critical Infrastructure Protection (CIP):* http://www.fas.org/ irp/offdocs/pdd/index.html — Presidential Decision Directive 63. Requires all federal agencies to take appropriate measures to protect America's critical infrastructure.
- *Presidential Decision Directives (PDD):* http://www.fas.org/irp/offdocs/ direct.htm — Electronic copies of PDDs and other Executive Department documents.

Federal

- *Federal Acquisition Regulations (FAR):* http://www.arnet.gov/far/ — Regulations governing acquisition within the U.S. federal government.
- *Federal Information Technology Security Assessment Framework:* http:// cio.gov/files/federal_it_security_assessment_framework.pdf — A framework for assessing IT security with the U.S. federal government.

Government

- *Federal Information Processing Standards (FIPS) Publications:* http:// www.itl.nist.gov/fipspubs/ — Links to FIPS publications and related materials.
- *NIST Special Publications:* http://csrc.nist.gov/publications/nistpubs/ — Links to National Institute of Standards and Technology (NIST) Special Publications.

Military

■ *DoD Dictionary of Military Terms:* http://www.dtic.mil/doctrine/jel/doddict/ — Military terms, acronyms, and abbreviations.

■ *Military Lexicon:* http://www.fas.org/news/reference/lexicon/ — Military terms, acronyms, and abbreviations.

NCSC

■ *Rainbow Series Library:* http://www.radium.ncsc.mil/tpep/library/rainbow — The "Rainbow Series" and other IT security-related publications.

NIST

■ *Computer Security Resource Center (CSRS):* http://csrc.nist.gov/publications/nistpubs/index.html — Index of NIST Special Publications (SP) related to IT and security.

■ *National Information Assurance Acquisition Policy:* http://www.nstissc.gov/assets/pdf/nstissp11.pdf — National Security Telecommunications and Information Systems Security Policy (NSTISSP) No. 11. National Policy Governing the Acquisition of Information Assurance (IA) and IA-Enabled Information Technology (IT) Products issued by the National Security Telecommunications and Information Systems Security Committee (NSTISSC).

■ *NIST Special Publication (SP) 800–23:* http://csrc.nist.gov/publications/nistpubs/800–23/sp800–23.pdf — Guidelines to Federal Organizations on Security Assurance and Acquisition/Use of Tested/Evaluated Products.

Policy

■ *JITC Testing Policy:* http://jitc.fhu.disa.mil/policy.htm — Secure interoperability testing policy within DoD. Regulated by the Joint Interoperability Test Command (JITC), a component of the DoD Information Systems Agency (DISA).

SEI CMU

■ *CMU SEI Capability Maturity Models (CMM):* http://www.sei.cmu.edu/managing/managing.html — Capability maturity models for use in software development, systems engineering, and other areas.

■ *CMU SEI Information Repository:* http://www.sei.cmu.edu/products/repositories/repository.html — Publications covering a wide variety of software, information system, and systems engineering concepts.

Red Teams

DoD

- *Army Land Information Warfare Activity (LIWA):* https://www.acert. belvoir.army.mil/ACERTmain.htm. — Must be accessed from a .gov or .mil address or with special permission.
- *Navy Computer Incident Response Team (NavCIRT):* https://infosec. navy.mil/ — InfoSec products, services, tools and publications; must be accessed from a .gov or .mil address or with special permission.
- *Red Team Methodology:* http://www.mitre.org/pubs/showcase/diart/ diart2.shtml — Mitre's DoD Red Team methodology.
- *USAF Information Warfare Center (AFIWC):* http://afiwcweb.kelly.af.mil/ — Penetration testing.

Research

Academia

- *Center for Education and Research in IA and Security (CERIAS):* http:// www.cerias.purdue.edu/hotlist/ — Purdue University IA and InfoSec research center.
- *CMU Center for Computer and Communications Security (C3S):* http:// www.ece.cmu.edu/research/c3s/index.shtml — Security-related projects and research.
- *CMU Laboratory for Computer Systems (LCS):* http://www.lcs.ece.cmu. edu/ — Research, education, publications, and seminars.
- *CMU Software Engineering Institute (SEI):* http://www.sei.cmu.edu/ — The SEI exists to help others improve their software engineering capabilities by advancing the state of the practice of software engineering.
- *GMU Center for Command, Control, Communications and Intelligence (C3I):* http://bacon.gmu.edu/c3i/ — C3I research.
- *GMU Center for Secure Information Systems (CSIS):* http://www.ise.g., mu.edu/~csis/ — IS security research.
- *GMU Laboratory for Information Security Technology:* http://www.list. gmu.edu/ — InfoSec laboratory.
- *GMU Systems Architecture Laboratory:* http://viking.gmu.edu/http/ main.htm — Systems architecture research. Part of GMU C3I Center.
- *GWU Cyberspace Policy Institute (CPI):* http://www.cpi.seas.gwu.edu/ — Policy for information and information systems.
- *GWU Institute for Crisis, Disaster and Risk Management:* http://www.emse. g.,wu.edu/emse/research/inst/icdrm.html — Risk management.
- *GWU Institute for Reliability and Risk Analysis:* http://www.emse.g.,wu. edu/emse/research/inst/irra.html — Risk analysis.

- *GWU Laboratory for High Assurance Computing and Communications (HACC):* http://www.student.seas.gwu.edu/~hacc/ — Information assurance research.
- *MIT Center for Information Systems Research (CISR):* http://web.mit.edu/cisr/www/ — Research on issues related to the management and use of IT in complex organizations.
- *MIT Laboratory for Information and Decision Systems (LIDS):* http://lids.mit.edu/ — The fundamental research goal is to advance the field of systems, communications, and control.
- *Purdue University CERIAS:* http://www.cerias.purdue.edu/hotlist/detail.php?arg1 = 300&arg2 = Education±/±Cryptography — Center for Research in Information Assurance and Security (CERIAS). Links to a wide variety of IA projects, programs, and organizations.
- *Software Engineering Institute (SEI):* http://www.iwar.org.uk/cip/resources/cross.pdf — Cyber security.
- *Software Engineering Institute (SEI):* http://www.sei.cmu.edu/managing/managing.html — CMU SEI Management Practices.
- *Software Engineering Institute (SEI):* http://www.sei.cmu.edu/cmm/cmms/cmms.html — Capability Maturity Models.
- *Software Engineering Institute (SEI):* http://www.sei.cmu.edu/iso-15504/ — Software Process Assessment (ISO 15504).
- *University of Illinois Bechman Institute Human Perception and Performance Group (HPP):* http://www.beckman.uiuc.edu/research/hpp.html — Research into mechanisms of human perception and the relations between perception and action.
- *University of Illinois Bechman Institute Integrated Systems Laboratory (ISL):* http://www.beckman.uiuc.edu/research/isl.html — A facility where researchers perform integration of advanced technology and conduct experiments in human multimodal perception and cognition.
- *University of Illinois Beckman Institute Cognitive Science Group (CSG):* http://www.beckman.uiuc.edu/research/cogsci.html — Cognitive Science Studies. Research on learning and languages.

DoD

- *Defense Science Board home page:* http://www.acq.osd.mil/dsb — Defense Science Board Studies and Report.

Stanford

- *Stanford Center for Information Technology (CIT):* http://logic.stanford.edu/cit/cit.html — The central focus of the Center's activity is the development of advanced information technology, computer technology appropriate to the encoding, storage, communication, manipulation, and use of information in digital form.

Standards

Common Criteria

- *Common Criteria for Information Technology Security Evaluation:* http://www.commoncriteria.org — Relatively new criteria for measuring information system security. Replaces a number of national and international standards including the Trusted Computer Security Evaluation Criteria (TCSEC) in the United States.
- *Common Criteria v2.0:* http://csrc.nist.gov/cc/ccv20/ccv2list.htm — ISO Publication 15408. Used to assess security products. The National Security Telecommunications Information System Security Program #11 (NSTISSP#11) mandated in July 2002 that the U.S. Department of Defense (DoD) may only acquire security products that have been Common Criteria-tested by a National Institute of Standards and Technology-accredited laboratory using the Common Evaluation Methodology. This impacts the products a Program/Project Manager might acquire for or use within his system.

Cryptography

- *Cryptographic Module Validation:* http://csrc.nist.gov/cryptval/ — Federal Information Processing Standard (FIPS) 140–1 and 140–2.

DISA/JITC

- *Interoperability Directorate:* http://www.itsi.disa.mil/aboutcfs.html — DISA Directorate for Interoperability. Requirements, standards, organization, and links.

DoD

- *Architecture Working Group (AWG) Digital Library:* http://www.csi.osd.mil/org/cio/i3/awg_digital_library — C4ISR Architecture Framework Version 2.0
- *Common Operating Environment (COE):* http://diicoe.disa.mil/coe/coeeng/ — DISA, D6 Common Operating Environment (COE) links.
- *Defense Standardization Program (DSP):* http://www.dsp.dla.mil — Interoperability, sustainment, CMI, data, publications, and links.
- *DISA IA Support Environment (DISA IASE):* https://iase.disa.mil/documentlib.html — Available from .gov and .mil addresses only without prior approval.
- *Interoperability Directorate:* http://www.itsi.disa.mil/ — DoD interoperability specifics.

Glossary

- *NIAP Glossary:* www.niap.nist.gov/glossary.html — National Information Assurance Partnership (NIAP) Glossary of Terms.
- *NSA Glossary:* www.sans.org/newlook/resources/glossary.htm — National Security Agency (NSA) Glossary of Terms.
- *United Kingdom's Military Computer-Electronics Security Group:* http://www.cesg.gov.uk/about/index.htm — CESG is the Information Security arm of GCHQ and is based in Cheltenham, Gloucestershire, United Kingdom. It is the U.K. government's national technical authority for InfoSec/IA issues. CESG was formally established in 1969, although elements of the organization have been in operation since World War I.

International

- *International Organization for Standardization (ISO):* http://www.iso.ch/iso/en/ISOOnline.frontpage — Information, information system, computer and other standards including the Common Criteria.

Languages

- *Sun Microsystems Java home page:* http://java.sun.com — Links to Java-related web pages.

Methodology

- *Common Evaluation Methodology (CEM):* http://cs-www.ncsl.nist.gov/cc/cem/cemlist.htm — Methodology associated with the Common Criteria.

Microsoft

- *Microsoft & The Common Criteria:* http://www.microsoft.com/TechNet/security/secureev.asp — Microsoft's position on security and the Common Criteria.

NIAP

- *National Information Assurance Partnership (NIAP):* http://niap.nist.gov/ — NIAP is a joint venture between NIST and NSA to sponsor and support the Common Criteria in the U.S.

NIST

- *National Institute of Standards and Technology (NIST):* http://www.nist. gov/ — NIST home page with links to a large variety of standards pertaining to information, information systems and interoperability.

Tools

DoD

- *DoD Information Assurance Technology Analysis Center (IATAC):* http:// iac.dtic.mil/iatac — IA Tools.

Interoperability

- *JITC Interoperability Tool:* http://jit.fhu.disa.mil — Automated tools to support Joint Interoperability testing.

Viruses

U.S. Army

- *Hoaxes:* https://www.acert.belvoir.army.mil/virusinfo/hoaxes.htm — Updates on virus hoaxes. Must be accessed from a .gov or .mil address or with special permission.
- *Trojan Horse Listing:* https://www.acert.belvoir.army.mil/virusinfo/trojan.htm — Trojan Horse updates. Must be accessed from a .gov or .mil address or with special permission.
- *Virus Listing:* https://www.acert.belvoir.army.mil/virusinfo/newvirus.htm/ — New virus updates. Must be accessed from a .gov or .mil address or with special permission.

Vulnerabilities

Commercial

- *BUGTRAQ:* http://msgs.securepoint.com/bugtraq/ — Best for latest IA information, vulnerabilities and tools.
- *Internet Security Systems (ISS) X-Force:* http://xforce.iss.net/index.php — Threats and vulnerabilities.

Mitre

- *Mitre Common Vulnerabilities and Exposures:* http://cve.mitre.org/ — All the known vulnerabilities.

Appendix D

References

[12 FAM 090]: U.S. Department of State. Definitions of Diplomatic Terms. Foreign Affairs Manual (12 FAM 090). Washington, D.C.: Government Printing Office, 1997.

[22 USC 4804]: Omnibus Diplomatic Security and Anti-Terrorism Act of 1986. 22 U.S. Code 4804. Washington, D.C.: U.S. Congress, 1986.

[40 USC 3502]: Paperwork Reduction Act of 1995. 40 U.S. Code 3502. Washington, D.C.: U.S. Congress, 1995.

[AAAI, 1999]: American Association of Artificial Intelligence (AAAI). AI Glossary. http://www.aaai.org/, 2 December 1999.

[Abriel, 1974]: Abriel, J.R. *Data Semantics*. Amsterdam, Netherlands: North-Holland, 1974.

[ACM, 1986]: Association for Computing Machinery. Proceedings: Conference on Object-Oriented Programming, Systems, Languages, and Applications. New York: ACM Press, 1986.

[ADW, 2002]: Information Assurance. Andrews Air Force Base. http://www.andrews.af.mil/89cg/89cs/scbsi/info.html, 30 May 2002.

[AISSIM, 1996]: U.S. Department of Defense (DoD). Automated Information Systems Security Implementation Manual (AISSIM). Washington, D.C.: National Reconnaissance Office (NRO), 1996.

[AJC, 1989]: *The Atlanta Journal and Constitution*. West German Attack Tied to Pro-Terrorists. 13 April 1989.

[Alagic, 1988]: Alagic, Suad. *Object-Oriented Database Programming*. New York: Springer-Verlag, 1988.

[Alashqur, 1989]: Alashqur, A.M., S.Y.W. Su, and H. Lam. OQL: A Query Language for Manipulating Object-Oriented Databases. Proceedings of the Fifteenth International Conference on Very Large Databases. Amsterdam, Netherlands: 1989.

[Alberts, 2000]: Alberts, David S. Information Superiority and Network Centric Warfare. Plenary Address. Proceedings of the 2000 Command and Control Research and Technology Symposium (CCRTS). Monterey, CA: U.S. Naval War College, 26–28 June 2000.

[Alter, 1999]: Alter, Steven. *Information Systems: A Management Perspective*. Reading, MA: Addison-Wesley, 1999.

[Andrews, 1990]: Andrews, Timothy and Craig Harris. Combining Language and Database Advances in an Object-Oriented Development Environment. *Readings in Object-Oriented Database Systems,* pp. 186–196. Stanley B. Zdonik and David Maier, Eds. San Mateo, CA: Morgan Kaufman, 1990.

[Andriole, 1986]: Andriole, Stephen J., Ed. *Microcomputer Decision Support Systems: Design, Implementation and Evaluation.* Wellesley, MA: QED Information Sciences, 1986.

[Andriole, 1988]: Andriole, Stephen J. *Handbook for the Design, Development, Application and Evaluation of Interactive Decision Support Systems.* Princeton, NJ: Petrocelli Books, 1988.

[Arkin, 1992]: Arkin, Stanley S. et al. *Prevention and Prosecution of Computer and High Technology Crime.* New York: Matthew Bender & Co., 1992.

[ASD(C3I), 1997]: Improving Information Assurance: A General Assessment. Comprehensive Approach to an Integrated IA Program for the Assistant Secretary of Defense for Command, Control, Communications and Intelligence (ASD(C3I)). Washington, D.C.: 28 March 1997.

[Athey, 1982]: Athey, Thomas H. *Systematic Systems Approach.* Englewood Cliffs, NJ: Prentice-Hall, 1982.

[AWST, 1991]: *Aviation Week & Space Technology.* Washington Roundup. 25 November 1991.

[BAH, 1998]: Booz, Allen and Hamilton (BAH), Inc. Analytical Risk Management. Report to the Central Intelligence Agency (CIA). McLean, VA: Booz, Allen and Hamilton, 1998.

[Bailin, 1989]: Bailin, Sidney C. An Object-Oriented Requirements Specification Method. *Communications of the ACM,* 32:5 (May), 608–623, 1989.

[Banerjee, 1987]: Banerjee, Jay et al. Data Model Issues for Object-Oriented Applications. *ACM Transactions on Office Information Systems,* 5:1 (Jan), 3–26, 1987.

[Bartimo, 1982]: Bartimo, Jim. Terrorism Vexing International DP Crime Experts. *Computer World,* 12 July 1982.

[Baskerville, 1988]: Baskerville, Richard. *Designing Information Systems Security.* New York: John Wiley & Sons, 1988.

[Bateman, 1998]: Bateman, Robert L. III. Avoiding Information Overload, Military Review, Headquarters, Department of the Army. Prepared by U.S. Army Command and General Staff College, Volume LXXVIII, July-August 1998, No. 4.

[Bates, 1992]: Bates, Tom. *Rads: The 1970 Bombing of the Army Math Research Center at the University of Wisconsin and its Aftermath.* New York: Harper Collins Publishers, 1992.

[Beadsmoore, 1986]: Beadsmoore, Michael. Terrorism in the Information Age: A Recipe for Disaster? *Computer World,* 7 July 1986.

[Bennett, 1990]: Bennett, Scott. Viewpoints: The Growth of Terrorism. *Dallas Morning News.* 11 January 1990.

[Bequai, 1983]: Bequai, August. *How To Prevent Computer Crimes: A Guide for Managers.* New York: John Wiley & Sons, 1983.

[Bequai, 1987]: Bequai, August. *Techno-Crimes: The Computerization of Crime and Terrorism.* Lexington, MA: Lexington Books, 1987.

[Blanchard, 1981]: Blanchard, B.C. and W.J. Fabrycky. *Systems Engineering and Analysis.* Englewood Cliffs, NJ: Prentice-Hall, 1981.

[Bloombecker, 1985]: Bloombecker, Jay, Ed. *Introduction to Computer Crime.* Los Angeles, CA: National Center for Computer Crime Data, 1985.

[Booch, 1987]: Booch, Grady. *Object-Oriented Development. Tutorial: Object-Oriented Computing, Volume II: Implementations,* pp. 5–15. Gerald E. Peterson, Ed. Washington, D.C.: Computer Society Press, 1987.

[Boorman, 1987]: Boorman, Scott A. and Paul R. Levitt. Deadly Bugs. *Chicago Tribune,* 3 May 1987.

[Boyd, 1986]: Boyd, J. Patterns of Conflict, December 1986. Unpublished study, 196 pp.

[Brooks, 1974]: Brooks, Fredrick. *The Mythical Man Month.* Reading, MA: Addison-Wesley, 1974.

[Brushweiler, 1985]: Brushweiler, Wallace S., Sr. *Computers as Targets of Transnational Terrorism. Computer Security.* North Holland, Netherlands: Elsevier Science Publishers, 1985.

[Burger, 1988]: Burger, Ralf. *Computer Viruses: A High-Tech Disease.* Grand Rapids, MI: Abacus, 1988.

[Busby, 1990]: Busby, Morris D. Address to the International Seminar on Maritime and Port Security, Miami, Florida. Current Policy No. 1243. Washington, D.C.: U.S. Department of State, Bureau of Public Affairs, 3 January 1990.

[C3I, 2002]: Command, Control, Communications, and Intelligence. U.S. Department of Defense. http://www.c3i.osd.mil/faq/#18, 30 May 2002.

[Campbell, 1997]: Campbell, Douglas E., Barry Stauffer, and Frank Pittelli. Refining the Management of IW-D Plans, Goals, Milestones, and Metric Based on Three Successful Navy Programs. Washington, D.C.: Space and Naval Warfare Systems Command (SPAWAR), 20 January 1997.

[Canter, 2000]: Canter, John. *An Agility-Based OODA Model for the e-Commerce/e-Business Enterprise.* Online: http://www.belisarius.com/modern_business_strategy/canter/canter.htm, 2000.

[CESG, 2002]: Computer-Electronics Security Group (CESG). United Kingdom. http://www.cesg.gov.uk/about/index.htm, 30 May 2002.

[Cetron, 1989]: Cetron, Marvin, President of Forecasting International, Ltd., as quoted in Terrorism: Home-Grown Threat to U.S.? *USA Today Magazine.* December 1989.

[Chambers, 1986]: Chambers, G.J. The System Engineering Process: A Technical Bibliography. *IEEE Transactions on Systems, Man, and Cybernetics,* 16:5, September-October, 1986.

[Chandler, 1977]: Chandler, John S. and Thomas G. Delutis. *Multi-Stage, Multi-Criteria Approach to Systems Evaluation.* Columbus, OH: Ohio State University Press, 1977.

[Chase, 1974]: Chase, W.P. *Management of Systems Engineering.* New York: John Wiley & Sons, 1974.

[Chen, 1976]: Chen, Peter P. *The Entity Relationship Model: Toward a Unified View of Data.Transactions on Database Systems.* New York: ACM Press, 1976.

[Chen, 1981]: Chen, Peter P., Ed. *Entity-Relationship Approach to Information Modeling and Analysis.* Amsterdam, Netherlands: Elsevier Science Publishers, 1981.

[Christakis, 1985]: Christakis, Alexander N. High Technology Participative Design: The Space-Based Laser. Proceedings of the International Conference of the Society for General Systems Research, Vol. II. Seaside, CA: Intersystems Publications, 1985.

[CIMPIM, 1993]: Corporate Information Management Process Improvement Methodology for DoD Functional Managers, Second Ed.. Arlington, VA: Appleton Company, 1993.

[Clark, 1980]: Clark, Richard C. *Technological Terrorism.* Old Greenwich, CT: Devin-Adair Company, 1980.

[Coad, 1990]: Coad, Peter and Edward Yourdon. *Object-Oriented Analysis.* Englewood Cliffs, NJ: Yourdon Press, 1990.

[Codd, 1970]: Codd, E.F. A Relational Model of Data for Large Shared Data Banks. *Communications of the ACM,* 13:6 (Jun), 377–387, 1970.

[Codd, 1979]: Codd, E.F. Extending the Database Relational Model to Capture More Meaning. *Transactions on Database Systems,* 4:4 (Dec), 397–434, 1979.

[Cohen, 1989]: Cohen, Benjamin. Merging Expert Systems and Databases. *AI Expert,* 4:2 (Feb), 22–31, 1989.

[Coleman, 1994]: Coleman, Derek et. al. *Object-Oriented Development: The Fusion Method.* Englewood Cliffs, NJ: Prentice Hall, 1994.

[Conner, 1987]: Conner, Michael. *Terrorism: Its Goals, Its Targets, Its Methods, The Solution.* Boulder, CO: Paladin Press, 1987.

[Cooper, 1989]: Cooper, James A. *Computer and Communications Security: Strategies for the 1990s.* New York: McGraw-Hill, 1989.

[Cowan, 2000]: Cowan, Jeffrey L. *From Air Force Fighter Pilot to Marine Corps Warfighting: Colonel John Boyd, His Theories on War, and their Unexpected Legacy.* Online: http://www.defense-and-society.org/second_level/boyd_military.html, 2000.

[Cox, 1986]: Cox, Brad J. *Object Oriented Programming.* Reading, MA: Addison-Wesley, 1986.

[Cox, 1987]: Cox, Brad J. *Message/Object Programming: An Evolutionary Change in Programming Technology. Tutorial: Object-Oriented Computing, Vol. I: Concepts,* pp. 150–161. Gerald E. Peterson, Ed. Washington, D.C.: Computer Society Press, 1987.

[CSIS, 1985]: Center for Strategic and International Studies (CSIS). *America's Hidden Vulnerabilities.* Washington, D.C.: Georgetown University, October 1985.

[Culnan, 1989]: Culnan, Mary. Electronic Terrorism: How Can We Fight It? *The Atlanta Journal and Constitution,* 13 April 1989.

[Curts, 1989a]: Curts, Raymond J. A Systems Engineering Approach to Battle Force Architecture. SCI TR 89–01. Fairfax, VA: Strategic Consulting, Inc., 1989.

[Curts, 1989b]: Curts, Raymond J. An Expert System for the Assessment of Naval Force Architecture. SCI TR 89–03. Fairfax, VA: Strategic Consulting, Inc., 1989.

[Curts, 1990a]: Curts, Raymond J. An Object-Oriented Approach to Naval Force Architecture Databases. SCI TR 90–01. Fairfax, VA: Strategic Consulting, Inc., 1990.

[Curts, 1990b]: Curts, Raymond J. Modeling Abduction. SCI TR 90–03. Fairfax, VA: Strategic Consulting, Inc., 1990.

[Curts, 1990c]: Curts, Raymond J. Automating the Architecture Process. Briefing/Lecture. Washington, D.C.: Space and Naval Warfare Systems Command, 1990.

[Curts, 1995]: Curts, Raymond J. Inference Methodologies in a Decision Support System: A Case Study. *Information and Systems Engineering,* 1:1 (Mar), pp. 39–54. Amsterdam, The Netherlands: Springer-Verlag, 1995.

[Curts, 1999]: Curts, Raymond J. and Campbell, Douglas E. Architecture: The Road to Interoperability. Proceedings: 1999 Command and Control Research and Technology Symposium (CCRTS), Newport, RI: U.S. Naval War College, 29 June–1 July 1999.

[Curts, 2000]: Curts, Raymond J. and Douglas E. Campbell. Naval Information Assurance Center (NIAC): An Approach Based on the Naval Aviation Safety Program Model. Proceedings: 2000 Command and Control Research and Technology Symposium (CCRTS). Monterey, CA: U.S. Naval Postgraduate School, 24–28 June 2000.

[Curts, 2001a]: Curts, Raymond J. and Douglas E. Campbell. Avoiding Information Overload Through the Understanding of OODA Loops, A Cognitive Hierarchy and Object-Oriented Analysis and Design. Proceedings of the Sixth International Command and Control Research and Technology Symposium (CCRTS). Annapolis, MD: U.S. Naval Academy, 2001.

[Curts, 2001b]: Curts, Raymond J. and Douglas E. Campbell. The Impact of Architecture and Interoperability on Information Warfare Systems. *Journal of Information Warfare,* 1:1, 33–41. Perth, Western Australia: JIW, 2001.

[CW, 1980]: Bomb Attacks on French Centres. *Computer Weekly,* 11 December 1980.

[CW, 1982]: Computer Crime Skeletons. *Computerworld.* November 29, 1982.

[DAD, 2002]: U.S. Department of Defense (DoD). Defense Acquisition Deskbook. http://web2.deskbook.osd.mil/default.asp, 19 June 2002.

[DARPA, 1977]: *Handbook for Decision Analysis.* Washington, D.C.: Defense Advanced Research Projects Agency (DARPA), 1977.

[David, 1988]: David, Thomas. Pentagon's Loss of Computer Control Opens Access to Data for Soviets. *New York City Tribune,* 22 January 1988.

[DCI, 1988]: Digital Consulting, Inc. (DCI). Computer Aided Software Engineering Symposium for Aerospace Defense and Engineering Proceedings. Andover, MA: Digital Consulting, Inc., 1988.

[DCID 1/16, 1988]: U.S. Director of Central Intelligence (DCI). Security Policy on Intelligence Information in Automated Systems and Networks. DCI Directive 1/16. Langley, VA: Central Intelligence Agency (CIA), 14 March 1988.

[DeMarco, 1979]: DeMarco, Thomas G. *Structured Analysis and System Specification.* Englewood Cliffs, NJ: Prentice-Hall, 1979.

[Denning, 1999]: Denning, Dorothy E. *Information Warfare and Security.* Boston: Addison-Wesley, 1999.

[Derrett, 1985]: Derrett, N., W. Kent, and P. Lunghaek. Some Aspects of Operations in an Object-Oriented Database. *IEEE Database Engineering Bulletin,* 8:4 (Dec), 1985.

[Dickinson, 1981]: Dickinson, Brian. *Developing Structured Systems.* Englewood Cliffs, NJ: Prentice-Hall, 1981.

[Dickson, 1989]: Dickson, David. Animal Rightists Claim Bomb Blast. *Science,* 3 March 1989.

[Dittrich, 1986]: Dittrich, Klaus R. *Object-Oriented Database Systems: The Notion and the Issue.* International Workshop on Object-Oriented Database Systems. Washington, D.C.: Computer Society Press, 1986.

[DMN, 1989]: *Dallas Morning News.* Army Captures Hit Squad Chiefs in Columbia. 10 September 1989.

[DMN, 1990]: *Dallas Morning News.* Probe Targets Klan; Tax, Rights Inquiry Includes Skinheads. 2 July 1990.

[Dobson, 1982]: Dobson, Christopher and Ronald Payne. *Counterattack: The West's Battle Against the Terrorists.* New York: Facts on File, Inc., 1982.

[DoD2167A, 1988]: U.S. Department of Defense (DoD). Defense Systems Software Development. DoD-STD-2167A. Philadelphia: Naval Publications and Forms Center, 29 February 1988. Superseded by Mil-Std-499, 5 December 1994.

[DoD5000, 2000]: U.S. Department of Defense (DoD). Operation of the Defense Acquisition System (DoDI 5000.2). Updated 04 Jan 01, Ch 1. Washington, D.C.: Government Printing Office, 2000.

[DoD5000, 2001]: U.S. Department of Defense (DoD). Mandatory Procedures for Major Defense Acquisition Programs (MDAPs) and Major Automated Information System (MAIS) Acquisition Programs (DoD 5200.2-R). Interim Regulation. Washington, D.C.: Government Printing Office, 2001.

[DoD5200, 1979]: U.S. Department of Defense (DoD). ADP Security Manual: Techniques and Procedures for Implementing, Deactivating, Testing and Evaluating Secure Resource Sharing ADP Systems. DoD 5200.28-M Ch1. Fort Meade, MD: National Computer Security Center (NCSC), 25 June 1979.

[DoD5200, 1985]: U.S. Department of Defense (DoD). Department of Defense Trusted Computer System Evaluation Criteria (TCSEC) (Orange Book). DoD 5200.28-STD. Fort Meade, MD: National Computer Security Center, 26 December 1985.

[DoD5200, 1988]: U.S. Department of Defense (DoD). Security Requirements for Automated Information Systems. DoD Directive 5200.28. Alexandria, VA: Defense Technical Information Center (DTIC), 21 March 1988.

[DoD8510, 2000]: U.S. Department of Defense (DoD). Department of Defense Information Technology Security Certification and Accreditation Process (DITSCAP). DoD 8510.1-M. Alexandria, VA: Defense Technical Information Center (DTIC), 31 July 2000.

[Dotto, 1979]: Dotto, Lydia. The New Computer Criminals. *Atlas World Press Review,* August 1979.

[DRC, 1986]: Datapro Research Corporation (DRC). Terrorism's Threat to Information Processing. Datapro Report, Delran, NJ, July 1986.

[Drogin, 1992]: Drogin, Bob. Aquino Touts Victory Over Communists But Clashes Raise Doubts That Government Has Beaten Insurgency. *Los Angeles Times,* 46A, 1992.

[DSB, 1993]: U.S. Department of Defense (DoD), Defense Science Board (DSB). Report of the Defense Science Board Task Force on Global Surveillance. Washington, D.C.: Office of the Under-Secretary of Defense for Acquisition and Technology, 1993.

[DSB, 1994]: U.S. Department of Defense (DoD), Defense Science Board (DSB). Report of the Defense Science Board Task Force on Readiness. Washington, D.C.: Office of the Under-Secretary of Defense for Acquisition and Technology, June 1994.

[DSD EB, 2000]: U.S. Department of Defense (DoD). Deputy Secretary of Defense Memorandum on DoD Chief Information Officer Executive Board, http://cno-n6.hq.navy.mil/gig/DoDCIOExecBoardCharter3–31–00.pdf. Washington, D.C.: Office of the Deputy Secretary of Defense, 3 March 2000.

[DSD GiG, 2000]: U.S Department of Defense (DoD). Deputy Secretary of Defense Memorandum on the Global Information Grid. DoD Chief Information Officer (CIO) Guidance and Policy Memorandum No. 8–8001. http://www.c3i.osd.mil/org/cio/doc/depsecdememo_gig3–31–00.pdf. Washington, D.C.: Office of the Deputy Secretary of Defense, 31 March 2000.

[DSD IA, 2000] : U.S Department of Defense (DoD). Deputy Secretary of Defense Memorandum on DoD Global Information Grid Information Assurance. DoD CIO Guidance and Policy Memo No. 6–8510. http://www.c3i.osd.mil/org/cio/doc/gigia061600.pdf. Washington, D.C.: Office of the Deputy Secretary of Defense, 16 June 2000.

[DSI, 1985]: Defense Security Institute (DSI). Soviet Acquisition of Militarily Significant Western Technology: An Update. Washington, D.C.: Defense Security Institute, September 1985.

[DSI, 1986]: Defense Security Institute (DSI). Real or Imagined? The Hostile Intelligence Threat to Computer Systems. Security Awareness Bulletin. Washington, D.C.: Defense Investigative Service (DIS)/Defense Security Institute (DSI), June 1986.

[DSMC, 1984]: Defense Systems Management College (DSMC). Department of Defense Manufacturing Management Handbook for Program Managers. Washington, D.C.: Government Printing Office, 1984.

[DSMC, 1986]: Defense Systems Management College (DSMC). DSMC Systems Engineering Management Guide. Washington, D.C.: Government Printing Office, 1986.

[DSMC, 1988]: Defense Systems Management College (DSMC). Mission Critical Computer Resources Management Guide. Washington, D.C.: Government Printing Office, 1988.

[EFP, 1992]: Ecodefense: A Field Guide to Monkeywrenching, Earth First Publishers, 2d ed., pp. 213–218, 1992.

[Egan, 1989a]: Egan, John. Interview with author. Washington, D.C.: 6 March 1989.

[Egan, 1989b]: Egan, John. EW Architecture Assessment Methodology. Unpublished research. Washington, D.C.

[EIA632, 1999]: Engineering Industries Alliance (EIA). Processes for Engineering a System. ANSI/EIA-632. Arlington, VA: EIA, 1999.

[Eisner, 1984]: Eisner, Howard. CASE: Computer-Aided Systems Engineering for C3I Systems. Signal, July 1984. Fairfax, VA: Armed Forces Communications and Electronics Association (AFCEA), 1984.

[Eisner, 1987]: Eisner, Howard. *Computer Aided Systems Engineering*. Englewood Cliffs, NJ: Prentice-Hall, 1987.

[Eisner, 1997]: Eisner, Howard. *Essentials of Project and Systems Engineering Management*. New York: John Wiley & Sons, 1997.

[Elmasri, 2000]: Elmasri, R. and Navathe, S., Fundamentals of Database Systems, 3rd ed. Reading, MA: Addison-Wesley, 2000.

[Entrust, 1999]: Annual Report. Plano, TX: Entrust Technologies, Inc., 1999.

[Entrust, 2000]: 10-K. Plano, TX: Entrust Technologies, Inc., 2000.

[Evans, 1997]: Evans, Phillip B. and Thomas S. Wurster. Strategy and the New Economics of Information. *Harvard Business Review,* Sep-Oct, 71–82, 1997.

[Farrell, 2002]: Farrell, Adrian. An Organisational Intelligence Framework for the Agile Corporation. White Paper. Melbourne, Australia: Woodlawn Marketing Services, http://www.worksys.com/agile.htm, 27 February 2002.

[FBIS, 1984a]: Foreign Broadcast Information Service (FBIS). Government Computer Destroyed in Bomb Explosion. 13 October 1984.

[FBIS, 1984b]: Foreign Broadcast Information Service (FBIS). Research Center Damaged in Bomb Explosion. 15 October 1984.

[FBIS, 1987]: Foreign Broadcast Information Service (FBIS). Bomb Damages Decoding Computer Plant in Bavaria. 13 April 1987.

[FBIS, 1990]: Foreign Broadcast Information Service (FBIS). Durban Bomb Fatality at Computer Center. 2 October 1990.

[FBIS, 1992a]: Foreign Broadcast Information Service (FBIS). Bomb Explodes Near Government Palace; More Attacks Reported. 14 May 1992.

[FBIS, 1992b]: Foreign Broadcast Information Service (FBIS). Update on Anti-Terrorist Operations in the Basque Country. 14 May 1992.

[FBIS, 1992c]: Foreign Broadcast Information Service (FBIS). Regional Guerrilla Activities 17–27 May. 29 May 1992.

[FBIS, 1992d]: Foreign Broadcast Information Service (FBIS). Roundup of Terrorist Activities. 5 June 1992.

[Firebaugh, 1988]: Firebaugh, Morris W. *Artificial Intelligence: A Knowledge-Based Approach*. Boston: Boyd & Fraser, 1988.

[Fischer, 1991]: Fischer, Dr. Lynn F. The Threat to Automated Systems. Security Awareness Bulletin. Richmond, VA: U.S. Department of Defense Security Institute, September 1991.

[Fites, 1989]: Fites, Philip, Peter Johnston, and Martin Kratz. *The Computer Virus Crisis*. New York: Van Nostrand Reinhold, 1989.

[FM 100–6]: U.S. Army. Information Operations. Field Manual 100–6. Washington, D.C.: Government Printing Office, 27 August 1996.

[Fowler, 1997]: Fowler, Martin with Kendall Scott. UML Distilled: Applying the Standard Object Modeling Language. Reading, MA: Addison-Wesley, 1997.

[Freeman, 1980]: Freeman, P. Requirements Analysis and Specification, The First Step. Transactions of the International Computer Technology Conference. San Francisco, CA: 12–15 August 1980.

[Futurist, 1988]: The Futurist. Terrorism and Computers. January-February, 1988.

[Gaines, 1956]: Gaines, B.R. Methodology in the Large: Modeling All There Is. Proceedings: International Conference on Cybernetics and Society. New York: IEEE Press, 1956.

[Gall, 1977]: Gall, John. *Systemantics*. New York: Quadrangle, 1977.

[Gallotta, 1985]: Gallotta, Albert A. EW and the Information War. *Journal of Electronic Defense,* March. Alexandria, VA: Association of Old Crows (AOC), 1984.

[Gann, 1975]: Gann, Richard G., Ed. Symposium on Halogenated Fire Agents, IS Symposium Series 16. Washington, D.C.: American Chemical Society, 1975).

[GAO, 1979]: General Accounting Office (GAO). Automated Systems Security: Federal Agencies Should Strengthen Safeguards Over Personal and Other Sensitive Data. Washington, D.C.: Government Printing Office, 23 January 1979.

[GAO, 1996]: General Accounting Office (GAO). Executive Report B-266140. Washington, D.C.: Government Printing Office, 22 May 1996.

[GAO, 1998a]: General Accounting Office (GAO). Report on Joint Military Operations: Weaknesses in DoD's Process for Certifying C4I Systems' Interoperability. GAO/NSIAD-98-73. Washington, D.C.: General Accounting Office, 13 March 1998.

[GAO, 1998b]: General Accounting Office (GAO). Measuring Performance and Demonstrating Results of Information Technology Investments. GAO/AIMD-98–89. Washington, D.C.: General Accounting Office, March 1998.

[Gertz, 1988]: Gertz, Bill. Hackers' Success Worries Pentagon. *Washington Times,* 19 April 1988.

[Harry, 1985]: Harry, M. *The Computer Underground: Computer Hacking, Crashing, Pirating and Phreaking*. Port Townsend, WA: Loompanics Unlimited Press, 1985.

[Hayes, 2000]: Hayes, Richard and David T. Signori. Report on the Information Superiority Metrics Working Group. Presented at the Command and Control Research and Technology Symposium. Monterey, CA: Naval Postgraduate School (NPGS), 28 June 2000.

[Heather, 1987]: Heather, Randall. *Terrorism, Active Measures, and SDI*. Toronto, Canada: The Mackenzie Institute for the Study of Terrorism, Revolution, and Propaganda, 1987.

[Henderson, 1989]: Henderson, Breck W. Experts Say Total Security Program Needed to Counter Terrorist Threat. *Aviation Week & Space Technology,* 20 November 1989.

[Higgins, undated]: Higgins, Mike. Polymorphic Viruses (Automated Systems Security Incident Support Team (ASSIST) 92–38). Defense Data Network (DDN), undated.

[Hillier, 1980]: Hillier, F.S. and G.J. Lieberman. *Introduction to Operations Research,* 3rd ed. New York: Holden-Day, 1980.

[Hitchins, 1992]: Hitchins, Derek. Putting Systems To Work. Chichester, UK: John Wiley and Sons, 1992. References from the electronic version downloaded from www.hith/cins.org/prof/ on 26 March 2002.

[Hodges, 1989]: Hodges, Parker. A Relational Successor? *Datamation,* 35:21 (Nov), 47–50, 1989.

[Hoffman, 1982]: Hoffman, L. Impacts of Information System Vulnerabilities on Society. NCC Conference Proceedings. Arlington, VA: AFIPS Press, 1982.

[Hofstadter, 1979]: Hofstadter, Douglas R. *Godel, Escher, Bach: An Eternal Golden Braid*. New York: Basic Books, 1979.

[Hong, 1988]: Hong, S. and F. Maryanski. Representation of Object-Oriented Data Models. *Information Sciences,* Vol. 52, pp. 247–284, 1988.

[Hosinski, 1989]: Hosinski, Joan M. U.S. Said to Be Vulnerable in Information War. *Government Computer News,* 7 August 1989.

[Hsaio, 1979]: Hsaio, David and D. Kerr. *Computer Security.* New York: Academic Press, 1979.

[Hull, 1987]: Hull, Richard and Roger King. Semantic Database Modeling: Survey, Applications, and Research. *ACM Computing Surveys,* 19:3, 201–260, 1987.

[IATF, 1999]: U.S. National Security Agency (NSA). Information Assurance Technical Framework (IATF). Release 2.0.1. Ft. Meade, MD: National Security Agency, September 1999.

[Icove, 1989]: Icove, David J. Modeling the Threat. A committee report presented to the Department of Defense Invitational Workshop on Computer Security Incident Response, Carnegie-Mellon University Software Engineering Institute, Pittsburgh, July 31–August 1, 1989.

[Icove, 1991]: Icove, David J. Keeping Computers Safe. *Security Management,* December 1991.

[IEEE, 1984]: Jay, F., Ed. *IEEE Standard Dictionary of Electrical and Electronics Terms.* New York: IEEE Press, 1984.

[IEEE, 1985]: IEEE Computer Society. Proceedings: International Conference on Entity Relationship Approaches. Washington, D.C.: Computer Society Press, 1985.

[IEEE, 1986]: Institute of Electrical and Electronics Engineers (IEEE). *The System Engineering Process: A Technical Bibliography. Transactions on Systems, Man, and Cybernetics.* New York: IEEE Press, 1986.

[INCOSE, 2002]: International Council on Systems Engineering. http://www.incose.org/ 19 June 2002.

[ISO 17799]: International Organization for Standardization (ISO). Information Technology — Code of Practice for Information Security Management. ISO/IEC Standard 17799. Geneva, Switzerland: International Organization for Standards, 2000.

[ISO15408, 1999]: International Organization for Standards (ISO). Information Technology — Security Techniques — Evaluation Criteria for IT Security. ISO/IEC 15408. Geneva, Switzerland: International Organization for Standards and International Electrotechnical Commission (IEC), 1 December 1999.

[ISO9000, 2000]: International Organization for Standards (ISO). Quality Management Systems — Fundamentals and Vocabulary. ISO 9000. Geneva, Switzerland: International Organization for Standards, 15 December 2000.

[ISSEP, 2000]: Information System Security Engineering Principles (ISSEP). Initial Draft: Outline. Washington, D.C.: National Institute of Standards (NIST), 18 Jul 2000.

[Jane's, 1989]: *Jane's All the World's Weapon Systems.* London, U.K.: *Jane's,* 1989.

[JCS3210, 1996]: U.S. Department of Defense (DoD). Joint Information Warfare Policy. Joint Chiefs of Staff Instruction 3210.01. Washington, D.C.: Government Printing Office, 1996.

[Jenish, 1992]: Jenish, D'Arcy. A Terrorist Virus: Michelangelo Stirs Fears of Future Shocks. *MacLean's,* 16 March 1992.

[Jenkins, 1991]: Jenkins, Brian. Defending Your Data. *Government Executive,* October 1991.

[JITC, 1999]: U.S. Department of Defense (DoD). Joint Interoperability Test Command (JITC) home page. http://jitc.fhu.disa.mil/. 2 December 1999.

[Johnson, 1989]: Johnson, John. "Dark Side" Hacker Seen as "Electronic Terrorist." *Los Angeles Times,* p. 1, 8 January 1989.

[JP 1–02]: U.S. Department of Defense (DoD). DoD Dictionary of Military and Associated Terms. Joint Publication 1–02 (JP 1–02). Washington, D.C.: Government Printing Office, 2001.

[JP 3–13]: U.S. Department of Defense (DoD). Joint Doctrine for Information Warfare. Joint Publication 3–13 (JP 3–13). Washington, D.C.: Government Printing Office, 1998.

[JP 6–0]: Doctrine for Command, Control, Communications and Computer (C4) Systems Support to Joint Operations. Joint Publication 6–0. Washington, D.C.: U.S. Department of Defense, 30 May 1995.

[JP 6–02]: Joint Doctrine for Operational/Tactical Command, Control, Communications Systems. Joint Publication 6–02. Washington, D.C.: U.S. Department of Defense, 1 Oct 1996.

[JROCM 134–01]: U.S. Department of Defense (DoD). Global Information Grid (GIG) Capstone Requirements Document (CRD), Final Version. https://jdl.jwfc.jfcom.mil. Washington, D.C.: Defense Information Systems Agency (DISA), 30 August 2001.

[JSC, 1994]: Joint Security Commission (JSC). Redefining Security: A Report to the Secretary of Defense and the Director of Central Intelligence. Washington, D.C.: 28 February 1994.

[JV 2020]: U.S. Department of Defense (DoD). Joint Vision 2020 (JV 2020). Washington, D.C.: Government Printing Office, 2000.

[Kaplan, 1992]: Kaplan, Robert S. and David P. Norton. *Translating Strategy into Action: The Balanced Scorecard.* Cambridge, MA: Harvard Business School Press, 1992.

[Katzan, 1976]: Katzan, H. *Systems Design and Documentation.* New York: Van Nostrand Reinhold, 1976.

[Kerschberg, 1976]: Kerschberg, Larry and Joao E.S. Pacheco. *A Functional Data Base Model.* Rio de Janeiro, Brazil: Pantificia Univ. Catalica, 1976.

[Kerschberg, 1987]: Kerschberg, Larry, Ed. Expert Database Systems: Proceedings of the 1st International Workshop. Menlo Park, CA: Benjamin Cummings, 1987.

[Kerschberg, 1988]: Kerschberg, Larry, Ed. Expert Database Systems: Proceedings of 2nd International Conference. Redwood City, CA: Benjamin Cummings, 1988.

[Kerstin, 1986]: Kerstin, Martin L. and Frans H. Schippers. Towards an Object-Centered Database Language. Proceedings: International Workshop on Object-Oriented Database Systems. Klaus Dittrich and Umeshwar Dayal, Eds. Washington, D.C.: Computer Society Press, 1986.

[Khoshafian, 1986]: Khoshafian, S.N. and G.P. Copeland. *Object Identity.* New York: ACM Press, 1986.

[Kim, 1989]: Kim, Won and Frederick H. Lochovsky, Eds. *Object-Oriented Concepts, Databases, and Applications.* Reading, MA: Addison-Wesley, 1989.

[Kim, 1990]: Kim, Kyung-Chang. Query Processing in Object-Oriented Databases. Lecture Notes. Austin, TX: University of Texas, 1990.

[King, 1986]: King, R. A Database Management System Based on an Object-Oriented Model. Expert Database Systems: Proceedings of the 1st International Workshop. Larry Kerschberg, Ed. Menlo Park, CA: Benjamin Cummings, 1986.

[Krutz, 2001]: Krutz, Ronald L. and Russell D. Vines. *The CISSP Prep Guide.* New York: John Wiley & Sons, 2001.

[Kupperman, 1979]: Kupperman, Robert H. and Darrell M. Trent, Eds. *Terrorism: Threat, Reality, Response.* Stanford, CA: Hoover Institution Press, 1979.

[Lam, 1989a]: Lam, Xia et al. *Prototype Implementation of an Object-Oriented Knowledge Base Management System.* PROCIEM, 1989.

[Lam, 1989b]: Lam, H., S.Y.W. Su, and A.M. Alashqur. *Integrating the Concepts and Techniques of Semantic Modeling and the Object-Oriented Paradigm.* COMPSAC, 1989.

[Lamb, 1986]: Lamb, John and James Etheridge. DP: The Terror Target. *Datamation,* 44–45, 1 February 1986.

[Laquer, 1987]: Laquer, Walter and Yonah Alexander. *The Terrorism Reader: The Essential Source Book on Political Violence, Both Past and Present.* New York: Meridian Books, 1987.

[LAT, 1985]: The World. *Los Angeles Times,* 3 September 1985.

[LAT, 1992]: *Los Angeles Times,* Bob Drogin, "Aquino Touts Victory Over Communists But Clashes Raise Doubts that Government Has Beaten Insurgency," p. 46A, 12 March 1992.

[Leedom, 2001]: Leedom, Dennis K. Final Report: Sensemaking Symposium. Command and Control Research Program (CCRP). Vienna, VA: Evidence Based Research, Inc., 23–25 October 2001.

[Livingstone, 1982]: Livingstone, Neil C. *The War Against Terrorism.* Lexington, MA: Lexington Books, 1982.

[Livingstone, 1990]: Livingstone, Neil C. *The Cult of Counterterrorism.* Lexington, MA: Lexington Books, 1990.

[Lloyd, 1980]: Lloyd, Andrew. DP: An Easy Target. *Datamation,* 100, 1 June 1980.

[Loeb, 2002] Loeb, Larry. "Conference at West Point Focuses on the Challenge of IA." *Information Assurance Powwow,* http://www.106.ibm.com/developworks/library/s-confnotes/, 30 May 2002.

[Loeb, 1999]: Loeb, Larry. *Secure Electronic Transactions: Introduction and Technical Reference.* Norwood, MA: Artech House, 1999.

[Long, 1990]: Long, David E. *The Anatomy of Terrorism.* New York: The Free Press, 1990.

[Maier, 1986]: Maier, D. et al. *Development of an Object-Oriented Database Management System.* New York: ACM, 1986.

[Manola, 1986]: Manola, F. and U. Dayal. *PDM: An Object-Oriented Data Model.* New York: IEEE, 1986.

[Manola, 1987]: Manola, Frank A. *PDM: An Object-Oriented Data Model for PROBE.* Cambridge, MA: Computer Corp. of America, 1987.

[Manola, 1990]: Manola, Frank A. Object-Oriented Knowledge Bases, Part I. *AI Expert,* 5:3 (Mar), 26–36, 1990.

[Markoff, 1988]: Markoff, John. Top Secret and Vulnerable: "Unguarded Doors" in U.S. Computers Disturb Experts. *New York Times,* 25 April 1988.

[Martin, 1973]: Martin, James. *Security, Accuracy and Privacy in Computer Systems.* New York: Prentice Hall, 1973.

[Mathwick, 1997]: Mathwick, James E. Database Integration, Practical Lessons-Learned. Proceedings of the DoD Database Colloquium. San Diego, CA, 1997.

[McCumber, 1991]: McCumber, John R. Information Systems Security: A Comprehensive Model Proceedings of the 14th National Computer Security Conference, 1: 328–337. Washington, D.C.: NIST/NCSC, October, 1991.

[McGinnis, 1994]: McGinnis, Lt. Col. Michael L. and Maj. George F. Stone III. Decision Support Technology, *Military Review,* 74:11 (Nov), 68, 1994.

[McKitrick, 1995]: McKitrick, Jeffrey et al. The Revolution in Military Affairs. Air War College Studies in National Security: *Battlefield of the Future,* 3 (Sep), 65–97. Maxwell AFB, AL: Air University Press, 1995.

[Mellor, 1988]: Mellor, Stephen J. and Sally Shlaer. *Object-Oriented System Analysis: Modeling the World In Data.* Englewood Cliffs, NJ: Yourdon Press, 1988.

[Menk, 1999]: Menk, Charles G. Assurance Overview. Washington, D.C.: U.S. Department of Defense (DoD), 1999.

[Menkus, 1983]: Menkus, Belden. Notes on Terrorism and Data Processing. *Computers and Security,* 2, 11–15, 1983.

[Meyer, 1987]: Meyer, Bertrand. Reusability: The Case for Object-Oriented Design. *IEEE Software,* 4:2 (Mar), 50–64, 1987.

[Meyer, 1988]: Meyer, Bertrand. *Object-Oriented Software Construction.* New York: Prentice-Hall, 1988.

[Michaels, 1999]: Michaels, Greg. DoN Data Interoperability. Briefing to Mr. Dan Porter, DoN CIO. Arlington, VA: GRC International, 18 February 1999.

[Mil232A, 1987]: U.S. Department of Defense (DoD). Red/Black Engineering Installation Guidelines. Mil-Hdbk-232A. Fort Huachuca, AZ: U.S. Army Information Systems Engineering and Integration Center, 20 March 1987.

[Mil498, 1994]: U.S. Department of Defense (DoD). Software Development and Documentation. Mil-STD-498. Philadelphia: Naval Publications and Forms Center, 5 December 1994. Cancelled 27 May 1998.

[Mil499A, 1974]: U.S. Department of Defense (DoD). Engineering Management. Mil-STD-499A. Philadelphia: Naval Publications and Forms Center, 1974. Cancelled 27 February 1995.

[MOP 06]: U.S. Department of Defense (DoD). Electronic Warfare. Memorandum Of Policy #06 (MOP 06). Washington, D.C.: Government Printing Office, 3 March 1993.

[MOP 30]: U.S. Department of Defense (DoD). Command and Control Warfare (C2W). Memorandum Of Policy #30 (MOP 30). Washington, D.C.: Government Printing Office, 8 March 1993.

[Moran, 1983]: Moran, William B. *Covert Surveillance and Electronic Penetration.* Port Townsend, WA: Breakout Productions, 1983.

[Morris, 1976]: Morris, William, Ed. *The American Heritage Dictionary of the English Language.* Boston: Houghton Mifflin, 1976.

[Nadler, 1984]: Nadler, G. Systems Methodology and Design. Proceedings of the IEEE Conference. Halifax: IEEE Press, 1984.

[NCSA, 1991]: National Computer Security Association (NCSA). Computer Viruses, 1 January 1991.

[NCSC004, 1988]: National Computer Security Center (NCSC). Glossary of Computer Security Terms (Teal Green Book). NCSC-TG-004. Fort Meade, MD: National Security Agency (NSA), 21 October 1988.

[NCSC005, 1987]: National Computer Security Center (NCSC). Trusted Network Interpretation (Red Book). NCSC-TG-005. Fort Meade, MD: National Security Agency (NSA), 31 July 1987.

[NCSC029, 1994]: National Computer Security Center (NCSC). Introduction to Certification and Accreditation Concepts (Blue Book). NCSC-TG-029. Fort Meade, MD: National Security Agency (NSA), January 1994.

[NDIA, 1999]: National Defense Industrial Association (NDIA), C4I Study Group. Information Assurance (IA) Study Final Report (draft pending release). Fairfax, VA: National Defense Industrial Association, August 1999.

[NDU, 2002]: Information Assurance. National Defense University. http://www.nduknowledge.net/information/infoassr_faqs.htm, 30 May 2002.

[NIAP, 1999]: U.S. National Information Assurance Partnership (NIAP). Glossary. www.niap.nist.gov/glossary.html. 2 December 1999.

[NIST, 1998]: National Institute of Standards and Technology (NIST). Guide for Developing Security Plans for Information Technology Systems. NIST Special Publication (SP) 800–18. Washington, D.C.: National Institute of Standards and Technology, December 1998.

[NIST, 1999]: National Institute of Standards and Technology (NIST). Common Methodology for Information Technology Security Evaluation. CEM-99/045. Gaithersburg, MD: National Institute of Standards and Technology, August 1999.

[NIST, 2000]: National Institute of Standards and Technology (NIST). National Information Assurance Certification and Accreditation Process (NIACAP). NSTISSI 1000. Washington, D.C.: National Institute of Standards and Technology, April 2000.

[Norman, 1985]: Norman, Adrian R.D. *Computer Insecurity.* New York: Chapman and Hall, 1985.

[NSA, 2002]: U.S. National Security Agency (NSA). NSA Glossary of Terms. www.sans.org/newlook/resources/glossary.htm. 19 June 2002.

[NSTISSI 4009]: National Security Telecommunications and Information Systems Security (NSTISS) Issuance. National Information Systems Security (INFOSEC) Glossary. Fort Meade, MD: National Security Agency (NSA), September 2000.

[O'Conner, 1990]: O'Connor, Rory J. Army Searches For New Weapon: Computer Virus. *Philadelphia Inquirer,* 7 May 1990.

[Ognibene, 1991]: Ognibene, Peter J. America the Vulnerable. *Los Angeles Times,* 16 January 1991.

[OMB A130, 1996]: Office of Management and Budget (OMB). Management of Federal Information Resources. OMB Circular A-130. Washington, D.C.: OMB, The White House, 8 February 1996.

[OPNAV, 1976]: Participation in a Military or Civil Aircraft Accident Investigation. OPNAV Instruction 3750.16B. Washington, D.C.: Chief of Naval Operations, 26 April 1976.

[OPNAV, 1989]: Naval Aviation Safety Program. OPNAV Instruction 3750.6Q. Washington, D.C.: Chief of Naval Operations, 28 August 1989.

[OPNAV, 1997]: NATOPS General Flight and Operating Instructions. OPNAV Instruction 3710.7R. Washington, D.C.: Chief of Naval Operations, 15 January 1997.

[OPNAV, 1998]: The Naval Aviation Maintenance Program (NAMP). OPNAV Instruction 4790.2G. Washington, D.C.: Chief of Naval Operations, 1 February 1998.

[Orlandi, 1984]: Orlandi, Eugenio. Data Processing Security and Terrorism. A paper given at the Second International Federation for Information Processing (IFIP) International Conference on Computer Security. Toronto, Canada: 10–12 September, 1984.

[Orr, 1983]: Orr, George E. Combat Operations C3I: Fundamentals and Interactions. Maxwell AFB, AL: Air University Press, 1983.

[Page, 1988]: Page-Jones, Meiler. *Practical Guide to Structured Systems Design.* Englewood Cliffs, NJ: Prentice Hall, 1988.

[Parker, 1975]: Parker, Donn B. *Computer Abuse, Perpetrators and Vulnerabilities of Computer Systems.* Menlo Park, CA: Stanford Research Institute, 1975.

[Parker, 1981]: Parker, Donn B. *Manager's Guide to Computer Security.* Reston, VA: Reston Publishing Co., 1981.

[Parsaye, 1989]: Parsaye et al. *Intelligent Databases: Object Oriented, Deductive Hypermedia Techniques.* New York: Wiley & Sons, 1989.

[Peckham, 1988]: Peckham, Joan and Fred Maryanski. Semantic Data Models. *ACM Computing Surveys,* 20:3 (Sep), 153–189, 1988.

[Peirce, 1934]: Peirce, Charles Sanders. *Collected Papers of Charles Sanders Peirce,* Vol. II. Hartshorne, Weiss, and Burks, Eds. Cambridge, England: Cambridge Press, 1934.

[Peirce, 1955]: Peirce, Charles Sanders. *Abduction and Induction.* Dover, England: Dover Press, 1955.

[Peltier, 1998]: Peltier, Thomas R. *Information Security Policies and Procedures: A Practitioner's Reference.* Boca Raton, FL: Auerbach Press, 1998.

[Peng, 1986]: Peng, Yun. A Formalization of Parsimonious Covering and Probabilistic Reasoning in Abductive Diagnostic Inference. Ph.D. dissertation. College Park, MD: University of Maryland, 1986.

[Peterson, 1987]: Peterson, Gerald E. *Tutorial: Object-Oriented Computing, Volume I: Concepts.* Washington, D.C.: Computer Society Press, 1987.

[PL 100–235]: U.S. Government. Computer Security Act of 1987. Public Law 100–235. Washington, D.C.: Government Printing Office, 1987.

[Pollak, 1983]: Pollak, Raoul. Implications of International Terrorism on Security of Information Systems. Proceedings of IEEE INFOCOM 83, 270–276. New York: IEEE Press, 1983.

[Pollard, 1988]: Pollard, James R. Systems Engineering: An Introduction to Architecture Development. Unpublished lecture. Dahlgren, VA: Naval Surface Warfare Center, 1988.

[Pollard, 1989]: Pollard, James R. Interview with author. Washington, D.C.: 1 March 1989.

[PRC, 1988]: Planning Research Corporation (PRC). Naval Warfare Tactical Data Base User's Guide. McLean, VA: Planning Research Corporation, 1988.

[Rand, 1975]: The Rand Corporation. *International Terrorism: A Chronology, 1968–1974.* Santa Monica, CA: The Rand Corporation, March 1975.

[Rawles, 1990a]: Rawles, James W. High-Technology Terrorism. *Defense Electronics,* January 1990.

[Rawles, 1990b]: Rawles, James W. The Viral Threat. *Defense Electronics,* February 1990.

[Reuters, 1990]: Counter-intelligence Hilite. *Reuters Newswire,* 17 February 1990.

[Reuters, 1992]: Dutch Computer Hackers Leave Global Trail of Damage. *Reuters Newswire,* 31 January 1992.

[Reuters, 1992]: U.S. General Wants Ray Guns for Commandos. *Reuters Newswire,* 5 May 1992.

[Roberts, 1989]: Roberts, Ralph and Pamela Kane. *Computer Security.* Greensboro, NC: Compute Books, 1989.

[Ross, 1977]: Ross, D.T. and K.E. Schoman, Jr. Structured Analysis for Requirements Definition. IEEE Transactions of Software Engineering. January 1977. New York: IEEE Press, 1977.

[Rowley, 1991]: Rowley, James. Libyans Indicted in Pan Am Blast. Pair Reportedly Intelligence Officers. *The Phoenix Gazette,* 14 November 1991.

[Rozen, 1988]: Rozen, Arnon and John Musacchio. Computer Sites: Assessing the Threat. *Security Management,* July 1988.

[Ryan, 1993]: Ryan, Daniel. Evaluation, Certification and Accreditation of Computer Systems and Networks. *The ISSA Journal,* 1:1, 1993.

[Ryberg, 1988]: Ryberg, August John, Jr. *Systems Engineering Tools.* Fairfax, VA: Unpublished, 1988.

[Sage, 1990]: Sage, Andrew P. *Decision Support Systems Engineering.* Fairfax, VA: Unpublished manuscript. 1990.

[Sage, 1995]: Sage, Andrew P. *Systems Management for Information Technology and Software Engineering.* New York: John Wiley & Sons, 1995.

[Santoro, 1984]: Santoro, Victor. *Disruptive Terrorism*. Port Townsend, WA: Loompanics Unlimited, 1984.

[Schmemann, 1987]: Schmemann, Serge. Computer Buffs Tapped NASA Files. *The New York Times,* 16 September 1987.

[Schum, 1986]: Schum, David A. Probability and the Process of Discovery, Proof, and Choice. Probability and Inference in the Law of Evidence, pp. 213–270. Peter Tillers and E.D. Green, Eds, Kluwer Academic Publishers, Amsterdam, 1986.

[Schum, 1989]: Schum, David, and Peter Tillers. *Marshalling Evidence Throughout The Process of Fact-Investigation*. Fairfax, VA: George Mason University (GMU), 1989.

[Schum, 1990]: Schum, David, and Peter Tillers. *A Technical Note on Computer-Assisted Wigmorean Argument Structuring*. Fairfax, VA: George Mason University (GMU), 1990.

[Schwartau, 1991a]: Schwartau, Winn. *Terminal Compromise*. New York: Interpact Press, 1991.

[Schwartau, 1991b]: Schwartau, Winn. Seven Weapons for the Well-Armed Computer Terrorist. *Information Security Product News* (September/October), 1991.

[SECNAV, 1995]: Department of the Navy Information Systems Security (InfoSec) Program. SECNAV Instruction 5239.3. Washington, D.C.: Office of the Secretary of the Navy, 14 July 1995.

[Seiber, 1986]: Seiber, Ulrich. *The International Handbook on Computer Crime: Computer-Related Economic Crime and the Infringements of Privacy*. New York: John Wiley & Sons, 1986.

[Seldon, 1979]: Seldon, M.R. *Life-Cycle Costing: A Better Method of Government Procurement*. Boulder, CO: Westview Press, 1979.

[Shlaer, 1988]: Shlaer, Sally and Stephen J. Mellor. *Object-Oriented Systems Analysis: Modeling the World in Data*. Englewood Cliffs, NJ: Yourdon Press, 1988.

[Sibley, 1977]: Sibley, E.H. and L. Kerschberg. *Data Architecture and Data Model Considerations*. Reston, VA: AFIPS Press, 1977.

[Simon, 1976]: Simon, Herbert A. *Administrative Behavior: A Study of Decision-Making Processes in Administrative Organization*, pp. 38–41. New York: The Free Press, 1976.

[Sitomer, 1986]: Sitomer, Curtis J. Crooks find computers useful; terrorists see vulnerable targets. *The Christian Science Monitor,* 4 December 1986.

[Smith, 1977]: Smith, J. M. and D.C. P. Smith. Database Abstractions: Aggregation and Generalization. *ACM Transactions on Database Systems,* 2:2 (Mar), 105–133, 1977.

[Solomon, 1992]: Solomon, Alan. Sneaking Past the Scanners: Stealth Viruses, Part II. *Infosecurity News,* November/December, 1992.

[Sowa, 1983]: Sowa, John F. *Conceptual Structures*. Reading, MA: Addison-Wesley, 1983.

[SPAWAR, 1987a]: Space and Naval Warfare Systems Command (SPAWAR). Weapon System Architecture and Engineering: History and Mission. Unpublished notes. Washington, D.C.: SPAWAR, 1987.

[SPAWAR, 1987b]: Space and Naval Warfare Systems Command (SPAWAR). Space and Naval Warfare Systems Command Consolidated Glossary. Washington, D.C.: SPAWAR, 1987.

[SPAWAR, 1989a]: Space and Naval Warfare Systems Command (SPAWAR). Physical Architecture for Sea Control for the Conduct of Electronic Warfare, Volume I, Part A. Washington, D.C.: SPAWAR, 1989.

[SPAWAR, 1989b]: Space and Naval Warfare Systems Command (SPAWAR). Functional Architecture for Sea Control for the Conduct of Electronic Warfare, Volume I, Part B. Washington, D.C.: SPAWAR, 1989.

[SPAWAR, 1989c]: Space and Naval Warfare Systems Command (SPAWAR). Battle Group Data Base Management (BGDBM). Washington, D.C.: SPAWAR, 1989.

[SPT, 1990]: Washington Digest. *St. Petersburg Times,* 8A. 6 December 1990.

[Stoll, 1989]: Stoll, Clifford. *The Cuckoo's Egg: Tracking a Spy Through a Maze of Computer Espionage.* New York: Doubleday, 1989.

[Stonebraker, 1987]: Stonebraker, Michael and Lawrence A. Rowe. *The Postgres Papers.* Berkley, CA: University of California, 1987.

[Stoneburner, 2001]: Stoneburner, Gary, Clark Hayden, and Alexis Feringa. Engineering Principles for Information Technology Security (A Baseline for Achieving Security). NIST Special Publication (SP) 800–27. Washington, D.C.: National Institute of Standards (NIST), 2001.

[Su, 1989]: Su, S.Y.W., V. Krishnamurthy, and H. Lam. *An Object-Oriented Semantic Association Model (OSAM*). Artificial Intelligence: Manufacturing Theory and Practice.* Kumara, Soyster, and Kashyap, Eds. Norcross, GA: Industrial Engineering Press, 1989.

[Sun, 2002]: Sun Microsystems, Inc. What is Java™ Technology? http://java.sun.com/java2/whatis/. 19 June 2002.

[Suplee, 1990]: Suplee, Curt and Evelyn Richards. Computers Vulnerable, Panel Warns. *The Washington Post,* 6 December 1990.

[Sutherland, 1975]: Sutherland, John W. *Systems Analysis, Administration, and Architecture.* New York: Van Nostrand Reinhold, 1975.

[Taylor, 1997]: Taylor, David A. *Object Technology: A Manager's Guide,* 2nd ed. Reading, MA: Addison-Wesley, 1997.

[TCSEC, 1985]: U.S. Department of Defense (DoD). DoD Trusted Computer System Evaluation Criteria (TCSEC). DoD Standard 5200.28. Washington, D.C.: U.S. Department of Defense, December 1985.

[Technautics, 1988]: Technautics, Inc. *Electronic Warfare Guidebook.* Arlington, VA: Technautics, 11 November 1988.

[TF, 1988]: Terrorism and Computers. *The Futurist,* January–February 1988.

[TGP, 1988]: Terrorist Group Profiles. Washington, D.C.: Government Printing Office, 1988.

[Thomas, 1989]: Thomas, Dave. Object-Oriented Databases and Persistent Objects. *Journal of Object-Oriented Programming,* 2:2, 59–60, 1989.

[Thomas, 1990]: Thomas, George et al. *A Survey of Object-Oriented Database Technology.* Fairfax, VA: George Mason University (GMU), 1990.

[TLB, 1986]: Time-Life, Inc. *Computer Security.* Alexandria, VA: Time-Life Books, 1986.

[USA, 1983]: U.S. Army. Countering Terrorism on U.S. Army Installations. Technical Circular (TC) 19. 16 April 1983.

[USAF, 1996]: 1995 Vulnerability Assessment of Air Force Networked Computer Systems. Air Force online survey study. May 1996.

[USAT, 1989]: Terrorism: Home-Grown Threat to U.S.? *USA Today* (magazine), December, 1989.

[USD(A&T), 1998]: U.S. DoD Under–Secretary of Defense (Acquisition & Technology). Strategic Direction for a DoD Architecture Framework. Memorandum. Washington, D.C.: U.S. Department of Defense, 23 February 1998.

[Van Eck, 1985]: Van Eck, W. Electromagnetic Radiation from Video Display Units: An Eavesdropping Risk. *Computers & Security,* 1985.

[Ward, 1984]: Ward, Paul T. *Systems Development Without Pain.* Englewood Cliffs, NJ: Prentice-Hall, 1984.

[Ward, 1985]: Ward, Paul and Steve Meller. *Structured Development for Real-Time Systems.* Englewood Cliffs, NJ: Prentice-Hall, 1985.

[Ward, 1988a]: Ward, Paul. *Structured Analysis and Design Workshop: Case Study and Exercises*. New York: Yourdon Press, 1988.

[Ward, 1988b]: Ward, Paul. *Structured Analysis and Design Workshop Lecture Notes*. New York: Yourdon Press, 1988.

[Warfield, 1972]: Warfield, J.N. and J.D. Hill. A Unified Systems Engineering Concept. Battelle Monograph, No 1. Columbus, OH: Battelle Press, 1972.

[Warfield, 1984]: Warfield, J.N. Principles of Interactive Management. Proceedings: International Conference on Cybernetics and Society. New York: IEEE Press, 1984.

[Warfield, 1985]: Warfield, J.N. Developing a Design Culture in Higher Education: Some Laws and Principles of Design. Proceedings of the SGSB Annual Meeting. Los Angeles, CA, 1985.

[Webster, 1984]: *Webster's II: New Riverside University Dictionary*. Boston: The Riverside Publishing Company, 1984.

[Weinberg, 1975]: Weinberg, Gerald. *Introduction to General Systems Thinking*. New York: John Wiley & Sons, 1975.

[Wells, 1985]: Wells, Timothy. *A Structured Approach to Building Programs*. Englewood Cliffs, NJ: Prentice Hall, 1985.

[Whitehouse, 1973]: Whitehouse, G.E. *Systems Analysis and Design Using Network Techniques*. Englewood Cliffs, NJ: Prentice-Hall, 1973.

[Whiteside, 1978]: Whiteside, Thomas. *Computer Capers: Tales of Electronic Thievery, Embezzlement, and Fraud*. New York: A Mentor Book, The New American Library, 1978.

[Wiersma, 1987]: Wiersma, Raymond. Warfare Systems Architecture and Engineering Process. Unpublished research. Dahlgren, VA: Naval Surface Warfare Center, 1987.

[Wilcox, 1984]: Wilcox, Richard H. and Patrick J. Garrity, Eds. *America's Hidden Vulnerability: Crisis Management in a Society of Networks*. Washington, D.C.: The Center for Strategic and International Studies (CSIS), Georgetown University, October 1984.

[WT, 1990]: Hackers Steal SDI Information. *Washington Times*. 24 December 1990.

[WTAP, 1987]: *Directory of American Firms Operating in Foreign Countries*. Volume I, 11th Ed.. New York: World Trade Academy Press, 1987.

[Yourdon, 1979]: Yourdon, Edward, and L.L. Constantine. *Structured Design*. New York: Yourdon Press, 1979.

[Yourdon, 1989a]: Yourdon, Edward. *Modern Structured Analysis*. Englewood Cliffs, NJ: Yourdon Press, 1989.

[Yourdon, 1989b]: Yourdon, Edward. *Structured Walk Throughs*, 4th ed. Englewood Cliffs, NJ: Yourdon Press, 1989.

[Zachman, 1987]: Zachman, John A. A Framework for Information Systems Architecture. *IBM Systems Journal*, 26:3, 276–292, 1987.

[Zaniolo, 1986]: Zaniolo, Carlo et al. Object Oriented Database Systems and Knowledge Systems. Expert Database Systems: Proceedings from the 1st International Workshop. Larry Kerschberg, Ed. Menlo Park, CA: Benjamin Cummings, 1986.

[Zdonik, 1990]: Zdonik, Stanley B. and David Maier, Eds. *Readings in Object-Oriented Database Systems*. San Mateo, CA: Morgan Kaufman, 1990.

About The Authors

Raymond J. Curts, Ph.D. (CDR, USN, Ret.), was born December 2, 1946 in Philadelphia, Pennsylvania, and is an American citizen. He graduated from Vandalia Community High School, Vandalia, Illinois, in 1965. He received his Bachelor of Science in Aeronautical and Astronautical Engineering from the University of Illinois in 1970, and was commissioned as an Ensign in the U.S. Navy. In December 1972, he earned his wings as a Naval Aviator and was assigned to the U.S. Naval Base at Guantanamo Bay, Cuba. Returning to the continental United States in 1976, he became an instructor pilot in the Navy's Advanced Jet Training Command in Beeville, Texas, where he earned a Master of Arts degree in Management and Business Administration from Webster College of St. Louis, Missouri. After tours of duty in Norfolk, Virginia; Rota, Spain; and Key West, Florida, he was stationed at the Space and Naval Warfare Systems Command (SPAWAR) in Washington, D.C., where he spent five years as the Navy's Electronic Warfare Architect. During this time, he earned a Ph.D. in Information Technology from George Mason University.

Douglas E. Campbell, Ph.D. (LCDR, USNR-R, Ret.), was born May 9, 1954 in Portsmouth, Virginia, and is an American citizen. He graduated from Kenitra American High School, Kenitra, Morocco, in 1972. He received his Bachelor of Science degree in Journalism from the University of Kansas in 1976, and was immediately commissioned as an Ensign in the U.S. Navy. He joined the U.S. Naval Reserve Program as an Intelligence Officer in 1980, and was transferred to the Retired Reserves as a Lieutenant Commander on June 1, 1999. Dr. Campbell received his Master of Science degree from the University of Southern California in Computer Systems Management in 1986 and his Doctor of Philosophy degree in Security Administration from Southwest University in New Orleans, Louisiana, in 1990, specializing in Computer Security. Dr. Campbell is president and CEO of Syneca Research Group, Inc., a certified 8(a) company under the U.S. Small Business Administration's program. www.syneca.com

Index

Printed and bound by CPI Group (UK) Ltd, Croydon, CR0 4YY

22/10/2024

01777636-0019